Explosive Conflict

This sequel to Randall Collins' world-influential micro-sociology of violence introduces the question of time-dynamics: what determines how long conflict lasts and how much damage it does. Inequality and hostility are not enough to explain when and where violence breaks out. Time-dynamics are the time-bubbles when people are most nationalistic; the hours after a protest starts when violence is most likely to happen. Ranging from the three months of nationalism and hysteria after 9/11 to the assault on the Capitol in 2021, Randall Collins shows what makes some protests more violent than others and why some revolutions are swift and non-violent tipping-points while others devolve into lengthy civil wars. Winning or losing are emotional processes, continuing in the era of computerized war, while high-tech spawns terrorist tactics of hiding in the civilian population and using cheap features of the Internet as substitutes for military organization. Nevertheless, *Explosive Conflict* offers some optimistic discoveries on clues to mass rampages and heading off police atrocities, with practical lessons from the time-dynamics of violence.

Randall Collins is the Dorothy Swaine Thomas Professor of Sociology at the University of Pennsylvania. His articles and books are influential in many academic disciplines throughout the world. His books include *Violence: A Micro-Sociological Theory*, *The Sociology of Philosophies: A Global Theory of Intellectual Change*, and *Conflict Sociology: A Sociological Classic Updated* (Routledge).

Explosive Conflict

Time-Dynamics of Violence

Randall Collins

NEW YORK AND LONDON

Cover image: © Larry Duenas

First published 2022
by Routledge
605 Third Avenue, New York, NY 10158

and by Routledge
4 Park Square, Milton Park, Abingdon, Oxon, OX14 4RN

Routledge is an imprint of the Taylor & Francis Group, an informa business

Library of Congress Cataloging-in-Publication Data

Names: Collins, Randall, 1941– author.
Title: Explosive conflict : time-dynamics of violence / Randall Collins.
Description: New York, NY : Routledge, 2022. | Includes bibliographical references and index.
Identifiers: LCCN 2021036160 | ISBN 9781032157733 (hardback) | ISBN 9781032157702 (paperback) | ISBN 9781003245629 (ebook)
Subjects: LCSH: Social conflict. | Violence. | Equality—Social aspects. | Social media—Political aspects. | Social media—Social aspects.
Classification: LCC HM1121 .C65 2022 | DDC 303.6—dc23
LC record available at https://lccn.loc.gov/2021036160

ISBN: 978-1-032-15773-3 (hbk)
ISBN: 978-1-032-15770-2 (pbk)
ISBN: 978-1-003-24562-9 (ebk)

DOI: 10.4324/9781003245629

Typeset in Garamond
by Apex CoVantage, LLC

Contents

Figures

Acknowledgments

Important parts of the argument draw on the researches of Michael Mann, Anne Nassauer, Isabel Bramsen, Stefan Klusemann, and Anthony King. I am indebted also for exchanges with Georgi Derluguian, Ralph Schroeder, Ido Yoav, Alessandro Orsini, Andreas Wimmer, Sinisa Malesevic, Peter Turchin, Alice Goffman, Elijah Anderson, Philippe Bourgois, David Gibson, David Grazian, Bridget Nolan, Erika Summers Effler, David Sorge, Jack Katz, Martin Sánchez-Jankowski, Jason Manning, Elizabeth Armstrong, Janet Vertesi, Jooyoung Lee, Randol Contreras, Mark Gross, Curtis Jackson-Jacobs, Waverly Duck, Lester Kurtz, Michael Biggs, Neil Ketchley, Lasse Liebst, Marie Heinskou, Marie Lindegaard, Poul Poder, Bo Paulle, Don Weenink, Giselinde Kuipers, Raheel Dattiwala, Jerome Ferret, Michel Wieviorka, Eddie Hartmann, Wolfgang Knöbl, Klaus Schlichte, Ugo Corte, Michael Staack and Tom Mallette.

Chapters 10–12 draw on discussions with US, UK and Israeli military officers and cyber-security experts, including seminars and conferences at U.S. Army War College; the U.S. Military Academy, West Point; Argonne National Laboratory; Mackinder Forum; Concepts and Doctrine Centre, UK Ministry of Defence; European Research Group on Military and Society, Amsterdam; Conference on Combat in Iraq and Afghanistan, Oxford University; Conference on Military Command in the 21st Century, University of Warwick.

Thanks also to colloquium participants at Wharton School; Kellogg School of Management, Northwestern University; Princeton University; Yale University; Graduate Center, City University of New York; Violence Research Center, University of West Virginia; University of California, Irvine; UCLA; McGill University, Montréal; International Sociological Association conferences at Toronto and Gothenburg, Sweden; Universidad National de Mexico; London School of Economics; University of Cardiff, Wales; European Association for Sociology of Sport, Dublin, Ireland; University of Copenhagen; University of Helsinki; University of Amsterdam; German Sociological Association conferences at Rostock and University of Trier; Humboldt University Berlin; Graduate School of North American

Studies, Freie Universität Berlin; University of Giessen; University of Gottingen; Instituto Carlo Cattaneo, Bologna, Italy; University of Trento; University of Milano; University of Genoa; Lisbon University Institute, Portugal; University of Zaragoza, Spain; Institut d'Etudes Avancées, Paris; Maison des Sciences de l'Homme, Paris; and University of Strasbourg.

Versions of Chapter 1 were published in *American Sociological Review*, Chapter 6 in *American Journal of Sociology*, and Chapter 9 in *European Journal for Sport and Society*.

I have not attempted comprehensive reviews of the literature, but wanted to present the analysis directly and clearly. Any such accumulation of knowledge is a collective enterprise. This book is dedicated to researchers past, present and future.

Abbreviations

ABS	anti-ballistics system
APC	anti-personnel-carrier
AWACS	Airborne Warning And Control System
BPM	beats-per-minute (heart rate)
C&C	command and control
C4ISR	command, control, communications, computers, intelligence, surveillance & reconnaissance
CCTV	closed-circuit television
C-escalation	counter-escalation
COIN	counter-insurgency
CT/F	confrontational tension/fear
D-escalation	de-escalation
DOD	Department of Defense
ECCM	electronic counter-counter-measures
ECM	enemy counter-measures
EDOM	emotional domination
EE	emotional energy
EO	electro-optical
F/A	fighter/attack
FOB	forward operating base
GPS	global positioning system
HARMS	high-speed anti-radiation missile
IED	improvised explosive device
IR	infra-red
IR	interaction ritual
IT	information technology
JSTARS	Joint Surveillance Target Attack Radar System
NCO	non-commissioned officer
NODs	night-observation devices
PRC	People's Republic of China
RMA	revolution in military affairs (computerization, remote sensors and precision weapons)

ROE	rules of engagement
SAMS	surface-to-air missiles
STARS	Surveillance Target Attack Radar System
TSA	Transportation Security Administration
UAV	unmanned aerial vehicle
WWI	World War I
WWII	World War II

Introduction

Emergent and Self-Propelling Conflicts

Introduction

Virtually all violence is emergent, in the sense that it does not inevitably happen because of long-standing structural conditions. Why does violence happen at one particular time rather than another? Most of the time it does not happen. Structural conditions for social antagonism are much more widespread than overt conflict, and conflict is more widespread than physical violence. Threatened violence often aborts; when it does break out, how long it lasts and with what severity of damage vary considerably. There appears to be a great deal of indeterminacy in all aspects of violence, from beginning to end.

Although violence is not structurally inevitable, emergent conflicts and their temporal life-spans are not inexplicable. By "inevitable," we mean following invariably from the particular causal conditions that we have in mind; for example, the theory that class conflict under capitalism is the cause of revolution has been widely rejected as a kind of historical inevitability that poorly fits the historical record. It does not follow that all theories of causal process fail; what we need are causal conditions that demonstrably operate at the level of time-dynamics we are concerned with. The crucial turning points in conflict and violence are matters of process and temporary situational configurations, rather than long-term structures. Processes have patterns, and discovering these patterns generates a predictive theory. This is not merely a hypothetical claim, since research in recent years on short-term patterns of violent situations has shown a number of situational configurations that promote violence and others that inhibit it.

Time-dynamics of social processes are concerned with when events begin and end and how long they go on. These time-patterns are a subject for empirical observation. Not all kinds of conflict and violence have the same time-patterns; why they differ is what we want to establish. The time-dynamics of conflict and violence are sensitive to scale: conflicts among small numbers of persons have different time-dimensions than

DOI: 10.4324/9781003245629-1

conflicts at larger degrees of organization, from crowds to movements to armies and states. This does not mean merely that small-scale fights take less time than struggles among bigger organizations. There are turning points in all sizes of conflict, and different time-patterns branch out from these turning points. In one-on-one face conflicts, repetitive gestures and insults (combined with an unsupportive audience) bring rapid boredom, and the threat of violence often aborts in less than 60 seconds. In a protest demonstration, there is a particular few hours when violence is most likely to break out, and if that period of vulnerability is passed, there is no violence that day. On a much larger scale, revolutions succeed rather quickly (in a matter of days) if a tipping point mechanism is present; without the necessary conditions for a tipping point, a would-be revolution turns into a civil war that can last years. These are the kind of time-dynamics we are seeking. As we shall see, differences in time-patterns are related to how much damage is done and the strength of people's emotions for continuing or ending a fight.

Violence, Volume 2

This volume, *Explosive Conflict: Time-Dynamics of Violence*, is the sequel promised in my 2008 book, *Violence: A Micro-Sociological Theory*. The original plan of that book was comprehensive, but there turned out to be far too many types of violence to handle in one volume. The *Micro/Violence* book analyzed 30 types, all focusing on here-and-now situational details. What was left out is the macro level, stretching out in time and space. This includes not only large-scale organized violence (war, revolution, genocide, guerrilla and terrorist tactics), but also the meso or middle-sized spectrum where protest demos can last for weeks. There are also violent events like mass rampage shootings, carried out by isolated individuals or duos (and thus in a sense are micro), but which have a preliminary build-up of months of secretly collecting weapons and making plans; and these connect to previous rampages because would-be mass killers obsess over spectacular attacks they want to imitate. Some kinds of violence have a backward trail that requires us to step out of the here-and-now dynamics, while other kinds of violence have sudden emergence but a long forward trail because of their scale of organization. *Violence: A Micro-Sociological Theory* bracketed the social background of individuals as well as their motives for getting into violence, in order to focus on situational dynamics. My aim was to start empirically at the point where a confrontation shapes up, and to watch it move forward—or not—to actual violence. This was a deliberate intellectual tactic. Obviously, I am aware of the large amount of research relating violence to social class, race, gang membership, gender, family, and childhood experience. It should go without saying that our explanations are multi-causal. My chief point is that having a background statistically related to violence still leaves most such people, most of the time, not committing violence. As I have noted about gang members: even if they committed half of all murders (and we know that a large proportion of homicides are domestic and other kinds), the ratio works out to 1 murder per 88 gang members (Collins 2008: 373); and even for these killers, what do they do the other 364 days of the year? Similarly with the causal power of motivations: being angry or wanting to hurt someone is not a sufficient explanation of whether violence will be carried out or not.

My key finding is confrontational tension/fear (CT/F), which makes committing violence difficult—when it comes to the sticking point, in the words of Lady Macbeth—not easy. This is an emotional and physiological process that tends to make threatening confrontations abort, except where there are situational conditions that allow persons to break through the emotional barrier. And even when they do start violence, CT/F generally makes them incompetent, with bad aim, out-of-control firing or striking, and hitting the wrong targets. Without social pressure to keep the fight going, most fights wind down rather quickly. My aim, then, was to shift the explanatory focus from background propensities to actual mechanisms in play in a threatening situation. What background conditions and current motives cannot explain are turning points and outcomes: that is to say, what determines whether a fight will break out or not; and if it does, who wins, loses, stalemates, and how much damage is done.

Explaining Outbreaks and Outcomes

This book continues the emphasis on turning points and emergent processes; but let us now remove the brackets around the immediate situation. Looking backwards from the threat of violence, what causes conflict in the first place? Do we have a general theory of the causes of conflict? Sociologists since the 1950s have worked with the three-dimensional stratification of Max Weber: economic class, cultural status-group identity, and political power are all domains of conflict. More recently, we have added gender and sexual preference as bases of domination and contention. Anything which is a resource for organizing and for social superiority can be grounds for conflict, between the haves and the have-nots.

Donald Black has argued that this kind of theorizing is insufficient. A constant cannot move a variable; only a change in one condition can cause a change in another condition. Racism, or capitalist inequality, as constant features cannot generate conflict. Black argues that change is what causes conflict; and that change can occur in either direction, and in three dimensions: an increase or decrease in hierarchy; an increase or decrease in social distance or intimacy; an increase or decrease in cultural similarity or difference. This gives conflict its moral quality: people feel their habitual arrangements and standards are being violated, and that they have the moral right to resist the change. Hence Black's title, *Moral Time* (2011): conflict is a movement in time, which people feel as a moral trajectory for the worse.

Black proposes that conflict is greater when changes on these dimensions are bigger and faster, and when changes occur on more dimensions simultaneously. His theory focuses less on large structural changes than on individual experience. Conflict occurs when a person or group rises or flaunts their success, thereby incurring hostility; but also when a person experiences downward mobility, lashing out in resentment at being fired. Thus, the prediction is about which persons set off conflict with whom. We should note two blank spots in the explanation. One is that there are a variety of ways persons can react to a shift in their relative position: losers can accept it; they can move away and avoid the situation; they can counterattack; they can displace their attack onto someone else; they can turn against themselves in suicide.[1] Black's *The Social Structure of Right and Wrong* (1998) spells out conditions under which people in particular network configurations choose one or another of these paths. For example, avoiding a conflict by moving away is typical both in hunting-and-gathering bands and in modern suburbs, where hierarchy and mutual dependence are low and it is easy to change networks. There still remains a gap on the micro-level of everyday life, because a person who wants to attack someone they feel has insulted them nevertheless will not carry out the attack, unless they have favorable situational conditions, such as emotional domination in a particular encounter.

Another kind of theoretical gap is the time-dynamics. An underlying mechanism in Black's theory is that people are habituated to being in a particular pattern of hierarchy and social distance, and feel that a sudden or large change is shameful or wrong.[2] By the same token, once they get used to a change in their social location, it again becomes taken for granted and no longer causes conflict. This means there must be a time-law about how long it takes for bland normalcy to be re-established. Putting the two kinds of theoretical gaps together, we can see that micro-interactional contingencies may keep an aggrieved person from engaging in overt violence, and if a favorable situation to attack never arises, enough time may elapse so that the new relationship becomes normalized. In other words, there is a danger-time zone between the initial change in "moral time" and habituation to the change. Once that time zone is passed, the chances of conflict fall away.

We need a three-step model: (1) changes in underlying conditions generate potential conflict; (2) potential conflict turns into overt conflict; and (3) overt conflict goes through a turning point to violence.

Step (1) is reasonably well theorized. Almost anything can become a source of potential conflict, especially changes in relative social position. Rapidity and extensiveness of these changes magnify the potential for conflict.

Step (2) needs further analysis. Potential for conflict is stored in people's emotions, but individuals can keep their emotions to themselves; or engage in backstage griping without confronting their target; or spend their time on private fantasies for revenge, even planning scenarios and collecting weapons for an attack. Posting such plans or rants on the Internet is another step along this path. But all these remain potential rather than overt conflict, until the two sides actually make contact expressing an "I-vs.-you" relationship. There are a number of ways this can happen. They could use official and organizational channels, such as making a complaint, calling the police, filing a lawsuit, organizing a political campaign. They could confront the opponent face-to-face, either as individuals or as a mass gathering, such as a protest demonstration. There are also some in-between steps, such as engaging in covert attacks. Robert Emerson's *Everyday Troubles* (2015) found that conflicts between roommates—over messiness, noise, or using each other's possessions—usually did not lead to overt complaints but to unvoiced tit-for-tat or other tactics expressing one's displeasure; and these moves were often misinterpreted by the other side because they were not overtly expressed. As yet we lack a good theoretical explanation of which kinds of moves are made, and whether they are made at all.

Step (3) has been theorized on the micro-level (Collins 2008) in the pathways circumventing confrontational tension/fear. A larger-scale theory of turning-points to violence is the subject of this book. And once violence breaks out, we need to theorize whether the result will be winning, losing, or stalemate, and how long it takes.

Steps (2) and (3) are the subject of this book.

Overview of the Book

Part I, "Time-Dynamics," is a series of steps toward establishing time-patterns and their mechanisms.

Chapter 1 uses a trendy title "C-Escalation and D-Escalation: A Theory of the Time-Dynamics of Conflict," to bring out some further points about the spiral of conflict: it is *counter*-escalation but also the less-studied but all-important *de*-escalation process. This is a micro-macro effort focusing on micro-mechanisms (from interaction ritual) plus meso-level structures that activists assemble by mobilizing networks and material resources. Together these drive the upward spiral, but also provide alternative ways for the downward process to happen.

Conflict escalates through a series of feedback loops. On the micro level, conflict generates conditions for intense interaction rituals, whose internal solidarity fuels external conflict. Perceived atrocities increase ideological polarization reciprocally between opponents, while real atrocities also happen because confrontational tension/fear makes violence incompetent at hitting its intended targets, and adrenaline surges plus emotional domination generate vicious overkill. Conflict groups build up meso-structure by seeking allies, driving out neutrals, and mobilizing material resources. Both sides counter-escalate through the same set of feedbacks. Who wins or loses depends on differences between opponents' rates of escalation, and by destroying the other side's organizational and material capacity.

Conflict de-escalates when both sides fail in conditions for solidarity, for overcoming confrontational tension/fear, and through exhaustion of material resources. Emotional burnout sets in through a time-dynamic of explosion (a few days), plateau (three months), and dissipation of enthusiasm (out to six months, somewhat analogous to the half-life of decaying radiation). Defection of allies opens the way for third-party settlement. When both sides remain stalemated, initial enthusiasm and external polarization give way to emergent internal factions—a victory faction (hard-liners) versus a peace faction (negotiators)—thereby creating a new dimension of conflict. Ideals promoted at the outset of conflict become obstacles to resolution at the end. Peace is not everybody's goal; a moral gulf develops between those who want to end a conflict through victory, and the combination of realists and idealists who want to end the costs of debilitating stalemate.

Chapter 2, "Time-Bubbles of Nationalism," introduces the concept of a "time-bubble," an emotional mood produced by a sudden event focusing public attention into a massive interaction ritual. But interaction rituals, like everything else, are subject to time-dynamics. How long does the bubble last before the air leaks out of it? We start by looking at the macro-historical causes of nationalism.

Modern nationalism is a by-product of the bureaucratic state penetrating society, creating cultural uniformity and national identity. But structurally based nationalism is not necessarily very intense. Even when institutionalized in periodic formal rituals like the Fourth of July, it can be routine, low in emotion—even boring. We need to explain sudden upsurges in popular nationalism, but also their persistence and fading in medium-length periods of time. Nationalist surges are connected with geopolitical rises and falls in the power-prestige of states: strong and expanding states absorb smaller particularistic identities into a prestigious whole; weaker and defeated states suffer delegitimization of the dominant nationality and fragment in sudden upsurges of localizing nationalities. Moving from macro-patterns to micro-sociological mechanisms, conflict producing solidarity is a key mechanism: dramatic events focus widespread attention and assemble crowds into spontaneous mass-participation interaction rituals. Evidence from public assemblies and the display of national symbols following the terrorist attacks of September 11, 2001 shows an intense period of national solidarity for three months, then a gradual return to normal internal divisions by around six months. Spontaneous rituals of national solidarity are produced not only by external conflict but by internal uprisings, where an emotional upsurge of national identity is used to legitimate revolutionary crowds and discredit regimes. But conflict-mobilized national solidarity lives in a three-to-six-month time-bubble, and needs to institutionalize its successes rapidly to have long-term effects.

Chapter 3, "Tipping Point Revolutions and State Breakdown Revolutions" examines why revolutions succeed or fail. After the fall of the Soviet satellites and then of the Soviet Union itself during 1989–1991, and a series of "color revolutions" in its successor states, the belief grew among activists in a formula for carrying out revolution. Assemble a huge crowd of demonstrators; stay civil and non-violent while letting the other side take the moral onus of committing atrocities against unarmed people; build up sympathy from the crowd-control forces so that they start intervening on your side; within a few weeks the authoritarian ruler becomes isolated and is removed by state elites going over to the revolution. This tipping point theory was widely emulated in the Arab Spring revolts in 2011, but with mostly poor results. It also runs contrary to the state breakdown theory of revolution formulated by Theda Skocpol, Jack Goldstone, and others on the famous historic revolutions in England, France, Russia, China, and Japan. This theory posits a sequence of three processes: first in time, a pervasive state crisis in finances and/or military defeat; second, a split within the ruling elite over how to solve the crisis; third, a popular revolt, after elite reformers have prepared the way for the downfall of the whole regime. The state crisis is inescapable because it undercuts the elite's means of coercion and control. The third component, a mass uprising, is similar to the tipping point theory. But the third component without the first two results in shallow or failed revolutions, which soon reverts to another version of the old regime, and produces no deep structural changes. The anti-Soviet revolution fits the state breakdown theory. The Arab Spring revolts, like other waves of attempted revolution (as in 1848), were set off by emulation of revolts elsewhere, without the prior internal components of state breakdown that made change inevitable. Not that the tipping point theory is useless as an analytical device; it adds to our theoretical repertoire—the causes of shallow revolutions and of deep structural revolutions.

Chapter 4, "Time-Dynamics of Violence from Micro to Macro," summarizes time-dynamics of conflict, on a scale from thresholds of small-scale violence within a few minutes or less; for crowds, violent danger-time zones of a few hours; for riots and revolutionary tipping points, a span of three days up to several weeks; the mass crisis solidarity and hysteria zone of three months, falling off by six months; and macro time-forks where wars or revolts get resolved quickly with relatively few casualties, or turn into prolonged civil wars and wars of attrition that go on for years.

Part II, "The Eye of the Needle: Emotional Processes," is about the collective moods that swing conflicts one way or another, from the threshold of outbreak, to the time they call it quits. This set of chapters makes two points. (Chapter 5, "Material Interests Are Ambiguous, So Interaction Rituals Steer Political Movements.") First, framing conflicts in terms of their conflicting interests is a poor predictor of what will actually happen. Not that material interests don't exist, but in practice they are ambiguous as to what people do to advance them. People still have to decide who gets included as having "the same interests," from narrowly self-centered personal advancement, to local protection, to grand coalition. And interests don't determine tactics; the history of the labor movement, or any reforming social movement, tends to revolve around splits over whether to be peaceful or violent; whether to seek incremental gains and pragmatic deals with opponents, or to strive militantly for rapid and total change: in short, compromisers vs. ultras. The same movement can switch among these paths (the Nazis and the early Chinese Communists are examples), and timely switching is often what makes them successful. This kind of split over tactics is similar to what we see in Chapter 1, in the downphase of a stalemated conflict between bitter-enders and the peace faction. If interests don't explain these emergent processes of conflict, what does? To readers of my previous books, it will come as no surprise: the success or failure of interaction rituals that bring people together as action groups.

Second point: How long do these collective moods last before they change? I examine mood swings in two historic revolutions. (Chapter 6, "Mood-Swings in the Downfall of the English Revolution.") The end of the English Revolution happened between the time Oliver Cromwell died in 1658 and the restoration of the monarchy in 1660. For most of this time, all the important actors wanted to continue the republic, the Commonwealth. Only in the last two months was there a switch, when the same people who vowed, "Monarchy never!" were cheering for the return of the King.

(Chapter 7, "When History Holds Its Breath: The Take-Off of the French Revolution.") The other case is the turning point of the French Revolution, the night of August 4, 1789, when the assembled notables of France decided to abolish the aristocratic regime, and with it the power of the chief hereditary aristocrat, the King. This is a theoretically important case because Ivan Ermakoff (2015) presents it as key evidence for a critique of Durkheimian interaction ritual theory. Yes, the assembly broke into collective effervescence, a wave of enthusiasm, emotional energy, a new basis of solidarity—but these happened *after* a period when the assembly was deeply divided, hesitant, and unenthusiastic about anything. The interaction ritual (IR), in other words, was just a victory celebration, once they finally hit on something they could agree upon. Ermakoff stresses this was an instance of genuine historical contingency, a cognitive and emotional standstill—they genuinely didn't know what to do. In Ermakoff's analysis, they suddenly shifted when the Duc de Châtelet made a speech declaring that aristocrats should voluntarily give up their privileges and become citizens like everyone else. (An extreme case of going against one's material interests!) Other speakers chimed in, and soon there was a cascade of aristocrats disavowing their privileges; and this created the conditions for Durkheimian solidarity. But the IR is an outcome, not a cause, in the time sequence.

My response is: look at the earlier events of the crisis through the experiences of the Duc de Châtelet. He was a strong monarchist, the commander of the royal guard, tasked with leading his soldiers to police the radicals of the assembly, and holding off the crowd at the Bastille. In all these events he failed. His emotional energy (EE) was dashed by his failed IRs with his own mutinous soldiers. Suddenly he had an emotional revelation: go where the EE is, on the side of the opponents he had tried to put down. This fits the motivational principle of IR chains: individuals avoid IRs that drain their EE, and seek those where they gain EE. How long does it take to make a total switch in trajectory? Trace the EE of the Duc de Châtelet from June 23 to August 4: six weeks.

Chapter 8, "Assault on the Capitol: 2021, 1917, 1792," compares the January 6, 2021 assault on the US Capitol with two similar scenes: the Bolshevik assault on the Czar's palace in November 1917 and the attack on the Tuileries palace in Paris in August 1792 that began the overthrow of the French monarchy. My focus is not on the background conflicts or the downstream consequences (the Capitol attack failed rather quickly while the others made historic revolutions), but on the process of crowds attacking the center of government. It is the similar details that first caught my attention: protestors sitting in the Senate presiding chair, and trashing the office of House Speaker Pelosi, scenes that echoed the French and Russian Revolutions. Similar, too, were the Capitol police retreating before the protestors, and officials wavering and disagreeing over what forces to send to repel the assault. The larger lesson is that at a revolutionary moment, it is a contest of which side can stay organized while the other side becomes disorganized—two spinning gyroscopes waiting to see which one will fall first.

This is one of two instances in this book where I was able to gather first-hand evidence on historic events while they were unfolding. The first (described in Chapter 1) was the day after the 9/11, 2001 attack on the Twin Towers in New York, when I realized it was an opportunity to investigate Simmel's classic theory that external conflict creates internal solidarity—in this case, by walking around and counting how many flags people put up and how long they were displayed. This became my first research measuring the time-dynamics of violent conflict. The second was in the days after January 6, 2021, when the news media and the Internet were full of photos and videos of militant demonstrators and the police at the Capitol. It was an opportunity to watch the details of revolution first-hand, instead of relying on documents collected by historians. Historic events are big and macro, but nevertheless they are human social processes, full of emotions and the collective actions of individuals. Today's era of visual data gives us unprecedented access to the dynamics of history—if we seize the opportunity to examine it with sociological eyes.

Part III, "War and Sport: Dynamics of Winning, Losing, and Stalemate," begins with the point that sports and violence model each other (Chapter 9, "The Micro-Sociology of Sport"). Sport is play-fighting, or in William James's term "a moral equivalent of war," and involves similar mechanisms for winning and losing. There is also a convergence in research methods. Close micro-observation was pioneered by using film and video recordings to plan game strategy and athletic training; and more recently taken a further step by body instruments measuring breathing and heart rate. We probably know more about what happens on an athletic field than anywhere else. This development was paralleled by micro-sociology of everyday interaction and violence. The upshot is we can spell out pretty clearly how play-conflict is won or lost; and this provides a useful addition to what we have observed about real violence. Both are contests of EE (emotional energy), solidarity, and EDOM (emotional domination).

There are of course some differences. Games are scheduled in advance and organized in leagues or tournaments, so that teams of about the same ability play each other. In war, especially in particular battles, leaders try to arrange it so that they fight when and where they have advantages of numbers and terrain; they *seek* an unequal playing field. Games are much shorter than battles, with time-dynamics in the 1-to-3-hour time zone rather than the all-day-to-several-days in battles of maneuver. Sieges and trench warfare stretch out into years, producing a level of attrition, and logistics problems, far beyond sports. Nevertheless, sport reveals the core of battle.

Chapter 10, "Battle Dynamics: Victory and Defeat": What happens in battle combines a number of different processes, but we can see fairly clearly how they flow toward victory, defeat, or stalemate by diagramming them in a flow chart with feedback loops. I try to avoid losing the path in a diagram with too many spaghetti loops, by walking our way through on two main paths. (1) How much *material resources* an army has, delivered by *logistics* of high or low quality, into *firepower* on the battlefield, which I call the intensity of *assault*. Simultaneously, (2) how high is the army's *organizational morale* (made up of the familiar sources of *EE*, *coordination*, and military *discipline*), which determine how good the army is at *maneuver*. (Think Napoleon, or Grant vs. Lee.) The main argument is that morale/maneuver is more powerful than material/logistics/firepower (Napoleon said 3-to-1), because the key to victory is breaking down the enemy's organization, making them unable to use the material resources that they have. But maneuver does not always win battles; if conditions for successful maneuver are weak, or if differences in material resources are just too strong (beyond 3-to-1, the precise ratio being more complicated than this), victory will go the other way.

Inventions of new military technology do not require a new theory, since technological innovations operate by changing the strength of the pathways in the basic model, but not eliminating these pathways. Chapter 11, "High-Tech War in Theory and Reality," takes up high-tech war, the "revolution in military affairs" since the computerization of battle in the 1990s. War has changed from commanders on the battlefield (Napoleon, Stonewall Jackson, Rommel, Patton) into remote control from the other side of the world. Sensors in space satellites and drones trace enemy movements by comparing high-resolution photos; infra-red sensors locate the heat of vehicles or human bodies; radar detectors pin-point the source of enemy firing and fire back immediately to destroy it. Does turning over fighting to computer-controlled technology penetrate the fog of war and eliminate Clausewitzian friction? Friction affects all parts of Chapter 10 battle diagrams. Friction in logistics—mechanical breakdowns, traffic accidents, running out of fuel—screws up scheduling all along the line, and reduces advantages in forces and firepower. Besides this physical drag, friction also takes the form of informational fog—not knowing where the enemy is, or even where all one's own forces are—and human emotions, which amplify enthusiasm or spread confusion and the passivity of defeat. Thus, friction also produces wild or inaccurate firing, and can stymie the morale-maneuver sequence. High-tech is designed to remedy this by turning to non-human sources of scheduling, targeting, and information, and by taking human emotions out of the loop.

Drawing on experiences of US and UK troops in the Iraq and Afghanistan wars, I spell out some reasons why friction remains. The enemy may also have high-tech and can use it to negate our own (an increasing concern in possible future conflict with China); and even in asymmetrical war against lower-tech enemies, cyberwar is often the technology most within their means. On the material/logistical side, high-tech equipment is expensive and difficult to maintain; expensive aircraft can carry only a limited number of smart bombs and missiles, and armored helicopters can be grounded by sandstorms or maintenance and not available when and where they are needed. On the morale/maneuver side, bored troops running battlefield computers can commit security breaches; nominally allied local forces can destroy trust and sow paranoia by green-on-blue attacks. Until the future invention of robot soldiers who can move around complicated spaces like buildings as well as humans can, boots-on-the-ground soldiers are going to be engaging other human beings in situations full of confrontational tension/fear.

Because of the expense of high-tech war, its vulnerability to countermeasures, and the morale-sapping effects of highly politicized communications media, contemporary wars tend to degrade back toward traditional war, the longer a war goes on. Adding together the sources of friction in a high-tech version of the battle flow-chart, there is an increasing tendency toward stalemate. This is the biggest morale deflator of all.

Chapter 12, "Terrorist Tactics: Symbiosis with High-Tech," applies the analysis to terrorism, which is an extension of guerrilla war. Both are a reaction by the low-tech side to fighting a more advanced army. Firepower was already becoming devastating by the end of the Napoleonic wars and during the American Civil War of 1861–1865, making frontal assault near-suicidal. There has been an increasing shift to long-distance bombardment—whether by artillery or by aircraft and missiles—throughout the last 200 years. In response to devastating firepower, battlefields have spread out; instead of big divisions marching into combat, infantry learned to infiltrate in small groups, whether through the trenches of WWI or the helicopter-delivered teams from Vietnam onwards. Increased mobility has made the battlefield into a checkerboard of outposts.

Guerrilla warfare (dating from the Spanish resistance to Napoleon) avoids major confrontations, instead hitting logistics lines that supply far-flung posts, whether by ambush or by improvised explosive devices (IEDs, a cheap, improvised version of minefields). Traditional guerrillas hid in inaccessible mountains and jungles; terrorists hide in the civilian population. Both follow the trend of spreading out the battlefield, to avoid massed frontal assaults against devastating firepower. As high-tech sensors have gotten better at detecting military formations, the preferred terrain for low-tech resistance has become concentrations of human population. This is a tit-for-tat response of low-tech warriors to superior high-tech enemies. A pre-modern conqueror would just annihilate the entire population, but the morality of modern democracies forbids it; and anything of the sort is publicized by ubiquitous high-tech news media. High-tech enhances the political side of war, as a contest of competing moralities (the "hearts-and-minds" cliché). Here the emotional side of war becomes even stronger.

Symbiosis between terrorism and high-tech war extends also to firepower. After the Vietnam War, the trend in artillery and bombing shifted from increasing the sheer destructiveness of explosives and incendiaries, to making their targeting more precise. But the world-wide communications and computerization that make this possible also mean that terrorists operate inside the same high-tech network as ourselves. Commands to detonate road-side IEDs against approaching Western military vehicles in the Middle East can be routed through Internet cafés thousands of miles away, using the same communication satellites as everyone else. The same world-wide network facilitates both the material side of war and its moral/

emotional side. Atrocities have become easy to publicize, whether they are committed by high-tech soldiers frustrated by terrorists who attack them under the guise of civilians; or the deliberate shock tactics of ISIS videos showing children cutting off the heads of captured enemies—a means of dramatizing their will to resist and of recruiting new volunteers to their side. Thus, the political side of war becomes even more a war of competing atrocities, as seen by opposing points of view. Ironically, the quest for clean "surgical strikes" in high-tech war has had consequences bringing back the emotional dynamics of wars in previous phases of history.

Part IV, "Violence in Everyday Life," updates the micro-level research on small-scale violence that is the topic of my 2008 book. One of the topics omitted there was sexual aggression and violence. Chapter 13, "Emotional Domination and Resistance to Sexual Aggression," asks if the patterns found in all face-to-face violence also apply to attempted rape: confrontational tension/fear that makes attacks difficult, not easy; micro-situational conditions that allow the barrier of CT/F to be circumvented, including attacking the emotionally weak, social support and audience effects. Data publicized during the take-off of the #MeToo movement makes it possible to test these points. These accounts are extensive enough to avoid the fallacy of sampling on the dependent variable (looking only at rapes that succeed); the movement's wider definition of sexual aggression makes it possible to see when potential sexual coercion succeeds or fails. Here we find that most potential rapes fail; and that the key process deterring them is not being emotionally dominated.

Chapter 14, "Clues to Mass Rampage Killers," looks at the sequence of action over time that culminates in mass rampage killings, especially school shootings. Most of the motivational conditions usually cited—being bullied, being an alienated isolate—are statistically far too common to explain the small proportion of students who make these attacks. One feature that stands out as a clue is that would-be perpetrators spend months collecting information about previous attacks, and assembling a clandestine arsenal of weapons, ammunition and costumes. The crucial point is that this is a clandestine activity; it needs to be distinguished from other patterns of gun ownership, even gun cults, which are out in the open, with no attempt at hiding.

Chapter 15, "Cool-headed Cops Needed (and Cool Heads on the Street): Heart Rate Monitors Can Help," examines the micro-dynamics of police shooting suspects when no real threat to the officers exists. Confrontational tension/fear is again at work, especially when exacerbated by a vehicle chase or high-speed arrival at the scene, by misleading rumors on police communications networks, or the confusion of large numbers of police present. We can zero in on a mechanism that makes violence incompetent—in the sense of hitting the wrong target, or applying more force than necessary. The physiological basis of CT/F is heart rate elevated to the level where perception blurs and officers lose fine motor control of their weapons. Recognizing the problem suggests a solution: heart-rate monitors and training to avoid going into action when one's own body-signs are out of control.

Finally, the "Conclusion: Optimistic Discoveries in the Sociology of Violence" argues that at least some kinds of violence can be prevented, by putting into practice what we have learned about turning points toward or away from violence. This can be done by participants right there on the ground. Large-scale violence is harder to control, but becoming aware of its time-dynamics can make policy-makers more sophisticated about where the danger-zones and turning points are.

Notes

1. These alternatives apply both to individuals and to groups that lose status. An example is lower-middle and working-class whites who see themselves squeezed out of the high-tech economy of the upper-middle class, and ignored in favor of efforts to raise previously discriminated minorities from below. This type of explanation has been prominent in political commentaries about Trump supporters. The latter three outcomes are evident here (especially if one counts the opiate crisis as a form of suicide).
2. This is my interpretation rather than Black's explicitly stated position, as he strives for a theory of pure sociology, without psychology.

References

Black, Donald. 1998. *The Social Structure of Right and Wrong*. New York: Academic Press.

Black, Donald. 2011. *Moral Time*. Oxford: Oxford University Press.

Collins, Randall. 2008. *Violence: A Micro-Sociological Theory*. Princeton, NJ: Princeton University Press.

Emerson, Robert M. 2015. *Everyday Troubles: The Micro-Politics of Interpersonal Conflict*. Chicago: University of Chicago Press.

Ermakoff, Ivan. 2015. "The Structure of Contingency." *American Journal of Sociology* 121: 64–125.

Part I

Time-Dynamics

Chapter 1

C-Escalation and D-Escalation

A Theory of the Time-Dynamics of Conflict

Introduction

A basic principle of social conflict was stated more than 100 years ago by Georg Simmel ([1908] 1955), and elaborated 50 years later by Lewis Coser (1956): external conflict increases group solidarity.

Solidarity also causes more conflict (Figure 1.1). Solidarity is a crucial weapon in conflict. Groups with solidarity are more capable of mobilizing and fighting; and groups that already have high solidarity are especially sensitive to threats to their boundaries.

The two most fundamental social processes—solidarity and conflict—are connected. The theory of social solidarity was classically stated by Emile Durkheim ([1912] 1964), in explaining how religious rituals produce feelings of group membership. Ingredients are: assembling the group face-to-face; focusing attention on the same object, and becoming mutually aware of each other's focus, thereby creating intersubjectivity; repeating the same actions so that people fall into a shared rhythm. These processes magnify whatever emotion participants are feeling. If the build-up continues without being interrupted or distracted, the group develops an excitement that Durkheim called "collective effervescence"—this is the exciting place to be, the experience that takes you out of your individual self and into something larger and more important.

The feelings and ideas experienced during these shared moments linger in participants' minds and bodies. They feel group solidarity, a sense of "we-ness." They acquire symbols of group membership, whatever they focused upon during the ceremony: Durkheim points to primitive tribal tokens as well as sacred objects of the literate religions (a cross, a Bible, a Koran), and notes that political rituals work the same way, making sacred objects out of a flag, a leader, or a slogan. And individuals get an emotional jolt out of taking part in such rituals: it makes you feel stronger, more dedicated, more energetic.

The ritual theory of solidarity was expanded by Erving Goffman (1967), who noted that not just formal ceremonies but also the common gestures of everyday greetings and politeness generate personal links of solidarity. Goffman called this "interaction ritual" (IR). Operating through the rhythms

DOI: 10.4324/9781003245629-3

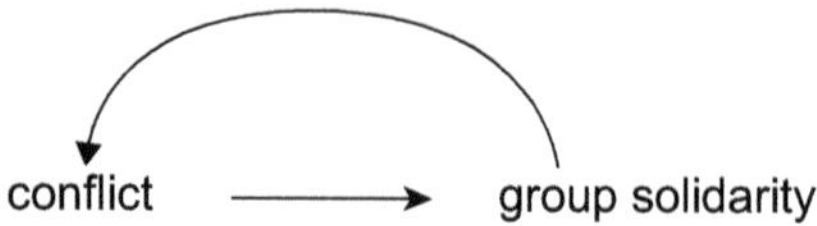

Figure 1.1 Escalation: conflict and solidarity

of talk and bodily alignment, IRs are the building-blocks of friendship, of networks, and of social classes and other groups with which we feel unconscious solidarity. I have stated the theory more formally in a set of ingredients and outcomes intensified by feedback loops (Collins 2004a). I emphasize a crucial point: rituals do not automatically produce solidarity. They can succeed or fail. Some rituals are extremely powerful (the rituals of a religion when one converts to it; the rituals of a political movement when its rallies are most intense). But many rituals fail; their ingredients are not strong enough to get off the ground (anyone who has gone to a dull party or sat through a boring speech knows what I mean). Many rituals, both formal macro-rituals and informal micro-rituals, are in the middle ground, mildly attractive and mildly influential, but fading away over a period of time if they are not repeated.[1]

Conflict is one of the strongest influences on social rituals; that is to say, conflict itself, insofar as it is conflict between groups, tends to produce very strong rituals. This is shown in Figure 1.2. The boxes on the

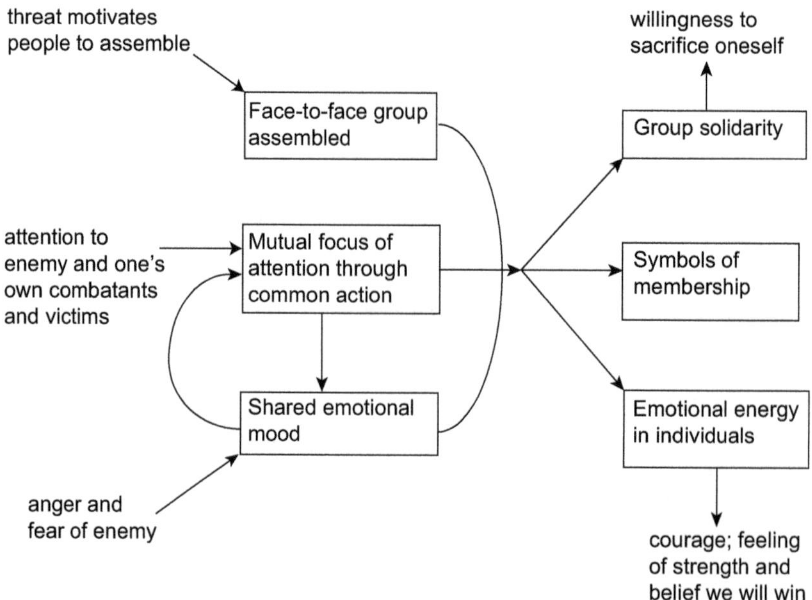

Figure 1.2 Conflict as an interaction ritual

left are three major ingredients. Conflict raises the level of each. Threat motivates people to assemble. Paying attention to the enemy produces a very strong mutual focus of attention—we can't turn our attention away, and we become acutely attuned to how the people around us are reacting to the threat. Anger and fear of the enemy are among the strongest and most contagious emotions.

On the right side of the model are three major outcomes of successful interaction ritual: Group solidarity, as Durkheim noted, makes you willing to sacrifice yourself for the group. Interaction ritual produces idealized symbols of membership, marking off good and evil at the boundary of the group. And it produces high emotional energy (EE), that is, confidence and enthusiasm; in conflict, emotional energy takes the form of courage, feeling strength in the group and belief that we will win in the end.

These outcomes are highest when the interaction ritual is at its most intense; interaction ritual is a set of variables, and we are going to trace their rise and fall over time. Conflict theory is not the opposite of a theory of human ideals, social cooperation and solidarity; we don't have a sentimental good theory of human beings, on one hand, and a cynical conflict theory, on the other. It is all part of the same theory.

C-Escalation

We now have a series of feedback loops, and I am going to add some more. Conflict and solidarity cause each other to rise, and thus we have the familiar spiral of conflict escalation. Plus, we add what I will call the atrocities/polarization loop (Figure 1.3).

Atrocities are actions by the opponent that we perceive as especially hurtful and evil, a combination of physical and moral offense that we find outrageous. Atrocities generate righteous anger, an especially Durkheimian emotion, bringing about the imperative feeling that we must punish the perpetrators, not just for ourselves but as a matter of principle.

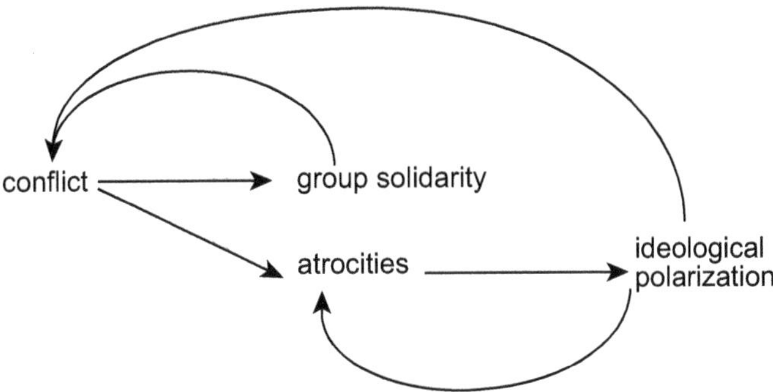

Figure 1.3 Escalating conflict: atrocities and polarization

The atrocities loop starts already at the level of conflict talk. This is apparent in small-scale conflicts, such as arguments, and trash-talking that precedes fights (Collins 2008: 337–369, and references therein). Conflict talk is a combination of insulting the other, boasting about one's own power, and making threats. On the micro-level, most of this is only Goffmanian frontstage performance, but in an escalating situation partisans take it as real; we remember our opponent's worst utterances and repeat them among ourselves, to keep up the emotional stimulus for our own high-solidarity ritual. In gossip as in politics, negatives are remembered much more strongly than positives (Baumeister et al. 2001; Rozin and Royzman 2001).

And as time goes along, stories circulate about atrocities the enemy has carried out, mobilizing more people onto our side, increasing the size of our interaction ritual. As conflicts escalate over time, some of the atrocities turn out to be real; but some of them are only rumors, and many are exaggerated. During the period of escalation, it is difficult to distinguish between rumors and realities; in the heightened interaction ritual, no one is interested in the distinction.

When conflict turns violent, there are several sociological reasons why atrocities really do occur. The most important point is that violence is generally incompetent and imprecise. Most persons in threatening situations stay back from the action, and relatively few actually fight; even those posing as belligerents usually do not get beyond threatening gestures and verbal bluster. Those who do fire guns, use weapons, or launch bodily blows miss their targets most of the time. This incompetence is a major source of atrocities.

Micro-sociological research looks at violence-threatening situations in as much detail as possible, seeking the micro-mechanisms that determine who does what and with what effect. It makes use of photos and videos, participants' accounts, ethnographic observations, forensic reconstructions (such as bullet paths and numbers of shots fired), data on bodily physiology, and subjective phenomenology. Becoming familiar with masses of such data makes a micro-sociologist skeptical of taking at face value what participants say about their motives for violence.[2] Good interviewing needs to probe what participants did in the interactional sequence over time, including opponents, supporters, and bystanders. We want as much situational context as possible, especially on what happens in the early part of the encounter and its escalation. This helps overcome fallacies arising from sampling on the dependent variable, seeing only those cases where violence comes about.

The main thing we see is that fighters are full of confrontational tension and fear. Photos of combat, riots, brawls, hold-ups and other kinds of violence typically show body postures are tense; facial expressions most commonly display fear—and not just the victim, but the perpetrator. Fighters are pumped up with adrenaline and cortisol; their heart rate accelerates to levels where fine motor coordination (i.e. control of your fingers) is lost and perception is blurred (Grossman 2004). As a result, combatants often hit the wrong target, whether by friendly fire—hitting their own side—or by hitting innocent bystanders. Confrontational tension/fear (CT/F) makes most violence incompetent—virtually the opposite of surgically precise.[3] This is a major source of atrocities.

For violence to actually happen, perpetrators must find a pathway around the barrier of CT/F. There are several such pathways, producing different types of violent scenarios. Most relevant here is the pathway of *attacking the weak*. The most successful tactic in real-life violence is for the stronger or more heavily armed to attack a weaker victim. In brawls, gang fights, and riots, almost all the damage is done by a group that manages to find an isolated victim. Thus, most violence is easily perceived as an atrocity, to be avenged by further violence, which the other side in turn also perceives as atrocity. As an exception, the ideal "fair fight" between evenly matched individuals does sometimes happen, but only in carefully arranged duels or exhibitions; such fair fights are not regarded as atrocities and do not result in escalation.[4] This supports my point that it is the perception of atrocities that produces polarization, not just violence per se.

The most dramatic kinds of atrocities are what I have called "forward panic": an emotional frenzy of piling on and overkill, that happens when a group engaged in prolonged confrontation suddenly experiences their tension released as dominance shifts overwhelmingly in their favor (Collins 2008: 83–133). The infamous Rodney King beating, captured on a camcorder in 1991, was of this kind; so are many instances of police beatings that happen at the end of a high-speed chase. Also typical are one-sided beatings of individuals or small groups caught by bigger groups in riots, and massacres in military battles after one side has given up. An important micro-interactional feature is that the victims have lost all their emotional energy, becoming passive in the face of the victors' onslaught.

The connection between atrocity and polarization is illustrated particularly clearly in an incident in the Palestinian *intifada* in October, 2000 (details, sources, and photo in Collins 2008: 421–423). Four off-duty Israeli soldiers had the bad luck to drive their jeep into a Palestinian funeral procession for a young boy killed the day before by Israeli troops. The outraged crowd of several hundred chased the soldiers into a building and killed them. In the photo, one of the killers waves his blood-stained hands to the crowd below, who cheer and wave back. Their faces show joy and solidarity, entrainment in the act of killing. From the Israeli side, this is an atrocity; for these Palestinians, it is an intensely moral interaction ritual, a celebration of what from their perspective appears are well-deserved justice.[5]

Atrocities cause atrocities in response. Neither side sees their own actions as atrocities, because of ideological polarization. From the opposing point of view, the enemy's moral blindness is taken as proof that they are morally sub-human. Angry denunciation of enemy atrocities frequently make this charge, in varying vocabularies.

Polarization is an intensification of the Durkheimian process of identifying the solidarity group with good, and evil as what is outside its boundary. Intense conflict unifies the group in a tribalistic ritual, giving the palpable feeling that Durkheim argued is the source of the sacred, and the social construction of good and evil. As conflict escalates, polarization increases: the enemy is evil, unprincipled, stupid, ugly, ridiculous, cowardly, and weak—negative in every respect. Our side becomes increasingly perceived as good, principled, intelligent, brave, and all the other virtues.

Polarization is the source of many aspects of conflict that in calmer perspective we would regard as immoral and irrational. Polarization causes atrocities. Because we feel completely virtuous, everything we do is good, whether it be torture, mutilation, or massacre. And because at high polarization the enemy is completely evil, they deserve what is done to them. Genocidal massacres, like Rwanda in 1994, start with build-up of emotional polarization, broadcasting the threat of atrocities that the enemy has already carried out, or is about to carry out if we do not forestall them.[6] Similar processes are found in the tortures carried out by US guards at Abu Ghraib military prison in 2004, in an atmosphere of small group ritualism and hilarity expressing intense emotional solidarity against a humiliated enemy (Graveline and Clemens 2010). Polarization is the dark shadow of the highest levels of successful interaction ritual. The more intense the feeling of our goodness, the easier it is to commit evil.

A second consequence of polarization is to escalate and prolong conflict. Even if a realistic assessment might show that further conflict is unwinnable, or that its costs would be too great, periods of high polarization keep partisans from seeing this. Because of polarization, both sides perceive themselves as strong and the enemy as, ultimately, weak; therefore we expect to win.

Mobilizing Allies through Atrocities and Polarization

The amount of escalation depends not only on emotional processes, but on numbers of participants and resources. Longer-lasting conflicts require further feedback loops. An embattled group first mobilizes its members locally; for large-scale conflict, it seeks sympathizers and allies (Figure 1.4).

This is done by activating prior network ties and by making exchange partners feel it is not only in their interest to join us, but that it is morally imperative to do so. Partisans try to mobilize the network by appealing to ideals, and above all by circulating atrocity stories, showing how

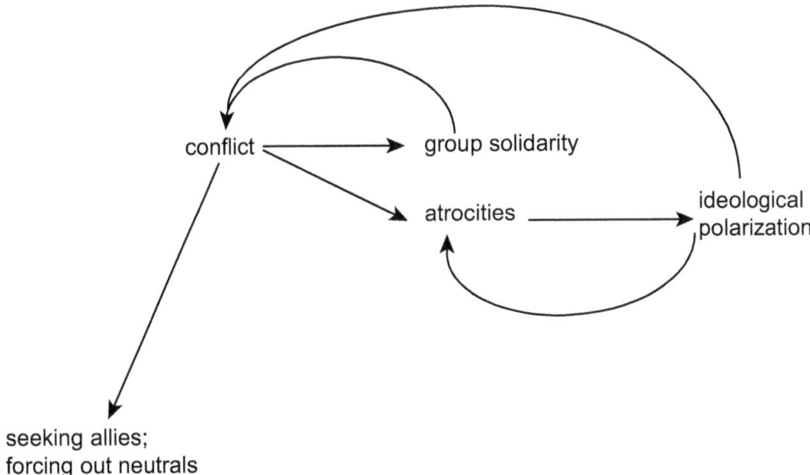

Figure 1.4 Escalating conflict: seeking allies

evil the other side is. The process of recruiting allies is done by spreading emotional polarization to others who are not originally involved. Slogans generally take such forms as: "Whoever is not with us is against us"; "No one is free as long as anyone is imprisoned." Since this is not literally true, belief in it depends on propagating a surge of collective emotion.

It is predictable whether third parties become allies of one side or the other, and with what degree of enthusiasm or reluctance, or whether they remain neutral. As Donald Black (1998) shows in *The Social Structure of Right and Wrong*, partisanship depends on the presence or absence of network ties and their relative social distance from each side.

If seeking allies and forcing out neutrals is successful, we add them to our coalition. This supports the last component of the process, mobilizing material resources (Figure 1.5). These include the numbers of activists, fighters, and supporters who take part in the effort; money, as you well know from fund-raising campaigns; full-time organization, if the conflict is to last for any considerable period of time; and weapons, if the conflict is violent.

One of the things that varies among conflicts is how much of their resources come from outside allies. In the Arab Spring uprisings of 2011, some groups relied heavily on outside intervention—notably in Libya and Syria, while others were local (Tunisia, Egypt). What difference does it make if resources are mostly external or internal? And whether they are military, economic, or merely communicative, such as journalistic sympathy and Internet activity?

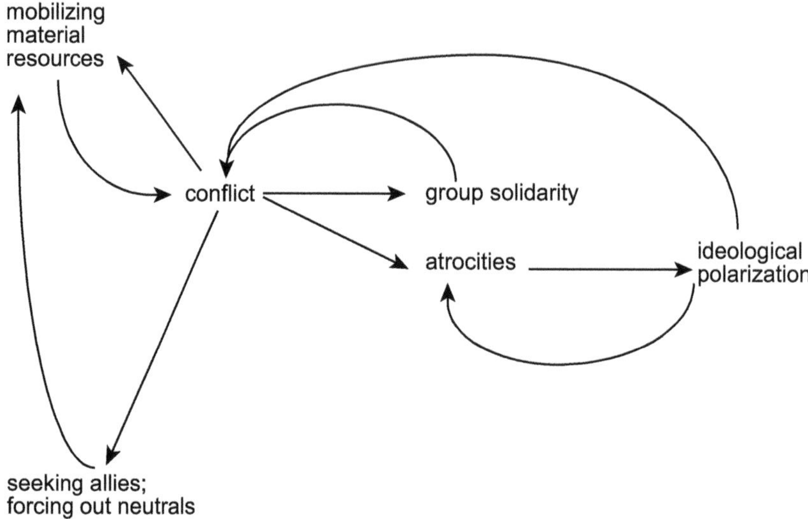

Figure 1.5 Escalating conflict: material resources

Locally-resourced uprisings are generally shorter. Outside military aid keeps violent conflict going much longer, especially when it is given to both sides. Worst of all is when many different states promote their local favorites, resulting in a truly chaotic situation (in the technical sense), where there is no clear equilibrium point.[7]

Sanctions, legal threats in international courts, and economic embargoes do not appear to be very effective, because their time-dynamics are very long-term, while most other C-escalation components are much faster. Direct military intervention can sway the balance in the medium run; but its effect is to keep the conflict going, if the opposing sides have equivalent military resources.

We now have the full model. All these processes are happening for both sides of a conflict simultaneously, so we need to model them twice. This gives us two interlinked flow-charts, each escalating in response to the other. Hence the term C-escalation, for counter-escalation (Figure 1.6).

Note that all feedback loops in the model are positive. If we were to do a computer simulation, conflict would escalate to infinity. What keeps this from happening in reality? Two processes introduce negative values into the variables. One process is victory or defeat, which is asymmetrical, as one side goes positive and the other side negative, or at any rate going negative at different rates. The other process is de-escalation.

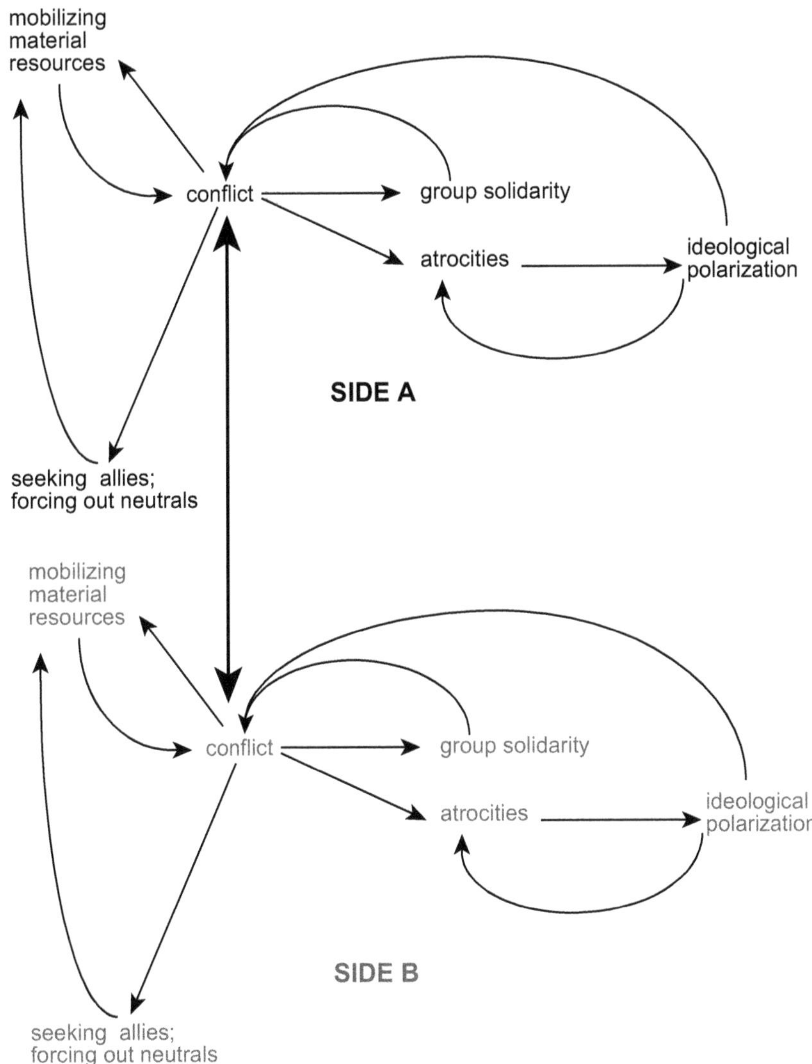

Figure 1.6 C-escalation (two-sided counter-escalation)

Victory, Defeat, or Stalemate

Moves against the enemy are attempts to destroy the major variables that support their ability to carry the conflict. There are three main paths (Figure 1.7).

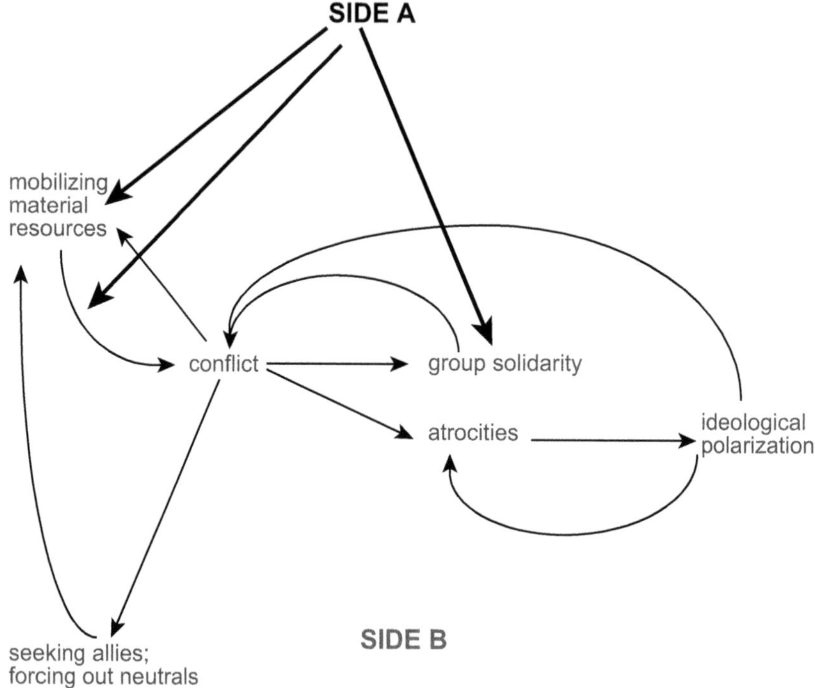

Figure 1.7 Winning, losing, stalemate

1. Attack the enemy's group solidarity. This is done by breaking up their organization; by taking the initiative or momentum, thereby putting them in a passive or indecisive position. In terms of micro-sociology, it means dominating the emotional attention space.
2. Attack the enemy's material base, physically destroying their resources.
3. Attack enemy logistics, their supply lines, cutting them off from moving people, supplies, and weapons to sustain the conflict.

I will illustrate this in Chapter 10 with a more elaborate model of victory or defeat in military battle.

The key point is that victory comes chiefly through breaking down enemy organization, rather than destroying their army by sheer firepower. In asymmetrical battles, organizational breakdown happens to one side while the other side retains its organization. Most casualties happen after a military organization has broken down; defeated troops have lost their solidarity and their ability to resist, and this is when they get killed or captured (Collins 2008: 104–112).

We see the same process on the micro level. In a photo from my collection, taken during the overthrow of the Serbian nationalist leader Milošević on October 6, 2000, we see a typical pattern in riots: four men are attacking one, who is covering his head and trying to escape. The attackers wield a stick, a tire iron, and their bare hands. But the retreating soldier is the only one with a gun, the pistol still in his holster. Physically he has superior force, and could kill the others. But he is isolated from support, and has lost momentum, falling into a passive mode as his attackers advance. Emotional dominance precedes and determines physical dominance. This pattern is documented in all areas of the micro-sociology of violence (Collins 2008: 71–72, 102–104, 156–189).

Victory and defeat are reciprocals of each other. But there is another possibility. Physical destruction and loss of social capacity may remain sufficiently balanced on both sides so that conflict goes on for a long time. This is stalemate. How long it goes on and why it varies remain unclear. But at a point yet to be specified, stalemate begins to send the C-escalation process into reverse: D-escalation or de-escalation.

D-Escalation

We come now to a series of diagrams showing how conflict can de-escalate. In winning or losing, it is largely a matter of how one side successfully attacks the key components of the enemy's ability to escalate. In de-escalation, the variables fall for a variety of reasons, not necessarily from opponents' action; and this decline happens at a rate where both sides lose their ability to sustain the conflict.

First: solidarity may fail because people avoid the conflict group. Small-scale quarrels and fights are especially likely to de-escalate in this way, as most people stay out of the fight. On a larger scale, a protest movement may fail to keep up attendance at demonstrations.[8] The conflict group may remain isolated and small. Or enemy attack may break up the group or prevent its supporters from assembling (Figure 1.8).[9]

Second: violent conflict has a special difficulty to overcome: confrontational tension and fear in face-to-face encounters (Figure 1.9). Verbal accounts by persons who have performed violence tend to focus on their own anger and motives, usually giving moralistic and polarized accounts of their rationale, implying that violence was inevitable. Here visual evidence of violent situations is especially valuable as a corrective. Photos typically show that at the moment of violence itself, the expressions on participants' faces are fear, not anger (Collins 2008: 42–45; 413–430). In photos of riots and other crowd violence, only a small number of those in the picture are actually performing any violence; this is typical also of virtually all close observations of fighting—most of the group is incapacitated by fear. Whatever they say their reasons for violence are, their verbal accounts

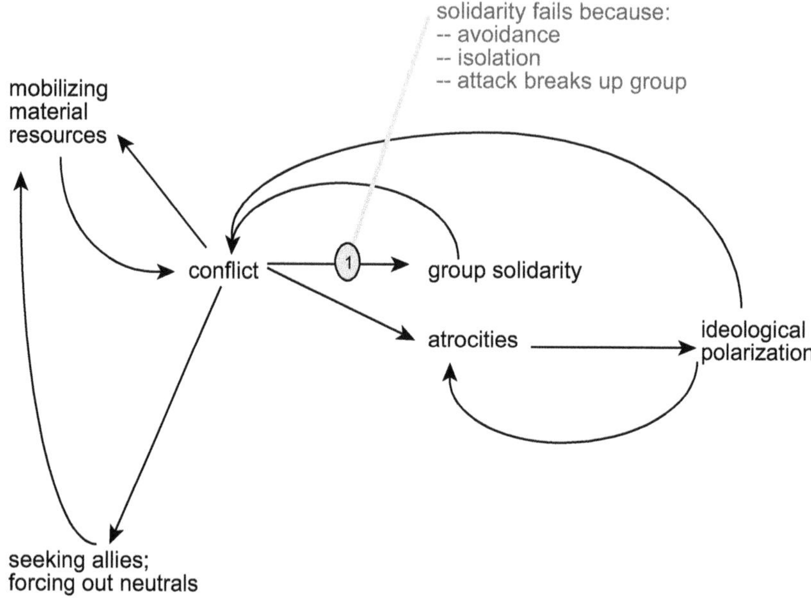

Figure 1.8 De-escalating conflict: solidarity fails

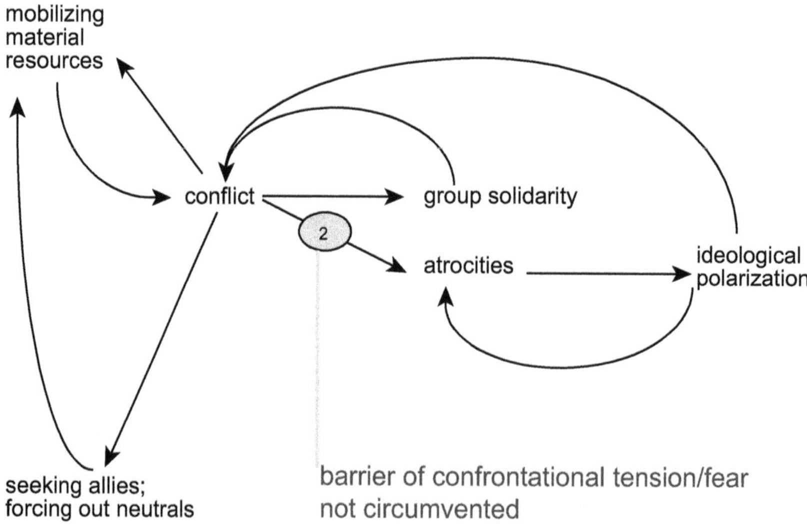

Figure 1.9 De-escalating conflict: confrontational tension/fear

tend to hide this crucial reality. In most of violence-threatening situations, it does not come off. Violence does not escalate because it cannot get past this point (Collins 2008: 361–369).

Most face-to-face threats consist of bluster, angry words, and gestures. This is not necessarily a bad thing, because many fights become stalled at the point of mutual equilibrium. The micro-details are displayed in a photo in Collins (2008: 365). It shows an Israeli soldier and a Palestinian militant, in angry confrontation on the Temple Mount in Jerusalem, the scene of many bloody incidents. But not this day; the angry quarrel eventually subsided without further escalation. The details of how to avoid escalation are visible here: both sides exactly mirror each other's gestures and emotional intensity. The two individuals are in a stare-down contest, their faces almost touching, brows expressing anger, mouths open and shouting. But they are in equilibrium. Neither one escalates ahead of the other. Neither side has established domination of the emotional attention space; neither has the emotional energy advantage, and eventually their EE falls off.[10] This is practical advice from micro-sociology: you can keep a confrontation from escalating by keeping it at the level of stalled repetitions, until it de-escalates quite literally from boredom. This is easiest to accomplish in small-scale confrontations; the higher the number of people, the more likely there will be some places where there are asymmetries, so that the equilibrium is broken.

Third: the entire set of feedback loops among solidarity, polarization, and conflict can become de-escalated through emotional burnout. This is an area we are just beginning to research, the time-dynamics of various kinds of conflict (Figure 1.10).

Conflict produces solidarity, but how long does it last? The day after the 9/11 attacks in 2001, I realized this would be an opportunity to find out (Collins 2004b). The first two days, people looked shocked and bewildered. On the third day, American flags started to appear; within a few days, they were sold everywhere, posted on cars and windows, sometimes worn on clothing. All public gatherings—such as athletic events and music concerts—began with huge flag displays, generally accompanied by the other newly-consecrated symbols of heroism, ranks of firefighters and police officers representing those killed in the Twin Towers. I surveyed the number of cars on the streets that displayed flags, as well as the numbers on buildings and windows, repeating observations of the same places at least weekly for a year (Collins 2004b). The time pattern that emerged was the following.

The first two weeks were an explosion of flag-displaying, rapidly reaching its peak.[11] It stayed at that peak for three months. This was also a period of intense national solidarity in other respects: Political debate largely disappeared. The popularity of the President—George W. Bush—reached 90

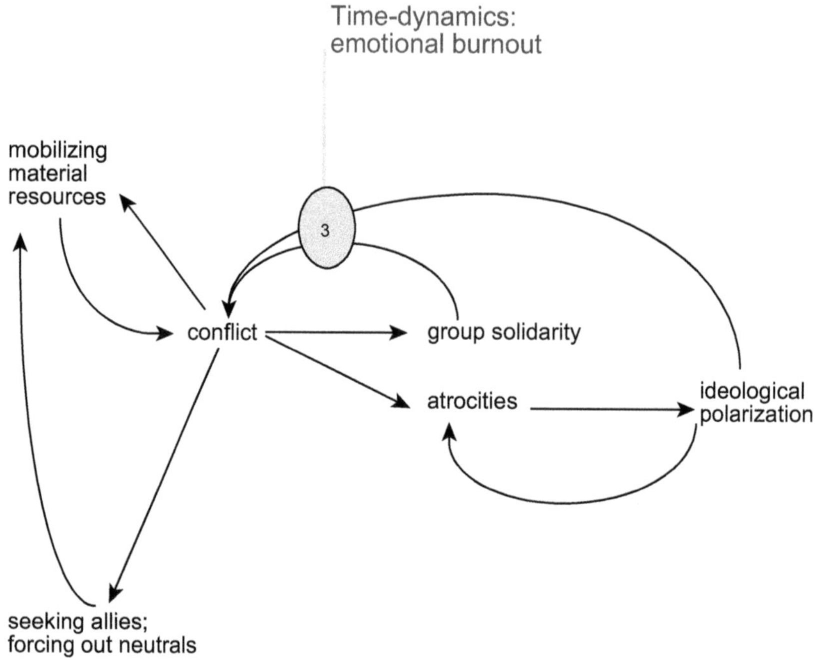

Figure 1.10 De-escalating conflict: emotional burnout

percent (the highest on record), a rise of about 40 percentage points from just prior to 9/11, 2001, and far above the levels to which it would fall later in Bush's administration. Around three months, political argument resumed, and articles began to appear asking, "Is it OK to take our flags down now?" The level of flag display began to fall off, reaching a moderate level around six months; thereafter it became a distinctly minority expression, with brief upward blips at the one-year anniversary and other commemorative dates (Figure 1.11).

Solidarity over time has the shape of a fireworks rocket: very rapid ascent, a lengthy plateau, and a slow dissipation. The actual length of these time-patterns varies with different kinds of conflict, and other conditions; here we need comparative research.[12] The three-month plateau and six-month dissipation fit popularity spikes for political leaders at times of dramatic turning-points in massive conflicts, i.e. conflicts on the size of entire nations. There are other correlates, such as the suppression of dissent during the explosion phase, and the tendency toward atrocities and paranoid rumors during the three-month plateau. Wars are almost always greeted by an initial burst of enthusiasm, which wanes within six months; not to say that wars cannot continue longer, but

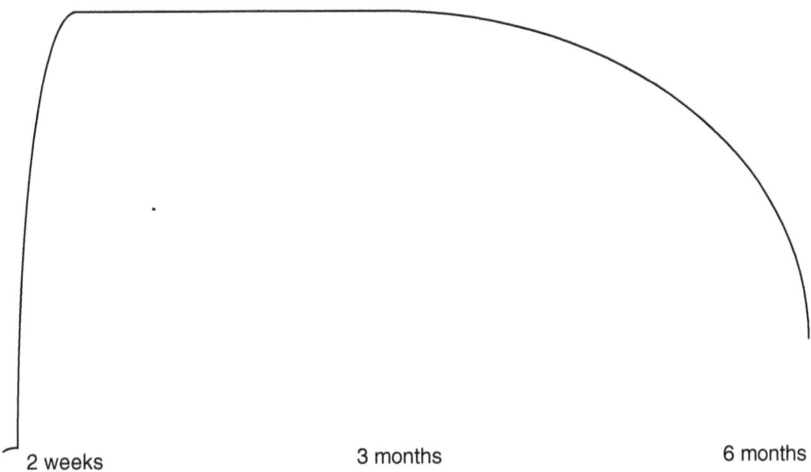

Figure 1.11 Time-dynamics of conflict solidarity: explosion, plateau, dissipation

Source: Collins (2004b).

they enter into another emotional phase, increasingly just grinding it through, accompanied by internal emotional splits that I will discuss shortly.

Fourth: we shift now to the left side of the model, which is where material and larger macro-conditions come in. Conflict de-escalates when material resources are no longer available to sustain it. This may happen because the resource base is exhausted; or because logistics channels fail to deliver the goods to the front line activists (Figure 1.12). War winds down when it becomes materially too costly to carry it on—more precisely, if both sides wind down resources at approximately the same rate, since a big disparity between the sides gives one of them the opportunity for victory. At a smaller scale, riots tend to be short, usually confined to a few days, because rioters have to go home and eat, and eventually to get back into their economic routines; small-scale conflicts lack the institutionalized organization to deliver material resources, that keeps larger conflicts going such as wars and social movements.

In principle, the third route to de-escalation is the opposite of the fourth route: in the former, material resources to keep on fighting may still exist but participants are emotionally burned out; in the latter, they may still want to go on, but materially they cannot. These are ideal types, and they interact in various ways. Like Napoleon's 3-to-1 ratio of morale to material, it may turn out that the emotional burnout path—indeed, the whole set of de-escalation processes on the right side of the model—tend to

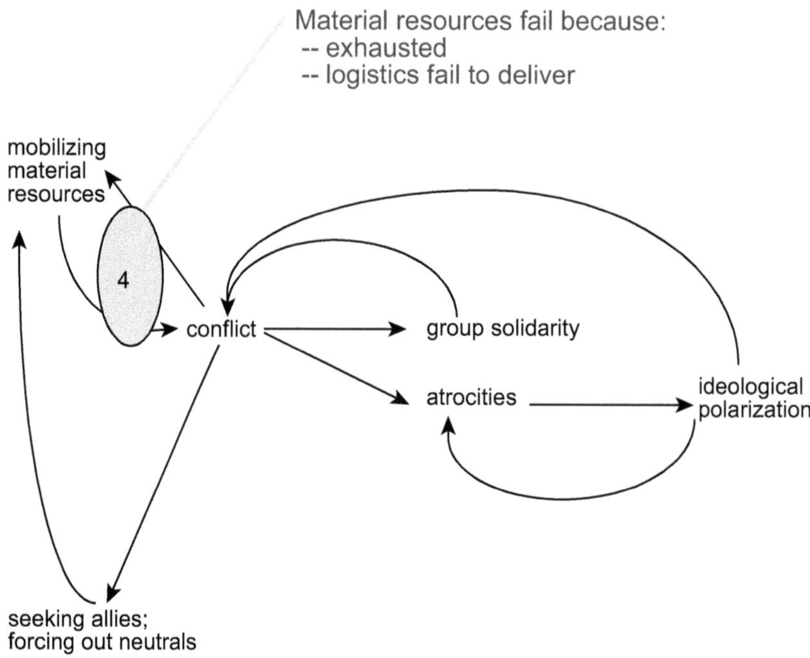

Figure 1.12 De-escalating conflict: material resources fail

outweigh the material route on the left. But material weakness can lead to the other side's successful attack, resulting in destroying one's organization and capacity to assemble for group rituals and by that route losing one's moral resources.[13]

Fifth and finally: the alliances which earlier supported a conflict fall away. Here neutrals reappear. As Donald Black (1998) and Mark Cooney (1998) have shown in their work on third parties, neutrals, equidistant from both sides while maintaining contacts with both, are in the crucial position to negotiate the steps that eventually bring disengagement. Neutrals, despised at the beginning, now take the idealistic high ground; and the mutual atrocities accumulated during the conflict begin to cast a pall on continuing polarization (Figure 1.13).[14]

Much of what I have said about de-escalating conflict can be put in terms of micro-sociological theory. Figure 1.14 again displays the Interaction Ritual model, used earlier to show how conflict generates solidarity during the escalation phase. During de-escalation, the variables go into reverse. Instead of assembling the group, it becomes dispersed. Mutual focus of attention is broken, as individuals pay more attention to nonmembers of the conflict group; worse yet, they may even fraternize with

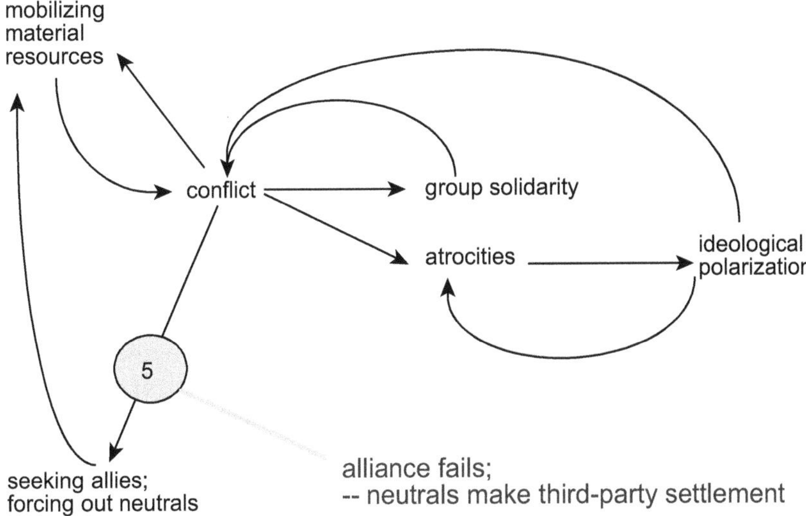

Figure 1.13 De-escalating conflict: third-party settlement

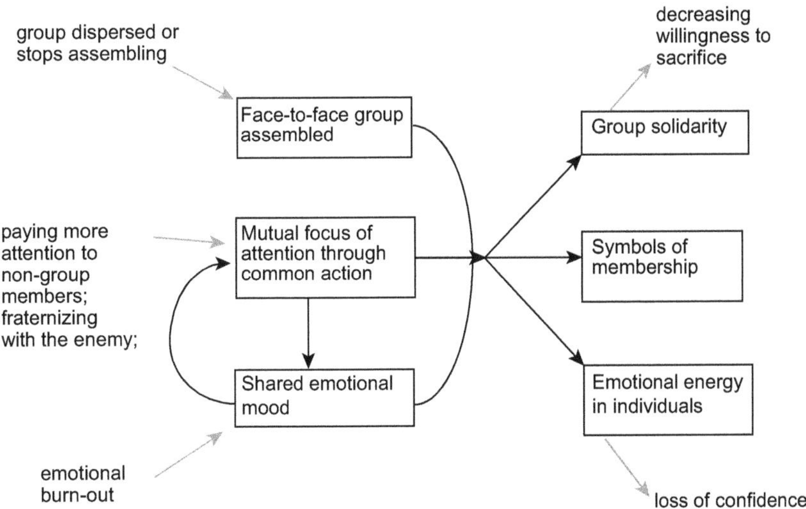

Figure 1.14 De-escalating conflict: interaction ritual fails

the enemy. And emotional burnout is the opposite of collective effervescence, reducing the shared emotional mood.

On the outcome side, group solidarity declines. And since solidarity is the source of idealism, individuals become less willing to sacrifice themselves for the group. Symbols of membership lose their intensity. Ideological polarization declines; the opponent becomes perceived as less demonic, our images of ourselves becomes less omni-righteous, less puffed up with our own virtues and collective omnipotence. And emotional energy falls away; since high EE means high confidence and enthusiasm, we lose confidence in our cause and pursue it with less energy. We are less exalted by the group, returning to the pragmatics of everyday life.

Victory Faction or Peace Faction

As we near the end, I want to emphasize a contradiction between the middle part of my theory and the latter part. The middle is asymmetrical: it is what one side attempts to do in order to gain victory, to impose defeat on the other. The latter part is symmetrical: de-escalation happens when both sides undergo degradation of their emotional and material resources, at a rate equal enough so that both become willing to end the conflict. This is a contradiction in real life, not just in theory. As de-escalating processes increase, the main obstacle to peace is those participants who feel they can still win. Thus, in the latter phase of a protracted conflict, a new set of factions appears: on one side, the hard-liners or militants, the victory faction; on the other, the peace party, the negotiators, the de-escalators. As we see in recent discussion about the Iraq and Afghanistan wars, the reasons of the peace faction or disengagement faction can be a mixture of ideals, burnout, and material costs. The motives and ideals of the war faction are also mixed, but above all they cling to the emotions and ideals of the phase of high solidarity through external conflict.

This new level of internal conflict muddies the purity of near-universal solidarity at the beginning of the conflict. The conflict between victory faction and peace faction can go either way; think of Churchill and Roosevelt in WWII, or the disgruntlements of US foreign policies from the Vietnam War to the present. I am not preaching about this one way or the other, but stressing an analytical point: if the strength of the various processes in the conflict model remain fluctuating long enough within a central range, this internal conflict will emerge.[15]

Theory should give the conditions for whether militants or compromisers prevail. On the theoretical level, a key point is that external conflict generates emergent lines of internal conflict. Hard-liners and compromisers are not the same as Left and Right; they are not rooted in pre-existing identities, such as classes, or religions, or ethnicities; they come into being because of the time-dynamics of conflict itself. They are, so to speak, latent possibilities in the structure of conflict space over time.

Hard-liners and compromisers are identities that do not easily fit into ideological categories; but in the latter phase of a prolonged conflict, it is this axis that takes over the center of attention. This is the time-period for the angriest accusations about traitors and sell-outs, and counter-accusations of blind fanaticism. A more advanced theory of conflict will tell us more about the process of emergent factionalization, conflict creating its own identities as it goes along, based more on tactics than on ideologies and interests.[16]

Perpetuating Conflict

We are not just theorists and researchers; we live through such conflicts ourselves. Does being aware of sociological processes help us navigate the real world?

Here is the most popular poem to come out of World War I. It was written by a Canadian officer who died on the Western Front in the last year of the war. It is a sentimental poem—maudlin, hokey. It's not true that men are unemotional; they're just emotional about different things than women. Men are sentimental about violence.

> In Flanders fields the poppies blow
> Between the crosses row on row . . .
>
> *We are the Dead.* Short days ago
> We lived, felt dawn, saw sunset glow,
> Loved and were loved; and now we lie
> In Flanders fields.
>
> *Take up our quarrel with the foe:*
> To you from failing hands we throw
> The torch; be yours to hold it high.
> *If you break faith with us who die*
> *We shall not sleep*, though poppies grow
> In Flanders fields.
> (John McRae, written in 1915.
> Emphasis added.)

The poem re-enacts the most effective of all conflict rituals: the funeral of a dead comrade-in-arms. My collection contains photos of motorcycle police mourning a fellow cop shot in action; they look the same as the photos of Hells Angels in their funeral procession; the same as photos of gang members making their gang signs over the grave of one killed in a drive-by. The message is the same: solidarity with the dead, to keep the fight going. What count as losses, for the de-escalators, are turned into symbols of our unstoppable drive toward victory.

I come down to being a sociologist. If there is anything we have to offer, it is clarity about a complex and dynamic situation. Polarization is the great enemy; it is false clarity, false simplification into one bundle in which we pack all the negative stereotypes about our opponents, and another bundle into which we pack self-righteous praise of our collective selves. Polarization is thinking through the categories of our insults. It makes for poor sociology; and generally it makes for unrealistic and inhumane action.

Yes, sometimes we have to plunge into the phase of escalation and polarization, if we hope to win and cause changes in the world, although there are always unintended consequences. But we need to be aware of what we are getting into, and be ready to pull ourselves back into sociological clarity when the first emotional binge is over. Max Weber threw himself into the war effort in the first months of enthusiasm of World War I, but then he returned to being a sociologist and worked for a negotiated peace and for a way to reconstruct a democratic post-war Germany (Radkau 2009).

Above all, we have to be sociological about ideals, our own as well as everyone else's. Ideals are part of social reality; interaction rituals make us ideal-making creatures, attached to our symbols. But ideals and solidarity are the strongest weapons of conflict, and the main forces that drive conflict in the C-escalation phase. Ironically, abstract ideals and principles make conflict worse; merely pragmatic and self-interested conflict is easier to negotiate. In the de-escalation process, solidarity and ideals are the greatest obstacles. That is what sociological sophistication is about.

Notes

1. There is an element of time-dynamics already in Durkheim's formulation. He argued that the earliest time-systems were built around the number of days over which ceremonies were repeated. Ritual repetitions approximately every 7 days appear to be the average for keeping up moderately strong religious attachment; carrying them out every day, or several times a day, makes you devout or fanatical. I have estimated (from changes in political allegiance) that a year or two of failing to taking part in the meetings and demos of a political movement you once strongly supported is enough to reduce the feeling of identification to near zero.
2. In contemporary youth culture, violent persons often say they were disrespected by the victim, and that they were defending their honor (for examples, Collins 2008: 353–360). But micro-detail shows that such individuals are violent only when there is a particular situational configuration; not every conflictual encounter is taken as a necessity for punishing disrespect or defending honor. Statement of motives for violence is not a sufficient explanation for what happens; often it is an ideology that obfuscates what actually happens. Above all, popular rhetoric avoids mentioning the dynamics of confrontational tension and fear.
3. Shooters on a firing range, or in simulated situations, are far more accurate than in real face-to-face confrontations (Holmes 1985; Collins 2008: 57–60; 384). As long as participants (like police trainees and military recruits) know that it is not real, they don't experience the bodily surge of CT/F that makes combat so different.
4. The development of duelling in sixteenth-century Europe came as a substitute for vendettas. Death or injury in a duel could not be avenged, and thus duels were a

step toward limiting violence to self-contained individual incidents (Collins 2008: 193–241; Spierenburg 2008).

5. An Israeli security officer told me that the men in this photo were identified, tracked down, and killed by elite security forces.
6. Horowitz (2001) shows that deadly ethnic riots are always preceded by rumors. In the case of Rwanda in 1994, Hutu militants carried out a prolonged massacre of Tutsis, while rumors abounded of alleged Hutu massacres by Tutsis. On this case and the larger dynamics, see Mann (2005); McDoom (2021).
7. A large majority of armed groups in internal conflicts during 1945–2005 received outside funding or arms; with the end of the Cold War around 1990, such conflicts ended at a higher rate, because this balance of funding by opposing geopolitical blocs greatly declined (Schlichte 2009: 121–123). But following the Arab Spring, outside interventions in the Middle East surged; the result in Syria was a multi-sided civil war so severe that it continued into the decade of the 2020s and made three-quarters of the population refugees.
8. A Black Lives Matter demonstration at its height, in San Diego, June 6, 2020, had 3000 participants. Its anniversary demonstration in 2021 had 35 persons (*San Diego Union Tribune*, June 6, 2021).
9. This was the pattern of democracy protests in Hong Kong during 2019. See Chapter 4 for details.
10. The photo also shows other people in the background, both Israelis and Palestinians. None of these has the intense emotional expression of the two protagonists in the foreground. As is typical of the standoff phase of crowd confrontations, their behavior waits on a trigger from a small number who change the focus of attention by violent action. In this case, the trigger did not occur.
11. This level was never more than 38–46 percent of residences and 10 percent of cars. Mass solidarity is carried by substantial numbers, but it does require unanimity, as long as oppositional expressions do not disturb the dominant expression. We see this also in opinion polls showing support of leaders in times of crisis; typically these reach about 83–90 percent, but except in totalitarian regimes, never much higher. Sources in Collins (2004b).
12. My point is not how long individuals bear grudges—a topic needing empirical investigation in its own right—but how long overt conflict is mobilized at various levels of intensity.
13. The model applies to all kinds of conflict, across the size dimension from the smallest micro to the largest macro. One reason why micro-interactions among individuals and small groups usually cannot escalate very far is that they lack the formal organizational structure to get over to the left side of the model; hence whatever material resources they have at the moment will soon be exhausted, and the conflict will come to an end. This is so even if the conflict becomes extremely violent: if an individual is killed in a quarrel, the bodies are lacking to carry on unless there is a larger organized structure, such as a gang or clan, to exact revenge. But even these semi-formal structures tend to be rather ineffective at keeping vendettas going, and their hostility remains more often at the level of bluster than of actual fighting. The idea of a unending vendetta is a myth. Evidence is found in Collins (2008: 231, 489) and Spierenburg (2008).
14. The effectiveness of neutrals has its own time-dynamics. In general, third-party intervention as peace-makers is most effective when a conflict is in its emotional burnout phase, or one or more of de-escalating processes 1–4 have already taken effect. But once armed peace-keepers are introduced into a violent conflict, local enthusiasm for their presence appears also to be subject to time-dynamics (yet to be measured); within three months or less, the peacekeepers themselves may become regarded as the enemy. Even purely altruistic third parties, who merely offer humanitarian aid, and avoid

coercive power, can find their good intentions overridden by the prevailing dynamics of the conflict. If the conflict has not already greatly de-escalated, especially by falling solidarity and emotional exhaustion, the material aid they bring to the conflict zone may simply be appropriated by whichever party remains best organized and committed to continue the fight; in this case humanitarian aid becomes part of the material resource loop, keeping the conflict going (Kaldor 2001; Oberschall and Seidman 2005). The practical lesson is that humanitarian aid organizations cannot ignore the time-dynamics of conflict.

15. How long they have to remain in this range for the split to emerge is one of the time-dynamics to be established. Schlichte (2009) shows that in a prolonged stalemate, where a state cannot rely on the loyalty of its army for repression, it tends to create militias using more extreme tactics, which eventually spin off into independent movements. This reminds us that stalemate can lead the victory faction to escalate internally rather than externally. This is one of the sources of the most extreme atrocities and ideological polarization, and a pathway to genocide.
16. Such identities are far from trivial, since they can live for a long time after the particular conflict that spawned them is settled. For instance, the Bolsheviks took their identity from a tactical split inside the revolutionary workers movement in Russia in 1903 and kept their distinct identity for 20 years. Emergent factionalization is one of the key dimensions along which conflict structures and restructures groups and identities. Martin (2009: 283–320) shows that American party politics in the early 1800s began with a distinction purely internal to the political field—the Ins and the Outs—and later expanded to encompass exogenous interest groups and ideological movements.

References

Baumeister, Roy, Ellen Bratslavsky, Catrin Finkehauser, and Kathleen Vohs. 2001. "Bad Is Stronger than Good." *Review of General Psychology* 5: 323–370.

Black, Donald. 1998. *The Social Structure of Right and Wrong*. New York: Academic Press.

Collins, Randall. 2004a. *Interaction Ritual Chains*. Princeton, NJ: Princeton University Press.

Collins, Randall. 2004b. "Rituals of Solidarity and Security in the Wake of Terrorist Attack." *Sociological Theory* 22: 53–87.

Collins, Randall. 2008. *Violence: A Micro-Sociological Theory*. Princeton, NJ: Princeton University Press.

Cooney, Mark. 1998. *Warriors and Peacemakers: How Third Parties Shape Violence*. Albany, NY: New York University Press.

Coser, Lewis. 1956. *The Functions of Social Conflict*. Glencoe, IL: Free Press.

Durkheim, Emile. [1912] 1964. *The Elementary Forms of Religious Life*. New York: Free Press.

Goffman, Erving. 1967. *Interaction Ritual*. New York: Doubleday.

Graveline, Christopher, and Michael Clemens. 2010. *The Secrets of Abu Ghraib Revealed: American Soldiers on Trial*. Washington, DC: Potomac Books.

Grossman, Dave. 2004. *On Combat: The Psychology and Physiology of Deadly Combat in War and Peace*. Belleville, IL: PPTC Research Publications.

Holmes, Richard, 1985. *Acts of War: Behavior of Men in Battle*. New York: Free Press.

Horowitz, Donald L. 2001. *The Deadly Ethnic Riot*. Berkeley, CA: University of California Press.

Kaldor, Mary. 2001. *New and Old Wars: Organized Violence in a Global Era*. Stanford, CA: Stanford University Press.

Mann, Michael. 2005. *The Dark Side of Democracy: Explaining Ethnic Cleansing.* Cambridge: Cambridge University Press.

Martin, John Levi. 2009. *Social Structures.* Princeton, NJ: Princeton University Press.

McDoom, Omar. 2021. *The Path to Genocide in Rwanda.* Cambridge: Cambridge University Press.

Oberschall, Anthony, and Michael Seidman. 2005. "Food Coercion in Revolution and Civil War: Who Wins and How They Do It." *Comparative Studies in Society and History* 47: 372–402.

Radkau, Joachim. 2009. *Max Weber: A Biography.* Cambridge: Polity Press.

Rozin, Paul, and Edward B. Royzman. 2001. "Negativity Bias, Negativity Dominance and Contagion." *Personality and Social Psychology Review* 5: 296–320.

Schlichte, Klaus. 2009. *In the Shadow of Violence: The Politics of Armed Groups.* Frankfurt, Germany: Campus Verlag.

Simmel, Georg. [1908] 1955. "Der Streit." Chapter 4 in *Soziologie.* Trans. Reinhard Bendix and Kurt H. Wolff (Eds.), *Conflict and the Web of Group Affiliations.* Glencoe, IL: Free Press.

Spierenburg, Pieter. 2008. *A History of Murder: Personal Violence in Europe from the Middle Ages to the Present.* Cambridge: Polity Press.

Chapter 2

Time-Bubbles of Nationalism

Introduction

Nationalism is frequently explained in terms of macro-structural causes. Ernest Gellner (1983), Anthony Smith (1986) and others have debated its relationship to modernity and to pre-modern structures. A version of that historical transformation, developed by Gellner protégés, such as Michael Mann (1993) and Sinisa Malesevic (2019), as well as by Charles Tilly (1995) and others, may be called the theory of state penetration into society. I would put it in Weberian terms: patrimonial structures based on alliances among armed households were displaced by bureaucratic organization of the state, beginning with a permanent military and its centralized logistics, generating an expanded apparatus of tax extraction and the penetration of state agencies and laws that bring individuals into direct relation with the state.

Among the important consequences of state penetration was the invention of the social movement. In parcellized medieval society, protests could only be local and mostly ephemeral, but state penetration created both the means of large-scale political mobilization and a target to aim at. By fostering communications, transportation, education, and a dynamic economy, centralizing regimes provided the material means for group mobilization; by penetrating the walls of patrimonial households to inscribe persons on the rolls of the state, not as group members but as individuals, such regimes opened up new possibilities for identity-formation; by centralizing the seat of government, they provided a unifying target at which petition campaigns and revolutions alike could aim. Accordingly, as Mann (1993) and Tilly (1995; 2004) have emphasized, all kinds of social movements mobilized at the same time: classes, nationalisms, as well as a variety of reform movements ranging from anti-slavery to anti-vivisectionism. The social movement was a mold from which a variety of things could be poured. Nationalism was one of its products, just as class movements like socialism and conservatism, were likewise products of the invention of the social movement.

DOI: 10.4324/9781003245629-4

Solidarity Ritual in Lived Time

I would like to extend another angle of vision—the micro-sociology of nationalism. Nationalism may be defined, ideal-typically, as an intensely felt bond of solidarity. But as Billig (1995), Fox and Miller-Idriss (2008), and others have noted, in the day-by-day experience of modern people, national identity is largely a matter of routine. Most of the time, nationalism is low-strength; latent, perhaps, but far from the thoughts and feelings of most people. The institutionalized celebrations and monuments of nationalism are for the most part a backdrop whose meaning is hardly reflected upon, like the statue of the victorious general in the park splattered with pigeon droppings. National holidays, to speak of the ones I have observed, like the US Fourth of July, Mexico's Cinco de Mayo, or France's Bastille Day, are annually scheduled occasions for eating and drinking, fireworks displays, or just a day off from work, and invoke little sense of national solidarity; I have never seen people on such occasions encountering strangers, or even acquaintances, and warmly addressing them as fellow-citizens. It is a danger of symbolic analysis to presume that the analyst can identify the meaning of a symbol, without examining what participants actually are thinking and feeling at the moment. Symbols are alive only to the extent they are the focus of shared emotional attention; and thus symbols can be living, dead, or lukewarm. What I would like to add is a mechanism determining their intensity or lack thereof.

Even in societies where nationalism is institutionalized, it is not necessarily very strong or constant. Structural conditions are insufficient to explain the intensity of nationalism, the moments when it is indeed a living bond of solidarity, uniting strangers into a vast brotherhood, and when it is on the periphery of people's consciousness, or even non-existent in their lives. We need a dynamic theory of nationalism as a process of surges in time.

Hence my chapter title: "Time-Bubbles of Nationalism." These are capsules of collectively experienced time, on the whole, rather sudden in onset, lasting for a while, then declining back to banal normalcy. I could have used the metaphor of a balloon, getting puffed up with Durkheimian collective effervescence, floating high in the air in a mood of widespread social enthusiasm, then gradually coming down to earth as the air slowly seeps out. Social sciences have not been very good at explaining the temporal dimension, the time-patterns of social processes. The most common metaphor, the cycle, is not strictly applicable to most important events of social life, especially social conflicts and mass enthusiasms. The metaphor of the cycle, which may be graphed as a wave, is inaccurate because most real-life social events do not show the symmetrical patterns of an ideal-typical sine wave: the ups and downs do not recur at regular intervals; nor is the amplitude of the peaks and troughs generally so regular. The metaphor of the balloon gives a better picture of the asymmetry of such collective time-dynamics, and of its capsule shape: the balloon is inflated quickly, stays high for a while, then gradually floats down; its beginning is more sudden and dramatic than its ending. A better metaphor would be a rocket zooming into the sky, exploding in an eye-catching blast, then dispersing into fallout slowing fading from vivid to drab. But putting all that into the title would have been more mystifying than illuminating.

The 9/11 Pattern

In the aftermath of the 9/11, 2001 attacks in the USA (shown in Chapter 1, Figure 1.11), national solidarity exploded upward rocket-like in a week or two, remaining at its balloon-like ceiling for three months, then gradually declining toward normalcy by six months. I have referred to this as the three-month solidarity-and-hysteria zone, and adduced comparative evidence that it is within such three-month bubbles of extreme collective attention upon a common identity and a shared danger that both precipitous ventures and violent atrocities are most likely to happen.

The shape of mass solidarity in time or the shape of the time-bubble—the rocket-like ascent, the plateau-like ceiling, the slow dissipation—is similar for the wider class of such events, although much remains to be established by comparison of cases. What varies is how long such events take; here it appears, from cases that I will describe shortly, that the main variation is the length of the high plateau. This calls for theoretical explanation. The extent of mobilization is affected by structural conditions: the historical process of state penetration into society, breaking down local enclaves, fostering communications and transportation, and providing a central arena for political activity and a unifying focus of public attention. Linking these causal levels together, I suggest that the extent of state penetration determines the size of the group that can experience itself as a collective actor, a Durkheimian unity; and it is the size of this sustained collective attention that determines the length of the time-dynamics plateau of widespread symbolic/emotional solidarity. Societies with a high degree of state penetration, and where symbolic mobilization is easily perceived throughout the society, sustain plateaus of national solidarity in the three-month range, but societies that are more fragmented and less state-penetrated may sustain the plateau for about a month.[1]

A further theoretical issue concerns what happens after a collective mobilization has gone through its peak and dissipated. My hypothesis is that a refractory period follows, such that no similar mass enthusiasm can be generated for a period of time thereafter. To risk another metaphor, the nerves of the social animal are innervated after this orgy of attention upon the collectivity; once the air is out of the balloon, it can't get it up again until after a time of rest. The Thermidorian Reaction following the Reign of Terror during the French Revolution is a famous example of such exhaustion from sustained crisis. I will discuss the implications of this point presently.

I offer the metaphor of a time-bubble, to emphasize that the most intense events of social life are capsules in time. Their coming is not expectable in any precise way, certainly nothing like the periodicity of sine waves; it may be a long time before another rocket goes up, another balloon is filled with similarly uplifting enthusiasm. That is why such moments in time have the emotional character of high drama, both tragic and joyous surprise.

Peak Moments Collapse Micro and Macro

There is another and deeper theoretical reason for this sense of uniquely high experience, besides their rarity and unpredictability. What happens inside the bubble is felt to be qualitatively different from ordinary life outside it. Not only is life much more intense at those times, but it has a different structure of social attention. It is rare for us as members of large modern societies to be in a situation where we can be reasonably sure that most other people are paying attention to the same thing, and feeling the same emotion as ourselves. When you are in a mass demonstration, crowds stretching out as far as the eye can see, and even more people beyond them, all thinking the same thought and expressing the same emotion—the regime must go! the people will triumph!—this gives a sense of the solidarity of the whole that Durkheim called collective consciousness. At such moments it is not an abstraction or a myth, but what people feel as the highest reality. The moment does not last; but we are not thinking that now. It will not last because it takes special circumstances to create such a high degree of simultaneous focus of attention; but while it is there, its power of shaping emotions and forming symbols is unsurpassed.

A mass demonstration or focused crowd of this sort is a large-scale version of an interaction ritual. Nationalist demos check all the boxes for the ingredients: first, assembling people bodily in the same place, so that they are in full multi-modal intercommunication; second, focusing their attention upon the same thing, and becoming mutually aware of each other's focus, thereby generating a sense of intersubjectivity; third, feeling and expressing the same emotion. If the ingredients pass a threshold, mutual focus and shared emotion feed back into each other, driving them upwards to high levels of rhythmic entrainment that Durkheim called collective effervescence.[2]

At high levels, what the group focuses upon becomes symbolic, representing membership in the group, as well as depicting its boundaries and enemies; individuals are filled with emotional energy, the feelings of confidence and enthusiasm that motivate them to acts of heroism and sacrifice;

and they are filled with a sense of morality, the palpable experience of good and its fight against evil. Nationalism is such a symbol.

It is through these symbols, in subsequent days, that people can recall the feelings of solidarity and morality that pumped them up at the peak moments of collective experience. The group cannot stay assembled forever; indeed, it is difficult for them to stay for even as long as a few weeks. The collective emotion fades after the assembly disperses. The symbols keep it alive to a degree; but as Durkheim recognized, periodic reassemblies and periodic rituals are needed to rejuvenate the symbols with emotion. I have added an argument about a refractory period; this holds that after an intense period of mass mobilization, people cannot experience the same intensity again for some time; they necessarily have to come down. Thus symbols must vary over time, between moments of high intensity significance, and milder levels, even banality.

My discussion of the mass demonstration as an interaction ritual is on the micro-sociological level. Let us recombine it now with the macro-historical level with which we started, the long-term transformations of state penetration and the invention of the social movement. The modern social movement became possible because it was provided with a target, the central organization of the state; this created a physical place to assemble, and a mutual focus of attention. Whether a movement wants to petition for redress of grievances, or overthrow the regime and take power for itself, it focuses attention upon the state, and elevates it into an image of omnipotence, an all-encompassing will or agency, which at the moment of maximal struggle is now endowed with the ability to carry out the will of the crowd, if it only would. This is a mythical view of the power of the state, ignoring all practical contingencies of organization and implementation, but it has very important ideological effects. The unifying focus on the state as the target of movement mobilization makes it easy, indeed natural, to invoke the unity of the people. Whatever the specific demands of the movement, it is "WE," the unified Durkheimian collectivity, who are demanding it. At the moment of mobilization, the sovereignty of the people is not a philosophical abstraction, but a felt experience. For this reason, mass movements engaged in state confrontation tend toward a nationalist tone, because this is an easy identity to evoke at the moment when seemingly everyone is assembled and united in their demands. It is rituals of this intensity that make primordialism plausible, at least for their own participants.

An example, which I have observed from videos, photos, news reports, and eye-witness accounts, is the two-and-one-half weeks protest at the Wisconsin State Capitol in the US (during February and March 2011). The issue was the plan of the Republican-dominated legislature to pass a bill eliminating most of the organizing rights of public sector employees unions. Because the State Capitol building is very close to the state university, it was easy for the teaching assistants union to mobilize a mass protest, which occupied the state building and attempted to block the legislation. The protest attracted large numbers of supporters, including even police officers—a fact that delighted the protestors. Although in fact it lost in the end on the legislation, it generated a mood of euphoria, with chants of "This is what democracy looks like!" and "We are the people!"—ringing through the halls and galleries of the building. In fact, in the election, three months previously, the Democrats and union supporters had lost control of every branch of the legislature and the governorship; so it cannot be literally the case that the protestors were the whole or even the majority of the people. My point is that the micro-structured experience of a mass demonstration itself generates the feeling of totality. One is aware there are enemies outside the collectivity, but they are defined away, not part of the people, but as an alien taint to be combated, much like theological views of the omnipotence of God and the shadow-reality of the devil. Thus the Wisconsin demonstrators displayed themselves surrounded by symbols, American flags, references to democracy and the People. Although the issue was specifically the rights of labor unions, the discourse and symbolism were not largely about unions; this was played down, a particularistic interest that had to be reinterpreted in the context an all-encompassing unity.

I have been arguing that the shape of the social movement is what creates nationalism; and that this operates through a micro-sociological mechanism, the mass interaction ritual mobilized at the place of the centralizing state. Historically, we can see this same process of micro-foundations of movement mobilization in the history of nationalism, specifically in the shift from nineteenth-century elite nationalism to the mass nationalism of the twentieth century and today. It has been widely argued that nineteenth-century nationalism, particularly in less modernized states, was a matter of small numbers of intellectuals.

Micro-sociologically, their chief tactic was the banquet. A few dozen gentlemen gathered in private mansions, restaurants, or hotels to dine; they made speeches, drank toasts, passed resolutions. It was a banqueting campaign of this kind that led up to the French Revolution in Paris in February 1848, and that carried the nationalist revolution to Germany and elsewhere (Tocqueville [1850] 1970). It was a banqueting campaign that mobilized reformers in Russia in 1904 during the opening provided by the defeat in the war with Japan, and prepared the way for the attempted revolution of 1905. I am drawing here on research by Stefan Klusemann (2010), who shows that the restricted settings of indoor banquets, extending the polite rituals of upper-class sociability, gave a very limited class character to nationalist mobilization; a widening came about when the labor unions in St. Petersburg demanded entry to the banquets, and eventually transferred such meetings to larger, more public buildings, thus setting off the movement for councils—soviets. It was the shift in the micro-organization of participation in a social movement that generated the key ideological shifts. Radicalization is a practical process and not merely an ideational one.

To summarize the key points so far: social movements were facilitated by the structural changes of modernization through state penetration; movements at their peak mobilize into huge interaction rituals directed at the central state; the micro-sociological experience at such moments is the feeling of universal solidarity in the crowd, which can be attached to a variety of ideologies but is especially compatible with ideas of popular sovereignty and the nation. And these peak moments are time-bubbles, lasting for a few weeks or months, then fading, and subject to a refractory period during which they cannot be mobilized at that same intensity.

I want now to continue with the dynamics of such mobilization as they stretch out in time. A key point is the difference between the pristine experience of the Durkheimian collectivity when mass solidarity discovers itself in a large-scale mobilization, and the change that comes in subsequent mobilizations. There is a refractory period of some length after intense mobilization dissipates. Under some circumstances, the demonstrators can go home; the struggle may go on, but in a different and milder form. After their 18 days occupying the Wisconsin State Capitol, the crowds dispersed; the struggle shifted to lawsuits in the courts and electoral campaigns to recall officials. But sometimes crisis can follow crisis, and renewed mobilization may be forced upon a population, however exhausted they are. In 1917 Russia, there were two great peaks of revolutionary mobilization, in February and in November, separated by 9 months during which the collective identity of the People was, if not in abeyance, at least fragmented and incapable of mobilizing as a unitary or near-unity force. But after the November revolution, all was not settled forever; in fact there were renewed crises, with civil wars beginning already in December 1917 and continuing through 1920, a period of three years.

These subsequent mass arousals have a different emotional atmosphere, less filled with the sense of shared solidarity and glory, more soldiering through. The peak Durkheimian moment, the fusion of the individual and the collective, is replaced by doing one's duty, going on under pressure of an organization; leaders stop being symbols of ourselves and become authorities, not part of the shared flow but a separate force impinging from outside.[3]

There are numerous instances where revolutions or attempted revolutions follow each other in a close sequence; on the whole, the later ones have both a different tone and a different micro-sociological structure. The French Revolution of February 1848 was a quick and almost bloodless transition to popular rule; but by the time of the June insurrection, collective solidarity had split into factional conflict and a great deal of violence—an extreme mood shift in four months. National unity gave way to class conflict. On the micro-level, interaction rituals can succeed or fail. The key variable is maintaining a mutual focus of attention, which thereby channels shared emotions into a feeling of solidarity and common identity. More precisely, the amount of mutual focus of attention is a continuum. At high levels there is unity of one group, the People as a whole, foregrounded in the mass mobilization we see all around us, with just one goal, to win out against the enemy we are all confronting. At low levels of the continuum, people do not assemble at all, do not pay attention to much in common, but are taken up with the myriad private concerns of everyday life. In between these levels, there can be mass mobilizations, but split into factions; they can't agree on goals; they go off into different collective actions; their discourse is splintered and off-message.

Centered or Dispersed Revolutions

Accordingly, there are two kinds of revolutionary or peak movement struggle. One is the Durkheimian collective consciousness, stretching as far as the eye can see, and beyond that, the sentiment that the whole world is watching. Once the struggle is won, that common focus of attention is lost. The regime that is the target of protest is gone. The subsequent regime is in a different micro-sociological situation; that is why the post-revolutionary situation is necessarily different from those days of high euphoria and high danger when the revolutionary coalition was at its height.

The second type of revolt is one in which the unity of the revolutionists is never achieved. Instead of one central focus of mobilization, there are many; dissidents against the regime are also dissidents among themselves. Such revolutions are more difficult. They are more violent, often turning into civil wars. The regime may fall, but it is not replaced by anything of similar unity. Such revolts are characterized not by overarching Durkheimian collective consciousness but by smaller pockets of ritual solidarity, mutually hostile. Group consciousness is split. The first type of revolt, the Durkheimian bandwagon, is maximally suited to produce moments of pure idealistic nationalism. The second type is less nationalist; that is, nationalism may be one of the ideological strands put forward during the movement, but it is contested and unconvincing, not the dominant identity; in the aftermath, a self-conscious nationalist movement may be prominent, but in the special form of a reactive nationalist militancy, struggling against other mobilized movements which are the enemy of nationalism. The White and Red factions of the Russian civil war are an example, but there are many others.

In the wave of Middle East revolts of the year 2011, we can point to the Egyptian revolution as an archetype of the Durkheimian bandwagon revolution; and the Libyan and Yemen revolts as cases of the fragmented type, with the Tunisian revolution combining elements of both. The Syrian civil war, growing out of the Arab Spring uprisings in 2011, strongly underscores the pattern of protracted violence when there is no central organizing place and no possibility of a rapid tipping point revolution. Let me review a few salient points, chiefly their time-dynamics, micro-interactional patterns, and the situational evocation of nationalist symbols.[4]

The Egyptian revolution covered 18 days of mass demonstrations, from January 25, 2011, when the first big crowd gathered in Cairo's Tahrir Square, to the fall of Mubarak on February 11, 2011. Actually there was a preliminary period of a week, beginning January 17, the day of one-month remembrance of the self-immolation which set off the Tunisian protests; a man attempted to set himself on fire in front of the Egyptian parliament, and five others made similar attempts, all stopped by the police. This week-long lull before the storm was given over to organizing, so what we count as day 1—January 25—had pre-arranged wide support from many political, civil, and ad hoc groups. The date was chosen to take advantage of a national holiday in honor of the police. Hijacking a national holiday is a not unusual tactic in authoritarian regimes that allow no other way to assemble, turning a banal mechanism of national solidarity into a mobilizing device for revolt. A similar tactic was used to set off the Tiananmen Square democracy demonstrations in China in 1989, using the occasion of a state funeral for a CCP leader.

The Egyptian police were also ready and violence quickly escalated, beginning with tear gas and water cannons against crowds wielding rocks and firebombs. For the first four days, violence took place at demonstrations not only in Cairo but Alexandria, Suez, and several other cities. An important swing occurred on day 5: the army was called out, but refused to intervene between police and protestors; by day 7, the army was announcing it would not hurt the protestors. At the same time, violence in other cities fizzled out; attention was centered on Tahrir Square in Cairo, where crowds now reached 250,000, while in Alexandria they had fallen to hundreds. As of day 5, Mubarak began offering concessions, but these were not accepted.

By day 8, the Tahrir Square protest had grown to a million, and had become mostly peaceful. There was one more important episode of violence, the so-called Battle of the Camel, when Mubarak supporters invaded the square, causing many injuries and several deaths, while the army attempted to separate the sides. This was day 9; from day 10 onwards, there was no notable violence in Cairo and most of the rest of the country. A sign of the tipping point was visible already on day 16, when a small demonstration in a provincial town was attacked by the police, killing several; but the following day the police were arrested. Mubarak, on the defensive, offered more concessions, which were rejected as unacceptable; and he finally resigned on day 18. This led to one last big day of rejoicing in Tahrir Square (with imitations in other cities), then the square was cleared. In following days, there were demonstrations in various places but no longer big heterogeneous crowds; instead separate occupational groups pressed their specific demands. The honeymoon was over, replaced by interest group politics.

It was in the gatherings at Tahrir Square that expressions of Egyptian national unity were most in evidence. Many women took part, some in full *abaya*, others flaunting western styles, even smoking and kissing. Christian and Muslim clerics ostentatiously appeared together expressing religious unity. These sectarian and gender divisions soon reappeared after the euphoria of the mass demonstrations had broken up. Some women were sexually molested and assaulted in the vast crowd on victory celebration day, day 19. When Egyptian women assembled again in Tahrir Square for International Women's Day (March 8, three-and-a-half weeks after the downfall of Mubarak—i.e. day 43), they were heckled and threatened. On the following day, Muslim/Christian violence broke out again in the Cairo suburbs, killing 13 and wounding 140. During subsequent months, Tahrir Square was used as a symbolic rallying-point, but on the whole the huge crowds of the peak period were not reassembled. Intermittently, from April to July 2011, militant crowds demanded speeding up the process of transition from military control, and stronger prosecution of the old regime; on July 23, a violent crowd attacked the Defense Ministry building.

By August 1, when military forces cleared Tahrir Square of hold-out demonstrators camping there, most Egyptians appeared to be tired of the conflict and supported their removal. The old regime as an opponent diminished as a focal point holding together a unified opposition; in the remaining months of 2011, and through 2012, intermittent clashes among Muslim, Coptic Christians, and secularists came increasingly into the center of attention. Egyptian nationalism was no longer a symbolic weapon with any potency either to generate solidarity or to overcome opposition. The ostentatious waving of Egyptian flags and signs referring to the unity of the people of Egypt were largely confined to the high points of collective assembly, inside the time-bubble of nationalism. For the Egyptian revolution, the time-bubble was 18 days (or 26 days if we include the previous week of initiation, the time it took to first inflate the balloon). Six months later, it was a distant mood-memory.

The Tunisian revolution did not make much use of nationalist slogans and symbols. The revolution was made possible by the temporary unity against the regime, as common enemy, between the Arab underclass in the hinterlands, and the liberal cosmopolites of the tourist zone. Its big coastal cities are the main tourist route, touted in the West for their beaches, ancient ruins, colorful but tamed Islamicism, and café enjoyments. The contrasting directions of orientation between the two components of the revolt tended to keep nationalism out of the center of attention.

In Libya and Yemen, revolutionary struggle was much more dispersed and prolonged, both in time and space. This pattern in itself is enough to limit the strength of Durkheimian collective consciousness, and to prevent resolution of the conflict by a tipping point abdication of power and flight to the winning coalition. In Libya, the revolt broke out almost immediately after the success of the Egyptian revolution, taking it as a sign that the unraveling of authoritarian regimes would proceed across the Arab world like a worn-out sweater. It might also be regarded as the transmission of Durkheimian collective consciousness vicariously, by the mass media and by the new electronic social media. The nationalism of such collective high points is propagated as a kind of generic enthusiasm for the nationalist tactic, not for any nation in particular but as a device for generating the experience of the people united in action.

In Libya, the spread of popular enthusiasm went on for about 8 days (beginning February 16). Gadhafi's forces did not crumble, but took the time to mobilize their superior weaponry. At first, military repulses of the rebels were attributed to an anti-national force, foreign mercenaries. During the second week, as rebels began to be pushed back, African guest workers in rebel-held territory were attacked in a wave of xenophobic nationalism. Hysteria about alien mercenaries settled down in the third week, when it became apparent that Gadhafi had tribal support of his own, an apparatus of clients, and a military force much better organized than the almost completely spontaneous rebel army. There were no equivalents of Tahrir Square. In rebel strongholds like Benghazi, at the other end of the country, quick success meant there was no need or purpose in prolonged crowd assembly, and the revolt soon turned into a civil war spread out across 500 miles of battle. In March, just as the militarily superior regime forces were about to extirpate the rebel center—four weeks after the revolt began—international military intervention by largely NATO-membership air power, along with covert ground support, turned the military balance. The Gadhafi regime was finally overthrown when its military strongholds were captured in late August 2011. Stable government was not restored. Within six weeks, rival militias were fighting in Tripoli, the old capital; clashes went on also in remote areas of the south during 2012, with attacks even in revolutionary Benghazi. Efforts failed at disarming and unifying the various rebel groups, adherents of the old regime, and regional tribes. Neither monopoly over the means of force, nor a focal center of government was reestablished—a situation that continued to exist 10 years later.

For such cases, revolution is the wrong word; a unified regime is replaced by a fragmented one, and no revolutionary policy or restructuring can be carried out. Although nationalist slogans and symbols were displayed early in the revolt, the bubble of nationalism was hardly inflated at all, at most, a popular mood in a limited part of the territory and lasting little more than two weeks.

In Yemen, there were indeed versions of crowd solidarity assembling heroically against the regime, especially in the capital city; but struggles took place in several cities, many of them already strongholds of rival factions. Although the Tunisian revolution provided a catalyst for a new round, it merely added to long-standing and multi-sided conflicts: a 50-year history of civil war, partition and reunification, and ongoing wars against secessionists, religious and ideological enemies. Although there were instances of heterogeneous crowds assembling in temporary unity against the regime of President Saleh, there is no unifying axis of conflict. No predominately peaceful tipping-point transition was possible. Fighting took place in the three major cities, among coalitions of tribes and militia; splits within the army produced further battles; secessionist movements and de facto autonomous regions split the structure of political control. President Saleh maneuvered and backtracked among numerous deals, withdrew to Saudi Arabia after an assassination attempt, returned unexpectedly, and finally in February 2012—13 months after the "Arab Spring" period of demonstrations began—agreed to step down in favor of the Vice President. But the Presidency had never been strong enough to serve as a revolutionary turning point; decentralized and fragmented conflict cannot be resolved by replacing a token individual in such a structure.

Symbols of popular unity, under such circumstances, do little to galvanize a movement for taking power. A momentary scene is described in an Associated Press report from the capital of Yemen, March 22, 2011, when protests had been going on for about 40 days:

> Protesters massed by the tens of thousands in the downtown Sana'a plaza they have dubbed "Change Square". Crowds ululated, chanted and painted each other's faces in the red, white and black colours of the national flag. Conservative tribesmen brought their wives to the protest, and the women brought their children, all basking in a carnival atmosphere.

Similarly, one can view photos of supporters of the Libyan rebels with flags of the old monarchist pre-Gadhafi regime, or their faces painted with that particular brand of nationalist colours. Similar uses of national symbols are seen in revolts all over the Middle East. It is striking how many of these photos are of women. I read this as a strategic use of nationalism: women in the Arab world take advantage of mass political mobilization to join in public life. Unity of the people is of special concern for them, since they have been most excluded from the arena in which people-hood is enacted. Perhaps shared memories of participation in these revolts will help—a little. It needs more structural transformation for women to be accepted, not as militant nationalists but as banal, taken-for-granted citizens.

The overwhelming conclusion one takes away from such cases is the illusory quality of nationalist time-bubbles, if the structural conditions for national unity, the state penetration and economic and cultural integration articulated by Gellner, Mann, and Tilly are not present. This is certainly the case with revolts like Yemen and Libya. The Egyptian revolution, even with its greater success in assembling a massive collective consciousness, did not have more integrating consequences. This became apparent within months after the event, with splits persisting through the rest of the decade.

Banal Nationalism and Divisive Nationalism

To be sure, there is also a calmer, everyday nationalism than the impassioned displays of revolutionaries at the height of mass mobilization, what Michael Billig (1995) has dubbed banal nationalism. But national identity is important in ongoing social relations chiefly when it is not the default setting, the unmarked case, but the foregrounded gestalt that immediately strikes the eye. The national identities of self and other are most inescapably present when there is a conflict or at least latent hostility founded on palpable differences in privilege: British or French or Dutch colonialists in their day; or American soldiers abroad in the early twenty-first century, irrevocably marked off by their intrusiveness, hence gathered together in consciousness of their nationality.

National identity is most salient in everyday life when it is divisive. Wars, too, heighten nationalism, although chiefly in the first three months or so after breaking out. Banal nationalism may not be much, but on the whole it reflects better conditions of everyday life than the contentious mobilizations and violence that are the platforms on which stronger national identities are staged.

To end with a methodological exhortation: Nationalism is visible; it is measurable. It is a varying quantity of emotion-laden belief during the rising and falling intensities of interaction rituals in everyday life. Many scholars are now engaged in close observation of nationalism. What is needed is more detailed attention to the dynamics that generate locally successful or unsuccessful ritual solidarity: what conditions exist for assembling or disassembling crowds; how much mutual focus of attention, and what breaks up attention; what kinds of emotions; what degree of intensification through rhythmic entrainment; how long solidarity rituals can be sustained. Our theoretical frontier is to explain their trajectories in time.

Notes

1. In Rwanda, a very poor rural country, the genocide of Tutsi by Hutu militants in 1994 lasted 11 weeks. McDoom (2021) shows that ideological consciousness was initially low, even among most of the subsequent perpetrators, but skyrocketed quickly within a few days after the precipitating crisis, the assassination of the President while an army of exiled Tutsis advanced on the border. Genocide in the name of ethnicity is the most extreme form of nationalism-in-action—in this case, a time-bubble in which the same people afterwards could hardly believe what they had done.
2. The theory of the critical mass (Marwell and Oliver 1993) describes the dynamics of this same situation. The main difference is that critical mass theory confines itself to individuals' cognitive assessment of whether it is safer to join the movement or to stay out. But it is also an emotional experience, and a collective one. At the moment when the critical mass is formed, its symbolic focus of attention becomes a huge emotional attractor, an electric generator, so to speak, pumping up the emotional energy of participants to a maximum.
3. The mixtures of ideological discourse and banal realities are nicely illustrated by the writings of Isaac Babel ([1924–1926] 2002), based on his experiences with Red Army troops in the civil war.
4. Sources: reports by the BBC, Associated Press, and al-Jazeera.

References

Babel, Isaac. [1924–1926] 2002. The Red Cavalry Stories. In *The Collected Stories of Isaac Babel*. New York: W. W. Norton.

Billig, Michael. 1995. *Banal Nationalism*. London: Sage Publications.

Fox, Jon and Cynthia Miller-Idriss. 2008. "Everyday Nationhood." *Ethnicities* 8: 536–576.

Gellner, Ernest. 1983. *Nations and Nationalism*. Oxford: Blackwell.

Klusemann, Stefan. 2010. "After State Breakdown: Dynamics of Multi-Party Conflict, Violence, and Paramilitary Mobilization in Russia 1904–1920, Germany 1918–1934, and Japan 1853–1877." PhD dissertation, University of Pennsylvania.

Malesevic, Sinisa. 2019. *Grounded Nationalisms*. Cambridge: Cambridge University Press.

Mann, Michael. 1993. *The Sources of Social Power*. Vol. 2. *The Rise of Classes and Nation-states, 1760–1914*. Cambridge: Cambridge University Press.

Marwell, Gerald, and Pamela Oliver. 1993. *The Critical Mass in Collective Action: A Micro-Social Theory*. New York: Cambridge University Press.

McDoom, Omar. 2021. *The Path to Genocide in Rwanda*. Cambridge: Cambridge University Press.

Smith, Anthony D. 1986. *The Ethnic Origin of Nations*. Oxford: Blackwell.

Tilly, Charles. 1995. *Popular Contention in Great Britain, 1758–1834*. Cambridge, MA: Harvard University Press.

Tilly, Charles. 2004. *Social Movements, 1768–2004*. London: Paradigm Publishers.

Tocqueville, Alexis de. [1850] 1970. *Recollections: The French Revolution of 1848*. New York: Doubleday.

Chapter 3

Tipping Point Revolutions and State Breakdown Revolutions

Why Revolutions Succeed or Fail

Introduction

In recent years, many people have come to believe they have a formula for overthrowing authoritarian governments and putting democracy in their place. The method is mass peaceful demonstrations, persisting until they draw huge support, both internally and internationally, intensifying as government atrocities in putting them down are publicized by the media. This was the model for the "color revolutions" (orange, pink, velvet, etc.) in the ex-Soviet bloc; for the Arab Spring of 2011 and its imitators; further back, it has roots in the US civil rights movement.

Such revolutions succeed or fail in varying degrees, as has been obvious in the aftermath of the different Arab Spring revolts. Why this is the case requires a more complicated analysis. The type of revolution consisting in the righteous mobilization of the people until the authoritarians crack and take flight may be called a tipping point revolution. It contrasts with the state breakdown theory of revolution, formulated by historical sociologists Theda Skocpol (1979), Jack Goldstone (1991), Charles Tilly (1991), and others, to show the long-term roots of major revolutions such as the French Revolution of 1789 and the Russian Revolution of 1917, and that I used to predict the 1989–1991 anti-Soviet revolution (Collins 1986; 1995). Major revolutions are those that bring about big structural changes (the rise or fall of communism, the end of feudalism, etc.). I will argue that tipping point revolutions, without a long-term basis in the structural factors that bring state breakdown, are only moderately successful at best; and they often fall short even of modest changes, devolving into destructive civil wars, or outright failure to change the regime at all.

Tipping Point Revolutions with Easy Success

Tipping points revolutions are not new. Some of the early ones were quick and virtually bloodless. For instance, the February 1848 revolution in France (Tocqueville [1850] 1970; *CMH* 1909). There had been agitation for six months to widen the very restrictive franchise for the token

DOI: 10.4324/9781003245629-5

legislature. The government finally cracked down on the main form of mobilization—a banqueting campaign in which prominent gentlemen met in dining rooms to proclaim speeches and drink toasts to revolutionary slogans. The ban provided a rallying point. The day of the banquet, a crowd gathered, despite 30,000 troops called out to enforce the ban. There were minor scuffles, but most soldiers stood around uneasily, unsure what to do, many of them sympathetic to the crowd. Next morning rumors swept through Paris that revolution was coming. Shops did not open, workers stayed home, servants became surly with their masters and mistresses. In the eerie atmosphere of near-deserted streets, trees were chopped down and cobble-stones dug up to make barricades. Liberal members of the national legislature visited the king, demanding that the prime minister be replaced. This modest step was easy; he was dismissed; but who would take his place? No one wanted to be prime minister; a succession of candidates wavered and declined, no one feeling confident of taking control. Mid-afternoon of the second day, just after the prime minister's resignation was announced, a pumped-up crowd outside a government building was fired upon. The accidental discharge of a gun by a nervous soldier set off a contagious volley, killing 50. This panicky use of force did not deter the crowd, but emboldened it. During the night, the king offered to abdicate. But in favor of whom? Other royal relatives also declined. The king panicked and fled the palace, along with assorted duchesses; crowds were encroaching on the palace grounds, and now they invaded the royal chambers and even sat on the royal throne. In a holiday atmosphere, a Republic was announced, the provisional assembly set plans to reform itself through elections.

In three days the revolution was accomplished. If we stop the clock here, the Revolution was an easy success. The People collectively had decided the regime must go, and in a matter of hours, it bowed to the pressure of that overwhelming public. It was one of those moments that exemplify what Durkheim called collective consciousness at its most palpable.

This moment of near-unanimity did not last. In the first weeks of enthusiasm, even the rich and the nobility—who had just lost their monopoly of power—made subscriptions for the poor and wounded; the conservative provinces rejoiced in the deeds of Paris. The honeymoon began to dissipate within three weeks. Conservative and radical factions struggled within the volunteer national guard, and began to lay up their own supplies of arms. Conservatives in the countryside and financiers in the city mobilized against the welfare-state policies of Paris. Elections to a constitutional assembly, two months in, returned an array of conservatives and moderates; the socialists and liberals who led the revolution were reduced to a small minority, upheld only by radical crowds who invaded the assembly hall and shouted down opponents. In May, the national guard dispersed the mob and arrested radical leaders. By June, there was a second revolt, this time confined to the working-class part of the city. The Assembly was united against the revolution; in fact, they provoked it by abolishing the public workshops set up for unemployed workers. This time the army kept its discipline. The emotional mood had switched directions. The provinces of France now had their own collective consciousness, an outpouring of volunteers rushing to Paris by train to battle the revolutionaries. Within five days, the June revolution was over; this time with bloody fighting, 10,000 killed and wounded, and more executed afterwards or sent to prison colonies.

The tipping point mechanism did not tip this time; instead of everyone going over to the victorious side (thereby ensuring its victory), the conflict fractured into two opposing camps. Instead of one revolutionary collective consciousness sweeping up everyone, it split into rival identities, each with its own solidarity, its own emotional energy and moral righteousness. Since the opposing forces, both strongly mobilized, were unevenly matched, the result was a bloody struggle, and then destruction of the weaker side. In the following months, the mood flowed increasingly conservative. Elections in December 1848 brought in a huge majority for a President—Napoleon's nephew, symbol of an idealized authoritarian regime of the past—who overturned democratic reforms and made himself emperor three years later. The revolutionary surge had lasted just four months.

Egypt in January–February 2011, the most famous of the Arab Spring revolutions, fits most closely to the model of 1848 France. By day 18, everyone had deserted the dictator Mubarak and swung over to the bandwagon, including his own former base of support, the military. This continuity is one reason why the aftermath did not prove so revolutionary. The Islamist movement elected in the popular vote June 2012 relegated to a minority the secularists and liberals who had been most active in the revolution. President Morsi bears some resemblance to Louis Bonaparte, who rose to power on the reputation of an ancestral movement—both had a record of opposition to the regime, but were ambiguous about their own democratic credentials. Ongoing violence between Muslims and Christians led to a military coup in July 2013, and restricted elections in favor of a military dictator in May 2014. Within three years, Egypt was back to the same condition it had been in before the Arab Spring.

Tipping Point Revolutions that Fail

The sequence of revolts in 1848 France shows both the tipping point mechanism at its strongest, and the failure not so far downstream to bring about structural change. Modern history is full of failed revolutions, and continues to be right up through the latest news. I will cite one example of a tipping point revolution that failed entirely, not even taking power briefly. The democracy movement in China centered on protestors occupying Tiananmen Square in Beijing, lasting seven weeks from mid-April to early June 1989 (Zhao 2001; Wikipedia, "Tiananmen Square Protests of 1989"). Until the last two weeks, the authorities did not crack down; local police were unsure what to do, just like French troops in February 1848; some even displayed sympathy with the demonstrators.

The numbers of protestors surged and declined several times. Initially, students from the prestigious Beijing universities (where the Red Guards movement had been launched 20 years earlier) set up a vigil in Tiananmen Square to mourn the death of a reform-oriented Communist leader. This was China's center of public attention, in front of the old Imperial Palace, the place for official rituals, and thus a target for impromptu counter-rituals. Beginning with a few thousand students on April 17 (day 1), the crowd fell to a few hundred by the fourth day, but revived after a skirmish with police as militants took their protest to the gate of the nearby government compound where the political elite lived. Injuries were slight and no arrests were made, but indignation over police brutality renewed the movement, which grew to 100,000–200,000 for the state funeral on day 5. Militants hijacked the ritual by kneeling on the steps of the ceremonial hall flanking Tiananmen Square, in the style of traditional supplicants to the emperor. The same day rioting broke out in other cities around China, including arson attacks, with casualties on both sides. Four days later (day 10) the government newspaper officially condemned the movement—the first time it had been portrayed negatively. Next day 50,000–100,000 Beijing students responded, breaking through police lines to reoccupy the Square. So far, counter-escalation favored the protestors.

The government now switched to a policy of conciliation and negotiation. This brought a two weeks lull; by May 4 (day 18), most students had returned to class. On May 13 (day 28), the remaining militants launched a new tactic: a hunger strike, initially recruiting 300; over the next two days it recaptured public attention, and grew to 3000 hunger strikers. Big crowds, growing to 300,000, now flocked to the Square to view and support them. The militants had another ritual weapon: the arrival on May 15 (day 30) of Soviet leader Gorbachev for a state visit, then at the height of his fame as a Communist reformer. The official welcome had to be moved to the airport, but the state meeting in the ceremonial hall flanking Tiananmen was marred by the noisy demonstration outside. On May 17 (day 32), as Gorbachev left, over one million Beijing residents from all social classes marched to support the hunger strikers. The militants had captured the attention center of the ceremonial gathering; the bandwagon was building to a peak. Visitors to Tiananmen were generally organized by work units, who provided transportation and sometimes even paid the marchers. A logistics structure was created to fund the food and shelter for those who occupied the Square. The organizational base of the Communist regime, at least in the capital, was tipping toward revolution. Around the country, too, there were supporting demonstrations in 400 cities. Local governments were indecisive; some Communist Party committees openly endorsed the movement; some authorities provided free transportation by train for hundreds of thousands of students to travel to Beijing to join in.

The tipping point did not tip. The Communist elite met outside the city in a showdown among themselves. A collective decision was made; a few dissenters, including some army generals, were removed and arrested. On May 19 (day 34), martial law was declared. Military forces were called from distant regions, lacking ties to Beijing demonstrators. The next four days were a showdown in the streets; crowds of residents, especially workers, blocked the army convoys; soldiers rode in open trucks, unarmed—the regime still trying to use as little force as possible, and also distrustful of giving out ammunition—and often were overwhelmed by residents. Crowds used a mixture of persuasion and food offerings—army logistics having broken down by the unreliability of passage through the streets—and sometimes force, stoning and beating isolated soldiers. On May 24 (day 39), the regime pulled back the troops to bases outside the city. But it did not give up. The most reliable army units were moved to the front, some tasked with watching for defections among less reliable units. In another week, strong forces had been assembled in the center of Beijing.

Momentum was swinging back the other way. Student protestors in the Square increasingly divided between moderates and militants; by the time the order to clear the Square was given for June 3 (day 49), the number occupying was down to 4000. There was one last surge of violence—not in Tiananmen Square itself, although the name became so famous that most outsiders think there was a massacre there—but in the streets as residents attempted to block the army's movement once again. Crowds fought with stones and gasoline bombs, burning army vehicles and, by some reports, the soldiers inside. In this emotional atmosphere, as both sides spread stories of the other's atrocities, something on the order of 50 soldiers and police were killed, and 400–800 civilians (estimates varying widely). Some soldiers took revenge for prior attacks by firing at fleeing opponents and beating those they caught. In Tiananmen Square, the early morning of June 4, the dwindling militants were allowed to march out through the encircling troops.

International protest and domestic horror were to no avail; a sufficiently adamant and organizationally coherent regime easily imposed its superior force. Outside Beijing, protests continued for several days in other cities; hundreds more were killed. Organizational discipline was reestablished by a purge; over the following year, CCP members who had sympathized with the revolt were arrested, jailed, and sent to labor camps. Dissident workers were often executed; students got off easier, as members of the elite. Freedom of the media, which had been loosened during the reform period of 1980s, and briefly flourished during the height of the democracy protests in early May, was now replaced by strict control. Economic reforms, although briefly questioned in the aftermath of 1989, resumed but political reforms were rescinded. A failed tipping point revolution not only fails to meet its goals; it reinforces authoritarianism.

If the Chinese government had the power to crack down by sending out its security agents and arresting dissidents all over the country, why didn't they do this earlier, instead of waiting until Tiananmen Square was cleared? Because this was the center of the tipping point mechanism. As long as the rebellious assembly went on, tension existed as to which way the regime would go. If it couldn't meet this challenge, the regime would be deserted. That was in question as long as all eyes were on Tiananmen. Once attention was broken up, all those security agents could fan out around the country, picking off suspects one by one, ultimately arresting tens of thousands. This is why centralized and decentralized forms of rebellion are so different: centralized rebellions potentially very short and sudden; decentralized ones long, grinding, and much more destructive.

We like to believe that any government that uses force against its own citizens is so marred by the atrocity that it loses all legitimacy. Yet the 1990s and the early 2000s were a time of increasing Chinese prestige. The market version of communist political control became a great economic success; international economic ties expanded and exacted no penalty for the deaths in June 1989; domestically Chinese poured their energies into economic opportunities. Protest movements revived within a decade, but the regime has been quick to clamp down on them. Even the new means of mobilization via the Internet have proven vulnerable to a resolute authoritarian apparatus, assigning many thousands of surveillance agents to control political messages and monitor activists to head off any possible Tiananmen-style assemblies before they start.

The failure of the Chinese democracy movement, both in 1989 and since, tells another sociological lesson. An authoritarian regime that is aware of the tipping point mechanism need not give in to it; it can keep momentum on its own side by making sure no bandwagon gets going among the opposition. Such a regime can be accused of moral violations and even atrocities, but moral condemnation without a successful mobilization is ineffective. It is when one's movement is growing, seemingly expanding its collective consciousness to include virtually everyone and emotionally overwhelm their opponents, that righteous horror over atrocities is so arousing. Without this, protests remain sporadic, localized, and ephemeral at best. The modest emotional energy of the protest movement is no rushing tide; and as this goes on for years, the emotional mood surrounding such a regime remains stable—the most important quality of "legitimacy."

State Breakdown Revolutions

Tipping point revolutions are too superficial to make deep structural changes. What does? Three ingredients must come together to produce a state-breakdown revolution.

1. Fiscal crisis/paralysis of state organization. The state runs out of money, is crushed by debts, or otherwise is so burdened that it cannot pay its own officials. This often happens through the expense of past wars or huge costs of current war, especially if your state is losing. The crisis is deep and structural because it cannot be evaded; it is not a matter of ideology, and whoever takes over responsibility for running the government faces the same problem. When the crisis grows serious, the army, police, and officials no longer can enforce order because they themselves are disaffected. This was the route to the 1789 French Revolution; the 1640 English Revolution; the 1917 Russian Revolution; and the 1853–1868 Japanese revolution (which goes under the name of the Meiji Restoration). The 1989–1991 anti-Soviet revolution similarly began with struggles to reform the Soviet budget, overburdened by military costs of the Cold War arms race (Collins 1995; Kotkin 2001).
2. Elite deadlock between state faction and economic privilege faction. The fiscal crisis cannot be resolved because the most powerful and privileged groups are split. Those who benefit economically from the regime resist paying for it (whether these are landowners, financiers, or even a socialist military-industrial complex); reformers are those who are directly responsible for keeping the state running. The split is deep and structural, since it does not depend on ideological preferences; whoever takes command, whatever their ideas, must deal with the reality of organizational paralysis. We are not dealing here with conflict between parties in the public sphere or the legislature; such partisan squabbling is normal, and it may also exist at the same time as a state crisis. Deadlock between the top elites is far more serious, because it stymies the two most powerful forces: the economic elite and the ruling officials.
3. Mass mobilization of dissidents. This factor is last in causal order; it becomes important after state crisis and elite deadlock weaken the enforcement power of the regime. This power vacuum provides an opportunity for movements of the public to claim a solution. The ideology of the revolutionaries is often misleading. What they say is the problem and its solution may have nothing to do with the causes of the fiscal crisis itself (e.g. claiming the issue is political reform, democratic representation, or even returning to an earlier religious or traditional image of utopia). The importance of ideology is mostly tactical,

a slogan for unifying the militant coalition at the time of maximum excitement. And, in fact, after taking state power, revolutionary movements often take actions contrary to their ideology: the early Bolshevik policies on land reform, for instance. During the government breakdown of 1853–1868, Japanese revolutionary factions shifted from anti-western antipathy ("Expel the barbarians!") to imitating the West, first in military matters, then in everything else (Klusemann 2010). The important thing is that the revolutionary movement is radical enough to attack the fiscal (and typically military) problems, to reorganize resources so that the state itself becomes well-funded. This solves the structural crisis and ends state breakdown, enabling the state to go on with other reforms. That is why state breakdown revolutions are able to make deep changes in institutions: in short, why they become "historic" revolutions.

Reconciling the Two Theories

Tipping point revolutions are far more common than state breakdown revolutions. The two mechanisms sometimes coincide; tipping points may occur in the sequence of a state breakdown, as the third factor, mass mobilization, comes into play. In 1789, once the fiscal crisis and elite deadlock resulted in calling the Estates General, crowd dynamics led to tipping points that are celebrated as the glory days of the French Revolution. In 1917 Russia, the initial collapse of the government in February was a crowd-driven tipping point, with a series of abdications reminiscent of France in February 1848; what made this a deep structural revolution was the fiscal crisis of war debts, pressure to continue the war from the Allies who held Russian debt, and eventually a second tipping point in November in favor of the Soviets. But state breakdown revolutions can happen without these kinds of crowd-centered tipping points: the 1640 English Revolution (where fighting went on from 1642 through 1651; *CMH* 1907); the Chinese revolution stretching from 1911 to 1949; the Japanese revolution of 1853–1868 with aftershocks until 1877 (Klusemann 2010). Conversely, tipping point revolutions often fail in the absence of state fiscal crisis and elite deadlock. An example is the 1905 Russian Revolution, which had months of widespread enthusiasm for reform during the opportunity provided by defeat in the Japanese war, but nevertheless ended with the government forcefully putting down a six weeks insurrection by a workers' Soviet in the capital, and several months of sporadic violence in the provinces; after these defeats of the revolutionists, the moderate reformers too lost their gains (*CMH* 1910; Deutscher 1954).

A tipping point mechanism, by itself, is a version of mass mobilization which is the final ingredient of a state paralysis revolution. But mass mobilization also has a larger structural basis: resources such as transportation and communication networks that facilitate organizing social movements—sometimes in the form of revolutionary armies—to contend for control of the state. If such mobilization concentrates in a capital city, it may generate a tipping point situation. But also such mobilization can take place throughout the countryside; in which case, the revolution takes more the form of a civil war.

Tipping Point Revolutions and Imitative Revolutions

At times, waves of revolution spread from one state to another; the success of one igniting enthusiasm for another. It is the mass mobilization of the tipping point, the huge crowds and the widespread feeling of solidarity in the pro-revolutionary majority, that encourage imitations. We can see this because some of the famous ignition-revolutions were not very effective in making changes, but they were still imitated. One such wave was in 1848, spreading from Switzerland and Sicily to the fragmented states of Italy, and most spectacularly to France (Weyland 2009). Soon after news propagated of events in Paris, Europe's most famous city, crowds demanded constitutional reforms in Vienna, Berlin, and most of the German states, and in the ethnic regions of the Austrian Empire. Some rulers temporarily fled or made concessions; troops mutinied; parliaments and revolutionary assemblies met. All of these were put down within a year and a half. Some were extirpated by the intervention of outside troops, as conservative rulers supported each other in regaining control. Of these revolutions, hardly any had a permanent effect.

The wave of Arab Spring revolts began with a successful tipping point revolution in Tunisia, imitated with temporary success in Egypt; but failed in Bahrain; had little effect on an ongoing civil war in Yemen; led to a full-scale military conflict in Libya that was won by the rebels only through massive outside military intervention with air power. In Syria, an imitative revolutionary movement set off a prolonged and extremely destructive civil war sustained by outside military aid to all factions. The lesson is that if tipping point revolutions themselves are not very decisive for structural change, further attempts to imitate tipping points in other countries have even less to go on. Regimes may or may not be removed but the downstream situation does not look very different, although there may be a prolonged period of contention amounting to a failed state.

The major exception would appear to be the wave of imitative revolts from 1989–1991, as the Soviet bloc fell apart. The states of eastern Europe overthrew their communist regimes one after another; some with relatively easy tipping point revolutions as in Czechoslovakia,

Hungary, Poland, and East Germany, and bloodier battles in Romania and eventually Yugoslavia. A second round of revolts began in 1991 as the USSR disintegrated into its component ethnic states. Here was indeed a structural change, dismantling communist political forms and replacing them with versions of democracy (some continuing control by ex-communist elites), and shifting the property system to capitalism. But this series of revolutions were not mere tipping points alone; they were all effects of a deep structural crisis in the linchpin of the system, the Soviet empire, that underwent a state breakdown revolution. Revolts can spread by imitation; but what happens to them depends on what kinds of structural conflicts are beneath the surface.

The Continuum of Revolutionary Effects, from Superficial to Deep

If we use the term "revolution" loosely to mean any change in government which is illegal—outside the procedures provided by the regime itself—there are many kinds of revolutions. They range from those with no structural effects at all, through those which change the deepest economic, political, and cultural institutions.

A *coup d'état* is the most superficial; there is no popular mobilization, only a small group of conspirators inside the circles of power, or in the military, who replace one ruler with another. Often there is not even the pretense of structural change or appeal to the popular will.

Tipping point revolutions are more ambitious; emotional crowds who are at the center of the mechanism for transferring power are enthusiastic for grand, if often vague, ideological slogans. But such revolts often fail, if the government is not itself paralyzed by a structural crisis. When tipping points succeed in bringing down the government, the new regime often has only ephemeral support, and may peter out in internal quarrels, civil war, or reactionary restoration.

State breakdown revolutions are not so ephemeral. The state cannot come back into equilibrium until its own organizational problem is solved; and since this means its fiscal, military, and administrative basis, reforms must go deep into the main power-holding institutions. Whether or not the same ideological brand of revolutionaries continues in office, these structural changes lay down a new order that tends to persist—at least, until another deep crisis comes along.

The Contemporary Era of Tipping Point Revolutions

After the fall of the Soviet Union and its empire, there have been many repetitions of tipping point revolutions (Serbia 2000, Georgia 2003,

Ukraine 2004, Kyrgyzstan 2005) mixed with personal power-grabs that are little more than coups masked as popular revolutions. The Arab Spring revolts relied heavily on the tipping point mechanism. Where the government has had a strong faction of popular support, tipping point attempts have brought no easy transition; the result has been full-scale civil war (Syria), or defeat of the revolutionary mobilization by a mass counter-mobilization in favor of the regime (the Green uprising in Iran 2009) (Harris 2012). The popularity of tipping point revolts in recent decades appears to have all the weaknesses of their genre.

The chief causal factor that determines the timing of an attempted tipping point revolution is imitation of other protests currently going on—contagious international enthusiasm over the news and social media. To reiterate a point recognized throughout modern sociological research of revolutions: grievances are not the crucial cause (although they are central to protestors' narratives). The grievances are generally long-standing, and do not explain why the outbreak of revolutionary protest occurs *now*. Because they lack the structural basis of revolution, it is realistic to recognize that they do not have strong prospects for success, even when they do manage to bring about a change of government. It is more important to look for elite splits over deep structural problems.

This is not to say there will never be any more structural revolutions. The twenty-first century portends several such issues, including the disappearance of middle-class jobs with the advance of robotics and artificial intelligence; and the environmental crisis with its growing conflicts over who should sacrifice what to mitigate it (Wallerstein et al. 2013). Such revolutionary conflicts, although foreseeable, will have to be dealt with, one way or another.

References

CMH = *Cambridge Modern History*, Vol. 4, 1907 (on the 1642–1651 English Revolution); Vol. 11, 1909 (on the 1848 French Revolution); Vol. 12, 1910 (on the 1905 Russian Revolution). Cambridge: Cambridge University Press.

Collins, Randall. 1986. "The Future Decline of the Russian Empire." Chapter 8 in Randall Collins, *Weberian Sociological Theory*. Cambridge: Cambridge University Press.

Collins, Randall. 1995. "Prediction in Macro-Sociology: The Case of the Soviet Collapse." *American Journal of Sociology* 100: 1552–1593.

Deutscher, Isaac. 1954. *The Prophet Armed: Trotsky 1879–1921*. Oxford: Oxford University Press.

Goldstone, Jack. 1991. *Revolution and Rebellion in the Early Modern World*. Berkeley, CA: University of California Press.

Harris, Kevan. 2012. "The Brokered Exuberance of the Middle Class: An Ethnographic Analysis of Iran's 2009 Green Movement." *Mobilization* 17: 435–455.

Klusemann, Stefan. 2010. "After State Breakdown: Dynamics of Multi-party Conflict, Violence, and Paramilitary Mobilization in Russia 1904–1920, Germany 1918–1934, and Japan 1853–1877." PhD dissertation, University of Pennsylvania.

Kotkin, Stephen. 2001. *Armageddon Averted: The Soviet Collapse 1970–2000*. New York: Oxford University Press.

Skocpol, Theda. 1979. *States and Social Revolutions*. New York: Cambridge University Press.

Tilly, Charles. 1991. *Coercion, Capital, and European States. AD 990–1990*. Oxford: Blackwell.

Tocqueville, Alexis de. [1850] 1970. *Recollections: The French Revolution of 1848*. New York: Doubleday.

Wallerstein, Immanuel, Randall Collins, Michael Mann, Georgi Deluguian, and Craig Calhoun. 2013. *Does Capitalism Have a Future?* New York: Oxford University Press.

Weyland, Kurt. 2009. "The Diffusion of Revolution: '1848' in Europe and Latin America." *International Organization* 63: 391–423.

Zhao, Dingxin. 2001. *The Power of Tiananmen*. Chicago: University of Chicago Press.

Chapter 4

Time-Dynamics of Violence from Micro to Macro

Introduction

What can we say so far about the time-patterns of violence?

Since ancient times, a favorite image of large-scale social fluctuations has been the cycle. In modern times, too, the preferred model has been sine waves, periodic oscillations of constant amplitude. This has been preferred, not because oscillations of conflict are in fact regular in periodicity or amplitude, but because the mathematics of sine waves are easy to work with. I suggest that we abandon the mathematics of cycles for simpler numbers, as we try to establish generalizations and time-dynamics. The following summarizes some well-documented examples of violent processes where time-patterns have been found.

Overview: Time-Dynamics within Different Scales of Violence

1. *Micro-seconds*. Micro-rhythms of entrainment and disentrainment in face-to-face interaction. These include rhythms of voice, heart rate, gestures, and bodily movements; and are measured in speed and frequency ranging from 0.5 MHz of vocal sounds, to the scale of human conscious awareness in tenths of seconds. Solidarity or conflict is manifested in synchronization or lack of synchronization among persons in these encounters. Dominance in setting the micro-rhythm largely determines who wins the conflict. What is referred to as "micro-aggressions" operate on this time-scale.
2. *Minutes*. Violence-triggering and boredom thresholds in small-scale conflicts between individuals and small groups. These typically occur in a few minutes or less. Boredom thresholds bring confrontations to an end. The bigger and better organized the group, the longer it can sustain boredom without breaking off. It sounds boring, but being boring is the best way to keep a small-scale conflict from escalating.

DOI: 10.4324/9781003245629-6

3. *Hours.* Tension-building and violent danger-time zone in organized crowds. In protest demos, the danger-zone is approximately between 1 and 3 hours since the beginning. A related type of tension-building process is a *forward panic,* in which tension between antagonists builds over a period of hours or days, and violence is triggered by a sudden shift from stalemate to the palpable weakness of one side. The resulting violence, characterized by emotional out-of-control overkill—an adrenaline rush of self-entrainment in the rhythms of attack—lasts from a few minutes to several hours, depending on the size of the groups involved.
4. *Days, months.* Revolutionary tipping points; violent protests and riots. These typically cover three days or less. Riots can last a few weeks longer if they spread from place to place. Larger protests can keep going for several months if they have organizational coordination.
5. *Three to six months.* Mass crisis solidarity and hysteria zones: the time-bubble of national unity when under attack, sometimes called the "rally-around-the-flag effect," lasting three to six months.
6. *Days or years?* Macro-time-forks: when conditions allow tipping point dynamics, a few days of intense confrontation result in rapid and relatively low-casualty resolution of a conflict. When tipping point conditions are absent, regime-level violence leads to years or decades of dispersed war with high attrition costs.

1. Micro-Rhythms of Entrainment, Disentrainment, and Dominated Entrainment

Rhythmic synchronization is the basis of human solidarity. It varies among situations, depending on the degree of mutual focus of attention and shared emotion among participants (Collins 2004a). People report feelings of solidarity when their vocal micro-frequencies converge on a common frequency. Talk that flows smoothly has the pattern of "no-gap, no overlap," with the ending of one speaker's utterances finely timed to the beginning of the next speaker. Pauses as short as a few tenths of a second signal alienation. Conflict talk is characterized by both persons talking at the same time, with rising loudness and attempting to force the other to shut up. Everyday life contains pockets of solidarity where people are drawn to interaction rituals that produce high rhythmic entrainment (Gibson 2010; Draper 2019). But there are many situations of weak solidarity, such as unfocused public encounters while passing on the street that Goffman (1963) called "civil disattention."

Hierarchy and conflict are asymmetrical interaction rituals where the focus of attention and the rhythm are set by one side who dominates the encounter, over other persons who are passively caught up in it. Nassauer's (2018) analysis of robberies recorded on CCTV shows that successful robbers immediately establish the rhythm of interaction, getting the store clerk to fall into passively doing what the robber demands. This is not merely a matter of verbal commands, but a visible rhythm of body movements and reciprocal postures. Store clerks do not always fall into the robber's rhythm; it can be disrupted, if a robber trips in vaulting the counter, or if the clerk is obliviously talking on the phone. When micro-moves on either side create uncertainty and disrupt the expected script, there is an opening for a shift in emotional domination, leading to a failed hold-up. Mosselman et al. (2018) (from an Amsterdam video research group) similarly found that robberies were resisted when the robber showed insecure body movements or lost the non-verbal body profile of dominance; guns and knives were important mainly as props for imposing a robbery frame, and the need to use them signaled its failure.

Conflict on the micro-level of face-to-face encounters is action at cross-purposes, while simultaneously making antagonists mutually focused on each other's actions and generating a contagious emotion. This antagonistic intersubjectivity has two important consequences (Collins 2008). First, emotional domination is the key to winning a violent conflict. Establishing emotional domination typically precedes establishing physical domination; not weapons nor strength are crucial but the rhythm and emotional impact with which they are displayed. Second, conflict that remains in antagonistic equilibrium generates high levels of bodily tension, that I have called confrontational tension/fear (CT/F), visible in faces and body postures. Such photographic evidence corresponds on a physiological level to high levels of adrenaline and heart rate (Grossman 2004: 31).

Sustained CT/F on both sides tends to make fights abort. Heart rates above about 145 beats per minute (BPM) tend to incapacitate complex motor coordination, and around 175 BPM bring perceptual distortions in hearing and vision, and physical clumsiness. At 180–220 BPM, fighters go into uncontrollable forward panic attack (if they have the momentum) or freeze up (if they don't), along with losing sphincter control. Persons with high CT/F become incompetent in their use of weapons, and are beaten by those skilled in violence—which is to say emotional self-control during violence—who keep their CT/F down with heart rates in the 115–145 BPM range. In many violent encounters, both sides have CT/F high enough to make both relatively incompetent, thus causing out-of-control, adrenaline-driven prolonged beatings, over-firing, poor aim, and hitting bystanders or one's own side ("friendly fire").

As a general formula, a violent conflict is won by those who keep their CT/F lower while raising the CT/F of their opponent, thereby imposing dominated entrainment. These micro-processes are ingredients of higher-order time processes (2) and (3).

2. Violence-Triggering and Boredom Thresholds

In confrontations between individuals, escalation to violence tends to happen very quickly if it happens at all, often within 10 seconds once hostility is expressed. In most instances when antagonists raise their voices, shout, utter insults, point fingers, and clench fists, they become bored by the repetition and break off the encounter within a few minutes, with a ritualistic parting insult or a slammed door. Informants have told me that a fight will take off very quickly; and that the first person to decide there will be a fight, usually wins. In police arrests, experienced officers tend to escalate quickly to higher levels of force if the suspect shows initial micro-signs of resistance (Alpert and Dunham 2004). This can also lead to police atrocities, if the officer perceives the suspect as very strong and dangerous.

These patterns vary with the numerical imbalance of participants. Violence is more likely when a small group outnumbers an opponent by a ratio of 3-to-1 up to 6-to-1; beyond these numbers, most of the persons present stand back and observe the attack. At these ratios, the symmetry of micro-threats between the antagonists that generates boredom is not present; if the attacking team is strongly synchronized with each other, piling on starts quickly. Fights among duos (1-to-1) usually break off quickly if the opponents are evenly matched and no audience encourages them; larger audiences cheering and jeering produce longer fights. When third parties try to break up a fight among individuals, they usually succeed; here verbal and gestural hostility may continue for a number of minutes, but winding down through boredom. (Ethnographic accounts, photos and video data in Collins 2008; Jackson-Jacobs 2013; CCTV data in Levine et al. 2011.)

As we see in the following points, when contending groups are bigger and better organized, the time periods for building up tension prior to violence become longer.

3. Tension-Building and Violent Danger-Time Zones

Researching when political demonstrations turn violent or stay peaceful, Nassauer (2019) found that demos that announce they are going to use violence nevertheless may remain peaceful, because militant protestors do not find an opportune moment for breaking into violence. That moment happens when there is a two-part sequence of heightened tension (visible in the shift from loose to tense body postures), followed by a sudden shift to emotional domination among the protestors or police locally on the spot, unleashing them against a temporarily off-balance opponent. Falling down while running away from police tends to create a contagious reaction in which the cops behind the first line will join in striking at the fallen person.

Protestors who outnumber and surround an isolated cop car are emboldened to attack. But protestors are never violent from the first minutes of a demonstration, but only if a sufficient period of collective tension has passed. Nassauer found the danger time-zone was between 1 and 3 hours after the protest began. Prior to this period, isolated individuals may try to goad the cops with taunts or throwing stones, but we can see in photos that the rest of the crowd is not paying attention to them (Collins 2008: 417).

Once violence starts, either side may get into a self-reinforcing rhythm of repeating their own violence: a frenzy of beating or kicking a fallen victim; an overkill of firing bullets. A high level of emotional self-entrainment is especially characteristic of a *forward panic*, a three-part sequence in which (1) both sides have high confrontational tension; (2) suddenly the tension is released by one side showing itself weak and helpless; and (3) whereupon the now-dominant side launches an attack featuring piling-on, and a temporary inability to stop their own violent movements (becoming self-entrained in one's bodily rhythms). The physiological mechanism is a sudden onset of a high-adrenaline peak, reported in research on soldiers and police, which likely exists in all instances of sustained, out-of-control violence.

McCleery (2016), using detailed investigative reports, applies the forward panic model to "Bloody Sunday," January 1972 in Northern Ireland, when British paratroopers shot 26 unarmed civilians, killing 13. A civil rights-style peaceful demo of 15,000 Catholics planned to march from a Protestant area to the city center. Prevented by barricades manned by soldiers, most marchers changed route, while others attacked barricades, throwing bottles, bricks, and iron bars. Paratroopers responded with tear gas, rubber bullets, and water cannon—sticking to non-lethal weapons. Paras were then ordered to move forward and arrest violent demonstrators; but as the non-violent march had split and the crowd was fleeing, soldiers couldn't distinguish between the two groups. Paras with guns cocked disembarked their vehicles in a neighborhood stronghold of IRA paramilitaries, previously a no-go area for the army, and immediately began firing. In fact, there was no resistance; the Para company advanced into a military vacuum.

Soldiers had been manning barricades since early morning until rioting broke out about 3.30 p.m. The demo deviated from its planned route; the Paras shifted from passively waiting to a sudden advance into IRA turf. Expecting opposition but finding none, one sub-unit burst into contagious firing at fleeing civilians (possibly upon hearing what some soldiers thought was a rifle shot). All shots were fired by one company within 10 minutes and in a half-mile radius. Overall, the strain of being in combat formation went on for about 7 hours; then came a half-hour of intense confrontation, moving to a new position, followed by 10 minutes of lethal violence. McCleery offers comparisons to other occasions when the same Para unit had maintained discipline. Two weeks previously, demonstrators attempted to break into an internment camp where IRA suspects were held; the demo was confronted on the beach by the Paras, who fired rubber bullets and baton-charged the crowd, causing injuries but no deaths. Unlike the city terrain of Bloody Sunday, they were on an open beach where everyone was visible; negotiations between the sides went on, antagonistic but with no surprises, no organizational breakdown, and no forward panic.

A longer period of tension build-up is shown by Gross (2016) in interview-based research on participants in vigilante groups that burn captured robbers to death with a rubber tire around their neck. In the South African slums, where police protection is non-existent, householders are constantly in fear of violent crime; this background tension exists for weeks or months. When neighbors believe a burglary or attack is going on, they alert each other through alarm signals—whistles that people signal from house to house, and raising tension to a high level over a period of minutes. The mob that answers the alarm signal is full of contagious excitement; when they capture an alleged perpetrator, the shared emotion tends to spill over into "necklacing." This creates a solidarity ritual among the crowd of on-lookers as well as participants in the violence, a temporary island of collective strength in a sea of ongoing tension and fear.

Gross shows that vigilante justice is more prevalent in neighborhoods that have a higher feeling of community solidarity. Contrary to what might be supposed, it is not social disorganization that causes lynching, but the collective alerts of community solidarity. Here lynching is Simmelian solidarity, and a way of working off the adrenaline surge felt during chasing and capturing the suspect. The lynching ritual follows the three-part dynamics of a forward panic: long-term tension over neighborhood crime; the excitement of the alarm signals and the chase of an isolated enemy; the necklacing carnival, an attention-commanding community street-assembly. The victim is outnumbered by dozens or 100s-to-1, who stay emotionally energized for an hour or so.

Another case of long-standing tension suddenly released is the massacre of Bosnian Muslim forces by the Bosnian Serb army at Srebrenica in 1995. Klusemann (2010) analyzed a news-team's videos of the hours leading up to massacre. In the background were two years of military stalemate, with periodic artillery fire, ground raids, and air-strikes. The two sides were separated by 400 Dutch peace-keeping troops, but these had become increasingly demoralized over the last six months: Muslim troops set up positions close to UN outposts to shelter from Serbian artillery, and attacked Dutch troops whom they accused of failing to protect them. Lightly armed Dutch troops relied upon NATO air strikes to keep belligerent sides from attacking (chiefly the aggressive Serbs). But air strikes were limited by a complicated political chain of command, and often refused by higher-ups. Dutch forces became openly distraught, feeling attacked by both sides. Perceiving this atmosphere, Serb forces attacked for six days, growing bolder as resistance crumbled. Demoralization of the peace-keeping forces spread to the Muslim forces, who gave up all resistance even though they still had most of their ammunition and outnumbered the Serb forces by approximately 5000 to 1800.

In a confrontation between the Serbian commander and the Dutch commander, the latter was browbeaten into apologizing for calling in NATO air strikes. Videos show emotional domination was visible in their respective body postures and voice tones. This shift tacitly gave the Serbs a free hand with their captives. Serbian soldiers now began to ostentatiously dominate the Dutch peace-keepers, taking their vehicles and weapons and mockingly donning their blue helmets. In this emotional atmosphere of triumph, Muslim men were crowded into vehicles, taken to remote areas, and killed. Time-dynamics followed the pathway from tension (the Serbs look wary as they take over the city, expecting Muslim or peace-keepers' resistance); to an emotional turning point where the defenders are dominated; to an atmosphere of joyous triumph and humiliating the defeated, culminating in a forward-panic-type massacre of demoralized and unresisting victims. The mood of collective emotional domination continued for 12–16 hours, losing enthusiasm over the next few days as Serbian soldiers became perfunctory in their executions, allowing victims to escape.

Forward panic does not continue beyond a few days. Deliberate genocidal extermination campaigns require more centralized organization.

Also within the time-scale of violent danger time zones are high-speed police vehicle chases and standoffs between police and suspects resisting arrest. Here we should count the period of building up high tension as beginning when police start a vehicle chase; or from the time police are notified to rush to the scene. In the Rodney King incident in Los Angeles in 1991—infamous because it was the first video-recorded police beating—the chase took 6 minutes, the confrontation 3 minutes and the beating 90 seconds. Other high-speed chases have lasted up to an hour, with 15 seconds of violence at the end (Collins 2008: 88–90). Out-of-control shooting in standoffs or mistaken identity shootings have happened within seconds of police arriving on the scene, but also up to an hour later in the confusion of large numbers of police arriving and noisy helicopters overhead (see Chapter 15).

Why do organized protest marches and demos have their violent danger-time zone between 1 and 3 hours in, while the corresponding period in police arrests of individuals is more variable but often much shorter? A hypothesis is that it lengthens with the number of persons involved; a systematic comparison of cases is needed.

4. Revolutionary Tipping Points: Duration of Violent Protests

Some revolutions are surprisingly rapid and easy. Fastest were the 1848 French revolutions: three days for the government to fall in February; five days in June for insurrection and counter-mobilization to put it down (Tocqueville [1850] 1970). The key mechanism is the tipping point or bandwagon effect. There is a tense period of confrontation between regime and mass uprising; there may be sporadic efforts at dispersing the crowds, a brief and hesitant use of force by authorities; but if the crowd holds on, sustained by the courage of mass solidarity, the regime tends to split. Elites go over to the opposition; soldiers and police waver and change sides; leaders feel isolated and lose their nerve. This is Durkheimian collective consciousness (Durkheim 1912) as a process in time, not a permanent entity but an emotionally compelling center of attention that sucks everyone in.

There were two brief tipping point periods in the 1917 Russian Revolution. The March revolution lasted eight days, beginning with four days of demonstrations, a general strike, and army mutiny. On day 7, the Czar abdicated in favor of a family member, who also abdicated the next day, leaving a provisional government in power. This was similar to the February 1848 revolution in France: during two days of confrontation, an army unit fired on the crowd but was withdrawn; the King dismissed the conservative Ministry but two successive candidates for Prime Minister declined through lack of confidence. On day 3, a crowd invaded the legislature; the King abdicated; no other royals accepted the throne; conservatives fled, and remaining legislators declared a Republic. The failure of nerve is part of the emotional mechanism of the tipping point.

The micro-dynamics of the tipping point have been documented by Ketchley (2014), combining interviews with on-line videos and photos of the first success of the Arab Spring in Egypt at Tahrir Square in 2011. The Egyptian revolution took 18 days of mass demonstrations, with the army turning neutral over days 5–7. When the regime turned from its unreliable soldiers to ad hoc paramilitary forces to violently clear the square ("the Battle of the Camel," on day 9), the army was forced to choose sides, and intervened to support the crowd. Protestors made friendly gestures toward soldiers tasked with repressing them, climbing on tanks and shouting "The Army and People are one hand!" The resulting solidarity ritual (building shared focus, emotion, and rhythm) created the turning point that brought down the authoritarian regime.

Violence Disperses, Solidarity Concentrates[1]

The period of violent contestation was almost entirely in the first four days, and spread among many different sites around the country. After that, the Durkheimian collective consciousness became an overwhelming center of attention, as virtually all other action stopped to focus on Tahrir Square.[2] The massive assembly, unmoved by violent attack, soon broke the will of the regime; the army had shifted to the crowd's side, and the army chief—temporarily a hero—ended up in charge of the transitional regime. The Durkheimian solidarity of the assembled crowd was so great that the revolution acquired an image as a non-violent, virtually bloodless revolution. This was not strictly true; including both sides, about 400 were killed and 6000 wounded, most of them in the first four days, when fighting took place in many different cities, before Tahrir Square established its primacy in the attention space.

In Tunisia, there was a progression from violent conflicts dispersed around the country, to the eventual formation of a peaceful revolutionary crowd in the capital city. The revolution in Tunisia took four weeks in December–January 2010–11, with an additional two weeks of demonstrations after the president fled, while protestors pressed for further changes. The first week began with two spectacular public suicides in an outlying town, spreading to protests in other small towns within a 30-mile radius of the capital.[3] These first protests spread by word of mouth. The first killings of demonstrators by the police happened on day 8, as demonstrators became increasingly destructive, burning tires, police cars, and public buildings. In the second week, protests spread to the three second-rank cities of the country, as the national labor union became involved; in the capital, two days of relatively small and peaceful protests were organized by the lawyers' association. Bigger and more modern organization was now becoming involved.

During days 18–27, violent protests occurred in still other provincial towns, especially in the remote western region near the Algerian border. Here violence became increasingly two-sided, as police escalated from tear gas and water cannon to live ammunition; crowds threw stones and petrol bombs, and snipers fired from rooftops. Simultaneously, in the Mediterranean coastal cities where labor and professions were well organized, more peaceful tactics were used, including protest marches, strikes, and blogging. The combination of street-fighting in the small towns and the provinces, plus more peaceful, politically sophisticated demonstrations in the urban centers, created an omnipresent sense of crisis. On days 29 and 30, the tipping point came: the president attempted to impose a state of emergency, then tried to escort his family out of the country; the military staged a coup, and the government fell. Thereafter, almost all the action was centered in the capital city, where demonstrations kept up pressure for a more radical change in the transitional government; at this point, the demonstrations were more peaceful, and the police were eager to accommodate their demands. Here the process of forming a turning point covered a little more than a month.

We see a contrast between the tactics and levels of violence in the two kinds of sites of confrontation. In the small towns where the protests began, and the remote provincial regions where it escalated to guns, bombs, and arson, it is likely the police had only small detachments. The fact that the violence spread from one town to another—rarely in the same place more than a few days—meant that the police were always heavily outnumbered and on the defensive; when their forces were beefed up by reinforcements, protests moved somewhere else. In the big cities, with their Westernized cosmopolitan style, protests had more centralized organization behind them; violence was restrained on both sides, and the protestors generated a better sense of legitimacy and responsibility. This created a magnetic attraction for government officials who would cross the line in a tipping point for regime change. The combination of both violent tactics in dispersed places and non-violent demos in the center played a part.

I will discuss revolutions that fail to have a tipping point in section (6), since these shift to another scale of time-dynamics.

The duration of violent protests resembles the tipping point period of a rapid revolution. In most riots, the violent crowd action is confined to one day, following a period of tension build-up. Violent protests last longer if they move from place to place, such as the rural arson campaign in England in 1830 called the Captain Swing rebellion, with most violence during two months (Tilly 2003: 178–187). Other cases of extended rioting are the Newark riot (or black ghetto uprising) in June 1967, which spread to adjacent locations in New Jersey over four days; the so-called Paris Banlieue riots of 2005 went on over 20 days, but spreading to different suburbs and distant cities, with a maximum of 5–7 days in any one place (Collins 2008: 492). The outer limit of continuous rioting appears to be a week, although most are much shorter. Riots lose emotional intensity, in part because they are not big enough to sustain the feeling that the majority of the people support them (unlike when a revolutionary crowd feels itself nearing a tipping point); in part because of logistical difficulties of an ad hoc crowd keeping themselves supplied. Riots that move from place to place last longer, but they are not usually the same persons, but others from nearby areas who take a day or two to imitate what they have heard from elsewhere.

Intermittent Demonstrations Extend the Time-Line

Tactically sophisticated movements like the French *gilets jaunes* (yellow emergency vests) of 2018–2019 have developed the tactic of scheduling intermittent demos every Saturday, so that they can provision themselves in everyday routine during the interims. These demonstrators protested rising fuel prices and taxes, government-imposed lower speed limits on country roads, and perceived bias by the newly-elected government of

President Macron in favor of the rich. The first protest in mid-November 2018 brought out 300,000 persons all over France, organized in a leaderless horizontal network by Internet social media. It blocked roads, constructed barricades, attacked superhighway toll booths, and destroyed traffic enforcement cameras. The movement was centered in rural and small-town France, by people dependent on cars and alienated by what they regarded as the contemptuous attitude of cosmopolitan city-dwellers and the formal news media. The movement hit its peak numbers in its first week, preceded by a five-month on-line campaign started in May for a protest petition, which had 300,000 signatures by October, and reached 1 million in the first month of protests.

Over time, the movement shifted in its numbers, targets, and tactics. The initial 300,000 at week 1 was down to 120,000 for weeks 3 and 4; dropped to 65,00 and then 40,000 by weeks 5 and 6; after a rather quiet period in the Christmas holidays, reviving in weeks 9 and 10 at 80,000, dropping to 70,000 in week 1; it was down to 40,000 in week 14, steadily declining to a few thousands in June—about 30 weeks overall.[4] This approximates the six-month solidarity/hysteria zone, with the two peak surges occurring within the first two months and the falling off starting around the third month.

These two surges also changed in location; the later surge took place mainly in big cities. Paris typically had 8000 protestors, but rising to 10,000–15,000 in week 12, as the movement wound down nationwide, before dropping to 5000, 2000, and below. Big city centers were not their home turf, and tactics there less involved using their cars to block roads (but burning city-dwellers' cars); protestors concentrated on marching in upscale areas, smashing display windows, looting luxury stores, and attacking famous public monuments. They also fought with the police, whom the government brought out in massive numbers (reaching 80,000), and gradually overwhelmed the outnumbered protesters. A relatively small number of persons (about a dozen) were killed, mostly in traffic accidents at road barricades in the early weeks; but 4000 were injured (approximately evenly) on both sides in fighting with the police. The movement petered out, in part by declining enthusiasm, and by massive and determined police repression aided by the increasing concentration of protests in big city centers. Government concessions on some issues came in the early months but had little immediate effect. (This was also true in Hong Kong.) We see also a pattern, common to big protests everywhere, that the longer the movement goes on, the more the non-violent participants drop out and the militants become more violent.

A similar tactic of intermittent demonstrations was used by the 2019 Hong Kong pro-democracy movement against influence by the government of China.[5] Big marches were held on Saturday or Sunday. Other protests targeted particular days: when the city legislature met to consider a controversial extradition law; the anniversary of the PRC take-over of Hong Kong; the big celebration in Beijing of the 70th anniversary of Communist China. A sit-in to block police headquarters went on overnight; some big marches were followed by violent action on the next weekday. Here, too, numbers were highest in the early weeks: large peaceful marches in week 1 (estimated between 250,000 and 1 million) and week 2 (2 million—i.e. about 25 percent of Hong Kong's population); a peaceful march in week 4 (550,000), but followed by a violent night-time attack by several hundreds on the legislature, smashing glass walls and trashing the interior. A peaceful rally on the following Sunday (perhaps trying to change the atmosphere) was down to 30,000–50,000; and the next three weeks were relatively calm. Violence escalated again for week 10, with a two-day sit-in blocking passengers at the international airport. Publicity exploded when videos went viral of protestors beating isolated individuals accused by the crowd of being Chinese spies. This led to a huge public outcry in China against the Hong Kong demonstrators—illustrating the familiar dialectic of counter-escalation by perceived atrocities on each side.

Week 11 had another big peaceful Sunday march (1.7 million), pushing back against China, and perhaps a last gasp at peaceful methods. Week 12 was back to violent street demonstrations, this time attacking surveillance lamp-posts, as protestors kept finding new targets. Over the following weeks, protestors closed major streets and highways downtown; barricaded and burned subway stations, and shut down public transport; then as police guarded public targets, protests shifted to residential neighborhoods. The message became increasingly hostile to Chinese people as well as government, as protestors attacked Chinese banks and other mainland-associated businesses. Protests became increasingly violent, as numbers of protestors were down (often in the hundreds) but comprising the most militant. In weeks 17–19, peak violence happened when tens of thousands spread out across the city, locally outnumbering police. Battles with police grew steadily worse: protestors attacking with bats, metal bars, bricks, and gasoline fire-bombs; police using tear gas, paint-spray, and by weeks 18–19 firing live ammunition, causing the first gunshot woundings, which further enraged the protestors. By week 20, the city was mostly locked down, except for a few hundreds of militants.

We started by looking at the time-pattern of tipping points and riots; traditionally these lasted a few days, with protests up to a few weeks if they acquired fresh participants by moving from place to place. But protestors learn new tactics and access new organizing technologies; the combination of the social media (allowing spontaneous coordination without formal hierarchy or charismatic leaders) and scheduling of intermittent protests at chosen places appears to have greatly increased the time-range of protest demonstrations. Nevertheless, we see a falling off in numbers, and a shift to the violent extreme to make up for the weight of peaceful demonstrators. This suggests there is an outer limit, even in the new era of sophisticated scheduling.[6]

5. Mass Crisis Solidarity and Hysteria Zones

As we have seen in Chapters 1 and 2, public focus of attention on an enemy attack or outbreak of war brings a rapid display of enthusiastic solidarity, lasting three to six months and then declining into normal partisan dissent and the local concerns of everyday life. Most political atrocities happen within this time zone. The initial three-month solidarity-and-hysteria zone is when violent atrocities are most likely to happen. Following the outbreak of the Spanish Civil War in July 1936, massacres of civilians on both sides were most intense in the first two months and fell off by six months; the internment of Japanese-American citizens happened 10 weeks after the Pearl Harbor attack in December 1941 (Collins 2004b). I have documented this for the period after the 9/11 attack in the United States in 2001, and for public enthusiasm on all sides at the outbreak of World War I. Section (4) of this chapter suggests that current Internet-organized techniques for protest demonstrations have extended their lifespan to this range as well.

Several other types of mass violence fit into this time frame. Martin Sánchez-Jankowski (2016) observed conflict between black and Hispanic students over three school years in high schools in Los Angeles and Oakland, and between white and black students in Boston. He tracked violence over the weeks and months, giving a rare picture of the time-process of escalation and de-escalation, and explaining how one kind of violence morphs into another. He documented what the students were concerned about in their daily lives from overheard conversations, including the fights they talked about; he also observed fights directly and on the streets to and from school. From the beginning of the school year in autumn, the shift over time went from *small fights* (typically the attacking-the-weak pattern ranging between 2-to-1 and 5-to-1), to *medium-sized brawls* (15–25 total participants), to *large-scale riots* (50–100 participants).

By winter term, smaller fights and brawls declined as they were supplanted by large-scale, mass participation riots. Some riots physically attacked the school itself; another type of riot consisted in mass fights between ethnic groups. A third type of collective action was *stampedes*—where virtually the entire student population, upon hearing of a violent disturbance, got up and spontaneously left the school. Stampedes became increasingly common in the latter part of the school year (winter–spring), outnumbering riots. Since only a fraction of the students took part in riots (ranging from an estimated 6–23 percent; an estimated 3–18 percent took part in small fights), the great majority of students were opting out of the fight scenario even as an audience. Stampedes de-focused and de-mobilized riots, sending an emotional message that it was not supported by the hitherto passive majority. By the third year, riots had disappeared, and fights were mostly confined to 1-on-1 scuffles.

The patterns found by Sánchez-Jankowski fit two generalizations about violence:

1. The attitude of an audience encouraging or discouraging violence strongly affects the length and intensity of violent events.[7]
2. The time-dynamics of ethnic violence in a school communty is roughly similar to the three-to-six-month duration of crisis escalation and mass hysteria. Although in the school violence there is no sudden onset and no external attack, but there is a similar plateau and gradual decline. In both cases, these are mass phenomena, spontaneously playing themselves out without formal organization or hierarchy. Thus, we would expect such phenomena to have different time-dynamics than in organized war.

Another type of mass violence that fits into this pattern are rampage mass shootings at schools and other institutions (Newman et al. 2004; see Chapter 14). This is mass violence, even though the perpetrator is typically a lone individual, at most, a duo. It is large-scale because large numbers of victims are killed or wounded, and the killer aims not at any particular individual but has a grudge against an entire organization or category of persons. It also has an extended time-pattern: the perpetrator spends several months in clandestine preparation, collecting weapons (usually far more than he actually uses in the attack), costumes, information about similar attacks, and planning the location that is to be attacked.[8] This period of preparation (as we know from survivors) is intensely exciting for the planner; keeping it successfully hidden from family and other people adds to the fantasies and emotions of adventure and doing something important in their life.

This period of clandestine excitement fits within the three-to-six-month horizon of public mobilization against an enemy. In both cases, there is a great deal of display of symbols that represent solidarity against an enemy. For the individual preparing a rampage, this has to be done alone (rarely with an accomplice). But clandestine preparations generate a feeling of tension (which must also be disguised) with the people around him from whom he must keep his preparations secret. The period of tension spent building up fantasy/symbolic emotional intensity by lone individuals corresponds to the time-period of Simmelian solidarity of an embattled people against an external enemy, and is a variant on similar mechanisms. Since collective solidarity falls off after three-to-six months, we would expect to find would-be rampage shooters who give up their planned attacks if their preparation period goes on longer than three months or so.

6. Macro-Time-Forks

A time-fork is a period when a violent uprising will go either in the direction of a rapid tipping point, or spread into far-flung civil war. A similar time-fork exists in interstate wars, which are sometimes rapidly settled by a crucial battle or *Blitzkrieg*; sometimes long drawn-out wars of attrition. Military time-forks have longer time-dynamics than revolutions, but their causal dynamics are similar.

There are two key conditions for a tipping point:

1. A *central place* where protestors can gather, and where the attention of the entire country is focused. Here protestors confront regime forces, with the feeling on both sides that whichever way the tipping point goes will determine regime change or not. Paris became such a place after France developed a strong central administration in the seventeenth century. Such places include St. Petersburg, and more recently Moscow; modern Cairo; Tehran. Such central places are not available in countries that have multiple important cities, with government administration, finance, and cultural institutions dispersed among them. These (Germany, the United States, India, Japan) have never had a tipping point revolution, although they have had prolonged civil wars.
2. A tipping point becomes possible where there is a confrontation between *one massive crowd* and the regime. The contrary case is when *two or more crowds* mobilize, especially where they have separate home grounds where they gather; in this configuration, the perception cannot be established that one crowd represents the People. Sometimes the government has its own mass supporters who mobilize against the revolutionary crowd. Revolutionists may be split into rival crowds, as in the post-Arab Spring struggle between Islamists in their own quarter of Cairo and cosmopolitans and Coptic Christians in theirs, sometimes attacking each other. A new authoritarian regime took advantage of these struggles, ostensibly to restore peace in Egypt by deposing the elected Islamist regime.

The two sets of conditions can follow in sequence. In 1917 Russia, the two peaks of revolutionary mobilization were separated by eight months during which time anti-Czarist parties were fragmented and incapable of bringing about a tipping point. But after the November Revolution (an eight-day period propelled by mutinies in the military), power was not settled; civil wars began already in December 1917 and continued through till 1920, a period of three years. The tipping points happened at a central focus of attention, St. Petersburg; the civil wars were against regional military forces, aided by foreign intervention. The 1917 revolutions were nearly bloodless; the civil war produced many thousands of casualties.

We see a similar fork in the series of Arab Spring uprisings, which ranged from tipping point revolutions that either succeeded (Tunisia, Egypt) or failed (Bahrain) within a few weeks; and geographically dispersed uprisings that turned into civil wars (Libya, Yemen, Syria) lasting 10 years or more. Bramsen (2017) analyzed videos from the Arab Spring uprisings in Tunisia, Bahrain, and Syria, culled from viewing hundreds of videos and selecting those that meet the criteria of showing both sides in the conflict, the presence of violence or visible threat, sufficient detail, and unaffected by editing. She also interviewed protestors and participated in protest marches.

Emergent processes shifted demonstrators away from their avowed strategy. Initially, demonstrators strenuously attempted to stay non-violent and to avoid religious and ethnic splits. The uprising in Bahrain initially chanted for Sunni/Shi'a unity. Following an early violent confrontation with the united demonstrators, regime forces allowed demonstrators to occupy a circular road intersection on the outskirts of the city. After a month, protestors became bored and lost numbers, precipitating a split between moderates and those who wanted to use aggressive tactics of stopping traffic in the city center. This had the effect of angering motorists and escalating violence against vehicles, splitting the population not only over tactics but along religious/ethnic lines. In this mood of falling confidence among participants, the regime was then able to arrest them piece-meal. Sporadic protest marches continued for three years, but with declining emotion and energy. Geographical dispersion and multi-sided conflict led to higher destruction as well as defeat.

This pattern was even more pronounced in Syria, where uprisings in far-flung cities, and local struggles between militants and those who wished to stay out of the conflict, led to an extremely destructive civil war fed by foreign military supplies and interventions in favor both of the regime and multiple factions. There was no Tahrir Square in Syria. Bahrain had one but abandoned it. Only Tunisia was able to centralize demonstrations and eventually compel a tipping point. The three cases had similar structural root causes of conflict (highly unequal, authoritarian regimes), but very different pathways of violence en route.

Conceptually, there is a similar dichotomy between wars or battle campaigns that end quickly through decisive battles, and those that grind down through the years by attrition. Examples of *rapid victory* are the 1871 Franco-Prussian War (four weeks); the 1940 *Blitzkreig* on the Western Front (six weeks); Japanese conquests of British Empire Malaya, Singapore, and Burma from December 1941 to May 1942 (six months); the Gulf War of 1991 (four days). Examples of *long attrition war* are World War I on all fronts 1914–1918; the US Civil War of 1861–1865; the US-led

Afghanistan War 2001–2021. Napoleon's campaigns were largely rapid victories, until the Spanish campaign of 1808–1813, and the six-month Russian campaign of 1812. The early victories all had decisive battles; the latter were shaped by guerrilla resistance, and by the Russian refusal to offer battle after the capture of Moscow, shifting instead to harassing French columns during their withdrawal.

Rapid victories were those that destroyed enemy morale, typically by speedy maneuver forcing organizational collapse, and by the inability of defensive forces to reorganize a front to meet a fast-moving attacker. Long attrition campaigns were either static fronts with massive firepower on both sides; or guerrilla-style resistance where an advancing army ostensibly holds territory but insurgents hide in the civilian population and sporadically attack spread-out logistics lines. Rapid victory campaigns typically had low casualty percentages, as most of the defeated were captured rather than killed on the battlefield, while attacking forces were largely unscathed. Attrition wars pile up very high casualties by massive bombardment and frontal assault; or in the case of dispersed guerrilla wars, by fighting among civilian populations and ambushing not just combat soldiers but the entire logistics structure in a war without a front.

Conclusion: Nested Time-Patterns and Meta-Time

What we have so far are empirical generalizations. Nevertheless we are beginning to see their theoretical basis. Time-dynamics take longer as numbers of participants and formal organization increase. At each time-scale, disrupting opponents' rhythm, and imposing one's own rhythm, result in ending the conflict. This happens by destroying the opponent's ability to coordinate itself (whether as an individual, a small group, large crowd, or formal organization). The end point can be victory of one side and defeat of the other; or a mutual feeling of stalemate leading to breaking off the fight. Among the causes of such variations in the time-dynamics of macro-conflict are those spelled out in Chapter 1.

Generalizations span time-segments from micro-seconds, minutes, and hours, to days, months and years. Conceptually, the smaller time-periods must be embedded in the larger ones; to put it another way, longer expanses of time are composed of smaller bits of time. This implies that the mechanisms of the smaller kinds of violence are parts of the mechanisms of the larger time-patterns. But this is not strictly a micro-basis of macro. In some ways, yes; emotional coordination and imposing micro-rhythms are the central process of group solidarity and hence the building-block of organization for violence; and the individuals or groups who maintain their own emotional energy, rhythm, and solidarity win out over those who lose their EE and become disorganized.

But in some ways the answer is no; revolutions are not just prolonged forward panics. Particularly important for the transition from micro-patterns to macro are longer periods where no one dominates, where tension stretches out; where formal organizations overcome the tendency to drop out from boredom or emotional burn-out or from confrontational tension/fear. Macro-organization overcomes some of the weaknesses of micro-processes in sustaining violence over longer periods of time; and it can vastly increase the scale of destructiveness. The mechanisms toward the micro-end of the continuum predominate in rapid tipping points, but when these are stalemated and drawn out, we are in the realm of time-forks, and these are what generates attrition and massive destruction. Time-forks are perhaps the ultimate form of explosive violence, launching us onto a meta-level of time-dynamics. This is not really a good place to be, but it is where a lot of history has been made. The following sections of this book explore this level.

Notes

1. We see this pattern also on a smaller spatial scale in photos of demonstrations around the world (Collins 2008: 415–421): when demonstrations are peaceful, they are compact crowds; when violence is happening, people are running around, widely spaced apart.
2. The chief exception was after the last violent episode on day 9, which was followed by a brief upsurge of violence and looting in Alexandria.
3. Since there was news censorship, probably these first protests spread by word of mouth, like traditional rural protest movements. According to the BBC, 34 percent of the Tunisian population of 10 million were Internet users, mostly in the coastal cities, as half the population lived in the impoverished countryside.
4. Sources: *Wall Street Journal*, June 12, 2019; Wikipedia, "Timeline of Yellow Vest Movement Protests."
5. Sources: *Wall Street Journal* and *New York Times*—June 9–October 22, 2019; and the BBC.
6. Does duration of protests depend on how successfully police use violence? On the other hand, violent repression tends to promote outrage and increases violence by the remaining protestors (the C-escalation pattern). The latter pattern predominated in the Black Lives Matter protests in the summer on 2020 (from June through September). Especially violent were protests in Seattle and in Portland, Oregon, where Federal forces used tear gas, baton charges, and mass arrests, while protestors attacked and attempted to burn Federal buildings and, subsequently, most downtown commercial areas. Numbers of protestors dwindled over time but intermittent arson and attacks on property continued through the spring months of 2021 (sources: Associated Press; *Wall Street Journal*; *Washington Post*; *New York Times*). This fits the generalization: over time, numbers of protestors decline but become increasingly violent.
7. This is similar to the pattern for smaller-scale fights found in Collins (2008: 202–204, 236), except that there the fights were prolonged or cut short on a scale of minutes; Sánchez-Jankowski shows it applies to riots over a timeline of a year.
8. In all cases so far examined, the killer has been male. I don't want to preclude the possibility that such killings are gendered, by using the conventional "he or she," or worse yet, making all personal pronouns female.

References

Alpert, Geoffrey, and Roger Dunham. 2004. *Understanding Police Use of Force*. Cambridge: Cambridge University Press.

Bramsen, Isabel. 2017. "Route Causes of Conflict: Trajectories of Violent and Non-Violent Conflict Intensification." PhD dissertation, University of Copenhagen.

Collins, Randall. 2004a. *Interaction Ritual Chains*. Princeton, NJ: Princeton University Press.

Collins, Randall. 2004b. "Rituals of Solidarity and Security in the Wake of Terrorist Attack." *Sociological Theory* 22: 53–87.

Collins, Randall. 2008. *Violence: A Micro-Sociological Theory*. Princeton, NJ: Princeton University Press.

Draper, Scott. 2019. *Religious Interaction Ritual*. New York: Lexington Books.

Durkheim, Emile. 1912. *Les formes élémentaires de la vie religieuse*. Paris: Presses Universitaires de France.

Gibson, David. 2010. "Marking the Turn: Obligation, Engagement, and Alienation in Group Discussions." *Social Psychology Quarterly* 73(2): 132–151.

Goffman, Erving. 1963. *Behavior in Public Places*. New York: Free Press.

Gross, Mark. 2016. "Vigilante Violence and Forward Panic in Johannesburg Townships." *Theory and Society* 45: 239–263.

Grossman, David. 2004. *On Combat*. Belleville, IL: PPTC Research Publications.

Jackson-Jacobs, Curtis. 2013. "Constructing Physical Fights: An Interactionist Analysis of Violence Among Affluent Suburban Youth." *Qualitative Sociology* 36: 23–52.

Ketchley, Neil F. 2014. "The Army and the People Are One Hand! Fraternisation and the 25th January Egyptian Revolution." *Comparative Studies in Society and History* 56: 155–186.

Klusemann, Stefan. 2010. "Micro-Situational Antecedents of Violent Atrocity." *Sociological Forum* 25: 272–295.

Levine, Mark, Paul J. Taylor, and Rachel Best. 2011. "Third Parties, Violence, and Conflict Resolution." *Psychological Science* 22(3): 406–412.

McCleery, Martin. 2016. "Randall Collins' Forward Panic Pathway to Violence, and the 1972 Bloody Sunday Killings in Northern Ireland." *British Journal of Politics and International Relations* 18: 966–980.

Mosselman, Floris, Don Weenink, and Marie Rosenkrantz Lindegaard. 2018. "Weapons, Body Postures, and the Quest for Dominance in Robberies: A Qualitative Analysis of Video Footage." *Journal of Research in Crime and Delinquency* 55: 3–26.

Nassauer, Anne. 2018. "How Robberies Succeed or Fail: Analyzing Crime Caught on Camera." *Journal of Crime and Delinquency* 55: 125–154.

Nassauer, Anne. 2019. *Situational Breakdowns: Understanding Protest Violence*. Oxford: Oxford University Press.

Newman, Katherine, et al. 2004. *Rampage: The Social Roots of School Shootings*. New York: Basic Books.

Sánchez-Jankowski, Martin. 2016. *Burning Dislike: Ethnic Violence in High Schools*. Berkeley, CA: University of California Press.

Tilly, Charles. 2003. *The Politics of Collective Violence*. Cambridge: Cambridge University Press.

Tocqueville, Alexis de. [1850] 1970. *Recollections: The French Revolution of 1848*. New York: Doubleday.

Part II

The Eye of the Needle

Emotional Processes

Chapter 5

Material Interests Are Ambiguous, So Interaction Rituals Steer Political Movements

Introduction

In talking politics and writing history, we typically explain what people do by their interests. But interests are often in dispute; people are accused of doing things that aren't in their own interests and failing to recognize their best interests—when they vote, go to war or not, or support a particular economic policy. "Interests" are the rhetoric of modern politics, not an accurate predictor of how people go into action.

Of course, there are other motives besides material interests: power, honor, prestige, sympathy, religious or ideological values. But even if we put these aside, and confine ourselves to material interests—people seeking money, property, and the necessities and luxuries of life—interests still do not predict very well what people will actually do in a specific circumstance. There are two main reasons: (1) interests are generally ambiguous; and (2) interests do not determine the tactics people will use to reach them.

If interests aren't a good predictor, does this mean the political and social struggles of history are inexplicable, a chaotic fumbling in the dark? Not necessarily; a better theory is the success or failure of interaction rituals (IRs) in motivating individual and collective action. IRs that focus group attention and generate high levels of shared emotion create emotional energy (EE)—confidence in and enthusiasm for symbolically-defined goals. These shape the cognitive component of action—how people define their goals; who are their fellows and opponents in seeking them; and what tactics seem appropriate. I am not arguing for a dichotomy between material interests, on one side, and "irrational" or "emotional" forces, on the other; I am pointing out that material interests by themselves are too vague to determine specific courses of action in most situations. Even the most hard-nosed material interest becomes a motive for action only when a successful IR focuses attention on it, making it a conscious goal with enthusiastic energy mobilized toward attaining it. Strong commitment to material interests does exist, but it has to be socially created, through interaction rituals.

DOI: 10.4324/9781003245629-8

Interests Are Ambiguous as to Compatriots

Take, for example, the interests of the working class. Presumably these are better wages, better job conditions, and job security. But who does one share these interests with? Possibilities include: (1) a class-wide organization of all workers; (2) a particular occupational sector, such as all skilled crafts, or just one particular profession seeking monopolistic licensing; or (3) a local organization of workers in a particular place or business. Within each of these choices, there are further sub-choices. Taking (1) again, what does the class-wide organization do: aim for massive strikes? for political influence to bring government intervention? for socialist ownership of production? All of these, in the abstract, can be said to be in workers' interest; but the interest doesn't determine which one to seek. Any program that claims to be in someone's interest is a theory, better yet, an ideology, that tries to persuade people this is the best way to attain their interests.

Ideology and organization thus become a crucial part of interests. Ideologies try to argue that this (______ *fill in the blank*) is the only way to truly secure your interest; but that is not true. The (1, 2, 3) list above is ordered roughly from the most inclusive to the least inclusive coalition, and the argument tends to be that bigger is stronger and will deliver more goods. But it is also in someone's interest to descend even further on the continuum and pursue advantage for a small group of friends or kin, or just for oneself. We get the best-paying jobs and others don't; I get the promotion and too bad for you. Ideologists trying to organize as a larger group condemn this as unethical, and organizers often claim that everyone will do better if they all stick together, even the token favorites; but that depends on other conditions—the argument that going your own way is not in your interest is an iffy one. Enthusiasm for joining a larger organization does not typically come by rational calculation; strong unions don't just try to persuade individualists that it is in their interest to join the union, they establish coercive rules (if possible enforced by state regulation) to make individualists join. One reason white-collar workers are hard to unionize is that they tend to think their careers have a chance of moving upward into management; they lack class solidarity because they regard their situation as temporary. I am not making an argument here for or against unions or individualists, but pointing out that it is not simply a matter of material interests. If everyone pursues what they think is their own best interest, all sorts of organization (or lack of organization) are possible.

Even with a union organization, a segment can pursue their interest over other members. Seniority rules protect older workers' jobs while younger workers are laid off. Another variant is an ethnic/racial group that monopolizes jobs for themselves. This can be condemned as immoral, but it is certainly not against the interests of the ethnic group that can get such privilege. The argument for inter-racial solidarity has to be made by moralistic rhetoric, not by simple appeal to interests. A similar logic applies to racial tokens; a black man taking a position as a conservative Supreme Court Justice, for instance, might be accused of selling out his people, but there is nothing irrational about it from the point of view of his interest. Similarly with gender. Feminists demanding equal access and equal pay in all jobs would seem to be in every woman's interest; but there is nothing irrational about an individual woman who decides that her best career path is to marry a wealthy man, especially if she has the opportunity and the personal qualities to do well on the marriage market. This is not to say that a rich lady could not join a feminist movement (and in fact this is how the movement originated in England); but that comes from other conditions than their own material interests. Arguments for the widely inclusive, high-solidarity path cannot sway individual motivations just by appeal to interests.

The same problem of compatriots arises in every interest, in every economic class and sector. When declaring something is in your interest, who is included in the "you"? It cannot simply be decided by an abstract calculation: choose the course of action that has highest probability of benefits vs. costs. In real life, not only do you rarely know those probabilities, but the deciding conditions are much more in the tactics than in the goal.

Interests Are Ambiguous as to the Short, Medium, and Long Run

The wider the scope of the organization, the more it can appeal to long-term interests. The party claiming to represent all workers is most likely to push a long-term solution to their interests, such as socialism. The trouble is, the more long-term the solution, the less certain that it will actually come about; if the event is a long way in the future, the present generation of members is not pursuing their own interests at all, but an altruistic dedication to someone else's interests. The key to long-term commitments, then, cannot be strictly in the realm of interests, but must depend upon social mechanisms of moral commitment.

It has been a trope of moralizing ever since the ancient Greek philosophers that very short-term gains can be foolish diversions from your own interests, even in the not-so-distant future. True enough, but how far into the future is it rational to calculate? If you never enjoy anything in the short run, you will never enjoy it in the long run, since every moment of time arrives as another short run. Weber's concept of the Protestant Ethic and similar theories of economic motivation solve this problem not by rationally calculated interests, but by religious and other emotional dispositions to work, invest, or consume. It is sometimes assumed that very short-run attraction to material benefits is due to being irrationally overcome by emotion, but one can argue just the opposite, that long-term self-discipline is also due to emotional forces. What I want to emphasize are two points: that viewing one's interests in the short-, medium-, or long-term perspective is an extrinsic condition, not contained in the interests themselves; and which time-frame persons happen to focus upon comes from outside themselves, from the social groups in which they experience emotional rituals.

Interests Do Not Determine Tactics

Once an economic or political interest group has gotten organized, that is still not the end of it. Take the example of a working-class movement; or an ethnic/racial movement; or a gender movement. This history of modern politics, ever since parties came on the scene in the nineteenth and twentieth centuries, has been made up of parties that defined themselves as representing a particular interest; but over time all parties twisted or split along lines of what tactics to use. Liberal/left parties have had the choice of being *reformist*, seeking small incremental changes where they could get them; *radical and militant*, using strong rhetoric, demanding big changes, and (another variant) using demonstrations, strikes, and disruptions instead of (or along with) electoral politics and courts; or *revolutionary*, seeking the overthrow of government and property by violent means. This is a continuum, and factions could take up positions nearer or farther from the different main points (left and right wings of socialist parties, or of anti-clerical/anti-monarchist republicans, etc.).

The key point is that the major splits and controversies of party politics happen along tactical lines within groups espousing similar interests. This is especially true of organizations identifying themselves as workers' movements. In early twentieth-century Germany and most other European states, the labor party split into a parliamentary/ gradualist wing, and a militant wing; a series of such leftist splits generated the Spartacists (whose uprising failed at the end of WWI), and the Communists. On the centrist side, liberal or Catholic parties from outside the working class might join the gradualist wing, supporting workers' interests out of charitable motives or a concern for social peace. On the revolutionary side, another tactical split was between socialists or communists who aimed to change the property system through control of the state; and anarchists who aimed for the same thing but by avoiding the state entirely—regarding parliamentary politics as a fraud that always worked against them, and the state as an instrument that would introduce new forms of inequality. The anarchists were mostly right on both counts, but their own tactics—such as, in Spain, their violent seizures of local property, assassinations, and destruction of churches as their hated symbolic enemy—were too uncoordinated to produce victory, and chiefly stirred up resentment. Although in the abstract it might seem workers' interests would be stronger if held together in one organization, which organization this should be could not be agreed upon. Political organizations became passionately committed to their particular tactics, and often their most bitterly fought enemy was their former compatriots who split over just such tactical issues.

The terms Left and Right, since the time of the French Revolution, have generally been used to refer to the degree of militancy in tactics. But the usage is confusing—Left/Right could also designate lower vs. upper classes; or it could mean change-oriented versus stability-oriented. None of these usages yields a clear and uncontradictory picture; revolutionary militancy could appear on the Right, with the Fascists, especially if the liberals or the Left held political power. The contradiction comes from assuming there is a perfect line-up between a social class, its interest both in economic matters and in stability, and its tactics. This is empirically wrong, and tactics almost always swamp the neater identities as classes and interests. Nevertheless, it is hard to resist falling into Left/Right terminology, and this is all right in particular historical contexts, provided we think through just what we are talking about.

Besides splits along the continuum of reformist-vs.-revolutionary, there is what might be called a meta-split between opportunists and principled ideologists. This is not merely the same thing as reformists (who are willing to make deals with parliamentary opponents to attain some of their interests) in contrast to more militant or revolutionary groups. Principled ideologists can occur at any point in the political spectrum. The Tea Party movement in the US in the years after 2010 is an instance of a conservative single-issue movement, that refuses to make deals and regards consistent defense of their principle as the cardinal virtue. But unyielding ideologists vs. opportunists are found on the revolutionary left as well.

The success of the Russian Bolsheviks in autumn 1917 came from a willingness to appeal to peasants in overthrowing the government by endorsing their seizure of farmland. Since the peasants were taking land as individual private property, the Bolsheviks were going against their own principle of collective organization of agriculture, although eventually once they got secure power, they went back on their promise. The Bolshevik slogan "Bread! Land! Peace!" also was opportunistic about ending the war; this was a temporary expedient to stop the futile fighting against the victorious German army, but almost immediately the Bolsheviks resumed fighting in a three-year civil war that lasted until 1920. The analytical lesson here is not that the Bolsheviks were especially perfidious bad guys. They were part of a spectrum of liberal and left groups that had been struggling against the Czarist regime for almost a century; broadening our perspective, they were part of a European family of squabbling reform-minded parties. The

Russians were very familiar with the different options. Instead of regarding the Bolsheviks as genetically imprinted from the outset, we should regard them as the movement that happened to fill the opportunistic niche as it emerged at a particular moment. The Bolsheviks were not opportunists of the parliamentary type (like the Social Democrats in Germany of the 1890s, or later the Mensheviks in Russia); they were opportunists among revolutionists (Klusemann 2010).

The Superior Success of Opportunism

Opportunism has a bad name, but it is generally the most successful tactic, especially if it is employed by a militant, violence-wielding organization. The Bolsheviks triumphed in Russia because they opportunistically sought state power; their tactical line was to do anything that strengthened the cohesion of their own party and the strength of the state. Hence the creation of the Red Army, the security commissars, and all the other means of organizational discipline. This could be justified theoretically in terms of interests—the strong state will get us to the workers' interest—but so could all the other tactics chosen by rival left movements. Russian-style Communists thus became the organizational identity embodying the left-opportunistic style. Their opportunism was a great advantage in struggles with other left organizations. During the Spanish Civil War of 1936–1939, the Anarchists' scatter-gun tactics and extreme consistency of revolutionary ideals made them unpopular with most other members of the anti-Fascist coalition; the Spanish Communists burgeoned because they advocated social order and group discipline, and could opportunistically declare the defense of private property during the emergency of the civil war, thereby gaining allies both in the Republican middle class and in the army (Thomas 1986). A similar opportunistic line was taken by Mao's Chinese Communist Party as it fought a guerrilla war in the countryside in the 1930s and 1940s; theoretically they favored the landless peasants, but they were willing to make deals and protect the rich peasants if they needed them in a particular circumstance.

Of course, the Communists were lying when they publicly took one of these opportunistic stances, ostensibly against their socialist aims. They knew that their line was only temporary and tactical, and that they would go back on it when the opportunity came to push through full communism. Here we need to explain why there are different types of opportunists. Why didn't the Communists become like the German Social Democrats or the British Labour Party, wedded to the parliamentary route and gradually becoming indistinguishable from a non-revolutionary party working inside the framework of capitalism? The Communists maintained more long-term consistency, even throughout their tactical opportunism, because they had a dual inner/outer structure not found in other leftist parties: a core of dedicated, career-professional revolutionaries organized in a hierarchy of small groups, holding secret meetings where they encouraged and criticized each other, renewing their commitment not only to doctrine but to discipline as a group. Philip Selznick (1960) called this *The Organizational Weapon*. What made the Communists strong was a conscious recognition that their organization was the key to victory, and that their ideological line was secondary.

These Communist cells, meeting frequently (often weekly or more) were also a discovery of political Interaction Rituals, carried out at the small-group level. They were successful IRs with all the ingredients: the secret meetings excluding outsiders and keeping up a strong focus of attention; the shared emotions of revolutionary danger, of secrecy itself, and the immediate emotions of mutual criticism issuing in solidarity on their public line at the end of the meeting. A close-up picture of what life was like in a secret cell is provided by Alessandro Orsini (2009), who interviewed members of the Red Brigades active in Italy during the 1970s and 1980s. They were dedicated to overthrowing capitalism by kidnapping and assassinating politicians and businessmen, and they spent their days shadowing their targets to find vulnerabilities in their routines. How did they keep themselves going despite little success in their political goals? They lived together in small groups crowded into an apartment, cutting off all ties with their former lives outside the group. Their days were spent shadowing their enemies and planning possible attacks; every evening they interrogated each other about the details of what they did, constantly wary of any minor mistakes that might give themselves away to the police. Everything they did was emotionally intense; life was a continuously powerful IR generating exclusive commitment to their high-pressure group.

This inner *cadre* organization had been created originally in Czarist Russia to fend off police agents, but it unexpectedly enabled the Communists to be successfully opportunistic. Where a parliamentary workers' party might stray from their original interests by befriending bourgeois politicians and enjoying the perquisites of office (what Robert Michels charged against the German socialist SPD in his ([1911] 1962) *Political Parties*), Communists did not pal around with their erstwhile allies, at least not on the backstage. The Communists had a superior backstage that generated much more emotional energy, along with more solidarity and more commitment to their sacred objects and beliefs. But this was a sophisticated, two-level belief: what we are really doing, and what we are pretending to do temporarily for practical reasons, and this sophistication was built into their organization. The Communists dominated in so many countries because they consistently took the opportunistic niche in revolutionary political space; because they developed an organizational structure that supported this; and because they harnessed IRs not just at the level of mass public meetings, but in backstage small groups to keep up revolutionary dedication.

Opportunism vs. principled consistency is a fundamental, but generally unrecognized, dimension of politics. The opportunists usually win, in any part of the political spectrum, whether the deal-making center or the militant wings. (When opportunists lose we will consider later.) This dimension operates on the militant Right as well. The Nazis differed from other right-wing movements in Germany of the 1920s, not because their interests and ideologies were different—there were nearly 100 movements calling for social order, invoking the solidarity of the Nation and the People, and spewing anti-Semitism. The Nazis gradually outcompeted their rival movements, recruiting better and eventually absorbing the others, because they were opportunists of the violent revolutionary wing. The Nazis were not the type of opportunists fostered by parliamentary participation; the core of their organization were their street-fighters. As Stefan Klusemann (2010) shows, the Nazis were innovators in political IRs, not only in their pageantry of uniforms and swastika-symbols and *Heil Hitler!* greeting rituals, but the tactic of using violence as a ritual, marching into workers' neighborhoods and taverns and provoking fights that they were better organized to win. Thus, both Bolsheviks and Nazis were IR-innovators, although of different kinds.

Nazi ideology reflected their preferred tactics, "Action!" rather than decadent parliamentary discussion that never led anywhere. But once they had dominated their rival Right-wing street-demonstration movements, around 1930, the Nazis violated a cardinal principle of their own ideology by running candidates for parliament. This shift in tactics provoked a split between the SA (street-fighters) and Hitler's more political followers, and eventually led to the bloody purge of the former. But Hitler's opportunism enabled Nazis to become a dominant faction in the despised parliament, enabling him to become chancellor and then to dissolve parliamentary government from above. The most important Rightist revolutionary movement, whose primary tactic and explicit ideology extolled violence, nevertheless took office legally through the electoral process. This was also true for Italian Fascists, whose showily dramatic march on Rome in 1922 paid off with the King appointing Mussolini prime minister (just as German President Hindenburg appointed Hitler). On Right as well as Left, opportunism pays off more than intransigent ideologies.

Interests Don't Predict Outcomes, Because of Multiple Causality

So far I have argued that interests are too ambiguous as to compatriots and time-frames to guide action; and the spectrum of tactics is not determined by interests but is the main source of organizational splits and loyalties in the political arena. Here I add a third reason why interests are poor predictors: whatever happens in a conflict is the result of all the different forces in play. A socialist or revolutionist line will not reach its aim if anti-revolutionary and capitalist forces are too strong. But neither will a reformist, parliamentary deal-making tactic necessarily yield much; with sufficiently strong political opponents on the right, and disillusionment from its own militant wing provoking splits on the left, reformists may simply become ineffectual or personally corrupt. Not only cannot the payoffs be predicted from the interests; nor can they be predicted from their choice of tactics alone—it is always the tactics of each group as they stack up against each other.

And there are many other contingencies that affect which interest group will take power: economic crises; wars won or lost; religious, ethnic and other cultural controversies. Timing of a crisis is especially important. If a party is strong enough to be in office (possibly as part of a coalition) when disaster happens, it will get the blame for it. All over the world, elected parties in office at the outbreak of the 1929 Depression were punished by being voted out, whether they happened to be right or left. The Russian government in spring 1917 that decided to continue a losing war thereby set themselves up for takeover, even though Kerensky himself was ideologically socialist. The best crack at revolutionary or deeply transformative power is to be a strong second, outside of office at the moment when confidence in government breaks down through a major crisis; the worst position is to be in charge during war defeat or economic collapse. On a milder scale, this was the problem of the Obama administration, which inherited an economic crisis, peaking just after the 2008 election.

Electoral Politics Is a Blunt Instrument When It Comes to Making Major Policy Changes

Voters essentially have a yes/no choice; either you take the incumbent government as a whole and keep it in office; or you throw them out. The non-controlling party (or parties) always tries to argue that the crisis (economy, war, social unrest, etc.) can be solved by their own ideology; this may or may not be true (and given multiple causality, can hardly be a very reliable predictor); so it may often be irrational for voters to get rid of the incumbents, since the policy of who will replace them could be even worse. But the extent to which people vote by the "misery index," indicates they are making a binary choice; they know what they don't like, but they cannot articulate what they really want and how to get it. The structure of an election as an interaction ritual focuses attention on the binary, the ins vs. the outs; the more emotional the mobilization for the election, the more people brainwash themselves into believing that flipping the binary will make all the difference.

Another reason why interests do not predict outcomes is that politics often goes through enormous swings on rebounds. The all-out effort of one side to put their program into action can result in a massive conflict; a revolutionary's best efforts can lead to a victory for the authoritarian right; this was a result of the anarchist mobilization in Spain in the early and mid-1930s. But also the Fascists' program of conquest provoked enough counter-mobilization in the world to destroy and delegitimate fascism both in Europe and Japan. Whatever your interests, no political pathway will predictably get you there.

Having an interest and a tactic doesn't mean you will get it; virtually no one gets what they aim for. Conversely, almost anything you do can be construed as against your interest, on some theory in hindsight about what would have been the correct thing to do. Hindsight has among its advantages over real life that it is never experienced through the same emotions that prevailed at the time when the future was still unknown. History-writing in this mode is a retrospective game of blame or praise played by fantasy advisors outside the action. It is the chief fault of writing by journalists.

Who benefitted from some particular policy does not show why it happened. Wars often cost much more than the victor gets out of them. Capitalists might think that a war is needed to protect property, or gain markets and materials, or just as a matter or patriotism or xenophobia; these become causal forces, not because they are true, but because of the fervor with which they are believed. Bad reasons are just as good explanations of what happens as good reasons (if we restrict that to mean economic calculation). In either case, the reasons people consciously give for whatever they do become powerful motives only to the extent that reasons are formulated in IRs, and thereby are pumped up with confidence, commitment, and belief.

Successful Interaction Rituals Predict Choices by Focusing Ideologies and Interests

Does the argument apply only against the left? Workers' interests, tactics and calculations may be ambiguous but capitalists might be better at it. After all, Weber describes modern capitalism as the omni-calculation of all factors of production. But it is dubious that this applies to capitalists as political actors. As Michael Mann shows in his four volumes (1986; 1993; 2012; 2013), whether a national economic policy succeeds or not depends on timing and what other economic powers in the world are doing. Interest-oriented policies only fit particular situations, and capitalists on the whole are not much better than workers at choosing policies that will pay off. Capitalist monetary policy during the Great Depression shows that capitalists do not necessarily have a clear idea of their own interests downstream; capitalism was rescued by liberal policies that capitalists resisted at the moment. One might assume that capitalists (or at least their economic advisors) become shrewder over time, but events since 2000 hardly bear that out. Empirically, the case for capitalists being more rationally calculating in political matters is far from proven; theoretically, all the generic problems apply as to time-frames, political tactics, and multiple forces bearing on outcomes.

To be clear: my argument is not about whether political people talk about interests—they often do, although sometimes they also talk in idealized rhetoric. They may even believe what they say about their interests, and, for that matter, what they say about their ideals. Sincerity is not an important question in politics, because sincere belief is a social product: successful IRs make people into sincere believers. People become insincere and manipulative mainly when they go through a range of different IRs, switching from one camp to another; or in the case of the Communist backstage organization, when they use one strong IR to anchor their beliefs against another more public IR which is not as emotionally intense.

This leaves room for the cosmopolitan opportunist, who believes in nothing because s/he surveys all factions but belongs emotionally to none. Such persons are fairly common in politics, but they rarely achieve much popularity or emotional sway, because strong EE, which is so impressive in leading others, comes from being deep into emotional IRs. Pure manipulators are uncharismatic and off-putting. Opportunists have their biggest success when they learn how to manipulate rituals and generate emotional entrainment, but then become caught up in it themselves. Yes, Hitler was manipulative; but he lived at the center of very strong IRs, and Nazi ceremonial made him a true extremist for Nazi ideals. In the end, he was so pumped up with self-confidence (EE) that he destroyed his regime by taking on overwhelming geopolitical odds.

Donald Trump is the most prominent recent example of a cosmopolitan opportunist. He supported both parties during his life, and chose to run as a Republican in 2016 because it was an easier opportunity to capture a presidential nomination. But he was also a master of political rituals, using his show-biz techniques—the campaign rallies which he continued throughout his presidency because they generated such emotional enthusiasm among his followers and EE for himself as the center of the crowd's attention. Trump did not initially believe in any particular policy, but in the slogans which he led his supporters in chanting. His rallies were such intense experiences that he and his followers could not give them up, chanting a new mantra that he could not possibly have lost the 2020 election. Once he launched into his successful series of crowd rituals, he too became swayed into believing in the reality he was projecting. Like Hitler, he became a prisoner of his own rituals.

At any point in time, we can predict the line-up of persons with varying degrees of commitment to ideas and ideals, by looking at the degree of success or failure of the IRs they experience. IR theory is an explanation of what people will think, as well as what they will do. At any particular moment, people are speaking certain words or thinking certain thoughts; the thoughts that go through one's head are internalized from previous talk with other people; more innovative thoughts are assembled out of the ingredients of verbal ideas already internalized. The world is a network of conversations, and what people think at any point in it is a product of what has circulated in previous conversations. There is a crucial emotional component: ideas are better remembered, and make more sense, if they were associated with emotion when they were previously talked about. Thus, even in spontaneous private thinking, it is those emotionally-laden ideas that spring to one's mind. When persons strategize, or vent, or otherwise try to express their aims in words, these are the words that arise in one's head, and flow from one's tongue.

Put more fully: the world is a network of conversations with different degrees of success or failure as IRs. Successful IRs are those in which the assembled group attains a high degree of mutual focus of attention, sharing a common emotion, and experiencing Durkheimian collective effervescence. Successful IRs in political life can be speeches and rallies, if they generate enough emotional high for everyone; especially dramatic are riots and atrocities. For some professional politicians, the most important IRs are their private discussions with other political devotees—their passions are about their backstage strategies. What kind of IR it is will have an effect on what kind of political commitment it creates. The mentalities of the street-fighter, the parliamentarian, and the campaign planner differ because of the contents of the IRs that are most successful for them. The important contrast is with IRs that fail, or are merely mediocre; rallies can be unenthusiastic, parliamentary sessions can be droningly routine or exasperatingly gridlocked; riots and wars can end in dispersion as well as in solidarity. In political life as in everything else, each person gravitates toward the emotionally successful IRs and is pumped up with their way of thinking. We move away from the IRs that don't work, and lose the attraction of thinking in their symbols.

I have argued that material interests are ambiguous as to compatriots, time-frames, tactics, and estimates of success. But in the flow of real life, people who take part in political action–going to public meetings, talking with their acquaintances, engaging in backstage planning, joining rallies, riots, wars—become part of a discourse that defines what interests we think we are furthering, while it defines the identity of who is in it with us. It is not the interests that holds us together, but our shared talk about interests. It is these symbol-formulated-interests that carry the Durkheimian solidarity of membership.

For that reason, people in a political interest group can become committed to material interests in a moralistic way. At one time in my life, I contributed regularly to an organization dedicated to lowering utility bills; eventually I realized that I was putting more money into the organization than I could possibly get out of it. That is typical of supporters of many, perhaps most, material interest groups. No researcher has yet shown empirically that most contributors to political campaigns—including the candidates themselves—make a profit on what they contributed. Some do; most don't; we need a more refined theory of conditions.

The same mechanism of success or failure of IRs determines whether people think of their interests in a short, medium, or long time-frame. On the whole, they need stronger IRs to sustain belief in long-term interests. The more "fanatical" movements have the strongest IRs, including the greatest barrier to outsiders, to prevent contaminating their members' attention.

The IR mechanism also chooses which tactics people become committed to, and which tactics they reject. Tactics become a focus of attention, and often the most heated topic of conversation. Most political factions do not differ among themselves so much in what they are aiming for, as in their tactics for how to get it; and it is around these tactical issues that the most vehement splits have taken place. A political group's favorite tactic becomes the basis of their identity; their opponents' favorite tactic becomes the symbolic dividing line which emotionally frames their worst enemy.

A good example is the "struggle meeting" developed by Chinese Communists in their guerrilla strongholds of the 1930s. In a struggle meeting, the poor peasants of a village criticized the rich peasants and put pressure on them to mend their ways. The presence of armed communists gave the oppressed peasants confidence; but the meeting was not just an angry outburst or a lynch mob—as in traditional uprisings—because it was institutionalized, i.e. repetitive and official. The communists restrained the poor from killing their class enemies, and instead encouraged them to apply continuous group pressure, to make their change their views (Mann 2012: 401–410). This became the prototype of "thought reform" tactics—really an application of small group psychology, in a deliberately manipulative mode—that were used up through the 1960s Red Guards movement, no longer purging class enemies but communist administrators themselves (Walder 2009). Like the Russian Bolsheviks (and in a different way, the Nazis), the Chinese Communists were both distinctive and successful because of their innovations in micro-sociology of group discipline and emotional commitment. And it was these innovations that made them appear so sinister to their enemies.

Interests do not become conscious motives until they are socially defined. There is no basic instinct of private property, or of collective property, or gift-giving, or plunder; all these have been practices, in many variants, in different societies since human origins. People have to be taught to be capitalists, or union members, or reformers or revolutionists (or, for that matter, gang members). The way they are "taught" is not so much by admonition as by their own experiences in IRs that give them emotional energy in talking about and performing these practices.

True, some material interests are easier to focus upon than others. If you already have a routine material practice, having it disrupted makes you pay attention, and that will generate a protest or a counter-attack if other persons gather with you to focus on the same grievance. Negative interests are easier to see clearly and easier to mobilize around than positive interests. Workers who are fired, or peasants who have their rents raised, can more easily see their interests than workers pondering what might they do in the future to give them higher incomes. Hence reactive movements—responses to economic downturns, threats to property from the state or other political movements—are easier to mobilize, and generally more emotionally aroused than positive movements seeking a better future. All this flows through the micro-mechanism of IRs.

Negative interests—losing or feeling a threat to one's material resources—tend to easily fulfill the conditions for successful IRs: assembling a group, focusing attention, enhancing a shared emotion about the object of attention. Positive interests, because they are more ambiguous and lead into a multiply branching future, are harder to focus on clearly; and emotions are harder to attach to them—joy and hope have to be generated in the group assembly itself, whereas in a loss or threat to what one already possesses, the emotion is generated individually and then is amplified by the group process. Movements for transformation have to do more IR work than movements defending the status quo.

Defensive interests are not always unambiguous. If landlords are taking more of the peasants' crops, that is clear; but if an anarchist or socialist movement threatens your property, the movement may not be as threatening as it appears—their threat is pumped up by their rhetoric (which may be sheer ritualism), and they may be incapable of carrying it out. On the other side, an anti-leftist movement may be successful at generating emotional hysteria about the alleged threat—one of the main tactics in conservative crackdowns. Property threat from the left is not always a myth; but at the moment of conflict it is hard to judge how serious it is, and hence there is a large element of social construction, via IRs, even in negative interests.

To summarize: material interests do not simply exist and thereby drive struggles among classes and interest groups. They must always be socially formulated, in words and symbols; and this is done when Interaction Rituals are successful in generating more focus of attention and more shared emotion around certain ways of construing interests than other ways. Not to say the material world doesn't exist; of course it does, and our bodies (and the numbers of people who take part in one ritual camp or another), weapons, vehicles, money, and all the other economic and technological resources make a difference in how the action is mobilized, and who wins. But it all has to go through the eye of a needle, which is the social definition of what we perceive our interests to be, and that is done by the degree of emotionally shared focus in IRs. Material resources are inert and blind until they are put in action by focused networks of humans in full emotional/cognitive communication. Different ways of organizing and focusing interaction rituals are the key to political action. It is not surprising that the most colorful movements throughout history, for good or for evil, have been those that generated the most political energy.

References

Klusemann, Stefan. 2010. "After State Breakdown: Dynamics of Multi-party Conflict, Violence, and Paramilitary Mobilization in Russia 1904–1920, Germany 1918–1934, and Japan 1853–1877." PhD dissertation, University of Pennsylvania.

Mann, Michael. 1986; 1993; 2012; 2013. *The Sources of Social Power*. 4 vols. Cambridge: Cambridge University Press.

Michels, Robert. [1911] 1962. *Political Parties*. New York: Free Press.

Orsini, Alessandro. 2009. *Anatomy of the Red Brigades*. Ithaca, NY: Cornell University Press.

Selznick, Philip. 1960. *The Organizational Weapon: A Study of Bolshevik Strategy and Tactics*. New York: Free Press.

Thomas, Hugh. 1986. *The Spanish Civil War*. New York: Simon & Schuster.

Walder, Andrew. 2009. *Fractured Rebellion: The Beijing Red Guard Movement*. Cambridge, MA: Harvard University Press.

Chapter 6

Mood-Swings in the Downfall of the English Revolution

Introduction

The first modern revolution took place in England. It eventually failed. Parliament revolted against the King in 1642 and chopped off his head in 1649. In 1660, the King's son was invited back and the monarchy re-established. The 18-year experiment in rule by a parliamentary Republic was ended.

Oliver Cromwell, Protector of the Commonwealth, died in early September 1658. In the little more than a year-and-a-half that followed, there were three *coups d'état* and four armed revolts. There was no immediate shift in public opinion in favor of monarchy. The Commonwealth went from crisis to crisis, the popular mood each time swinging sharply and overwhelmingly toward one center of power or another. The groundswell of opinion in favor of Restoration of the monarchy happened at the end, nine months after a Royalist revolt ignominiously failed. But in the final surge of the political storms, the London stronghold of the Republic celebrated through the night and Parliament itself voted overwhelmingly for Restoration.

How can people shift their position so sharply? Political conflicts are generally analyzed in terms of group interests or ideologies; but most of the opinion swings in the death phase of the Commonwealth were strongly enthusiastic and near-universal. How can people forget what was their strongly-held belief only a few months earlier?

The puzzle is solved once we recognize that people's behavior in crisis situations—i.e. in massive mobilization of the entire community—is not determined primarily by their interests, nor by their deep-seated beliefs and values, but by the shared emotional mood of the time. The mass focus of attention in each crisis creates a pervasive Durkheimian ritual, and thus a temporary but powerful pressure to share the same emotions, rhythms, and public demonstrations of solidarity; the result is to create temporarily strong beliefs, and to submerge narrower calculations of material interests. Then comes another crisis, another mass mobilization, focused on some other object of conflict; older political

DOI: 10.4324/9781003245629-9

beliefs are washed away and replaced by a fresh one riding on the public expression of emotion.

Not quite everyone goes along with these swings. There are some strong ideological activists, who hold on firmly even when the vast majority swings against them. These are the fanatics, die-hards, or heroes, depending on your point of view. But they are a small minority—even within the political class of activists who regularly take part in politics, whether by discussion, demonstration or violence. I want to underline the point: the biggest swings of enthusiasm from one position to another happen in London, in the Parliament, and in the army—exactly the people who are most ideological. Even the ideologues, those most committed and experienced in politics, are subject to the strongest swings of public emotion. This is not really a paradox, once we examine the social interaction that happens in their daily lives during these agitated events. Political activists are closest to the center of attention and most tightly surrounded by the swirling bodies of their compatriots; no wonder they are most strongly swept up by the Durkheimian tides.

What I am investigating here is a theory of political mood-swings. This is a theory of emotional time-dynamics. *How fast can these emotional swings happen, and how long do they last? How long can a series of such swings go on before it breaks down in emotional exhaustion?* The English Revolution came to an end because most people got tired of the emotional roller-coaster, and found returning to non-democratic rule a way out. These processes happen in most revolutions. Something similar happened in the French Revolution that started in 1789, swung through wild gyrations until 1794, then turned toward authoritarian rule.

Eight Mood-Swings in the Fall of the English Revolution

Mood-Swing 1. Months 1–3, September–November 1658

From Honeymoon to Army Dissent

Oliver Cromwell dies, having named his son Richard as successor. Richard is well-liked and easy-going, devoted to country sports like fox-hunting. The first two weeks are a honeymoon. Richard is accepted by all political factions around the country, and the military officers stationed in London unanimously deliver a loyal address. By the six-week mark, there is agitation in the army. Richard and his friends calm things down, but by November, officers in London are holding weekly meetings. Their demands are for more autonomy and security in their commissions: no officer to be removed without court-marshal; General Fleetwood to be named commander of all forces, interposing a step between them and Richard's control. Richard agrees to appoint Fleetwood and things calm down again. But veteran revolutionaries are reviving their customary suspicions and political paranoias, fearing the son will be like his father.

Mood-Swing 2. Months 6–8, February–April 1659

First Coup d'état

Richard calls Parliament to deal with finances. Republicans in Parliament debate whether to recognize Richard as Protector, or to remove his veto power and shift control of militia forces directly to Parliament. But the Republicans are out-voted and his powers as Protector are confirmed. It was an arrangement that Oliver Cromwell had set up to end the incessant quarreling of political factions. In fact, Protectors had existed before, acting as Regent when an English monarch was still a child. Now the Protector was a quasi-king, called Your Highness, living in a palace in London. Oliver had refused the title of King, preferring the constitutional façade of ruling in the name of Parliament, that he controlled by the device of excluding intractable members.

The army was now splitting into factions. One group favored abolishing the Protectorate and restoring the Commonwealth under direct Parliamentary rule. Another group organized themselves into a Council of Officers, meeting regularly at General Fleetwood's mansion in London. Fleetwood and other high-ranking aristocrats in the army wanted to keep the Protectorate, seeing Richard as a weak puppet whom they could manipulate.

A couple of things worth noting already at this stage: First, the army itself is relatively democratic; the officers call meetings among themselves and vote on their course of action. Higher officers do not insist on rigid lines of authority. Their recurrent demand is that no-one can remove a officer without the verdict of a court-marshal, which is to say, an independent judiciary made up of a body of officers judging each other.

Moreover, there is a degree of dual sovereignty built into the way that each faction has its own meeting place, its home base where it can debate among themselves and organize its own forces.[1] London now has three such bases: General Fleetwood's Wallingford House; Whitehall Palace where Richard resides; and Parliament meeting in Westminster Abbey. It would acquire more bases, and they would move to invade each other's space.

In early April, there is a mass meeting of all officers at Wallingford House, concerned that the dominant faction in Parliament will vote to make Richard—like his father—commander-in-chief of all forces. Another group of lower officers and common soldiers are upset by the opposite rumor: that Parliament in going to recall the monarchy. That would be Charles Stuart, son of King Charles I, whom they had executed in 1649, now living in exile in France and waiting an opportunity to return. Many officers now demand that Richard should dissolve Parliament.

There follows a confused 10 days. Wallingford House declare themselves a Council of War. Richard visits their assembly, hears them debate for an hour, then rises and announces that he is dissolving the Council. They leave quietly. But they keep on meeting, now clandestinely, out of Richard's sight. On the other side, Parliament does the same thing, voting in closed-door session that no Council of the Army can meet without Parliament's consent. The same day, Richard calls the leading officers to Whitehall, demands again that they dissolve their Council, and threatens them with force if they do not.

Three days later, another faction is heard from: the Mayor and Aldermen of the City of London present a petition in favor of Parliament and the Protector. At the same time, troops stationed in London march through the streets in favor of the army petition. Richard calls his Life Guards to protect Whitehall Palace, but most of them marched away, and his friendly colonels could raise only a few companies.

That night, every regiment in London was under arms. Richard's own bodyguards faded away in the dark, and the army marched into Whitehall without opposition. General Fleetwood shut himself in a room with Richard until the late hours. Next day Richard dissolved Parliament.

It was a *coup d'état*, but it solved nothing. The Council of Officers at Wallingford House spent the next week debating what form of government they wanted. Lower officers split off, meeting independently at St. James Palace, demanding a Republic, direct Parliamentary rule without a Protector. The higher officers had made their coup in order to keep Richard as their figurehead, but now the revolutionary surge swept beyond them. The lower officers outvoted their superiors, and the Council of the Army voted to bring back the old Parliament.

In May, the old Parliament reassembled, and Richard bowed out. If the coup was launched by General Fleetwood and other aristocrats to keep Richard as a puppet, they got the opposite result, abolition of the Protectorate and revival of Parliamentary rule.

Mood-Swings 3 and 4. Month 12, August 1659

Revolts by Royalists and Presbyterians

Since winter, Royalists had been starting to meet secretly on country estates. For months they wavered about when the opportunity was ripe. August 1 was set as the date for armed revolt. There were scattered gatherings in eastern and western regions of England, but most of the King's party held back. Not only did they fail to muster sufficient numbers, but their divided and timid attitude spoiled the possibility of a tidal wave of emotion sweeping the country, the most important ingredient for successful revolt. Those who did rise in arms were easily put down, and the Royalist cause sank lower than ever.

But also in August, a more serious revolt broke out from a different political direction: an army of Presbyterians, 5000-strong, in northwest England and north Wales. The Presbyterian Church had been the strongest backer of the original revolution in 1642, although they had been pushed aside by Oliver Cromwell and the Independents— Protestants who wanted no religious control other than local congregations; no Pope, no bishops, no assembly of Presbyters, no central control of any kind. Now the Presbyterians, feeling the London Parliament weakened by the back-and-forth conflicts of the spring, took up its own demands by force. Their slogan: return to the full and freely elected Parliament of revolutionary days—the Parliament before it had been pared down to a Rump of Oliver's supporters by his forced exclusions.

Armies were not large in those days. A pro-parliamentary army under General Lambert marched north, with 4000 men. On August 23, in a single day of fighting, Lambert's parliamentarians defeated the Presbyterians. One reason they collapsed may well have been confusion. Although the Presbyterians did not advocate restoring the King, their forces were joined by scattered bands of Royalists, shouting their proclamations in favor of the King. Usually the more unified force wins on such occasions.

The crisis was over in three weeks. Two revolts had been put down. Moreover, Parliament's financial situation suddenly improved, adding the confiscated property of the defeated leaders to their treasury.

Mood-S.wing 5. Months 13–14, September–October 1659

Second Coup d'état, in the Flush of Military Victory

Full of emotional energy in the aftermath of victory, General Lambert's officers assembled in a country town, and petitioned Parliament to make Lambert, along with Fleetwood, commanders-in-chief. During three weeks from late September to mid-October, conflict with Parliament escalated. The House of Commons refused to appoint more top commanders. The officers pushed back with more demands for autonomy. Escalation on both sides came to a head on October 11–12. The House voted to annul all acts of previous Parliaments unless confirmed by themselves; declared it treason to raise money for the army without Parliament's consent; and cashiered Lambert and other officers. October 13, Lambert's troops, now back in London, sent a military guard to close the doors of the House of Commons. One loyal officer attempted to defend the House with a couple of regiments. But their "ranks thinned by desertion, at night they abandoned their posts without a blow" (*CMH* 1907: 434–458, 539–559).

It was another bloodless coup, the emotional tides flowing entirely in one direction. "London was apathetic and indifferent. On the thirteenth, in all the hurly-burly the streets were full, everyone going about his business as not concerned." Parliament asked the City of London for help, but these usual supporters replied "it would not meddle in the dispute."

Lambert's forces control London. Parliament locked out of its base. Acquiescence everywhere. For how long?

Mood-Swing 6. Month 16, December 1659

Army in Scotland Revolts Against Coup

The only opposition was in Scotland, where General Monck declared his intention to restore Parliament. Monck had 10,000 men, but the army in England expected the trouble would go away, as it had before. Monck made a truce with General Lambert, which the latter took as a sign there would be no fighting. But in fact, Monck was buying time; to make arrangements to keep Scotland quiet in his absence; and to replace officers whose loyalty he doubted. (This was the same issue as in Mood-Swing 1.)

Up to now, there was no real difference between General Lambert and Monck. Both were strong Republicans, devoted to Parliament and Constitutional rule. But now they were on opposite sides. They had become enemies, not over principles, but tactics. Or just because of where they happened to be located when events emerged.

Opposition started to gather around Monck. In late November, leaders of the deposed Parliament sent Monck a commission as head of all forces in England and Scotland. In London, merchant bankers refused a loan to Lambert to support his troops. Only six weeks before, all of London was accepting and pusillanimous; now the apprentices took to the streets, getting up a noisy petition for the restoration of Parliament. When troops were sent to put up notices that their petition was refused, they were mobbed in the streets. On December 5, there was a riot in which several apprentices and citizens were killed. Now the City Corporation pushed back, demanding a free Parliament without exclusions, control of their own militia, and the removal of soldiers from the City. Army control of London was beginning to waver in its own base.

Tides were also turning in the north. Top officers of the army in Ireland supported Lambert, but subordinate officers took Dublin Castle by surprise, and entered into communication with Monck. Other garrison cities did the same. The Portsmouth navy base on the English Channel was taken over by Parliamentary supporters; in early December, troops sent by Lambert arrived, but the besiegers went over to the rebels.

On December 8, Lambert's troops massed at Newcastle (near the Scottish border) confronted Monck's army for battle. Both sides were evenly matched at about 8000 each.

> But Lambert's men had no heart in their cause. They felt it was not their quarrel. As they marched north some said boldly they would not fight, but would make a ring for their officers to fight in; and when the scouts of the two armies met, they fired their pistols into the ground and indulged in a friendly gossip.

On December 15, the Army's Committee of Safety, holding power in London, got a series of bad news: the navy fleet had declared for restoration of the old Parliament; the desertion of troops at Portsmouth, the sudden revolution in Ireland. On December 24, "soldiers about London assembled in Lincoln's Inn Fields, declared for Parliament, and marched in the streets with the Speaker of the House at their head." General Fleetwood, switching sides again, sent the keys to the House of Commons and withdrew guards from the doors. Two days later, Parliament was resumed.

Over a period of four weeks, the tides had completely turned. In early January, Newcastle opened its gates to Monck's army. York and other northern cities were taken by uprisings. Lambert's army melted away as Monck advanced south, taking his time to cashier disloyal officers and reorganize regiments along the way. In London, Parliament took its revenge. Lambert and other leading officers were dismissed—although the House, perhaps not feeling strong enough, did not arrest them, but ordered them to live far from London, a kind of domestic exile. The army list was purged of officers who supported Lambert and Fleetwood; and the Members of Parliament who had supported them were expelled.

Mood-Swing 7. Months 18–19, February–March 1660

General Monck Occupies London, Wavers, Switches Sides, Carries Out Third Coup d'état

Parliament seemingly is riding high. They propose a bill requiring all high government officials to swear an oath never to support restoring the monarchy, and a similar oath for all current and future Members of Parliament. But half the Council of State refused to swear, and even Parliament is becoming reluctant to tie its own hands for future maneuver. "Oaths were said to be useless, and had but multiplied the sins of the nation by perjuries." Too many side-switches had happened in the past, and at an increasing rate in recent months.

Now the public mood is in favor of Parliamentary government, but it surges beyond the one we have now. Former MPs come forward demanding to be readmitted, having been excluded by force in the purges of the past. Parliament promised to reform their grievances, but the contemporary observer Pepys wrote in his (1660) diary: "They declare for law and gospel, but I do not find the people apt to believe them." The historian notes: "Contempt and hatred were the dominant feelings in the public mind toward the little gang of Republicans who cling with such avidity to power."

Parliament gets a new nickname. Back nine months ago when Richard Cromwell had been thrown out as Protector, one of the debaters had referred to "the fag-end of the Long Parliament, the Rump." Now in January the nickname becomes a veritable media hype, in the media of the day: "Every day a new derisive ballad about it was sold and sung in the streets of London: 'The Resurrection of the Rump,' 'A New Year's Gift for the Rump,' 'The Rump Roughly but Righteously Handled,'" etc. The overpowering forces of humor and scorn were now against it.

This was the public mood that greeted Monck when he arrived in London on February 3 with his victorious army. Rural counties were sending petitions demanding readmission of the excluded members, and convocation of a full and free Parliament—not the present Rump. The House, still full of triumph, sent some of the petitioners to prison in the Tower, but they kept on coming. Petitioners turned to Monck, perceiving him as the true source of power; but Monck rebuffed them, declaring himself strongly against monarchy, against the return of the excluded members, and for submission to Parliament.

He did attempt to keep power in his own hands, demanding that all regiments quartered in London be withdrawn and replaced with his own troops. This was granted, and Monck dispersed the troops which had supported Parliament as far away from London as possible. "The citizens received him coldly; and as he passed through the streets, there were repeated shouts for a free Parliament." The Republicans in the House greeted him effusively. Monck declared his devotion to the Commonwealth, but refused the oath adjuring the Stuart monarchy, "telling the House that the fewer oaths they imposed, the sooner they would obtain their settlement." On the burning issue of the day, Monck was already shifting: he declared in favor of a full and free Parliament, but not for readmitting the excluded members. It was a compromise, halfway between the rival demands, and somewhat contradictory to put into effect. Already Monck, the resolute man of principle, was being affected by the cold mood that met him as he rode through the streets.

London crowds continued to push. On February 8, the City refused to pay taxes until Parliament was filled up. The Rump Parliament responded with force, ordering Monck to march into the City (i.e. the walled part of old London), arrest the Common Council, and remove its defensive gates. Monck complied but refused to break down the gates "because it would exasperate the citizens, and he hoped to bring them to submission by milder means." The House reiterated its orders. It was a showdown of sorts. Monck carried out its orders, but "determined no longer to be the tool of the Republicans." The historian comments that Monck recognized "the impracticable character of its leaders. Prolongation of crisis would lead to fresh civil war."

Monck now changed his tone. He was giving the orders, not they: Parliament must fill up all vacant seats in the next six days, and dissolve itself for a freshly elected Parliament in May. Turning to a new base, he "marched back into the City, where he was welcomed by universal acclaim. Bells and bonfires celebrated the impending downfall of the Rump, and it was burned in effigy in every street in London."

One more time, Parliament fought back. It removed Monck as commander-in-chief, downgrading him to one of five joint commanders, hoping to tie his hands by controlling his colleagues. Their pushback pushed Monck off the fence. He called together the excluded MPs and told them he would have them readmitted to the House. He effected this simply on February 21 by ordering the officers in charge of the guard to let them in.

> The other members of the House heard nothing of all this till they found them in the House, insomuch as the soldiers that stood there to let in the secluded members they took for such as they had ordered to stand there to prevent their coming in.

"This peaceful Revolution was hailed with no less joy in London than Monck's declaration against the Rump ten days earlier." Pepys noted: "It was a most pleasant sight to see the City from one end to another with a glory about it, so high was the light of the bonfires, and so thick around the City, and the bells rang everywhere."

Monck was man of the hour, but his waverings over the past three weeks revealed him to be more reading the public mood than strengthening his own position. The Republicans in Parliament offered to make him Protector, strongman under any title, but he refused. Already the public mood was swinging, not just back to equilibrium at its victory demands, but beyond. Pepys reported: "Everybody now drinks the King's health, without any fear, whereas before it was a very private man who might do it." Monck now was removing officers whom he judged to be too fanatical Republicans, and replacing the governors of many garrisons around the country.

On March 16, Monck dissolved the Long Parliament, in advance of the May elections. It was widely expected that pro-Royalists would win throughout the countryside. On the same day, "the inscription '*Exit tyrannus Regum ultimus*' (the last tyrant king departs) which had been set up in the Merchant

Exchange where the King's statue had once stood, was blotted out by noon." Monck and the new Council of State were already entering into negotiations to bring back Charles II from France.

Monck has now made a complete turn-about within six weeks, from resolute supporter of Parliamentary government, to return of the monarchy. Perhaps being realistic, he doesn't even trust the newly elected Parliament to carry it off without further complications; he is going to make it a fait accompli before they assemble.

Mood-Swing 8. Month 20, April 1660

Army Revolts Against Restoration of Monarchy; Fails

The army, better organized than anyone else, also was able to make more of a stand against public opinion. Already in early March, officers of Monck's own army, parliamentary loyalists who had marched with him from Scotland, "were beginning to show signs of alarm and insubordination." On April 10, as Royalist enthusiasm was spreading around the country, and local elections were carrying Royalists to an overwhelming majority, officers of the London regiments were meeting, declaring their loyalty to Parliament "knowing Parliament only can secure us our religious and civil rights." General Lambert, who had been arrested, escaped from the Tower and raised an insurrection. It was a repeat of the failed Royalist revolt in August of the previous year, only with the sides reversed. Troops mutinied in a few towns of central and north England, but in London, the old Republican stronghold, no one stirred, not even their Parliamentary members. Lambert managed to raise no more than 1000 men. On Easter Sunday, they met a government force of the same size, about 70 miles north of London. "Lambert's men would not fight, and the insurrection collapsed without a blow. So ended the rising of the fanatics, which for some months all men had dreaded." When Lambert was brought back to London as a prisoner on April 24, Pepys wrote: "Their whole design is broken, and things now very open and plain, and every man begins to be merry and full of hopes."

Next day, the newly elected Parliament met. The King's conditions were soon read: amnesty and pardon to former rebels, liberty of private religion (although restoration of the state church), sales of confiscated lands to be determined by Parliament, army to receive its arrears of pay. "Both Houses received the King's declaration with enthusiasm." The navy met in a Council of War and resolved in favor of the King, without a dissenting vote; Pepys says "the fleet took it in a transport of joy." General Monck was made a Duke and awarded a large fortune, but not without some recriminations, in the years after the enthusiasm had died down, for his double dealings.

Why Did Violent Conflicts Almost Always Abort in Those Mood-Swings?

Four armed revolts and three coups: you would think there would be quite a few casualties along the way. But surprisingly not. There were only two points where there was much violence at all: in the defeat of the Presbyterian revolt in August 1659, where there was one battle; and in the riot in London on December 5, 1659, when the mood was starting to turn against Lambert's coup. Is it because the English had learned to become civil and merciful? Certainly, General Monck was praised for his bloodless revolutions. But these events in 1658–1660 were not long after a prolonged civil war that began in 1642, the execution of the King in 1649, massacres and near-genocidal ethnic cleansing in Ireland during its conquest by Cromwell's army in the early 1650s. Surprisingly, no one got his head chopped off this time, not even General Lambert. One could even say it was an English tradition: during the reign of Henry VIII and his three children (including "Bloody Mary" and Queen Elizabeth I), six male and four female members of the royal house were executed or murdered; and in the previous generation of the House of York, almost every male relative of Richard III was killed (Doran 2009). Nor was the Restoration the end of medieval butchery and the beginning of modern civility. By the late 1680s, there were bloody crack-downs and revolts; there were plenty of atrocities in the Scottish rebellion of 1745, and so on.

No, what we are seeking is a dynamic that made the intense period of conflict at the end of the Commonwealth so casualty-free. It was not for lack of threat and intention. But what happened when the armies actually met, or the troops were sent to defend or break down the gates of Parliament or one palace or city or another, was that almost every time one side backed down.

Richard Cromwell calls his guards, but they let him be taken prisoner anyway. When Lambert dissolves Parliament, its guards start deserting, and the rest abandon their posts at night as Lambert's troops march in. When Monck's troops are approaching, General Fleetwood sends the keys back to Parliament. Monck follows Parliament's orders to break down the gates of the City, but then decides he won't take any more orders. Parliament suddenly finds their own guards are letting in the excluded members who are going to out-vote them. These side-switches are the essence of a coup, as one bold move leads to a growing mood to abandon the perceptibly sinking ship, ending in something between a panic, indifference, and enthusiastic support for the victors.

Similarly, when troops actually take the field to fight. Most of the rebellions are half-hearted, most of their supporters do not show up, not judging the time ripe for rebellion; and this affects the ones who do show up, finding they themselves are not so ready to fight. First, the Royalist uprising fizzles; the Presbyterian army fights one battle but is beaten by a smaller,

BOX 6.1 TIMELINE OF THE ENGLISH REVOLUTION

Richard Cromwell's Protectorate

Month 1: two weeks of honeymoon of support, declining by six weeks.

Months 2–3: four weeks of army agitation; Richard makes concessions.

Two months calm.

First Coup

Month 6, dissent in Parliament, Richard wins moderate majority.

Months 6–7, army factions meet, split between abolishing Protectorate and keeping it as puppet.

Month 8, paranoid rumors in army, about Richard's dictatorship, or Royalist Restoration—all hysteria, since neither is realistic at the time.

10-day crisis: multi-faction mobilization. Richard's guards desert him, coup succeeds, Parliament is dissolved. But rival factions remain mobilized, Parliament is recalled, Protectorate abolished.

Three months calm.

Revolts by Royalists and Presbyterians

Month 12: two simultaneous revolts; put down in three weeks.

Four weeks victory mood.

Second Coup

Months 13–14: three weeks of quarrel between Parliament and victorious general.

Three days of showdown of opposing demands, ending in coup.

London population apathetic, refuses to support Parliament.

Six weeks acquiescence.

Army Revolt vs. Coup

Month 16: Monck's revolt in Scotland.

Four-week period: more army garrisons revolt in support; political opposition and riot in London; Lambert's army deserts to opposition or disintegrates.

Third Coup

Month 17: popular mockery of Rump Parliament in London.

Months 18–19: Monck's army arrives in London.

Three weeks of struggle between Parliament and City; Monck wavers, switches sides.

Another three weeks: popular surge for restoring monarchy; Monck begins negotiations with King.

Last Army Revolt

Month 20: two weeks of army revolt against Restoration, collapses.

Followed by one month-plus joyous celebration for the return of the King.

more resolute force. When Monck opposes Lambert's coup, garrisons quickly go over to the revolt, and besiegers sent to recapture them go over to the rebels. When pickets of the opposing armies meet, they fire their pistols into the ground and fraternize. Monck's army advances without a blow while Lambert's melts away. Finally, the army revolt against Royalist Restoration draws few activists, and when confronted in battle, even those refuse to fight.

Emotional Domination Rules the Day

What happens in every instance is emotional domination. Whoever is in the focus of attention with emotional support of those around, becomes pumped up with emotional energy—confidence, resoluteness, ability to act. When the focus becomes uncertain and emotions do not build around a dominating organization and leader, those present start to waver and to avoid being there at all. We see the details of this as General Monck marches into London. Up to now all the emotional energy is on his side; everyone has come over to him on his advance from Scotland. Accordingly, his purpose is resolute: to restore the Parliament that had been overthrown. But other groups have been mobilizing in the vacuum of power; they want not this Parliament but a more representative one. Monck, single-minded, refuses their petitions. But the crowd starts to sway him, by their cold reception, by the demands shouted at him. The London crowd for the past month has been jeering Parliament, singing parodies about the Rump, feeling the collective effervescence of crowd rituals carried off with impunity. They have been too pumped up with their own emotional success to be dominated by Monck's loyalties; and indeed Monck does not threaten them. Monck reports loyally to Parliament and reluctantly agrees to discipline the rebellious City; but after a few token gestures, he no longer feels like swimming against the tide, and puts himself at the head of it.

In the whole array of characters, the only one who seems entirely resolute is General Lambert; but after an early flush of success, his ability to raise followers becomes more and more feeble.

This is not a matter of personalities imposing their will on the situation. The situation pumps up the will of some persons while deflating that of others. After all, what we mean by "willpower" is high emotional energy sustained over time; this means imposing one's will against the resistance of other wills. Sometimes this is a tough fight (whether political or violent), sometimes a stalemate; it is only when an emotional tipping point occurs that one side wins decisively. That requires that the other side loses emotional energy. General Monck's resoluteness, then his period of wavering when he arrives in London, and his switch to the other side, are a real-life experiment on the conditions that determine the rise and fall of willpower. The fate of Lambert, or Fleetwood, or Richard, are also natural experiments. If we look at Oliver Cromwell's life, we would find the same thing. Emotional domination by one side requires being emotionally dominated on the other. One's side's willpower is the other side's lack of willpower.

Time-Dynamics of Emotion Switches

For the end of the English Revolution, we have the following series of events in Box 6.1.

First, notice the periods of calm: after each big shift in power, there are periods where the mood is stable, either supporting or acquiescing: 6 weeks, 2 months, 3 months, 4 weeks, 6 weeks, 4 weeks, 1-plus months. At minimum, these stable periods are 4–6 weeks long; sometimes stretching out to 3 months.

Second, periods when opposing sides are locked in intense conflict:

- ten-day crisis (first coup, preceded by two months mobilization and agitation);
- three weeks (military revolts mobilized, but defeated during a few days);
- three days showdown and second coup (preceded by three weeks quarreling);
- four weeks (surge to join Monck's revolt, preceded by six weeks preparation);
- three weeks struggle (Parliament vs. City, ending in third coup);
- three weeks (period of surge for restoring monarchy).

Crisis points where power decisively shifts revolve around a core period in a mood of showdown, when both sides (or indeed a series of sides) are all making peremptory demands. These take anywhere from 2–3 days out to 10 days. Moreover these crisis points do not usually end with a stable solution; the institutional center of power has been disrupted, and the first victors often are quickly outflanked by yet another faction mobilizing in the same crisis: Fleetwood's coup against Richard but overtaken by pro-Parliamentary forces; Lambert's loyal defense of Parliament against revolts, ending in Lambert's coup; Monck's rescue of Parliament ending in a coup, then sliding into the popular upsurge for restoring monarchy.

And crisis points do not come out of nowhere, but are preceded by a period between three weeks and two months when multiple contending factions mobilize on their own bases.

Altogether, this gives us three kinds of public moods:

1. The periods of building mobilization, when factions meet at their own base where they can build up collective emotions in their assemblies, hence the solidarity and emotional energy to confidently revolt.[2]
2. The crisis moments, full of energy but often without a resting place.
3. Finally, the calm or acquiescent periods, when power appears to be decisively located in one place again. Sometimes the mood is joyous and widespread; sometimes it is merely apathetic, such as when the populace of London gives in to the Lambert coup, even though it is not popular.

The latter case is easy enough to explain: sometimes you would like something else to happen, but are overwhelmed by things as they have turned out. But what produces the swings to popular and joyous celebration? It cannot be simply that the people are happy because they have finally gotten their long-sought wish. London had been a stronghold of Republican, Parliamentary sentiment; thus it is not too surprising that they were apathetic about Lambert's coup overthrowing Parliament. But after Parliament is restored in late December, why should they swing so quickly to recalling the King? And not just swing, but go into a veritable orgy of celebration after Monck defies Parliament—in mid-February, mind you, barely two months since the London riots and revolts favoring Parliament in December.

There are of course reasons why people would decide that recalling the King was better than going on with endless struggles in the Parliamentary Commonwealth. The question is, why did they start coming up with those reasons, abruptly in the winter months of 1660? Abruptly is only a figurative word here; but it conveys the point that *strongly held political beliefs can make a complete reversal in about two months*. Not overnight, obviously; people may give in to a sudden coup, but they do not become immediately enthusiastic about it. General Monck changed his beliefs more quickly than that, over a period of less than three weeks when he rethought his loyalty to Parliament, and a few more weeks in becoming pro-monarchy. A few weeks—with a number of small crises and quandaries along the way—are plenty of time for people to make a 180-degree turn in political ideologies.

Most people; not everybody. John Milton never swerved in his support of the Republic. But he was a studious intellectual, one of the ideologues of the English Revolution from beginning to end. There were royalists, too, living isolated in their country homes, who never gave up their belief in monarchy, although they kept quiet about it for over 10 years. As a sociologist, I make this comparison, not to extol the steadfast as heroes and the side-switchers as villains. Realistically, the side-switchers are usually better at bringing peace than the unmovables.

Notes

1. Trotsky (1932) stated the theory of dual sovereignty to explain what happened in the 1917 Russian Revolution, when the revolutionaries established their own independent base, the Soviet or Council, with its own building, acting as people's assembly in parallel to the official Russian legislature.
2. When more than two clearly defined mobilizations happen at once, the atmosphere turns chaotic, with paranoia and uncertainty of aims. We see this again in the French Revolution, 1789–1794, and in the Red Guards in China, 1966–1969 (discussed in the Conclusion).

References

CMH = Cambridge Modern History. 1907. Vol. 4, Chapters XV and XIX. Cambridge: Cambridge University Press.

Doran, Susan. 2009. *The Tudor Chronicles, 1485–1603*. New York: Metro Books.

Trotsky, Leon. 1932. *The History of the Russian Revolution*. New York: Simon & Schuster.

Chapter 7

When History Holds Its Breath

The Take-Off of the French Revolution

Introduction

Are there moments when people collectively do not know what to do?; moments when quite literally the assembled group has to make up their mind, and thereby decide which way history is going to go? Ermakoff (2015) locates such a moment on the night of August 4, 1789, when reformers who had protested against royal power for several months found themselves at a standstill, unable to decide what reforms they wanted. After much hesitation, they suddenly reach a momentous decision: to abolish the aristocracy, turning the reform into a revolution. And it is the nobles themselves who lead the movement to abolish their own privileges. This all happens in a emotional cascade of solidarity and altruism.

This looks like Durkheimian solidarity at its highest, and indeed Durkheim ([1912] 1961: 240–241) pointed to just these events of the French Revolution to show that his theory of religious ritual applies also to secular political action. But Ermakoff challenges the application of interaction ritual theory to this moment. By closely examining the debate of that evening in Versailles, he points out that collective effervescence does not precede, but follows a mood of collective indecisiveness; hence the outburst of mutual enthusiasm and shared altruism is consequence rather than cause, *explanandum* rather than *explanans*. The empirical pattern of a moment of contingency, its phenomenology, is that indeterminacy is palpably experienced by a group that feels routine courses of action—institutions—no longer guide or impel them, and that choices among multiple future pathways are open. Ermakoff argues that free and unmotivated choice of institutions can occur—not everywhere, to be sure, but on occasions that have a specific "structure of contingency." Hence this new theory "calls into question the significance of emotions in collective action settings" (Ermakoff 2015: 69).

This is a useful challenge. To begin with, let us bear in mind that the theory is Interaction Ritual *Chains* (Collins 2004), a chained sequence in time of interaction rituals (IRs), that affects people's motivation for action by attracting them in some directions and away from others. *Ingredients* for an IR are assembly of persons in close immediate communication; mutual

DOI: 10.4324/9781003245629-10

awareness of a shared focus of attention; and a shared emotion. The *intensification* process takes place by rhythmic entrainment of voices, bodily gestures, (and adrenaline levels), feeding back into strengthening mutual awareness and common emotion, building to the state of excitement Durkheim called collective effervescence. *Outcomes* are solidarity of the group, feelings of strength and energy, dedication to collective symbols (which set and guide goals), and standards of morality and righteous punishment.

Ermakoff's analysis of the meeting of the National Assembly on August 4, 1789, indicates a prolonged gap in time between the initial conditions, and the turning point toward the build-up of collective effervescence, and the eventual outcomes of revolutionary consciousness and its project to implement a new social order. All the initial conditions are present, but they are not causally efficacious. Other processes—which Ermakoff's analysis details—are necessary before the intensification process takes off and leads to the historic outcome.

Let us see. Everything in the IR model is variable. The IR may succeed or fail, may be stronger or weaker in intensity. Failed IRs are caused by the failure of ingredients: the group may be prevented from assembling, or members drift away; attention may be scattered or divided; emotions may be weak or diverse. Any of these failures tends to feed back into further weakening of the other ingredients. Instead of an intensification process, there is a process experienced as lassitude or boredom, like a political speech that falls flat or a party where the guests soon leave.

I will return shortly to whether this is what happened at any point during August 4. Now let us consider conflict situations as a particular kind of IR. In a conflict where antagonists are assembled, there is a strong mutual focus of attention on the object of conflict itself; and this tends to produce a shared emotion (in addition to whatever emotions individuals bring to the scene), including anger and fear. Collins (2008) provides evidence that as the conflict moves toward threatened violence, the predominant emotion is confrontational tension and fear—not just fear of injury but the tension of being locked into a mutual focus of attention but at cross-purposes, opposing trajectories of action, each attempting to impose one's will upon the other. This emotion is endogenous to the conflict situation.

Violent conflicts could be regarded as contingent, as there are three general types of outcomes possible: side A could win, side B could win, or the conflict could end in a stalemate. Empirically, at least on the level of small groups and crowds, threatened violence most often does not come off; the mutual tension often fades (especially through boredom when nothing disturbs the equilibrium between the opponents), and the conflictual assembly drifts away or goes back to routine. Nassauer (2019) shows such micro-turning points of protest demonstrations toward or away from violence. In this sense, most conflicts have a moment of contingency. But micro-research, especially using videos and other close evidence, shows what micro-moves lead to one or another of the three outcomes. The most important factor is emotional domination, where one side seizes the initiative, setting the rhythm while the other side turns passive, at best responding to the rhythm set by the other. Emotional domination does not necessarily arise through individuals deliberately manipulating the emotions of their adversary. Micro-interactional analysis as well as phenomenological accounts by participants (Klinger 2004) show that emotional domination often occurs without conscious planning. It is a matter of which side comes to set the collective mood; and this is predictable from a combination of immediate and prior interactional conditions.

Timing is important here. Being surprised by the other's moves is one of the things that produces emotional domination, i.e., the surprised side tends to lose initiative and the surprise-making side sets the rhythm of violent and/or expressive action that prevails.[1]

Emotional Standstill on the Night of August 4, 1789—and Its Antecedents

Let us turn now to the night of August 4. It is a conflict situation; the assembly is split among proponents of incompatible courses of action. As one side (arguing for compensation for nobles' property) attempts to seize the initiative, the majority of the assembly express uneasiness. This is not just lack of enthusiasm, and lack of unity; it is described as confusion, surprise, uncertainty. This widespread mood is already, in IR theory of conflict, an indicator that one side is emotionally weak; they are setting themselves up to be emotionally dominated. Certainly they are not carrying out a counter-mobilization of emotional energy among their faction that would enable them to stalemate or overawe the radicals.

Instead of continuing conflict, there comes a tipping point, a cascade of emotional flow toward aligning the conservative faction with the radical project. Ermakoff's micro-analysis of how this comes about is revealing. The Duc de Châtelet breaks through the moment of indecision among his conservative fellows, making an impassioned speech of exemplary altruism: the nobles should voluntarily give up their hereditary rights and become ordinary citizens. Is this course of action unpredictable? No; not only does it depend on the immediately prior moves in which it is situated and to which it responds, as Ermakoff shows; it also follows a causal principle of IR theory. The chief motivational principle is: individuals seek situations which raise their emotional energy (EE), and avoid situations which lower their EE. They are attracted to successful IRs, and repelled by failed IRs.

IRs are chained together across time; in each new situation, participants come in with emotions and memories from previous IR events; the strongest emotional events (both negatively and positively) are strongest in memory.

Châtelet had been Colonel of the Gardes Françaises, and thus the commander at previous events where authority was challenged by revolutionary crowds. His own troops had refused to fire on the National Assembly in June, and had changed sides at the Bastille in July. After these upsets, Châtelet resigned his commission, avoiding an emotionally debilitating situation. A few weeks later, on August 4, he switches to join the group with the high-EE-producing successful interaction rituals.

How do we know the revolutionaries' rituals were emotionally dominant? There had been three showdowns during the previous six weeks, all of which ended with the conservative forces backing down or defeated. (The following details draw on Montague 1904; Carlyle [1837] 2002; Doyle 2002.)

1. June 20–23

Saturday, June 20: royal officials attempt to deflate the National Assembly by denying them their meeting hall in the Versailles Palace; the approach is non-confrontational, merely declaring that the hall must be prepared by workmen for an appearance by the King on Monday. Members of the elite Gardes Françaises regiment shut the doors on the delegates. The delegates mill around on the road outside, until they find a meeting place at the Tennis Court, complete with seats for enthusiastic spectators. They generate solidarity and enthusiasm in swearing oaths of future resolve, joined by the crowd; and resolve to meet Monday before the King's *séance*. In response, the King's *séance* is postponed to Tuesday. On Monday, keeping up their momentum, the National Assembly/Third Estate meets in a church, where they are joined by liberal clergy, who make a ritual procession of the occasion, and are greeted with enthusiasm. Tuesday, the royal *séance* takes place; the King enters through a crowd described as "grim and silent," and his speech, making some concessions but declaring the Estates will vote separately, is silently received. The National Assembly delegates refuse to leave when the King and his loyalists depart; they are described as standing silent and uncertain what to do, until Count Mirabeau speaks loudly from the lectern, and confronts the royal minister who orders them to leave. Mirabeau denies his authority over them. The minister leaves, and orders troops to disperse them by force. But the Gardes Françaises refuse to act. Later this day the remaining clergy and 48 of the Nobles go over to the National Assembly—joining the direction of the tipping point.

2. June 24–26

The royal court shifts to direct threat, calling 30,000 troops to Versailles, parading them in front of the assembly hall and aiming cannon at it. But this is done half-furtively, "without drum-music, without audible word of command" (Carlyle 2002: 142), omitting the usual ostentatious military ritual. The army's sympathy shifts and it becomes regarded as unreliable. The Gardes Françaises are confined to barracks, as unwilling to fire when ordered. They make a secret agreement (another oath-taking ritual of solidarity) not to act against the National Assembly. On June 26, they are released from barracks, and embraced by a welcoming crowd. Simultaneously 11 ringleaders are put in prison; but the crowd breaks in and releases them at night. New forces are called from the provinces, but crowds "laid hold of their bridles," weapons were lowered, soldiers sat immobile, until brought liquor to drink toasts to King and Nation. (Drinking here operates as ritual fraternization, establishing new lines of solidarity.) Royalists lose their nerve and withdraw troops.

3. *July 12–22*

Sunday, July 12: Official street placards in Paris tell the people to stay indoors and not to gather in crowds; large numbers of troops and artillery are in the city, including foreign Swiss Guards. Presumably the regime is prepared to head off trouble when news of the dismissal of Necker (the reforming prime minister) gets around. A procession in favor of the reform ministry is attacked by German mercenary troops, who follow up by clearing out the fleeing crowd from the Tuileries Gardens. At the rumor that an off-duty member has been killed in the demonstration, the Gardes Françaises leave their barracks and attack the German mercenaries. Royal soldiers melt away. Crowds overrun the Hôtel-de-Ville; the Town Councilors flee, displaced by the Paris Electors who create a Municipal Government, and call on all districts of the city to create a Paris Militia.

Monday, July 13: The populace is called into widespread participation by several shared activities: forming militia groups, seeking arms, forging pikes; women sewing colored cockades as symbols of membership. The arming is not very militarily effective, but it is a collective ritual with high enthusiasm as well as sense of inescapable compulsion. The collective atmosphere is enhanced by a deliberate program of symbolically significant noise: tocsin bells (sounded in emergencies) are ordered to be rung continuously from all steeples; city criers with bells call all men to enroll in militias; new soldiers parade with drums beating; once gunpowder is procured, the city uses it not for fighting but to sound alarm-cannon. At night, militia patrol with torches, while all windows are illuminated by city orders. (Illumination was a chief tactic in the eighteenth-century repertoire of mass politics, designed to demonstrate unanimity: Tilly 2008.)

Attacks on prominent buildings begin a day before the attack on the Bastille, the last and most difficult royal stronghold. Crowds break into buildings looking for arms; finding or not finding arms, as well as finding stores of food, leads to looting and arson—more activities that give crowds something exciting and successful-feeling to do collectively. Crowds also find purposeful activity in taking over the city-wall barriers to stop the rich from departing. They build street barricades and prepare for street combat, which never comes.

In this omnipresent mood, soldiers desert individually to join the militia; they are heartily welcomed at enrollment sites. The Gardes Françaises regiment defects en masse, its organization still intact, giving the revolution some military proficiency. The military commander at the Champs de Mars finds his troops melting away; a Council of Officers is indecisive. This is one-sided indecisiveness, draining emotional energy from the official forces, at the same time that the populace is emotionally galvanized by their participatory rituals.

Tuesday, July 14: In the morning, following rumors that weapons are stored in the Hôtel des Invalides (army center), crowds descend on the building. The commander wants to parlay rather than fight; crowds scale walls, with no shots fired by troops, and open the gates; large numbers of muskets are seized. The army has now split; the Gardes Françaises are the only intact unit in Paris.

The commander of the Bastille garrison is indecisive but unwilling to surrender. The fortress is very strong, with a series of moats, courts, and drawbridges. Once the siege begins in the afternoon, heroic action by individuals only manages to take the outermost court. Only one defender is killed in action, while the crowd has many more casualties. The casualty ratio does not determine emotional domination; after a four-hour siege, individual soldiers start to offer to surrender; it becomes a cascade, surrenders are accepted, the inner drawbridges and gates are opened. The first wave of attackers embrace the surrendering soldiers—the typical ritual of side-switching; later waves of the crowd lynch prominent individuals in the excitement of victory.

Wednesday, July 15: The King appears at the National Assembly, humbling himself without ceremonial escort, and is welcomed when he speaks of reconciliation and goodwill. A royal delegation is joyfully received in Paris at the Hôtel-de-Ville, the new center of attention.

Thursday–Friday, July 16–17: Hard-line conservative officials at Versailles flee for the border. But on Friday, the King splits the conservative camp by visiting Paris in a conciliatory gesture, where he is received into the joyous celebrations—but on the crowd's terms.

Wednesday, July 22: Several former officials are discovered hiding; taken to the Hôtel-de-Ville for trial, but lynched by an impatient crowd, their heads paraded on pikes. Violent crowd rituals have now joined the repertoire of the victorious crowd.

From EE-Loss to EE-Gain: Switching Sides

Through this series of emotional events—large-scale IRs—royalists and conservatives find themselves repeatedly losing a confrontation, with emotional dominance going to the revolutionaries. It is not surprising that someone like Châtelet, who has been in the front line of several of these crises, would feel an emotional pull away from the conservative side, and toward the victorious side. And this is a general pattern in tipping point revolutions: the neutralization and fraternization of military forces with the insurgents, and the shift of second-level military officers to the other side. (This is the same pattern that Ketchley (2014) describes at Tahrir Square in January 2011.) The key actors at tipping points avoid the EE-losing side and join the EE-gaining side; whereupon they are temporarily greeted as heroes. Thus, after Châtelet's speech, one nobleman after another stands up and declares his renunciation of hereditary rank, in a swelling wave of exclamations, applause, and rapturous tears. It is a moment of exalted celebration of shared humanity, emotionally and bodily palpable to everyone present.

To summarize the theoretical conclusion: The trajectory and outcome of conflicts are strongly determined by whether emotional domination is established. Whether force is successfully used depends on whether the organization of force-users holds together; if that organization is emotionally dominated, it loses. Virtually all conflictual confrontations have a moment of apparent contingency, since the outcome can go either way, or remained stalemated. But causality is not exhausted here; micro-mechanisms exist that establish emotional domination. In the case of political conflicts where the issue is which coalition will prevail, the predictable pattern is that prominent individuals will lead the tipping point by the emotional mechanism of losing their attraction for EE-losing situations and shifting to join an EE-gaining situation. Châtelet's experiences in June–July 1789 are on a par with General Monck's experiences in London in February–March 1660.

How does this theoretical argument square with Ermakoff's analysis of contingency as an empirically experienced moment of uncertainty and indecisiveness? I agree empirically, while adding a chain of micro-mechanisms that determine what will happen. In that sense my argument is parallel to Ermakoff's, except that, in IR theory, emotion is central; in Ermakoff's theory, the cognitive processes in a series of communicative moves are central. Cognitions and emotions happen simultaneously in the flow of social interaction. All cognitions arise in particular situations, and which cognitions arise happens because they are neurologically marked by a degree of emotion that makes them come to persons' minds and tongues more readily than other cognitions.

Our aim should be a theory of cognition and emotion working together. It is these combined processes at moments of confrontation and uncertainty, and their trajectory as people regroup around ideas-as-social-slogans, that drive moments of seemingly inexplicable contingency in structural change. To call them "contingent" is just a challenge for us to get better at integrating micro- and macro-level social processes.

Note

1. Surprise is one of six basic emotions that are recognized worldwide from standard facial expressions (Ekman and Friesen 1978). The surprise face shows extreme passivity and disconnect from purposeful behavior; being surprised disrupts one's own line of action.

References

Carlyle, Thomas. [1837] 2002. *The French Revolution: A History*. New York: Modern Library.

Collins, Randall. 2004. *Interaction Ritual Chains*. Princeton, NJ: Princeton University Press.

Collins, Randall. 2008. *Violence: A Micro-Sociological Theory*. Princeton, NJ: Princeton University Press.

Doyle, William. 2002. *The Oxford History of the French Revolution*. Oxford: Oxford University Press.

Durkheim, Emile. [1912] 1961. *The Elementary Forms of Religious Life*. New York: Free Press.

Ekman, Paul, and Wallace V. Friesen. 1978. *The Facial Action Coding System*. Palo Alto, CA: Consulting Psychologists Press.

Ermakoff, Ivan. 2015. "The Structure of Contingency." *American Journal of Sociology* 121: 64–125.

Ketchley, Neil F. 2014. "The Army and the People Are One Hand! Fraternisation and the 25th January Egyptian Revolution." *Comparative Studies in Society and History* 56: 155–186.

Klinger, David. 2004. *Into the Kill Zone*. San Francisco: Jossey-Bass.

Montague, F.C. 1904. Chapters V and VI in *The Cambridge Modern History*, Vol. VIII: *The French Revolution*. Cambridge: Cambridge University Press.

Nassauer, Anne. 2019. *Situational Breakdowns: Understanding Protest Violence and Other Surprising Outcomes*. Oxford: Oxford University Press.

Tilly, Charles. 2008. *Contentious Performances*. Cambridge: Cambridge University Press.

Chapter 8

Assault on the Capitol: 2021, 1917, 1792

Introduction

The iconic image of January 6 is a protestor sitting with his feet up on Nancy Pelosi's desk, and another in the Senate Chair. These are reminiscent of Sergei Eisenstein's 1928 film, *October*, a documentary of the Russian Revolution of November 1917. Attacking the seat of government in St. Petersburg, the Winter Palace, revolutionary soldiers break into the Czarina's bedroom: amused by uncovering the jeweled top of her chamber pot, then ripping through her feather-bedding with their bayonets. The same in the French Revolution in its many repetitions between 1789 and 1792, and its replay in 1848, where the crowd took turns sitting on the vacant throne after the guards had collapsed and the royal family had fled (Tocqueville [1850] 1970).

There are differences, of course. The 1917 and 1792 revolutions were successful in overthrowing the government. The 2021 Capitol assault probably had few such ambitions in the minds of most protestors; and in any case, they occupied the outer steps of the Capitol for five hours and penetrated the corridors and chambers inside for three-and-a-half, with momentum on their side for less than an hour.

The similarities are more in short-term processes: The building guards putting up resistance at first, then losing cohesion, retreating, fading away; some fraternizing with the assaulting crowd, their sympathies wavering. They had weapons but most failed to use them.

Higher up the chain of command, widespread hesitation, confusion, conversations and messages all over the place without immediate results. Reinforcements are called for; reinforcements are promised; reinforcements are coming but they don't arrive. Recriminations in the aftermath of January 6 have concentrated on this official hesitation and lack of cooperation, and on weakness and collusion among the police.

In fact, it is a generic problem. Revolutions and their contemporary analogues all start in an atmosphere of polarization, masses mobilizing themselves, authorities trying to keep them calm and sustain everyday routine. Crowd-control forces, whether soldiers or police, are caught in the middle. At the onset of surging crowds, there is always some place where

DOI: 10.4324/9781003245629-11

the guards are locally outnumbered, pressed not just physically but by the noise and emotional force of the crowd. They usually know that using their superior firepower can provoke the crowds even further. Sometimes they try it; sometimes they try a soft defense; in either case, they have a morale problem. If there is a tipping point where they retreat, the crowd surges to its target, and is temporarily in control.

From this point of view, the lesson of January 6 is how protective forces regain control relatively quickly. Comparing the Winter Palace on the night of October 26, 1917,[1] or the Tuileries Palace on August 10, 1792, tells us what makes for tipping points that wobble for a bit but then recover; or not. The normal exercise of authority is above all a smooth and expectable rhythm. (That doesn't mean everything goes well, but the hitches are what we are used to.) In revolutions, it gets worse and worse until psychological equilibrium is re-established only when one leadership team entirely replaces the other.

The wavering and indecisiveness of the guards and the incoherence of the chain of command higher up are connected. We see this particularly strongly in the Russian and French cases; but the same pattern exists, on a less extreme scale, in the contemporary American crisis. In the weeks and hours leading up to the afternoon of January 6, there are strong splits inside Congress, as well as among the branches of government, not to mention the line-up of states across the federation, and the anomalous local position of the authorities of the District of Columbia. Revolutions and revolts usually begin with prolonged splits at the top, moods which are transmitted to their own security forces. Add to the mix popular crowds which are more than a puppet of elite factions. The energy, enthusiasm, and hostility of crowds have a power of their own (in fact, earlier theories of revolution usually focused entirely on this popular force from below). But even granting great causal significance to elite splits, how strong the popular hurricane blows at some point becomes the determining factor of events.

At the tipping point crisis, the two centers of emotional contagion—the two places the political authority machine can wobble, the crowds-and-cops scene, and the elites quarreling and sending for reinforcements—are both wobbling at the same time. The outcome depends on which gyroscope rights itself first—if at all.

From this point of view, we will look at the assaults on the Winter Palace in 1917, and the Tuileries in 1792. These were both revolutions from the Left; the Capitol assault of 2021 was from the Right. But the dynamics of crowd confrontation with a center of authority are much the same, regardless of Left or Right ideologies.

Assault on the Winter Palace, 1917

The insurgents launched their attempt to take over the capital city on October 25. The Bolshevik revolutionists had infiltrated and gained the support of most armed forces around St. Petersburg, units of sailors from ships stationed nearby and soldiers from fortresses and arsenals. Their officers had been arrested or reluctantly came over to the revolution, watched by political committees of their own troops. The Bolsheviks also had a strong base among factory workers and in the railroads and telegraphs, giving them control of communications. Armed workers were now moving throughout the city carrying rifles and revolutionary flags. Acting together with the troops on the first day of the insurrection, they took over most of the major buildings and installations in the city: the railroad stations, bridges across the river, the electric plant, banks, government offices—all except the Winter Palace (Reed 1919; Trotsky 1932).

This was the former palace of the Czars, now occupied by a coalition government of liberal reformers and former officials, since the Czar had abdicated in February. Here was concentrated what military forces the government still had in the capital city. Here they waited and sent out messages for reinforcements to put down the revolutionaries: recalling troops from the Front against the Germans: Cossack cavalry, long dreaded as the enforcers of the absolute monarchy; elite military units recruited from the respectable middle class; students from the military schools. The Winter Palace was the military stronghold and political command center; the center of political legitimacy, too, since it housed the Assembly that made the laws and the Ministry that made official decisions. As long as the Winter Palace held out, the success of the revolution hung in the balance.

On October 26, the Bolsheviks assembled their forces in a ring around the Winter Palace and began to close in. Both sides proceeded cautiously.

> The court of the palace opening on the square is piled up with logs of firewood like the court of Smolny (the building across town where the Bolsheviks have their meetings). Rifles are stacked up in several different places. The small guard of the palace clings close to the building . . . Inside the palace they found a lack of provisions. Some of the military cadets did sentry duty; the rest lay around inactive, uncertain and hungry. In the square before the palace, and on the river quay on the other side, little groups of apparently peaceful passers-by began to appear, and they would snatch the rifles from the sentries, threatening them with revolvers . . .
>
> (Trotsky 1932: 377–378)

Agitators also began to appear among the cadets, internal trouble-makers; the cadets quarrel about who they should take orders from, the civilian ministers or their own school directors. They opt for the latter—severing the chain of command. They take their posts but are forbidden to fire first.

Outside on the river bank, thousands of soldiers and sailors are being disembarked who have gone over to the insurgency. Their remaining officers "are being taken along to fight for a cause which they hate." The Bolshevik commissar announces: "We do not count upon your sympathy, but we demand that you be at your posts . . . We will spare you any unnecessary unpleasantness." The most militant of the troops volunteer for action on their own. "The most resolute in the detachment choose themselves out automatically. These sailors in black blouses with rifles and cartridge belts will go all the way" (Trotsky 1932: 390) The take-over of the city had mostly been by military units acting in regular order, encountering virtually no resistance, the token forces of the government letting themselves be disarmed. A real fight now looms ahead. The militants of armed workers meld with militants of the troops in a crowd-like surge.

> Hiding behind their piles of firewood, the cadets followed tensely the cordon forming on Palace Square, meeting every movement of the enemy with rifle and machine gun fire. They answered in kind. Towards night the firing became hotter. The first casualties occurred. The victims, however, were only a few individuals. On the square, on the quays, the besiegers hid behind projections, concealed themselves in hollows, cling along walls. Among the reserves the soldiers and Red Guards warmed themselves around campfires which they had kindled at nightfall, abusing the leaders for going so slow.
>
> In the palace the cadets were taking up positions in the corridors, on the stairway, at the entrances, and in the court. The outside sentries clung along the fence and walls. The building would hold thousands, now it held hundreds. The vast quarters behind the sphere of defense seemed dead. Most of the servants were scattered, or in hiding. Many of the officers took refuge in the buffet . . . The garrison of the palace was greatly reduced in number. If at the moment (of greatest reinforcement) it rose to a thousand and a half, or perhaps two thousand, it was now reduced to a thousand, perhaps considerably less . . . With angry and frowning faces the Cossacks gathered up their saddle bags. No further arguments could move them . . . The Cossacks were in touch with the besiegers, and they got free passes through an exit till then unknown to the defenders. Only their machine guns they agreed to leave for the defense of a hopeless cause.
>
> By this same entrance, too, coming from the direction of the street, Bolsheviks before this had gotten into the palace for the purpose of demoralizing the enemy. Oftener and oftener mysterious figures began to appear in the corridors beside the cadets. It was useless to resist; the insurrectionists have captured the city and the railway stations; there are no reinforcements . . . What are we to do next? asked the cadets. The government refused to issue any direct commands. The ministers themselves would stand by their old decision; the rest could do as they pleased. That meant free egress from the palace for

> those who wanted it. The ministers passively awaited their fate. One subsequently related: "We wandered through the gigantic mousetrap, meeting occasionally, either all together or in small groups, for brief conversations . . . Around us vacancy, within us vacancy, and in this grew up the soulless courage of placid indifference."
>
> (Trotsky 1932: 394–396, 401)

Artillery from the ships fired sporadically, the gunners unenthusiastic, hoping for an easy victory. Of 35 shells fired in a couple of hours, only two hit the palace, injuring the plaster (Trotsky 1932: 400).

> The inner resolution of the workers and sailors is great, but it has not yet become bitter. Lest they call down it on their heads, the besieged, being the incomparably weaker side, dare not deal severely with those agents of the enemy who have penetrated the palace. There are no executions. Uninvited guests now begin to appear no longer one by one, but in groups. The palace is getting more and more like a sieve. When the cadets fall upon these intruders, the latter permit themselves to be disarmed . . . These men were not cowardly; it required a high courage to make one's way into that palace crowded with officers and cadets. In the labyrinth of an unknown building, among innumerable doors leading nobody knew where, and threatening nobody knew what, the daredevils had nothing to do but surrender. The number of captives grows. New groups break in. It is no longer quite clear who is surrendering to whom, who is disarming whom. The artillery continues to boom.
>
> (Trotsky 1932: 403)

The siege began in earnest about 6 p.m. With periodic excursions and lulls, it went on until 2 a.m. (about 8 hours). Lenin and the Bolsheviks at their headquarters are getting anxious, sending angry notes for all-out artillery fire. The commander decides to wait another quarter hour "sensing the possibility of a change in circumstances." Time is almost up when a courier arrives: The palace is taken!

> The palace did not surrender but was taken by storm—however, at a moment when the power of resistance of the besieged had already completely evaporated. Hundreds of enemies broke into the corridor—not by the secret entrance this time but through the defended door—and were taken by the demoralized defenders for a deputation (of supporters). A considerable group of cadets got away in the confusion. The rest—at least a number of them—still continued to stand guard. But the barrier of bayonets and rifle fire between the attackers and the defenders was finally broken down.

They are now confronting each other face-to-face—psychologically the most difficult situation for effective use of weapons.

> Part of the palace is already filled with the enemy. The cadets make an attempt to come at them from the rear. In the corridors phantasmagoric meetings and clashes take place. All are armed to the teeth. Lifted hands hold revolvers. Hand grenades hang from belts. But nobody shoots and nobody throws a grenade. For they and their enemy are so mixed together that they cannot drag themselves apart. Never mind: the fate of the palace is already decided.
>
> Workers, sailors, soldiers are pushing up from outside in chains and groups, flinging the cadets from the barricades, bursting through the court, stumbling into the cadets on the staircase, crowding them back, toppling them over, driving them upstairs. Another wave comes on behind. The square pours into the court. The court pours into the palace, and floods up and down stairways and through corridors. On the befouled parapets, among mattresses and chunks of bread, people, rifles, hand grenades are wallowing.
>
> The conquerors find that Kerensky (head of government) is not there, and a momentary pang of disappointment interrupts their furious joy . . . Where is the government?

The government ministers have long since abandoned the great assembly hall overlooking the river now full of gunboats. They have retreated to an inner room, as far away as possible.

> That is the door—there where the cadets stand frozen in the last pose of resistance. The head sentry rushes to the ministers with a question: Are we commanded to resist to the end? No, no, the ministers do not command that. After all, the palace is taken. There is no need for bloodshed. The ministers desire to surrender with dignity, and sit at the table in imitation of a session of the government.
>
> (Trotsky 1932: 403–404)

The last guards are disarmed. The door crashes open. Backed by the crowd, the Bolshevik commissar takes the ministers' credentials and declares their arrest. The officers and cadets of the defense are allowed to go free. As the ministers are led away through square, there are shouts: "Death to them! Shoot them!" Some soldiers strike at the prisoners. The commissar and the Red Guards stick to the ritual of victory, escorting the overthrown authorities to prison, an act of taking their place.

Physically these scenes at the Winter Palace in 1917 look a lot like the Capitol in January 2021: Both buildings are labyrinths, huge complexes of assembly chambers, galleries, halls, stairwells, meeting rooms, offices. There are tunnels, secret passages, escape routes, hidden doors. There are main entrances, back entrances, side entrances. Especially when some people are evacuating and others intruding, there are plenty of mix-ups; sometimes crowded clashes, standoffs with barely room to swing about; sometimes guards or protestors, one side or another, find themselves outnumbered. Sometimes—as we see in photos—lone protestors striding through grand spaces with their flags or booty; sometimes arrestees sprawled on the floor under guard, sometimes a thin line of guards backed up against a door. Both attackers and defenders are swallowed up by the building, forces stretched thin and unable to be everywhere at once. Both sides are uncertain, confused, without chains of command on the spot; unclear what is behind a door, who has what weapons, how our forces are holding out or making inroads; how many are smashing through openings and preparing to rush inside. Members of Congress hunker down in the rows between the seats, and are led away by security forces to subterranean hallways, take refuge in a basement cafeteria like the Russian officers hiding in the buffet. Some attackers wander about in remote corridors; in 2021, getting into Congressional offices, taking selfies, rifling through desks. In 1917, Russian militants and defender cadets alike fill their pockets with expensive knickknacks from the sprawling palace. Some are fighting; many are not. We will come back to the points of violence.

To summarize the pattern, so confusing in detail and lived experience, let us invoke the tottering gyroscopes of organization in varying levels of breakdown: first, the point of view from below on the front lines, then the view of chains of authority from above. Start with 1917; then 2021.

Wavering among Government Forces

We have seen the Winter Palace guards, heavily armed but mostly tired, bored and discouraged. Sometimes they let their guns be taken away from them. Sometimes they fire across the courtyard, mostly missing (not unusual in the sociology of combat). Sometimes they are ordered not to fire first—but who can tell who starts it? Their sympathies are not at all with the revolution; they are elite military cadets, going into action for the first time. The mood and pressure of the situation determine whether they fire or not. They have moments of hope; the enemy is holding back, maybe they too are experiencing difficulties, maybe help is on its way.

The hardened Cossacks, an alien ethnic group amid the Russian population, used to administer whippings and massacres to uphold authority, are expected to be the bulwark of the defense. But now they hesitate. They will obey orders to support the Winter Palace; but—first they need assurances they will not be alone, there should also be infantry, artillery, armored cars. The government assures them these will be there. In fact, they are not; Cossacks get wind of it, or suspect it. They are preparing to move—telephone messages go between barracks and Palace—but they don't move. A few Cossack units reach the Palace; after assessing the situation, the atmosphere, the lack of chain of command, they negotiate with the besiegers a retreat through a secret exit.

And so it goes with reinforcements from the Front. The government wants to send unreliable units out from the capital, and bring back reliable units. But ministers can talk only to officers who are their sympathizers, or at least their yes-men. Chains of command are poor in the army as well; and the railroads are not under their control. Within the military units we know most about, mainly the naval forces who have mutinied to the Bolsheviks or have cowed their officers into going along with them, there remains hesitation about using force. Artillery assault is called for; but the gunners complain their guns are not ready; when they finally fire, it seems they don't want to hit anything, hoping the situation will resolve itself. They are holding open their options, waiting to see which side is going to lose.

Wavering among Government Politicians

The government is not set up to act with decisiveness, for it is a coalition of hold-overs from the czarist regime and a variety of parties of differing ideologies and militancy; of those who took part in the February Revolution and those who resisted it. This is particularly true in the military side of the administration; the government is now calling on its old enemies to defend it. Meetings in the Winter Palace agree on little except resisting a second revolution, but even here politicians are split between those who demand a vigorous crackdown and those who want a softer policy of conciliation. It all depends on how much of a show of force they can muster, but this boils down to putting up a frontstage of optimism that reinforcements are on their way. They waver between optimism and pessimism. Discussions and arguments take place over the telephone, making demands to military headquarters, to citizens militias, to Cossack regiments, to the military schools.

Moments of optimism come from the confusion of communications, and indeed the confusion of events themselves. To the extent there is any chain of command, the government ministers are talking with high officials whose own authority chains are out of order. Some talk a good show; they are willing to put down the insurrection, if only they can get some coordinated support. Others become increasingly exasperated; I agree with your orders, Minister, but where are the troops to carry them out? Sometimes the revolutionaries can't seem to get their act together either; with every lull and delay optimism of the defenders goes up a notch. It is not a bandwagon—yet. How long can the indecisiveness last?

Wavering among the Revolutionaries

Generically, their problems are similar, but quantitatively better. Their forces on the ground are a mixed bag; some ideological militants; some newly joined allies in the navy and army; old-line officers of dubious loyalty; many holding back to see what will happen. Politically, too, the left-wing assembly and the local soviets (councils) are coalitions, not just Bolsheviks but other factions and splits left over from 15 years of revolutionary politics. On present policy, the divisions are among those who want to press their advantage right now, and those who are cautious, worried, or hoping for a peaceful transfer of power—the usual split on tactics rather than ideology. Lenin, Trotsky, and their faction want to present the waverers with a *fait accompli*, and that means taking the Winter Palace before it is reinforced. Emotionally, they have a recent bandwagon in their favor, the successful take-over of the city the previous day.

But a bandwagon has to keep expanding to new adherents and new successes; if it stalls, the mood starts flowing away. The militants are mobilized; they must be put into action against the final target. But realistically, there are logistical and organizational problems to work out. Plans to use their military supporters to surround the Winter Palace, to bring combined arms into action—all these are too complicated for a newly improvised structure. And in any case, this is counting too much on organization from the top. Their biggest resource at the moment is the spontaneity of the self-propelling crowd. The Bolshevik network is capable of getting the most militant workers and sailors on the spot, if with enough lags and delays to give hopes to the defenders. At this point a crowd surge develops. Intersecting with the mood inside the Winter Palace, the tipping point tips.

Top-Down and Bottom-Up

Enthusiastic self-mobilizing crowds, and the strategies of political elites, play into each other. Politics in normal times is almost entirely the province of political elites. But when crowds repeatedly mobilize themselves with their own indigenous networks and organizations, they become social movements with momentum and tactics of their own. Such movements can change the career trajectories of politicians, on the whole more than vice versa. The world history of labor movements, or of racial/ethnic movements, gives ample evidence of this.

If we need recent examples of how energized crowds carry politicians along pathways with a vehemence they may not have anticipated, consider how Bernie Sanders' campaign in 2016 ballooned from token opposition to serious challenge to Hillary Clinton; Trump's discovery that his reality-TV methods generated such crowd enthusiasm that he kept feeding off of rallies throughout his four years in office; the Black Lives Matter demonstrations in spring and summer 2020, creating a political bandwagon whose stronghold became the Democrat-controlled House of Representatives. And which became the target for the counter-mobilization culminating in the January 6 assault. Trump's emotional addiction to rallies took him down the slope of political psychosis, the delusion that the size of his crowds meant he couldn't possibly have lost the popular vote—a delusion shared by the rallies themselves.

There is always a danger, as a sociologist, of being emotionally too close to an event to see what is going on, what the patterns are and the relative weight of the various forces. Our ideological labels, Left and Right, don't help. We have seen enough of St. Petersburg in 1917 to recognize the most general features of Washington in January 2021. But we have to abstract away from the particular names and issues, to get at the dynamics. If the Presidency is on their side, can the attackers at the Capitol be a revolution, or a counter-revolution, or a coup? Or is it again the Smolny Institute against the Winter Palace? Better to invoke the imagery of two spinning gyroscopes, tottering or staying upright. From this perspective, attacker and defender are subject to the same dynamics, differing only quantitatively. Look at who wavers when and how much:

Wavering among Official Forces at the Capitol, 2021

It needs to be appreciated that many different officials and organizations had a role in the defense of the Capitol, with no command center. Advance intelligence about possible attacks by militant groups and unorganized protestors came from the FBI, military intelligence agencies, and civilian organizations like the Anti-Defamation League. These differed widely on how seriously on-line rhetoric about violence should be taken. Advance estimates of the crowd size to be expected ranged from 2000 to 80,000.[2]

Forces that could be brought into action included: (1) the Metropolitan Police of the District of Columbia, reporting to the Mayor; (2) the Capitol Police, under a Police Chief, as well as a Sergeant-at-Arms for the House of Representatives, and another Sergeant-at-Arms for the Senate; these latter reporting to the Majority Leader and Speaker; (3) the Secret Service, armed plain-clothes officers protecting not only the President but all those in the chain of succession, notably the Vice President and Speaker of the House; (4) other federal officers, including FBI SWAT teams, Department of Homeland Security, and Bureau of Alcohol, Tobacco, Firearms and Explosives; (5) US military forces under the Secretary of Defense; the US Army specifically under the Secretary of the Army; (6) the National Guard forces of each state, which can be deployed under orders from each Governor, although coordinated with the Secretary of the Army; (7) the

National Guard of the District of Columbia, which not being a state, could only be called out by the President. Altogether these make up at least 15 quasi-autonomous officials and agencies (not counting the 50 state Governors and National Guards). The array gave plenty of room for communication and coordination problems, not to mention differences in policy and partisan splits—not least with President Trump urging on the protestors and resisting mobilizing Federal forces. Chains of command were sometimes upheld, sometimes breached.

To sample these disagreements: Washington, D.C. Mayor on December 31, 2020 (7 days before the Electoral College count) requested calling out the D.C. National Guard, but only to provide unarmed crowd management and traffic control; this was approved by the Acting Secretary of Defense on January 4, calling up 340 troops but no more than 115 at a time. There must have been splits in the Pentagon, since on January 3, some officials offered the National Guard; but Metropolitan Police Chief said later they had no intelligence that the Capitol would be invaded, and Capitol Police Chief said it would be unnecessary. The latter had 2000 uniformed cops, but assigned only normal staffing levels (ordinarily there are four 40-hours shifts per week, so the number available would be about 500, minus administrative personnel; at the peak of the emergency, reportedly 1200 were on site). Accustomed to dealing with tourists and peaceful protests, they counted on a soft, friendly style to keep the crowd in hand. The Capitol Police Chief also said he didn't like the impression it would give if armed troops were photographed around the Capitol; a sentiment echoed by some military officials.

Once the attack began, disagreements persisted for a while over how severe the breach was. Around 1 p.m., when hundreds of rioters pushed aside barriers and climbed to the higher terraces outside the Capitol, the House Representative chairing the Committee in charge of security called the Capitol Police Chief but couldn't get through; the House Sergeant-at-Arms, assured her that the doors are locked and no one can get in. Shortly after, Capitol Police Chief (who was not on site but at his headquarters) called the House and Senate Sergeants-at-Arms for emergency declarations from their respective chambers to call the National Guard; they replied they would "run it up the chain" of command. The Democrat-controlled House side got their approval about an hour later, after windows and doors were broken in and rioters entered the building. On the Republican-controlled Senate side, the Sergeant-at-Arms apparently never did notify the leadership. Rioters reached the Senate around 2.15, just after its doors were locked. At the same time, the House recessed briefly when Secret Service escorted the Speaker out; but resumed debate again at 2.25—apparently thinking the disturbance was minor. They recessed for good at 2.30, as rioters noisily banged on the doors.

By this time the Capitol Police Chief in a conference call was urgently requesting National Guard "boots on the ground." The conversation was described as chaotic as everyone asked questions at the same time. The General directing the Army Staff resisted, arguing "I don't like the visual of the National Guard standing a police line with the Capitol in the background," and that only the Secretary of the Army (who was in a different meeting) had authority to approve the request. Finally, at 3 p.m., the Secretary of Defense authorized deploying the 1100 troops of the D.C. National Guard, but restricted them from carrying ammunition and sharing equipment with police without prior approval. Since Trump resisted the order, Vice President Pence approved it on his own authority, breaking the chain of command.

In the event, it did not make much difference. Metro police sent 100 reinforcements within 10 minutes after the police line was pushed back at 1 p.m. The D.C. National Guard mobilization would take at least 2 hours for its members to assemble and get equipped at the D.C. Armory. In fact, 150 troops arrived at the Capitol at 5.40, just as the Capitol Police announced the building has been cleared of rioters. Meanwhile, between 2.30 and 2.50, calls from D.C. Mayor to the Virginia State Police promised reinforcements, the first of which began arriving in the city at 3.15; while a request for the Virginia National Guard was authorized by the Governor but not by the Defense Dept. About 3.40, the Maryland Governor ordered a mobilization in anticipation of a request, which comes from the General in charge of the Pentagon National Guard Bureau about 4 p.m. But Maryland National Guard forces are not expected until next day. At 5 p.m., the New Jersey Governor announced he was sending state police at the request of D.C. officials; and in the evening the New York Governor said he would send 1000 National Guards.

The invasion of the Capitol building itself lasted from about 2.10 to 5.40 p.m., the Senate having been invaded for only a few minutes around 2.30, and the House repelling an attack at 2.45 when one rioter is shot and killed by plain-clothes security. By 3 p.m., many people who entered the House side of the building were leaving. On the Senate side, clashes continued until after 4 p.m.

By this time, the mostly unarmed Capitol Police were reinforced by ATF tactical teams, and by SWAT teams of the Metro Police in heavy gear. Other buildings in the Capitol complex, including the Senate Office Building were cleared by FBI and Homeland Security forces in riot gear around 4.30 p.m. At 6.15, the Capitol Police, the Metro Police, and the D.C. National Guard had formed a perimeter around the Capitol, although several hundred rioters remained in the vicinity until around 8 p.m.

The promised reinforcements were mostly psychological in effect, building confidence among the victors. On the front line, the Capitol Police had put up a delaying resistance, taking about 60 casualties (15 seriously enough to be hospitalized), with one dead (later diagnosed as having died of a stroke). The Metro Police had 56 injuries. The rioters apparently got off easier, one killed by gunfire, five rioters known to be hospitalized: out of perhaps 300–500 who breached the Capitol, and the thousands (10,000?) who shouted support outside. Among these latter, three died of heart attacks or other emotional effects of extreme excitement. The shooting was done by a Capitol Police lieutenant, which appears to have turned the tide. Heavily armored SWAT teams effectively mopped up die-hard resistance.

Police Lines Retreat, Violence, and Crowd Management

Police retreated in two phases on the West (main) front of the Capitol; another sequence at the East (rear) of the building involved a smaller crowd and fewer police. On the East side, a crowd started gathering around 12 noon. On the West side, a larger crowd gathered by 12.30. By 12.53, the crowd began to push back police from barricades of waist-high portable fencing. (My counts from photos indicate about 2500 people visible in the crowd—with more further back and on the wings; against a single line of about 80 police behind the fencing, with somewhat less than that number spread out in the space behind them.) Over the next 10 minutes, the crowd overran three more rows of barricades, the officers retreating to the base of the Capitol steps. Photos and videos of this phase show what looks like a tug of war, three or four men on each side of a segment of fencing, which they push to tip over or hold upright. Occasionally someone on either side rushes forward to strike across the barrier with baton or stick. The cops are trying hard, pushing back vigorously.

Around 1.30, a large crowd arrives from listening to the Trump rally 14 blocks away. This increases the density of the crowd pushing the police up the steps to the Capitol terraces. But on the whole, there is an hour-long standoff, lasting from 1 to 2 p.m., until the break-in to the building itself.

Meanwhile, on the East side, a smaller police line loses control of the last barrier at 2 p.m. Information is lacking on when this crowd got inside, but they must have added to the chaotic situation of intruders in the corridors and tunnels of the Capitol building complex. They probably also were those who entered other nearby buildings including the Senate Office building, and breaking into and ransacking offices inside the Capitol complex that went on for several hours after the main assault crowd from the West front was dispersed.

Shortly after the police lines on the East side collapsed, on the West front about 2.10 p.m., police are pushed up the grand steps. The emotional momentum is with the crowd, who break through a side door and window at 2.12 and get inside. Within a few minutes they are on the second floor outside the Senate chamber. Videos show a lone cop rather coolly engaging a dozen intruders, gesturing at them, turning to climb a stairwell, looking back to make sure they are following; he has a pistol in his holster but never reaches for it. The intruders advance surprisingly slowly, hardly more than brisk walking pace; the cop misleads them away from the doors of the Senate. Alerted security locked the Senate doors at 2.15, a minute before intruders reached the gallery outside the chamber. The Senate was evacuated by 2.30, before some attackers briefly got into the viewers' gallery, and few climbed down to sit in the presider's chair and pose for photos.

Meanwhile, most of the crowd moved through the Rotunda into the House wing around 2.30 (the Representatives started evacuating after 2.20). As they pounded on the doors shouting to find Pelosi, a group of about a dozen followed a side corridor to reach a windowed door into the Speaker's lobby, near a staircase used just before to complete the evacuation. Videos show them arguing with three police who rather calmly guard the door; they wear no helmets or riot gear, and pass the word they are being relieved by a heavily armored tactical squad. In the two minutes when the police withdraw to make room for their reinforcements, the mob pounds on the door, shouting and breaking the windows in the upper doors with a helmet, fists and stick. Meanwhile, photos taken from the inside of the House chamber itself show five plain-clothes officers in suits, behind an improvised barricade of furniture, aiming handguns at the main doors where the crowd is clamoring to get in. These do not include the officer in the lobby at the rear of the House who shot and killed Air Force veteran Ashli Babbitt, climbing through the broken door window at 2.44 p.m. It was the last peak of momentum of the attackers.

On the whole, there is little evidence of panic among the police; they put up a strong resistance at each barricade outside the building until pushed back by crowd pressure. Inside, photos and videos show the police largely calm. The greatest tension is in the faces and body postures of the police getting ready to fire if the House door is breached.

Other photos show the most intense emotions at moments when the Rotunda is crowded with both sides mixed together: police in riot gear—helmets with plastic visors—rioters in MAGA hats, hockey helmets, stocking caps, bare-headed, a few flags visible and more than a few mobile phones taking pictures. My count gives about 150 persons pushed together at close quarters, approximately equal numbers of both sides. In the distance along the far wall, we can see about 50 cops lined up in riot gear; the impression is they are held in reserve, as the tide has turned and the rioters are being driven into retreat. There are more cops than rioters in the foreground.

How violent was it? Although news reports noted that rioters had guns and explosives, this seems to be based mainly on discoveries made away from the Capitol: home-made pipe bombs at the Republican National

Committee and Democratic National Committee headquarters. A street search found a parked vehicle with a handgun, assault rifle, ammunition, and homemade napalm bombs.[3] These reports raised alarm in the Capitol, and spread the belief that the rioters, including the one who was shot and killed in the House lobby, were an armed threat. Except for that shooting, the weaponry used on both sides was surprisingly low-level. The Capitol police had a considerable arsenal at their disposal, but initially the officers inside the building were in regular uniform; those at the barricades outside were in riot gear, with helmets, shields and batons. Within an hour after the breach, photos show forces inside mostly in riot gear.

Some rioters wore a version of riot gear, helmets, military-style vests. These were prominent among the dozen or so who scaled the West front of the Capitol to reach the top terrace. This appears to have been showing off, since photos show the crowd was already up the side steps and behind the police lines. It appears that the most heavily equipped rioters were either police or military personnel (current or former), including ideological militias. In fact, they seemed to believe they were taking part in a legitimate police mission of their own, carrying plastic handcuffs to arrest "traitors." But their "weapons" were more in the nature of accoutrements; handcuffs are not offensive weapons, although strongly identified with cops; similarly with the two-way radios some carried; and with reports of "stun grenades," what SWAT teams call "flash-bangs" used to confuse a hostage-taker, which is to say a device to avoid using lethal violence if possible.

The rioters' main high-tech offensive weapon was "bear spray"—high-intensity pepper spray used as protection against wild animals by outdoor campers and hikers.[4] What is most in evidence are flag poles (doubling as emblems), and sticks, chiefly used to break windows.

One of the most violent incidents of which we have a description took place during the peak moment of conflict outside the West front, when the crowd found a relatively lightly guarded side door where they eventually broke in. Three cops were pulled out of the defensive line (to make room for the attackers), and shoved down the steps. Cut off from support and surrounded by a large crowd, they were beaten with "hockey sticks, crutches, flags, poles, and stolen police shields"—on the whole, improvised weapons. In the sociology of violence, this is called a "forward panic," where a group that has been in an intense confrontation suddenly finds the balance has broken, one side is suddenly at the mercy of the other, and an emotional surge of adrenaline takes over and results in a beating characterized by piling on and overkill (Collins 2008: 83–94). Unlike in most military and police-chase situations, here the victims escaped alive—the difference being, no one had guns.

The most serious casualties caused by the attackers were from improvised weapons found on the spot: fire extinguishers. One incident happened, again at the flashpoint on the West front, after 2 p.m. as the police line was breached (*Wall Street Journal*, January 15, 2021). The attacker, retired from a Philadelphia-area fire department, threw a fire extinguisher at the police line, hitting three officers in the head. One was knocked down or hit from behind on the head by a fire extinguisher. (That officer was evaluated at a hospital and returned to duty.) Although details are lacking, this is in keeping with the typical pattern in deadly violence: no eye contact when the attack is made. The same is the case with Ashli Babbitt, who was unarmed, but the officer who shot her was at the climax of a tense situation, the House Chamber about to be invaded, a noisy threat outside the door, then a sudden intrusion right at the gun tensely held by both hands pointed at the entry window. In the micro-sociology of violence, close face-to-face confrontations are emotionally stressful on both sides, pumping adrenaline to the level where most participants are incompetent with their weapons, unable to fire accurately; perceptually, it becomes a blur. A minority of highly trained soldiers and police control their adrenaline enough to pull the trigger under such situations; an even smaller minority hit their target.

The most striking thing about the violence at the Capitol is that so little of it came from gunfire. Many hundreds of police on the scene had guns; except at the climax of the attack on the House, none were fired, and few were drawn or aimed. A rare photo of five captive rioters shows them lying prone on the floor, guarded by three cops with a baton but guns holstered. On the side of the protestors, five guns were seized, although it's unclear if these were inside the Capitol—if so, they were never used. Sociologically, this is nothing amazing: it is the most typical pattern of armed confrontations. Whether by police, gangs, robbers, or military in combat, in the vast majority of confrontations with guns, they are not used.

Victory or defeat, advancing or retreating, is far more emotional and psychological than physical violence itself. This pattern holds too at the Capitol, as it does in 1917 and 1792.

Fraternization

Fraternization between protestors and regime forces has played a major part in any successful revolution. In Russia, in 1917, agitation by Bolshevik sympathizers inside the army and navy prepared the way by bringing them over to their side; and it was these militants and the most convinced sailors who made the attack on the Winter Palace. And in the early hours of the attack, agitators inside created confusion and promoted the defection of most of the defending troops. There are numerous examples of this pattern. The downfall of the Soviet Union was consummated in August 1991 when tanks sent to take over the parliament building were surrounded by crowds, and Boris Yeltsin climbed on top of a tank to take command from its stunned and demoralized crew. In the most famous of the Arab Spring revolts in 2011, crowds in Cairo's Tahrir Square chanted "the army and the people are one hand," as security forces first refused to expel the protestors, then changed sides to protect them against last-ditch attacks by Mubarak's militia enforcers (Ketchley 2014).

Armed forces swinging over in a tidal wave happens when two conditions hold: when rebellion appears right and just to a vast majority of people (maybe just those who are most visible in the capital city); and when it seems inevitable, making it dangerous to hold back. The first of these conditions existed to a degree at the Capitol; the second hardly at all.

The attackers certainly made efforts at solidarity with the police. Reportedly some rioters showed police badges or military IDs as if expecting to be allowed inside. A Capitol police officer said one rioter displayed a badge and said, "we're doing this for you." Some intruders wore the "thin blue line" emblem of support for the police. Some videos showed police standing back and allowing rioters into the building; one officer was seen in a "selfie" with a rioter inside the building. Especially inside, where during the initial phases the police were not in riot gear, police tended to maintain normal demeanor and to talk quietly with the intruders. Afterwards, some Representatives accused the police of complicity, including giving them directions to specific offices, or giving them preliminary tours of the layout. Two Capitol police were suspended and ten or more were under investigation. Four officers later committed suicide.

The police were also criticized for making very few arrests (about 30 on the Capitol grounds, mostly outside), and for letting the hundreds of intruders get away once control was regained after 3 p.m. In fact, it appears the police were most concerned to clear the Capitol, and the most expeditious way to do it was to push or lead them out the doors. Making arrests is like taking prisoners in a battle; it is the most formal protocol, but prisoners take up manpower to guard them. Bear in mind that all this happened before reinforcements started arriving at the Capitol about 6 p.m. Most of the arrests that did happen were apparently outside in the evening, when a large number of police chased down the die-hards from the demonstration.

Most of this behavior was ambiguous. One gets the impression from watching videos made inside the building that the officers not in battle dress tried to maintain as much of an atmosphere of normalcy as possible. In the initial phase of entry, the intruders once inside walked rather tentatively, not rushing about in a frenzy but even staying inside velvet guide ropes set up for tourists. Photos in this phase generally showed thin numbers spread out in a lot of space; police presence in the halls and Rotunda at that time was sparse or non-existent.

Riot-equipped forces were concentrated outside, while tactical squads in riot gear, visible in later photos, had not yet mustered inside. Under these circumstances, it is not surprising the cops were not interested in putting up violent resistance. The exception, of course, was when the intruders reached their goal—the legislative chambers themselves; above all at the doors of the House, the only place where guns were drawn, and used. And these were the places where the crowds grew most agitated, shouting threats and slogans and trying to smash their way in.

Current or former police officers and military personnel were prominent in the front lines pushing back the barricades, and among those who got inside. Later investigations concentrated on persons identified by photos and videos or their own on-line posts; among these about one-fifth of the hundred or so investigations were police or military. Most prominent of all was Ashli Babbitt, veteran of many deployments in Iraq, who was a security officer (i.e. military police) in the Air Force.

Two comments: first, it is typical in riots that the great majority of the crowd are onlookers and noise-making supporters; only about 10 percent or less of the persons seen in riot photos are actually doing something violent, engaging the other side (Collins 2008: 413–430). It may well be the case that those who carry the battle are specialists in violence, as Charles Tilly (2003) calls them, tough guys, athletes, and weapons specialists on either side of the law. (One of those charged at the Capitol was an Olympic gold-medalist swimmer.)

Second: in the overall context of recent years and months, it is not surprising that some substantial portion of American police, as well as military, are disgruntled. Among veterans and active-duty military, the suicide rate has been at a peak; the psychological toll of fighting for almost 20 years in seemingly endless wars in the Middle East; a professional (non-draftee) force repeatedly deployed, isolated from the majority of the home population; wars where victories repeatedly proved temporary and reversible; and where news publicity concentrated more on atrocities against the enemy than on American accomplishments. Since a substantial portion of police are veterans (the job where their training is most relevant), there is a bond of sympathy between the two occupations.

The police themselves have experienced the historically strongest wave of criticism in the media and from liberal politicians. Starting in the 1990s, when amateur video of violent police arrests became publicized, protest has accelerated with the proliferation of mobile-phone cameras, CCTV, and near-instantaneous propagation through the Internet. Police shootings and violent arrests have resulted in a series of protest demonstrations nationwide periodically dominating the news cycle since Ferguson, Missouri, in 2014, Baltimore in 2015, and others. The most intense protests were those starting in late May 2020, in the midst of dissent over the COVID shut-down; these were the most widespread and long-lasting ever, extending into September and beyond in hot spots such as Seattle and Portland. More than in any previous protests, most news media supported these Black Lives Matter protests and related actions; publicizing and endorsing their calls to defund the police; blaming local police for racism; blaming violence on Federal intervention by the Trump administration; downplaying arson and attacks on police stations, courthouses, and government buildings. Many police felt they were being unfairly blamed for the actions of a few, with little understanding for doing a tough job in a period of sharply rising homicide in minority neighborhoods.

In the context of an election campaign, both parties rallied to the issue: Democrat politicians on the whole endorsed BLM demands for wholesale revision not only of policing but the historical legacy of slavery and racism. A wave of tearing down Civil War statues of Confederates expanded into renaming and expunging almost anyone in US history who could be implicated in slave-holding, words or deeds detrimental to Native Americans, or European settlement of North America in general. These included Benjamin Franklin, Thomas Jefferson, Andrew Jackson, Abraham Lincoln, Ulysses Grant, and Teddy Roosevelt. In June 2020, in the midst of the protests over the death of George Floyd, the Democrat-controlled House of Representatives voted to change the District of Columbia into a state renamed Douglass Commonwealth, replacing Christopher Columbus with the abolitionist Frederick Douglass. Corporations were pressured into re-education programs at which employees were told to avow their guilt in being white.

Conflict moves by escalation and counter-escalation. Social movements on both sides mobilized from below; politicians attached themselves to the emotional momentum. An attack, both verbal and physical, on the police led to counter-mobilization. Some of it built upon existing right-wing militias and conspiracy-publicists, gaining recruits to the Proud Boys and others who took the defense of police installations into their own hands. A strange coalition of extremists and police was created, at least in goals and sympathies, which only became manifest in the assault on the Capitol.

This was the atmosphere in which Trump supporters, polarized against the BLM protests, the left-dominated media, and the congressional Democrats, acquired the emotional conviction that their country was being taken from them. The slogan of the stolen vote was a symbol of this larger feeling. Trump fed it with his rallies, ritualistic emotional-energy generators that swing belief into line with a surge of collective feeling. The Durkheimian collectivity always feels like *we* are Society, *we* are the People; it is not quantitative but embodied and totalistic. Riding this emotional wave, they swarmed the Capitol. The effort to fraternize with the Capitol police came out of this conviction.

But a Durkheimian political groundswell must be overwhelming; it reaches its nemesis when there is a counter-mobilization on the other side. Two wavering bodies, with their usual disorientation and lack of smooth coordination at moments of crisis, do not create the ingredient that sways the behavior of security forces at the hinge of events: the feeling that revolution is inevitable, better to join it than be left in the minority opposing it. The Capitol police, whatever twinges of sympathy or moments of soft demeanor they displayed, for the most part stayed firm.

Looting and Ritual Destruction

By ritual destruction, I mean behavior that is seemingly purposeless, to outsiders and opponents. But it is meaningful, or at least deeply impulsive, for those who do it: a collective, social emotion for those involved.

Looting is generally of this sort (Collins 2008: 245–253). It rarely takes anything of value. In riots, including those that take place in electrical black-outs, the early looters tend to be professional thieves, but the crowds that come out to look and see broken-in store fronts are often caught with goods that they have no use for; they just join in the collective mood, a holiday from moral restraints when everything seems available for free. (This is also visible in photos taken during the looting phase of riots.)

In political protests and uprisings, looting does something else. Usually in the first phase of riot, especially a neighborhood riot, after the first confrontation with the police, there is a lull while the police withdraw from the outnumbering crowd to regroup and bring reinforcements. In this lull, the emotional mood will drain away unless there is something for the crowd to do. Looting is a way to keep the riot going—sometimes along with arson, even if it means burning your own neighborhood; the smoke and flames in the sky carry a visual message of how serious the situation is. And looting is made possible, and easy, because police are visibly absent. Without opposition, the atmosphere is like a holiday; and at least temporarily it is a victory over the absent enemy. Looting is emotionally easy; there is no face-to-face confrontation. It provides a kind of pseudo-victory over the symbols of the enemy.

This was the situation in the Capitol after about 3 p.m. The attackers had been driven back from their political targets. Heavily equipped and menacing-looking tactical police squads are now pushing back the crowd, chiefly in the dense areas of the Capitol around the Rotunda. But it is a building with several wings and multiple floors, numerous stairs, a labyrinth of offices. This is the period when rioters spread out, penetrating far-flung corners where the last would not be dislodged until after 5 p.m. This is when the looting and ritual destruction mostly took place.

A prime target was House Speaker Nancy Pelosi's office. Looters flipped over tables, ripped photos off the walls, damaged her name plate on the door. One of her laptops was stolen, as were those in other offices. The office of the Senate Parliamentarian was ransacked, as were other offices. Some places had graffiti: "Murder the media" was one of them, at Press rooms with damaged recording and broadcast equipment. These we can interpret as specific political targets.

Broken doors and cracked or smashed windows were throughout the building, leaving the floors littered with glass and debris. Some of this happened in the process of breaking into locked areas. But it continued in remote office spaces; presumably this was ritualistic destruction, just prolonging the attack—precisely in places where guards were not present, while their main force was concentrated elsewhere.

Photos taken in the aftermath do not show a great deal of trash or destruction in the main corridors. Some of the furniture piled up was from improvised barricades by the defenders. Art works in the main galleries and display areas were not attacked—presumably these had little meaning as enemy targets for the intruders. Some statues and portraits were covered with "corrosive gas agent residue"—this would include tear gas and smoke bombs set off by the defenders, and (perhaps a small amount of) bear spray used by the attackers. In other words, this damage was an unintended by-product of the fighting that took place. Note too that these were "non-violent" weapons, designed to drive away opponents and avoid lethal force.

If the looting and ritual destruction were intended to be a symbolic attack upon the Capitol, they succeeded in frightening and angering its officials. It was a ritualistic exercise on both sides—which is to say, a war of emotions.

A far more destructive instance is the last comparison we will consider.

Paris, August 10, 1792

It was the day the French Revolution turned radical. Up till now it was a Constitutional Monarchy, the King ruling together with the Assembly. But tension had grown as the King vetoed punitive laws against nobles who fled the country and priests who refused to become civil servants. Tension grew worse as foreign troops threatened French territory to restore the old monarchy.

The royal palace had already been invaded seven weeks before. On June 20, the third anniversary of the Tennis Court Oath in 1789, when reforming aristocrats had gone over to the National Assembly, a memorial demonstration of 10,000–20,000 surrounded the Tuileries. Carlyle summed up: "Immense procession, peaceable but dangerous, finds the Tuileries gates closed, and no access to his Majesty; squeezes, crushes, and is squeezed, crushed against the Tuileries gates and doors till they give way" ([1837] 2002: xl). The King held them off, declaring his loyalty to the constitution, even wearing a popular "liberty cap" (the emotional force of a MAGA cap), and drinking a toast with them. Finally, the Mayor of Paris arrived and persuaded the demonstrators to leave. In the aftermath, a wave of sympathy for the King split the Assembly. But efforts to swing back to moderation stalled, and news from the front raised further alarm as the enemy advanced. In Paris, everyone expected another assault on the palace, this time for keeps.

Security was beefed up. Courtiers in the palace went around armed and prepared barriers. The National Guard—an official militia—were urged to defend the crown against the *sans culotte* mob, but their loyalty was questionable, and a force of Swiss Guard was relied upon. On the other side, contingents of volunteers poured into Paris on their way to reinforce the front. The coming assault was an open secret. The "patriots . . . were now openly talking of storming the Tuileries as the Bastille had been stormed, and establishing a Republic" (Doyle 2002: 187).

The organizational center of power was slipping away from the Assembly. The radical political clubs of Paris, the Jacobins and others, agitated in the neighborhood sections to coordinate action in a revolutionary commune. Distrusting the National Guard drawn from the wealthier citizens, they called out the *sans culottes* (those without fashionable knee breeches) of small shopkeepers and artisans. In late July, panic over the invading Prussian and Austrian armies had moved the Assembly to distribute arms to all citizens—even though the arms could and would be used against themselves.

In the small hours of the night before August 10, the continuous ringing of the tocsin bell proclaimed emergency. The central committee of the Paris sections declared an insurrection and ordered all forces to march on the Tuileries. "Arriving there at nine the next morning, they found that the King and his family had fled to the safety of the Assembly across the road." Defending the palace were about 2000 National Guards, but these immediately defected to the Commune's side, a crowd of about 20,000. Courtiers had put up a brave show before the attack, but now withdrew. This left the 900 Swiss Guards, professional mercenaries, who began the action by opening fire. Their initial volley did not deter the huge crowd, and their allies melting away no doubt eroded their confidence. After about an hour,

> the Swiss began to retreat, pursued by mobs of bystanders without firearms who hacked them to pieces with knives, pikes, and hatchets, and tore their uniforms to pieces to make trophies . . . crowds rampaged through Paris destroying all symbols and images of royalty down to the very word "king" in street names.
>
> (Doyle 2002: 189)

Carlyle summarized contemporary accounts in his own rhetoric of the 1830s:

> Till two in the afternoon the massacring, the breaking and the burning has not ended . . . How deluges of frantic Sansculottism roared

> through all passages of the Tuileries, ruthless in vengeance; how the valets were butchered, hewn down . . . how in the cellars wine-bottles were broken, wine-butts staved in and drunk; and upwards to the very garrets, all windows tumbled out their precious royal furnitures: and with gold mirrors, velvet curtains, down of ripped feather-beds, and dead bodies of men, the Tuileries was like no garden of the earth . . . bodies of Swiss lie piled there; naked, unremoved until the second day. Patriotism has torn their red coats into snips; and marches with them at the pike's point.
>
> (Carlyle [1837] 2002: 499)

Paris was now in the super-dangerous situation of rival centers of power, the Assembly and the Commune. Both of them commanding armed forces; both internally split among mutually distrustful factions, fearful of what their rivals would do, and motivated to strike first out of fear of what would happen if they didn't. But the initiative had passed to the Commune, and its radical political clubs; they had won the big victory, and demonstrated the awesome force of the mobilized crowds of Paris. Awesome because of its emotional pressure, its all-encompassing noise, its sheer size, and its ferociousness, now several times demonstrated, when opponents wavered and it had them at their mercy. Guillotines were being set up. In future months, the King and Queen would be executed, along with thousands of others, aristocrats, priests, and just plain political rivals, anyone who aroused suspicion of whatever faction was temporarily dominant. This would go on for two years, until Robespierre was executed and a reaction began to swing back toward unitary authority and eventually dictatorship.

During these two years there was a veritable mania of renaming. Forms of address, Monsieur and Madame, were forbidden; everyone was to be called Citizen. Churches were declared temples of Reason. The old Christian calendar was abolished, its AD (*anno domini*) and BC (before Christ) replaced by Year One, starting with the declaration of the Republic in September 1792 (oops, old-style!). While we're at it, all the names of the months have to go too, for instance, the month of July is now called Thermidor. Symbolic politics glorifies the hopes and projects of the most radical intellectuals. These changes would remain in place until Napoleon brought back the church and reinstated the old calendar in 1801.

Lessons Learned?

What was different about the Capitol assault of January 6, 2021 was how quickly and easily it was defeated. Yes, it had factional splits and dispersed centers of command, wavering and dissenting about sending reinforcements; it had police retreating before an aggressive crowd; reluctance to shoot; some fraternization between attackers and guards; some ritualistic looting at the end. It had a background of long-standing and accumulating tension between two sides, counter-escalating social movements, politicians jumping on and off of bandwagons. But in historical comparison, it had no overwhelming consensus that the regime was toppling, much less that it ought to topple. The assault was defeated, in a momentum swing of about an hour, and with an historical minimum of serious casualties. That it could be put down so easily is a testament to American institutions. A federal democracy, with powers shared and divided at many levels among executives, legislatures, and courts, there is no place to turn the switch that controls everything. Decentralized democracies like the USA can have civil wars—if geographical splits are severe enough and include the armed forces; but it cannot have coups at the top or revolutions in the Capitol.

Notes

1. Russia in 1917 was still using the old-style calendar which had been updated by various states of Western Europe during preceding centuries. To convert these dates to the modern international calendar, add 13 days to the date. Thus October 26 (old style) becomes November 8 (new style).
2. Sources: Associated Press; *Wall Street Journal*; *Washington Post*; *Los Angeles Times*; published and on-line photos and videos.
3. This home-made arsenal is similar to those accumulated by school rampage shooters obsessed with a private cult of accumulating weapons, few of which they actually use. See Chapter 14, "Clues to Mass Rampage Killers."
4. The only such photo I have seen among several hundred posted is of a young man in helmet and gas mask, outside at the base of the Capitol, who sprays a brown liquid across an empty space in the crowd while running with his head turned the other way. This was probably around 12.50 p.m. when the crowd first surged against police lines. There are several photos of police spraying a clear liquid at protestors, in these external scenes.

References

Carlyle, Thomas. [1837] 2002. *The French Revolution*. New York: Modern Library.

Collins, Randall. 2008. *Violence: A Micro-Sociological Theory*. Princeton, NJ: Princeton University Press.

Doyle, William. 2002. *Oxford History of the French Revolution*. New York: Oxford University Press.

Ketchley, Neil. 2014. "The Army and the People are One Hand! Fraternisation and the 25th January Egyptian Revolution." *Comparative Studies in Society and History* 56(01): 155–186.

Reed, John. 1919. *Ten Days that Shook the World*. New York: Boni and Liveright.

Tilly, Charles. 2003. *The Politics of Collective Violence*. New York: Cambridge University Press.

Tocqueville, Alexis de. 1850/1970. *Recollections: The French Revolution of 1848*. New York: Doubleday.

Trotsky, Leon. 1932. *History of the Russian Revolution*. New York: Simon & Schuster.

Part III

War and Sport

Dynamics of Winning, Losing, and Stalemate

Chapter 9

The Micro-Sociology of Sport

Introduction

We live in a technological age of visual recording devices. Many of their practical uses were pioneered in sports. In the 1960s, American football coaches began to review films of past games to prepare strategies against upcoming teams. Now football and baseball players study the moves of their individual opponents, and film has become a tool of coaching everywhere to improve athletes' techniques. Referees review video of crucial plays to decide on scores and penalties, or hear about it from fans and TV commentators when the cameras show the refs didn't get it right. Advanced instrumentation is used for training in sports like track and field by monitoring real-time physiological signs of breathing, heartbeat, and adrenaline.

Similar observational technologies have led to big advances in the sociology of violence, and in the sociology of micro-interactions generally. CCTV cameras give real-life observations of crime and violence; crowd members at demonstrations and riots use mobile phone cameras to show what's going on and to expose atrocities. Sociologists can now go beyond retrospective accounts to see the actual dynamics of violence in police arrests; the turning points where violence breaks out in demonstrations, or what prevents it; when quarrels at pubs become violent, and how fights are stopped. On-line, there is an abundance of cell-phone videos of casual fights; in fact, these videos give an optimistic result, insofar as they show how easily most small-scale fights stalemate or break up. Really serious violence shows a different pattern of piling on an outnumbered victim—very ugly violence here, but we are beginning to understand what are the most dangerous situations.

In ordinary social interactions, close visual technologies together with research on the expression of emotions on the face and in bodily movements, enable us to see what kinds of emotions operate in different situations. Interaction ritual theory shows the micro-interactional conditions producing high solidarity, social alienation, and all degrees in between.

Putting all three together—micro-observational sociology of sports, of violence, and of the emotional dynamics of social interaction—gives payoffs all

DOI: 10.4324/9781003245629-13

around. For sports, we have both theory and research methods for understanding what happens on the field, including the dynamics of winning and losing. For the theory of violence and the theory of social solidarity, sports provides an accessible laboratory of data.

Three Ways of Winning a Game

1. Contests of Effort

One formula for winning lumps together sheer willpower, inspiring leadership, and *esprit de corps*. Ya gotta have heart—trying harder than the other guy; never give up. A popular variant in recent times is practicing harder and longer hours, getting oneself in better condition, making yourself stronger and more skilled by sheer effort. Nevertheless, close microsociological analysis shows that this pathway to victory is fallacious.

Chambliss (1989) analyzed winning and losing by observing swimmers at different levels of competition, from local club up to the Olympic team. Winners are those who have perfected the details that go into swimming faster (exact hand angles, timing of turns on the wall, etc.). An ensemble of such techniques, practiced to perfection, add up little advantages into superior speed. Chambliss found that winning swimmers do not practice longer hours or put in more effort than their also-ran competitors. It is not that they practice more; they practice better. And they enjoy their practice: it gives them a sense of being in rhythm with oneself, a zone where effort is eclipsed by smoothness and purpose. John Wooden's coaching strategy, described below, agrees on this point: feel yourself performing your best skills, and winning comes as a by-product.

Chambliss denied that the winning difference is innate bodily strength or muscle quickness; the same swimmer can make a quantitative leap in competitive level, once he or she has acquired the ensemble of skills and the mind-set to use them. Opponents who are strong contenders but rarely winners often think the habitual winner has something special, which they can't define in physical terms; hence they tend regard the winner as a higher realm of existence. They think that the top rank must be something alien to their own experience, and thereby put themselves in an inferiority zone of lesser confidence. But there is nothing mysterious about winning—in sports or anything else, Chambliss argues; writer's block is a version of the same problem of psyching oneself out by comparing oneself with the company of unreachable great writers. Excellence is the ability to maintain a normal, habituated attitude to being in the inner circle, just performing one's detailed techniques. Thus, Chambliss's title: "The Mundanity of Excellence."

Another variant on the winning-through-greater-effort strategy is to rely on emotional solidarity within the team. Solidarity and emotional energy are the traditional pep-talks of coaches: stick together, try your hardest, never give up, and you will win. But there is little systematic evidence that the most strong-willed or inspirational coaches are the most successful, if that is all there is to it. Publicity about particularly tough coaches who are winners is sampling on the dependent variable, if we don't compare them to coaches who aren't successful. Techniques of arousing solidarity are much the same on all sides, and one high-solidarity team is generally matched by another.

I have by-passed the simplest victory plan, sheer physical superiority: just have bigger and better athletes than the other side. It is this claim that the "ya gotta have heart" emotional/inspirational messages are designed to trump. But sports leagues try to separate levels of play so that the sides are fairly equally matched. Matching opponents primarily on the physical level leads to long, grinding contests, generally with low scoring. The grinding approach also becomes equivalent to wars of attrition. In sports, this takes the form of losing because your players get injured (whether in the game or in practice). In war, attrition is something that one army tries to inflict on the other; in sports, deliberately causing injuries is generally against the rules, so that winning or losing through injuries is just a random accident that makes games emotionally flat.

2. *Contests of Superior Rhythmic Entrainment*

Coaching methods are a good source of detail on the techniques of winning. John Wooden's coaching records in basketball at UCLA represent the best in any team sport: 10 NCAA national championships (in a peak period of 12 years); an 88-game winning streak covering almost 3 years; a 38-game winning streak in NCAA tournaments against the highest competition. Comparisons with other coaches and other sports are complicated: winning streaks, frequency of championships, winning percentages, all need to be combined, taking into account differences in level of competition. Top coaches are those who win consistently, against whoever, and are at their best in big games against the strongest opponents.[1]

Wooden did not believe in giving pep-talks, speeches to stir up emotion before big games:

> If you need emotionalism to make you perform better, sooner or later you'll be vulnerable, an emotional wreck, and unable to function to your level of ability.
>
> Hatred and anger motivate only briefly. They aren't lasting and won't get you through the ups and downs of a game.
>
> Mistakes occur when your thinking is tainted by excessive emotion . . . To perform near your level of competency your mind must be clear and free of excessive emotion.
>
> (Wooden and Jamison 1997: 124–125)

Top performance is being cool and professional. Micro-sociologically, this is high EE—emotional energy as confidence and enthusiasm, the very words that Wooden uses.

Star center Bill Walton described team practices at UCLA as

> non-stop action and absolutely electric, super-charged, on edge, crisp, and incredibly demanding, with Coach Wooden pacing up and down the sideline like a caged tiger, barking out instructions. He constantly moved us into and out of minutely drilled details, scrimmages, and patterns while exhorting us to "Move . . . quickly . . . hurry up!" . . . In fact, games seemed like they happened in a lower gear because of the pace at which we practiced. We'd run a play perfectly in scrimmage and Coach would say, "OK, fine. Now re-set. Do it again, faster." We'd do it again. Faster. And again. Faster. And again. I'd often think during UCLA games, "Why is this taking so long? Because we had done everything that happened during a game thousands of times at a faster pace in practice."
>
> When four guys touched the ball in two seconds and the fifth guy hit a lay-up, man, what a feeling! When things really clicked, the joy of playing was reflected by the joy on (Wooden's) face. He created an environment where you expected to be your best and outscore the opponent; where capturing a championship and going undefeated was part of the normal course of events.
>
> (Wooden and Jamison 1997: viii–ix)

Not that it is emotionless—Bill Walton speaks of the joyful feeling when a high-speed coordinated play involving the entire team clicks. This is a non-disruptive emotion, in the rhythm, not breaking it.

The coach's job includes criticism, pointing out mistakes not as punishment by to correct them and get better results. "The only goal of criticism or discipline is improvement." Above all, hard criticism in public is to be avoided, since it embarrasses and antagonizes players. Wooden's strongest punishment was to take away the privilege of participating in a UCLA team practice:

> If they weren't working hard in practice I would say, "Well, fellows, let's call it off for today. We're just not with it." The vast majority of the time the players would immediately say, "Coach, give us another chance. We'll get going."
>
> (Wooden and Jamison 1997: 118–119)

Practice was more central than the game. After Wooden retired, when people would ask him what he missed, he said "I miss the practices" (Wooden and Jamison 1997: 108). Practice was the high experience. Games were a pale imitation of rhythmic synchronization at its best.

The point of practicing was not just to learn the right physical moves—"body memory" in the current cliché. It had to be done in the proper rhythm, and that is intrinsically a social rhythm. Wacquant (2004) makes a similar point about practicing in a boxing gym: everything could be done alone at home except sparring. But doing stomach-building sit-ups, skipping rope, punching the light and heavy bags were more motivating when they were done together in the gym in 3-minute rounds punctuated by the trainer ringing a bell. Wacquant observed that the feeling of collective rhythm depended on an optimal number of persons working out in the gym; when they were only a half dozen or fewer, the rhythm was weak; when the number of boxers rose to 35, the excitement was intense. The gym scene gave a collective aspect to what was, during a match, an individual sport.

Mistakes happen, in practice and in games. This is inevitable. Wooden's point is not to blame yourself, or blame others, but to analyze the situation, locate the mistake that is under your own control, and fix it. This means not getting emotional when bad things happen.

Playing well under pressure against top competition, obviously, is the mark of a championship team. For Wooden, this was a by-product of long experience in his methods of practice. He also believed the most difficult experience would promote even higher effort—not just as individuals or in bodily endurance but in team rhythm. The apex was perhaps in the 1973 championship game when UCLA stretched its undefeated streak to 75 games and won the NCAA for the 7th year in a row; Bill Walton made 21 of 22 field goal attempts.

Wooden rated himself an average coach tactically; he said his advantage was in analyzing his players, and the fact that he enjoyed hard work. I would add: his hard work went into producing intensely focused, high-speed, rhythmically entraining team practices: the ingredients of a successful Interaction Ritual. The hard work of an intense IR pays off in high EE. The rhythm of success feeds on itself, at the very moment it is happening. Wooden's methods support Chambliss's point that winning swimmers enjoy their practice; it makes them feel high.

King and De Rond (2011) analyzed the central importance of shared rhythm in a boat race—in this case, the annual Oxford/Cambridge rowing contest on the Thames River. Detailed observations, covering the period when the Cambridge team began practicing through the events of the race itself, turned up a series of problems. The eight oarsmen were all experienced winners, but they had not rowed together before.[2] There were difficulties in settling on a coxswain, who sits in the rear of the boat and calls out the stroke of the oars. This is crucial because the boat moves most smoothly through the water when all oars enter and exit the water at exactly the same moment, and at the same angle. Feathering the oars as they move through the air in exactly the same way is essential. If one or more oar is off, the entire boat feels it as a rough jolt. The team was unable to achieve a sustained rhythm in its practices, and there was dissent among the members. Thus, when the race itself began, Cambridge fell behind Oxford by several boat lengths. Then, in the middle of the course, the rowers themselves gave out a cry: they clicked, they hit their rhythm, they knew it, and their boat shot ahead, overtook Oxford, and won the race. The analysis bolsters Chambliss's point that winners perfect the fine details of their technique; and add the collective rhythm on a team which gives them an extra jolt of emotional and physical energy. This particular boat race provides a natural experiment, because the crew had difficulties establishing their high-speed rhythm, and the moment of transition from failure to success was so palpably experienced by them all.

3. *Winning by Emotional Domination and Destroying Opponents' Collective Rhythm*

Emotional domination is when the emotional energy on different sides of a social assembly is very unequal. One side is full of initiative, confidence, and enthusiasm; the other is passive, out-of-sync, clumsy, and slow-moving. This pattern is usually referred to as momentum, when one side is pushing the other around and the latter is falling apart. Here emotional energy translates into physical energy. The sports commentator who says that the defence looks tired out because it has been on the field a long time, is ignoring the fact that both sides have been on the field equally long. But one side has been gaining energy while the other side is losing it.

Winning by emotional domination occurs above all by breaking down the opponent's solidarity. The winning team not only needs to keep up a high degree of rhythmic coordination among themselves, but also to disrupt the opposing team's coordination. This is not so much physical disruption, as disruption of the emotional signals that tie their players together. Physical disruption of the opponents can happen at times by beating the other players through greater speed, accuracy, or strength; to the fans, this looks like a dramatic display of skill or talent. But teams that maintain their rhythm and their solidarity are not beaten just because of a single play. In fact, the more spectacular it is, the less it may disrupt them, if they have high-level coordination to begin with. Instead, it is the more subtle interplay between the internal rhythms of the two teams that determines when there is a momentum shift.

Winning in team sports is a combination of keeping up one's own coordination, and disrupting the other team's. Sometimes this can be done by sheer physical domination, greater force and speed; that is similar to attrition in warfare, wearing the other side down, perhaps because of superior physical conditioning. Games of attrition are generally undramatic and unexciting, less of a spectacle for the fans.

The most dramatic games are when one side falls apart as an organized team, whereupon the scoring gets out of hand. This is what happened during Germany's 6-minute explosion of goals against Brazil in the 2014 World Cup semi-finals. Brazil was the perennial World Cup favorite, riding a 62-game winning streak at home, famous for their highly-coordinated passing. The game was tight at the outset, with Germany scoring on a corner kick in the 14th minute. In the 23rd minute, Germany scored again, picking up the rebound of a shot blocked by the Brazil goal-keeper. The Brazilian players looked upset, down 2–0 against a good team. A minute later, Germany scored again, on a cross deflected by the goalie. The goalie stomped around in unbelief, while the other Brazilian players wandered about waving their hands. After the kickoff, alert German players took the ball from a Brazilian star in his own half and scored again: the 26th minute. In the 29th minute, the Germans unleased a long-distance pass to a swift player racing down the field: 5–0. The 6-minute lapse in the Brazilian defense started with a bit of bad luck, compounded by the emotional reaction of the goalie and then of the entire Brazilian team, while the Germans stayed focused and took advantage of their opponents' unprofessional mood. Brazil had no shots on goal at all in the first half. The second half was more evenly played, but Germany scored two more goals, until Brazil got a consolation goal in the 90th minute, to finish 7–1. An usually well-coordinated team became emotionally disrupted, while the opposing side became super-energized.

The 2013 Superbowl game between the Denver Broncos and the Seattle Seahawks is another example of a top team suddenly collapsing. During the regular season, Denver quarterback Peyton Manning set records for the most prolific passing offense in history, passing for 5477 yards and 55 touchdowns, while the team scored an unprecedented 606 points in the regular season. Manning led a hurry-up offense, where plays were never called in the huddle but always by audibles at the line of scrimmage as he surveyed the line-up of the defense. Manning acquired a reputation for being completely in control, ordering his players into the positions he wanted. The team was a fine-tuned, high-speed instrument and Manning was its driver. When the first play from scrimmage of the Superbowl began, Manning was looking around and barking out orders in his usual manner, when the Denver center—perhaps distracted by crowd noise—snapped the ball over the quarterback's head and into the end zone, where it was recovered by Seattle for a safety (2 points and Denver had to punt the ball away from their own end zone). For the next 30 minutes, everything went wrong for Denver. Seattle led 22–0 at halftime, 36–0 before Denver scored at the end of the 3rd quarter, 43–8 final score. Manning threw two interceptions, one returned for a touchdown; the team didn't even make a first down until the second quarter. The TV commentators said that during the first half, every Seattle player outplayed his Denver opponent on every play—the collapse affected both Manning's offense and the defensive unit as well.

Teams playing at the championship level are obviously extremely good, both physically and in coordinated playing. Nevertheless, such games often hinge upon a dramatic series of plays, where one side loses its rhythmic coordination; and the other team jumps on the weakness, enforcing emotional domination and keeping them out of sync until they are so far behind they cannot recover. This tells us that rhythmic coordination—which is the essence of generating high emotional energy and effective performance—is a situational achievement at a particular moment in time. It doesn't matter how good you were in the past; rhythms can be disrupted at a high level as well as low.

In individual sports, rhythmic coordination is different than on a team; but there is an analogous process for top athletes in games like tennis. This can also be described as setting the rhythm of play and destroying the opponents rhythm. Bill Tilden (1950), who dominated men's tennis during the 1920s (ranked number one player in the US 11 years in a row, 8 years as world champion), wrote about his own methods: the keys were to observe carefully, to anticipate the opponent's moves and the flight of the ball, and to establish emotional domination. He would watch an opponent warming up, looking for his favorite and least-favorite shots; then he would attack his weaknesses. Tilden carefully observed the angle of the racket so that he could tell which way the ball was going even before it was hit; and he moved immediately to the spot, not where the ball would bounce, but where he could hit it with his own body in prepared position. The aim was to gain control of the back-and-forth rhythm of tennis.

Tilden commented that luck plays less of a role in tennis than in any other sport, so skill wins out consistently. But it was skill, not brute force: he disparaged the emphasis on hard-hitting serves of the younger players that he called "the California game," and was consistently able to beat them. Above all, it was a mind game: concentrating one's attention during play: "The man who keeps his mind fixed on his match at all times puts a tremendous pressure on his opponent" (Tilden 1950: 13). It is like playing an interaction ritual where the ingredients—focus of attention, shared emotional intensity, rhythmic coordination—are controlled by the winner. He relentlessly exploited the opponent's weaknesses. Against very good players, he would shift to the opposite approach, attacking their favorite moves to deflate their confidence.

Tilden illustrates Chambliss's point that dominant players do not rely on innate strength or quickness, as we witness their quantum leaps in competitive ability once they learn the winning skills and mind-set. Tilden was obsessed with tennis since age 6, but for a long time he was a klutzy player despite hanging out at a tennis club near his home (Hornblum 2017). By the time he was 26—following 20 years of sharpening his observations of what makes good tennis—he became unbeatable.

In contests between individuals or teams involving a great deal of precision, one often observes that losing teams beat themselves. They play below their normal level of competence; they miss their shots, make bad throws, fail to field a routine ball. These are often the crucial turning points in championship games or series. It has the look of being emotionally dominated, letting one's adrenaline level get out of control, so that the physiological incompetence and perceptual blurring found in violent situations also occur on the playing field. In baseball games, any particular error can be overcome, since the game is played for at least nine innings and it takes a series of successful plays by the offense (or bad plays by the defense) to move runners around the bases and score very many runs. Where games get out of hand—so far behind that the loser can't catch up—it often involves a series of errors by the team on defense. A good predictive rule is: when a team makes a series of unforced errors, it is losing its emotional solidarity, and is in a contagious spiral of rhythmic un-coordination. A cascade of errors on one side predicts losing the game.

Bodily Micro-Sociology in Violence and in Sport

This brings us to the borderline of sports and violence. In my research on the situations where violence breaks out during a game (Collins 2008: Chapter 8) I found that when players get into a fight, the side that wins the fight, goes on to win the game. Why is this the case? A fight is a dramatic instance of confrontation, an in-your-face contest over emotional domination. Most fights on the playing field are standoffs. Football players get angry at opposing blockers or at tackles at vulnerable body angles, but these scuffles rarely go beyond harmless pushing and shoving and are quickly broken up. Baseball games have a highly ritualized response to a pitcher hitting a batter with a pitch, where both teams empty their dugouts and mill around on the field, pushing and shoving usually to little effect. But when such fights have high intensity, its outcome has a strong effect on subsequent performance.

Violence is typically incompetent, all the more so when persons are in close face confrontation. We can put this in physiological terms: confrontation pumps high amounts of adrenaline. High adrenaline makes one lose fine muscle coordination as well as clear visual and auditory perception; we know from interviews after violent incidents (mostly from soldiers and police) that they typically experience time distortion, tunnel vision, blur, and temporary obliviousness to sounds (Artwohl and Christensen 1997; Klinger 2004). The same can be seen in comparing rates of breathing; at high levels of breathing and heart-beat, physical performance deteriorates and awareness of the environment blurs. No wonder soldiers and cops can fire inaccurately, or get themselves caught up in beating their targets after they have already been captured, or attack peaceful demonstrators who for the moment they cannot distinguish from the violent ones (Neville and Reicher 2011; for analysis of video evidence, see Nassauer 2019).

I have described this process in physiological terms, because we have the instrumentation to show it. But whether violence happens or not, and how it unfolds, are not primarily from physiological causes. Adrenaline is undifferentiated arousal, and it is social factors that determine whether it will come out in flight or fight. If it is fight, sheer uninhibited adrenaline release into an attack does not result in competent violence, but in a perceptual blur and clumsy use of weapons and one's own body. The most competent practitioners of violence have socially learned skills that bring their adrenaline down to a moderate level, keep their perceptions clear, and fine motor coordination intact; they also have learned how to push the opponent's adrenaline into the out-of-control zone.

The difficulty is getting one's adrenaline level just right is sometimes taken advantage of in football strategy. Recognizing that the opposing defence is likely to be especially hyped up with adrenaline at the beginning of the game, a coach can call for deceptive counter-movement plays, expecting that the defenders will over-pursue and thus be vulnerable to a cut-back pattern for a long gain. The essential skill of the professional quarterback is achieving calm and alertness, especially at the tensest moments of the game. Baseball pitchers are often successful at rhythm-breaking slow pitches when facing the most aggressive batters. There are similar examples from all sports, where the sophisticated move is to take advantage of the opponent's physiological arousal.

In violence-threatening encounters, relatively little physical damage is done unless and until emotional domination is established by one side over the other. Sheer battering at the other side does not usually produce victory; the biggest turning points, the most decisive victories and devastating defeats, happen when one side collapses emotionally and opens the way for the opponent to administer a physical beating against a demoralized and largely unresisting opponent.

Confrontational Tension/Fear in Violence and in Sport

Sports is less intense conflict than violence. But both involve a version of confrontational tension/fear. Winning and losing depend on how one finds a way around the barrier of confrontational tension/fear that inhibits successful aggression, and on using the opponent's CT/F against themselves. If no such path is found, the result is poor performance; in violence, this means an aborted fight or stalemate; in sports, it means a poorly played game on both sides.

Face-to-face violence is the most difficult kind, because it contravenes the main form of normal social interaction. Recall the basic ingredients of an interaction ritual: people are bodily assembled; they focus attention on the same thing and recognize the others are doing the same; they become caught up in a shared emotion and bodily rhythm, which strengthens all these shared processes. The result of this should be solidarity. But face-to-face conflict combines solidarity-producing elements with action at cross-purposes, attempting to impose one's will on the other against resistance. No wonder people feel tension in this situation: their nervous systems are straining to do two incompatible things once. It is this tension that generates further adrenaline, rising heartbeat, rapid breathing, and the incompetence that follows. That is why most face confrontations, however angry they may be at the beginning, empirically result in aborted violence, or are easily broken up by bystanders who intervene; or wind down after a display of incompetent violence.

Confrontational tension/fear is the barrier that prevents violence from happening, and makes it incompetent when it happens. For violence to occur, there must be pathways around this barrier (Collins 2008). To repeat a brief list:

1. *Attacking a weak victim.* This means, not just finding someone who is physically weak, but emotionally weak: a victim who is emotionally dominated. A small group attacking an isolated victim is the pattern most widely seen in riots, where a little cluster of about a half-dozen attackers beat up one opponent knocked helplessly to the ground. Also among individuals: techniques of successful robbers are finding the right moment to seize emotional domination by surprise and threatening bluster.
2. *Group cooperation in violence.* In military situations, soldiers who operate group-served weapons (like machine guns; or a team of sniper and spotter) have a much higher rate of firing and accuracy than soldiers with individual weapons. Street gangs rely on the solidarity of their blustering as a group, especially when they can isolate an intruder on their own turf.
3. *Audience-oriented violence.* This is where the confrontation takes place in front of a crowd, assembled for the purpose of seeing a fight. The fighters are face-to-face, the interactionally hardest situation, but they overcome this because much of their attention is on the crowd. The fighter who is most in sync with the crowd typically wins. Confrontational tension/fear is overcome by emotional domination provided by audience support.
4. *Distant violence.* Since the biggest problem is the tension of confronting another human being at cross-purposes, violence is easiest to carry out when it is done by artillery or aircraft, by bombs or hidden explosive devices.

5. *Avoiding confrontational tension.* By stealthy or clandestine violence, including suicide bombers and mafia assassins.

The *first* and *fourth* types are generally ruled out in sports. Games are designed to be fair fights. And they are microcosms of wars, much smaller in time and space, and pitting individuals or small groups against each other, body-to-body or face-to-face.

Sports fit the *third* type, audience-oriented violence. Sports are pseudo-wars, with varying degrees of similarity to actual violence. But sports are a spectacle designed to show an idealized form of violent conflict. Unlike most real-life violence, in sports, the opponents are selected to be evenly matched; piling-on and walkovers, typical in the real world, are considered unsporting and uninteresting, because insufficiently dramatic.

Street fights in front of a crowd manage to keep up face-to-face confrontations, because the attention of the fighters is heavily on the crowd—mainly by auditory support rather than visual contact. Even the losing fighter gets social esteem, because he or she is in the center of public attention. The basic social form of a sports event, then, is a crowd who get solidarity and emotional energy by focusing on the players; and the players who share a bond, even though antagonists, because they are the elite who are watched by the crowd. The tension that inhibits fighters in everyday life is overcome, not only because the crowd supports them in fighting, but because they have some solidarity among themselves over and above their staged antagonism.[3]

In everyday life, my data show that the attitude of a crowd toward a fight that breaks out in their midst strongly determines how long the fight will last and how much damage is done (Collins 2008: 203–204, 236). If the crowd cheers, the fight is longer and more intense; if the crowd is indifferent, the fight peters out.

The analogy in sports is how well an athlete performs when the crowd encourages him/her as a fighter for their side, or is indifferent or hostile to their performance. The pattern shows up most strongly in individual sports, where the athlete does not have the local support of team solidarity. Several incidents provide a natural experiment for what happens when a top athlete, used to having audience support, suddenly faces hostile crowds.

Tiger Woods, for many years the world's top-winning golfer, suddenly lost his touch. He was famously cool-headed especially on the tension-laden fourth day of a tournament, when most top golfers fall back, while Tiger played at his best. Now he missed his shots like everyone else, and more so. The turning point was a widely publicized domestic dispute in November 2009, when he was physically beaten by his wife, who was angry at discovering a sexual infidelity, and he crashed his car outside his home. The news became a cascade of women claiming to have had affairs with him, and commercial sponsors dropping him from their advertising contracts. As the new golf year began, formerly adulating crowds began to jeer him on the course. He fell from number 1 world ranking (which he had held almost continuously for 11 years) to number 58 in late 2011 (i.e. in the two years since his public scandal), with further ups and downs when he dropped out of the world's top 1000 golfers. Seemingly on his way to a record number of tournament victories, the once-upon-a-time "best of all time" golfer was destroyed by his public. Tiger became inconsistent, even tormented, as he repeatedly changed his swing, losing the natural approach he had developed since early childhood. In the later period, he had a series of back problems and operations, probably related to his bodily and emotional turmoil. Here again we see the pattern: suffering emotional domination precedes most physical damage.

John Rocker was a top relief pitcher, the closer for the Atlanta Braves, who won the National League pennant in 1999. Rocker was from a small town in the South and grew up in a conservative religious environment. During the off-season, a reporter for a national magazine asked if he would like to be traded to a New York team. Rocker said he would hate to play in New York City, riding on subway trains to the ballpark with drug addicts, ex-convicts, and unmarried welfare mothers, surrounded by people who don't speak English. He described the fans at the New York Mets stadium as the rowdiest in the country, throwing things at the players and yelling obscene insults. The interview was widely quoted in the media—above all in New York—and Rocker was suspended by the Commissioner of Baseball for the beginning of the 2000 season. When he resumed playing, he was booed and taunted by fans at opposing stadiums wherever he went. His pitching skills disappeared; he became wild, unable to locate the plate or get anyone out. The Braves quickly traded him; but he was never able to regain his skill as a pitcher, and was out of the league in three years.

Winning is not just a matter of sheer ability or highly-trained habits. Emotional disruption and being emotionally dominated happen even to the best performers when the audience turns against them.

Another violence-supporting technique that applies to sports is the *second* type, group-coordinated violence. This is most apparent in body-contact sports like American football or rugby. Because the teams are relatively large, they are able to provide their own internal support group. The tension of confrontation with the enemy is overcome by focus upon one's teammates. The more fine-tuned the coordination among one's own side, the less important tension is from facing the opponents. We can hypothesize that the most cool-headed performers are those who are most intensely focused on keeping up the most refined coordination on their own side.

Stealthy and clandestine violence (the *fifth* type) is prevalent in many forms of violent conflict (ranging from ambushes to suicide bombers), and is often a very successful tactic. It is relatively easy to carry out since it avoids confrontational tension, pretending that no confrontation exists until the moment of attack. Here there is a lesson for the sociology of sports, but in reverse. It is doubtful that trickery, surprise and deception win many games. Trickery generally happens so fast that it involves no emotional domination. It may win a particular point but it does not create turning points, shifts in emotional momentum. For similar reasons, Alexander the Great avoided surprise attacks and ambushes; he wanted his Macedonian army to be acknowledged as unquestionably dominant, and further resistance was useless; he did this by frontal attacks with his heavy cavalry against the place where the enemy king or commander was stationed (Arrian [150 AD] 1971; Collins 2014). Alexander's tactic was like a very forceful rugby team—since his heavy cavalry was physically superior to other troops; but he also could beat armies much bigger than his own, by breaking up their organization, essentially by frightening its commander and putting the whole thing in flight, whereupon they could easily be slaughtered. Physical domination at a key point of confrontation was combined with an effort to break down enemy organization and assert emotional domination; a short period of intense fighting leading to a walkover.

Sports without Face-to-Face Conflict

I have concentrated on sports with an attack and a defence, where emotional domination would appear to be most relevant. But there are also sports which are parallel contests (like golf, or track and field); and some sports which are skill demonstrations, like gymnastics and figure skating, scored by judges. Does the micro-sociological approach tell us anything about winning and losing in these latter kinds of sports?

Monahan (2007) interviewed judges on how they scored the performance of gymnasts. Judges are usually former gymnasts themselves, because they need to know exactly what are the sequence of moves that comprise a particular program; and they need to concentrate on details not readily visible to non-experts, such as the precise angle the gymnast holds his or her arms at a particular moment (not just the obvious differences like whether he or she sticks the landing). Moreover, these moves are happening in a fast sequence, so the judge needs to know where to look, every fraction of a second. The experienced judge can do this by imagining going through the sequence, anticipating what comes next, as if the judge were vicariously a performer. Hence the judges like best the gymnasts who perform in a good rhythm; everything flows in a palpable way, making it easier for the judge to feel what is coming next. Monahan concludes that the winning gymnast sets up a feeling of solidarity with the judge; and this is what comes out in the scores awarded.

The pattern fits interaction ritual theory: the tighter the mutual focus of attention— intersubjectivity, in this case, coming from being closely attuned on detailed bodily movements—and the stronger the common mood between gymnast and judge, the more it adds up to the kind of rhythmic entrainment that we find in high-solidarity conversations. Durkheim called it collective effervescence, and theorized that this shared rhythmic excitement results in symbolic objects that simultaneously represent an ideal and the participants in the group themselves. High rhythmic coordination and solidarity between performer and judge do not feel merely like personal sympathy, because they are perceived in terms of a collective ideal: the beautiful form of the gymnastic performance in time and space. The winning performer literally becomes the ideal, not just for the adoring fans, but above all for the judges in sync with him or her.

This account of winning in gymnastics is not merely an exposé. To regard it as a scandal that needs to be remedied by replacing human judges with more objective instrumentation would be to miss the point. Gymnastics (and similar performance-comparison contests such a figure skating) are not simply about technical precision of the movements, but above all the flow of rhythm that makes it beautiful in the same way that a piece of great music, say, Beethoven's Sixth Symphony, is beautiful. (This, too, is produced by rhythmic coordination among the instrument players in an orchestra.) The social nature of an ideal of rhythmic performance is inescapable. Monahan's analysis implies advice for aspiring gymnasts: aim not just at free-standing technical competence, but a higher level of solidarity with the judges; not by superficial smiles, but by the deeper social bonds that happen in a well-performed collective ritual. Perhaps imagining the ideal judge anticipating and mimicking one's smallest move is the way to do it.

On the negative side of the comparison, one can include technically powerful, superlative athletes like the ice skater Tonya Harding—infamous above all for her bad relationships with judges, culminating in a violent attack by Tonya's supporters on her chief rival, Nancy Kerrigan, just before the 1994 Winter Olympics.[4] Her tough working-class background did not fit the image of the sport the judges were trying to portray; and her failure to play up to them, and her defiant attitude, only made their relationships worse. Tonya did exactly what Monahan's analysis says one should not do.

Skill contests are at the opposite extreme of the continuum from team sports, where team solidarity during attack-and-defense is central. In the middle of the continuum are parallel contests such as races (but also golf), where competitors are in each other's physical presence but do not engage in attack-and-defense tactics and the emotional domination that goes with them. But there can be variation in this direction. The least amount of interpersonal interaction is where racers do not compete simultaneously but against a clock (as in most ski races), or where they are strictly required to stay in marked lanes (usually in short track races). Where they are all jostling for position on the same course, different degrees of interference may be allowed. Ancient Roman and Byzantine chariot races allowed for considerable violence in impeding each other. Bicycle races have an element of this where teams try to block rivals. Roller derbies, popular in the 1950s, featuring women skaters, played up exactly this kind of conflict, which is why these races were considered rather low-class.

Large numbers of competitors in middle-distance races frequently generate traffic jams of runners or horses. How closely these bodily contacts are judged depends not only on the rules but on the technologies of surveillance to allow judges to review recordings of the event. Two sociological comments: since the popularity of sports depends heavily upon their dramatic quality, the more technical the rule-enforcement becomes (and the more it disrupts the rhythm of the race—especially the climax of victory), the more likely it is to reduce audience enthusiasm. The 2019 Kentucky Derby is a case in point, where the race stewards spent 20 minutes examining videos before disqualifying the winning horse for interference, leaving a disgruntled audience.

A second point is that where races are influenced by traffic jams, the outcome becomes highly unpredictable. The prior track record of even the top winners can be negated by the chances of being boxed in or knocked down by competitors. The much-touted 3000-meter race between Zola Budd and Mary Decker in the 1984 Olympics is a famous example. Decker was heavily favored, as the world champion and women's record holder in the mile, 5000 and 10,000 meters; she was also a sentimental favorite because at age 26, she had yet to win an Olympic gold medal, due to various accidents. Zola Budd was controversial because at age 17 she had broken the women's world record in the 5000, but her native South Africa was under boycott by world athletic organizations and her record was not recognized. Controversy was heightened when she was granted British citizenship through family history and added to the British Olympic team. She was also famous for running bare-footed. Decker set a fast pace, running as usual from the front, but followed closely by Budd and the pack. Midway through the race, Budd passed her by running wide on the curve. As Decker struggled to regain the lead, the women's legs clashed, Budd was knocked off balance, then Decker's spiked shoes stepped on her ankle, Budd fell into Decker's path, got stepped on again, Decker fell to the curb and out of the race. Zola Budd regained her feet and continued to lead for a short time, but faded to 7th place. The collisions eliminated both champions, Decker seemingly out of frustration at her string of bad luck, Budd probably because she was knocked out of her rhythm and made self-conscious rather than single-minded.

The uncertainty posed by traffic jams on the track is part of the appeal of horse racing. Despite all the records of previous performance available, the best horse does not always win; and that uncertainty is a chief ingredient of gambling. Sports are not just a "moral equivalent" of war; they are constructed to be an emotionally attractive substitute.

The Micro-Sociology of Sports as a Laboratory

The sociology of sports promises insights for other kinds of sociologists. It is a good place to study the dynamics of solidarity, both at its height, and when it fails and breaks down. In sports, there is a growing instrumentation that taps many of the micro-dimensions: we can analyze the degree of coordination among body rhythms. We can look more carefully at eye gaze and intersubjectivity, both between teammates and opponents. The audio dimension here has not been much explored, but we can compare the rhythms and emotional tones that come through visual and auditory channels. There will be more to learn from instrumentation on breathing patterns and heartbeat (some of this is being done by the military). And there is nothing to prevent us from combining all these measures with interviewing the athletes themselves, since we have some theoretical guidance for what kinds of details we want to ask them about.

Here we study in detail the micro-interactional processes of social emotions, about energy ups and downs, about winning and losing. For micro-sociology, sports is a research frontier.

Warfare operates on a much larger level, and has much more extensive problems with logistics and attrition. War also produces much more severe physical damage. But the central pressure of confrontational tension/fear is not fear of death, but the tension of action at cross-purposes to human hard-wiring for rhythmic entrainment. Sports reveal the emotional core of battle.

Notes

1. See "What Made the Greatest Coach in Any Sport?" http://sociological-eye.blogspot.com/2018/12/ for Wooden's record compared to other top winning coaches in various sports. We are concerned here with team sports that have offense and defense, those which most closely fit "a moral equivalent of war." I will discuss below whether patterns are different in sports without defensive tactics.
2. Unlike American college teams, the Oxford and Cambridge boat teams are not restricted to undergraduates, and do not race in a yearly season of meets. The boat crew for this event represents the university as a whole, and can include faculty, medical doctors, scientists, as well as students. De Rond was himself a member of the Cambridge team.
3. This suggests a testable hypothesis: would a boxing match, held entirely without an audience, but under TV cameras, have a different rhythm and intensity? I would predict more clinching and fewer solid blows.
4. The 2017 film, *I Tonya*, provides an accurate picture of her career.

References

Arrian. [ca. 150 AD] 1971. *Campaigns of Alexander*. New York: Penguin Books.

Artwohl, Alexis, and Loren W. Christensen. 1997. *Deadly Force Encounters*. Boulder, CO: Paladin Press.

Chambliss, Daniel F. 1989. "The Mundanity of Excellence." *Sociological Theory* 7: 70–86.

Collins, Randall. 2008. *Violence: A Micro-Sociological Theory*. Princeton, NJ: Princeton University Press.

Collins, Randall. 2014. "What Made Alexander Great?" Available at: http://sociological-eye.blogspot.com/2014/02/what-made-alexander-great.html.

Hornblum, Allen M. 2017. *American Colossus: Big Bill Tilden and the Creation of Modern Tennis*. Lincoln, NE: University of Nebraska Press.

King, Anthony, and Mark de Rond. 2011. "Boat Race: Rhythm and the Possibility of Collective Performance." *British Journal of Sociology*, 62: 565–585.

Klinger, David. 2004. *Into the Kill Zone: A Cop's Eye View of Deadly Force*. San Francisco: Jossey-Bass.

Monahan, Kerry. 2007. "Micro-Sociological Coordination of Gymnasts and Judges." Unpublished paper, Department of Sociology, University of Pennsylvania.

Nassauer, Anne. 2019. *Situational Breakdowns: Understanding Protest Violence and Other Surprising Outcomes*. New York: Oxford University Press.

Neville, F. G. and Reicher, S. D. 2011. "The Experience of Collective Participation: Shared Identity, Relatedness and Emotionality." *Contemporary Social Science* 6: 377–396.

Tilden, William T. 1950. *How to Play Better Tennis: A Complete Guide to Technique and Tactics*. New York: Simon & Schuster.

Wacquant, Loïc. 2004. *Body and Soul: Notes of an Apprentice Boxer*. Oxford: Oxford University Press.

Wooden, John, and Steve Jamison. 1997. *Wooden: A Lifetime of Observations and Reflections On and Off the Court*. New York: McGraw-Hill.

Chapter 10

Battle Dynamics

Victory and Defeat

Introduction

There have been three main theories of military victory:

1. *Material resources*, sometimes referred to as force ratios. Here victory goes to the side that has more troops, and more and better weapons. Since resources have to be brought into action, a related component is logistics, and further back in the causal chain, economic capacity of a society. Material resource theories emphasize both immediate preponderance of forces on the battlefield, and long-term resources for a war. Over longer time periods, these are theories of attrition, wearing down enemy resources until the bigger and better-supplied force wins.
2. *Maneuver*. Victory comes through movement of forces; the side with greater speed or surprise disrupts the enemy and prevents it from using its forces effectively or even from responding at the point of attack. Through maneuver, a smaller force can defeat a much larger one, and major victories can be won with relatively few casualties on the winning side.
3. *Morale*, variously referred to as élan, bravery, or heroism. Victory happens when fighters impose their will on their opponents, fighting harder, more fiercely, and resolutely. In contrast to (1), which is material, rational, and calculable, (3) is considered to be distinctively human, harder to explain, but palpably real in the moment of battle. It is sometimes described as having better quality troops, implying that it is a long-term attribute, although some theories invoke situational conditions—immediate social processes. Tolstoy ([1869] 2005), describing the Napoleonic wars but applying his own observations as an officer in the Crimean War, argued that the morale of the common soldiers outweighs both (1) and (2), the province of generals and their plans. Napoleon famously declared that, in battle, morale outweighs material factors by three to one. Military doctrine, incorporating both factors, holds that to guarantee success, an attacking force should

DOI: 10.4324/9781003245629-14

outweigh its opponent by a factor of three to one (i.e. either in forces or in morale). Élan is manifested at the point of attack and repulse, and thus in direct frontal assault, in contrast to (2), which largely avoids prolonged confrontation.

The three theories, often presented as mutually exclusive, imply each other at various points, although differing greatly in emphasis. Maneuver ultimately comes down to some fighting, and hence requires some moment of élan; and maneuver's greatest success is often regarded as breaking through into the enemy's logistics lines, thereby disrupting the flow of material resources. Conversely, material resource superiority can take account of maneuver by persisting longer and forcing a war of attrition. This was the strategy of General Grant in the American Civil War, in which the North had over three times the resources of the South, while the South had more trained officers (initially) and better knowledge of local terrain, which resulted in better maneuver and élan.

Popular history, journalism, and political rhetoric extol yet another theory: Leadership—having a better general—is the main determinant of victory. However, military leaders operate through the main processes of the model; some are masters of maneuver; some induce particularly strong imposing of will, both on one's own troops and on the enemy; some are good at logistics and the organization of large forces. All generals must address all three components to a degree; Napoleon was considered masterful at all three. Tolstoy, in contrast, insisted that the crucial condition of victory or defeat was endogenous to the short-term processes on the battlefield—a position supported by micro-sociological analysis of violence (Collins 2008). We will be in better condition to understand the empirical realities of "leadership" if we see it through the lens of the dynamic model.

Technology is sometimes regarded as a separate theory of military superiority, and advanced technology is held to outweigh all other conditions. US strategic planning and budgeting since the 1940s have emphasized leading all potential opponents in technological innovation. Since the 1990s, it has been held that precision-guided weapons, sensor systems, satellite communications, and computers are creating the most profound change in the history of warfare (Hammes 2004; McIvor 2005). The extreme claim is that Clausewitzian friction has finally been overcome, and thus the causes of battle victory shift to a new theoretical perspective. But I will argue that technology operates through the same basic components of material resources, morale, and maneuver. The theory of military technological innovation has to be assessed as a further series of inputs to the basic model. I will provide this at the end of the chapter. At that point, we will be in a position to better understand the sources of Clausewitzian friction and how much of it can be eliminated.

The Basic Model: Material Resources, Maneuver and Morale, Organizational Breakdown

I present the theory in the form of a flow chart. First, we view the multiple causes in a sequence as they play out in time (Figure 10.1); next, the full model adding feedback loops (Figure 10.2). After this comes a sub-model for attrition (Figure 10.3); and an overview of how technological innovation affects the multiple causes of battle dynamics (Figure 10.4).

Figure 10.1 presents the central components of the model. It is not as complicated as it looks at first glance. There are two main causal paths, from left to right: (1) the material path of resources and damages; (2) a path combining morale and maneuver—the main argument here is that morale is the most important input for maneuver.

At the top of the flow chart, MATERIAL RESOURCES are mobilized by LOGISTICS, to bring force to the point of ASSAULT; this leads to CASUALTIES. At the bottom of the chart, MORALE leads both to intensity of ASSAULT, and also to MANEUVER; assault and maneuver jointly determine ORGANIZATIONAL BREAKDOWN. The two paths come together to determine BATTLE VICTORY OR DEFEAT.

The chief peculiarity of the model is that organizational breakdown is more important than the material force of assault—sheer firepower delivered—in causing casualties. It is after an army has broken down organizationally that it suffers most of its casualties, and not primarily through sheer physical battering. Here military combat parallels the pattern of small-scale micro-sociology of violent interactions (Collins 2008). And in the next steps of the causal chain: both casualties and organizational breakdown determine BATTLE VICTORY OR DEFEAT, but breakdown is the stronger condition.

At the upper-right of the flow chart are two additional variables, ATTRITION and WAR VICTORY/DEFEAT. Attrition is distinguished from casualties because there are more ways to lose troops and equipment besides casualties; as we shall see later in Figure 10.3, several different paths besides enemy firepower cause losses. BATTLE VICTORY/DEFEAT is short-term; WAR VICTORY/DEFEAT is long-term, and accumulates both from battles and from other factors, that I have simplified here to attrition.

Throughout the model, all variables are in terms of relative standing of both sides in a war.[1] For instance, material resources are always expressed as relative advantage or disadvantage to the enemy; level of assault is relative amount of firepower compared to what the enemy delivers; etc. This has the important implication that *an army does not have to operate at a very high level, but only higher than its enemy.* In Clausewitzian terms, both armies suffer friction, but the one that undergoes less friction wins.

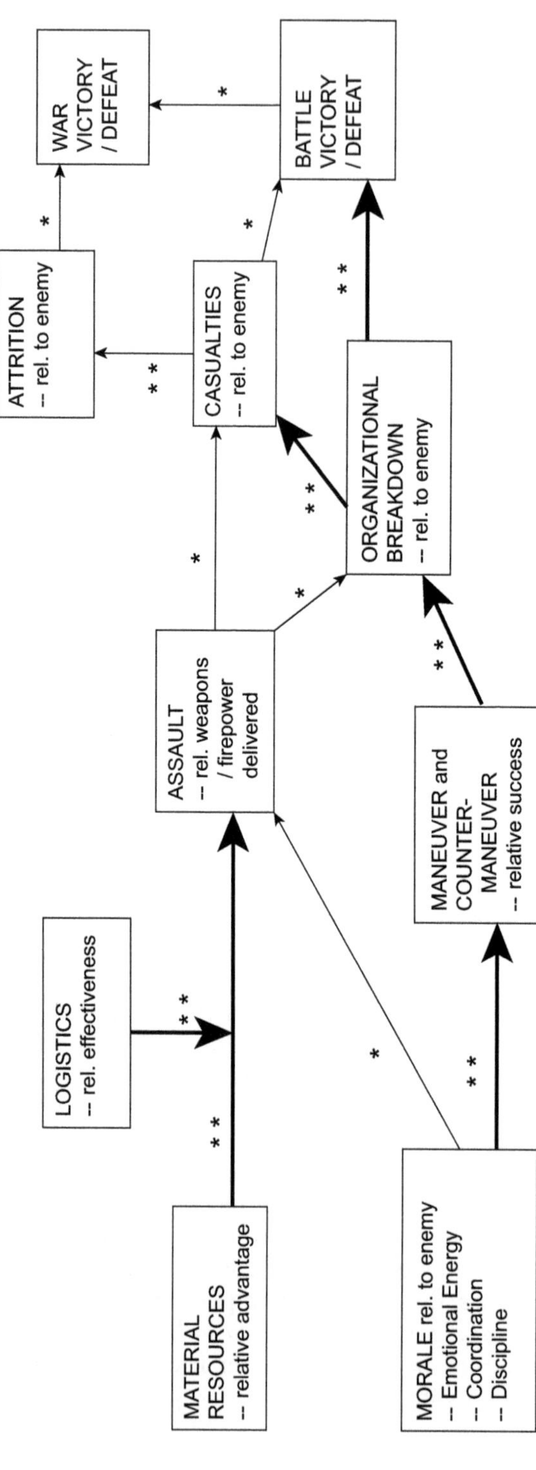

Figure 10.1 Battle victory and defeat: basic model

Notes: ** = strong causal path; * = moderate causal path.

Consider now the upper pathway starting with MATERIAL RESOURCES. These are the numbers of troops and their equipment. To bring them to the battlefield and the point of attack requires LOGISTICS, which again has a relative level of effectiveness compared to the enemy. Some resources are always used up in logistics; and accidents, traffic problems, the speed and coordination of movement (or lack thereof) subtract some proportion of material resources by the time it reaches the point of attack. ASSAULT—i.e. firepower delivered sufficiently accurately on target—results in the material destruction of violence: CASUALTIES suffered by each side, in troops killed and wounded, and in loss of equipment. Firepower is a term of convenience; the model is general and encompasses all other use of weapons, including pre-modern ones.

So far, the model is straightforward and commonsensical. It is sheer slug-it-out with victory going to the more richly supplied army and the big battalions. The only complication is the effectiveness of logistics, the comparatively banal side of combat that nevertheless tends to prove crucial, at least in battle campaigns that are more than brief and local (Van Creveld 1977).

Turn now to the lower line of causal flow. MORALE, again relative to the enemy, is made up of a number of components. It includes emotional energy (EE), a continuum ranging from feelings of confidence, enthusiasm, and initiative at the high end, down through foreboding, depression, and passivity at the low end. EE can exist at the level of the top command (highly energetic and aggressively confident generals, such as Alexander, Napoleon, and Robert E. Lee); at the level of the officer corps in general, or its subcomponents; and at the level of ordinary soldiers. The strength of the modern US military is considered to be in the high level of initiative taken by NCOs and junior officers, a quality also found in the German army in WWI and WWII (Shils and Janowitz 1948; King 2013). In contrast, many Third World armies are considered to be very weak at the NCO level, because of excessive subservience to hierarchy. As we shall see, feedback loops from combat events affect EE in intense short-run moods, which have very strong consequences for victory and defeat.

MORALE includes discipline, the extent to which troops and the chain of command obey orders; and coordination, the degree that the different components, both within and across units, act together smoothly, or are out of synch and mutually disrupting. Here I depart from the narrower concept of morale as fighting élan. An effective fighting force might not be very fierce, but have very strong discipline to obey orders. Or it might not be very respectful to authority, but have a high capability of acting together in battle. Here I will lump all of these together as social processes—as contrasted with material conditions—that set off a series of consequences in the conduct of battle.

MORALE, together with MATERIAL RESOURCES delivered through LOGISTICS, jointly determine ASSAULT. I propose that the strength of the upper (material) pathway is greater; the sheer volume of firepower delivered is more strongly determined by the material flow of armaments and munitions than by troop morale. This may be over-simplified; troops with high emotional energy, and/or coordination, and/or discipline may fire their weapons at a higher rate compared to troops lower in these social qualities.

The most important thing that flows from MORALE is MANEUVER. This includes counter-maneuver: the response of one side to the opponent's maneuver. Sometimes the response is inadequate, in which case the maneuvering forces produce a breakthrough or at least bring superior forces to bear on a point where they gain a local victory through a higher level of assault. Sometimes the second-mover successfully blocks the maneuver, resulting in a renewed stalemate; on occasion, the second-mover caps the first maneuver with an even more striking counter-maneuver. Maneuver generates a lot of friction, and thus is hard to carry out; many maneuvers fail because the troops cannot move fast enough, lose their way, become uncoordinated, etc. This friction is overcome by factors from the MORALE box. Strong discipline is one of them. The enthusiasm of sheer emotional energy also can enable an army to maneuver successfully.

An example of successful counter-maneuver is the celebrated battle of Chancellorsville, in 1863. The Northern General Hooker made a successful encircling movement around the west end of Lee's line. Lee responded by sending part of his army on an even more extended circling movement around the west end of Hooker's line, taking his army from behind. The result was heavy casualties and breakdown of the Union forces and an ignominious retreat by a larger army in the face of a smaller one (McPherson 2005). It is also an example of victory through strong discipline: Confederate General Stonewall Jackson, who carried out the flanking counter-move at Chancellorsville, was a ferocious disciplinarian who treated his troops harshly but made them move considerably faster than other troops.

In military history, maneuver is frequently considered a matter of brilliant strategy; but when successful it often has an element of improvisation, rapid seizing of opportunities, and these are results of MORALE. Aggressive initiative falls within the definition of emotional energy. This applies above all to the field commanders, but there also has to be high EE among the troops, as well as coordination and discipline if the movement is to be carried out. Strategic brilliance is more in the social conditions of situational flow and execution than in detached strategic planning. Most American Civil War victories did not result from strategies actually carried out as planned (Griffith 1989; McPherson 2005). Strategy does not need to be modeled separately.

The most important result of MANEUVER is to bring about ORGANIZATIONAL BREAKDOWN. More precisely, both sides need to maintain organizational coherence; the variable could be called that, but I have put it in the negative, to highlight the importance of an organization breaking apart, as the key to victory and defeat. ORGANIZATIONAL BREAKDOWN is relative. Both sides are always breaking down to a degree, under the stress of combat. Both are suffering Clausewitzian friction, and the more they attempt to move from one place to another, to disassemble one formation and reassemble it somewhere else, the more friction they risk. Thus, both combat—the physical destruction of ASSAULT—and MANEUVER tend to break one's own organization down. Offsetting this is the extent to which the enemy's organization breaks down. (ORGANIZATIONAL BREAKDOWN should be read as a positive quantity for the side which has the advantage.)

At Chancellorsville, as in most clear-cut victories, most of the casualties taken by the loser happened after its organization had broken down; disoriented troops were unable to fight back, and took many casualties from forces that suffered few. (For evidence of this process, including both ancient and modern battles, see Collins 2008: 104–111.) Thus, the path from ORGANIZATIONAL BREAKDOWN to CASUALTIES is stronger than the path from ASSAULT to CASUALTIES. There is also a path that leads from ASSAULT to ORGANIZATIONAL BREAKDOWN, but this is weaker than the path leading in from MANEUVER.

This point is so central that the entire theory might be called *the organizational breakdown theory of battle*. Social processes are central to holding an army together as an organization. When social cohesion is high—not just sufficient but enthusiastic—it can result in successful tactical maneuvers. If these catch the enemy's timing off, they can lead to rapid turning points, where one organization deteriorates rapidly, and the other battens on it to destroy it physically. Without turning points where the organizational coherence of the two opponents diverges rapidly, battles are mostly matters of attrition, either stalemate or slow gains and losses without decisive consequences.

This is so even though élan can also be channeled into sheer frontal assault. Napoleon and Lee were sometimes successful at this; but they also failed—Napoleon at Waterloo, Lee at Gettysburg—since frontal attack on a prepared defensive position costs very high casualties when high-firepower weapons are used (Biddle 2004). Thus, although MORALE can flow directly into ASSAULT, its more powerful effect is when it flows into MANEUVER.

The biggest victories tend to come about via the lower path in Figure 10.1. Left to itself, the upper path has few decisive results unless one side is greatly superior to the other in resources (well beyond the 3-to-1 rule of thumb). On the right side of Figure 10.1, ORGANIZATIONAL

BREAKDOWN has a strong path to BATTLE VICTORY/DEFEAT, while the latter has only a moderate path from CASUALTIES. What is considered a victory or defeat is a social construction of the participants themselves. In decisive battles, there is general agreement on both sides as to the outcome, and the publicly announced label is not contested (although credit and blame may be). Some battles are indecisive, a stalemate with no victor announced. What determines the amount of consensus is chiefly the feeling of emotional dominance. Victory and defeat are, above all, emotional conditions. Physical destruction contributes to a degree, but jointly with the more powerful causal lines flowing from morale and organizational coherence.

At Chancellorsville, all three of the usual criteria favored the Confederates: one side was routed and felt itself beaten; the same side took the most casualties; the victors ended up in possession of the ground. Sometimes the criteria diverge: an army can take heavy casualties and still be regarded as victorious, because the other side is emotionally dominated, one side exultant and the other depressed; one organization more broken down than the other, even though the victor took a great deal of physical battering in bringing about this result. An example is Grant's victory at Shiloh in 1862, where the North lost 13,000 to the South's 10,000, but nevertheless repelled an initially successful surprise attack (McPherson 2005). Moreover, holding ground is not a necessary criterion of victory. Stonewall Jackson's campaign in the Shenandoah Valley in 1862 was considered a brilliant series of victories through fast-moving maneuver, although he never stayed to occupy the battlefields where he defeated the enemy (McPherson 2005). In some routs, the defeated army is so badly disorganized that it does not take very high casualties. An example is the German *Blitzkrieg* victory in France in 1940, where so many French troops were encircled and captured that the physical casualty rate was low relative to the size of forces (Keegan 1997).

The main point of this analysis is so important that I will repeat it for emphasis: *Clausewitzian friction is everywhere in combat.* Ordinary logistics is subject to wear and tear, accidents, maintenance problems, not to mention enemy attacks; supply chains and coordination schedules get broken; firepower and morale suffer. Maneuver is superior to frontal assault when it can be carried out, but maneuver adds its own sources of friction and risks organizational breakdown on its own. Historians have paid more attention to the famous victories through successful maneuver than to maneuvers which failed.[2]

The key point is that *both sides have some degree of organizational breakdown in battle. The winning side only has to break down less than the enemy.* Big victories happen when the ratio of organizational breakdowns between the sides reaches a turning point, where one side's breakdown cascades into emotional demoralization, rendering them incapable of doing nothing but retreat or surrender. Battle, like team sports, is a contest of breaking down the opponent's rhythm while preserving one's own.

Short-Term and Long-Term Feedback from Battle Processes

Consider now Figure 10.2, beginning with the lower pathways.

Here I have added causal arrows feeding into the relative success of MANEUVER and into ORGANIZATIONAL BREAKDOWN, from *accidents and local conditions*. This indicates chance can play a role in affecting how successfully the movement of troops is carried out, including local terrain, weather, and other incalculable events and conditions. These were omitted from Figure 10.1 in order to present the basic model more clearly. Technically, these can be entered into the model by multiplying each path by a random fraction. The role of chance variations is important in fitting real historical conditions, since otherwise a model dominated by positive feedback loops would make initial advantages cumulate inexorably without the reversals so often seen in real battles.

ORGANIZATIONAL BREAKDOWN feeds back into MORALE; army units that have made an enemy break down feel more confident and enthusiastic (EE). Conversely, an army that has been broken down has plummeting morale—low confidence and energy; all the worse when the disciplined chain of command is weakened and coordination suffers, even after the battle is over and organization is nominally restored.

MORALE and ORGANIZATIONAL BREAKDOWN appear to be two boxes containing the same thing. They differ in their placement in the time-sequence: ORGANIZATIONAL BREAKDOWN is the moment of combat and its immediate aftermath; MORALE is the more long-term condition of the army. These should be measured separately.[3]

Taken in isolation from other factors, ORGANIZATIONAL BREAKDOWN (read as a positive quantity for the side that has the advantage) feeds back into MORALE. The successful army gains emotional resources that will make it better fighters in the future; the broken army tends to reproduce the conditions for future defeats. For example, the long series of successes by Lee's Army of Northern Virginia during 1862 and early 1863 gave it energy and aggressiveness, even though its material logistics were poor and it was generally outgunned on the battlefield (McPherson 2005).

But these processes do not happen in isolation. An organizationally-broken army can be replaced or reorganized, given sufficient material resources and logistics. After each of the major defeats suffered by the Northern armies at the hands of Lee and Confederate generals in 1861–1863, they would withdraw, replace officers and men, and eventually come back in sufficient strength to where their superior numbers began to tell. After late 1863, morale in Union armies tended to rise. This was a period of rising

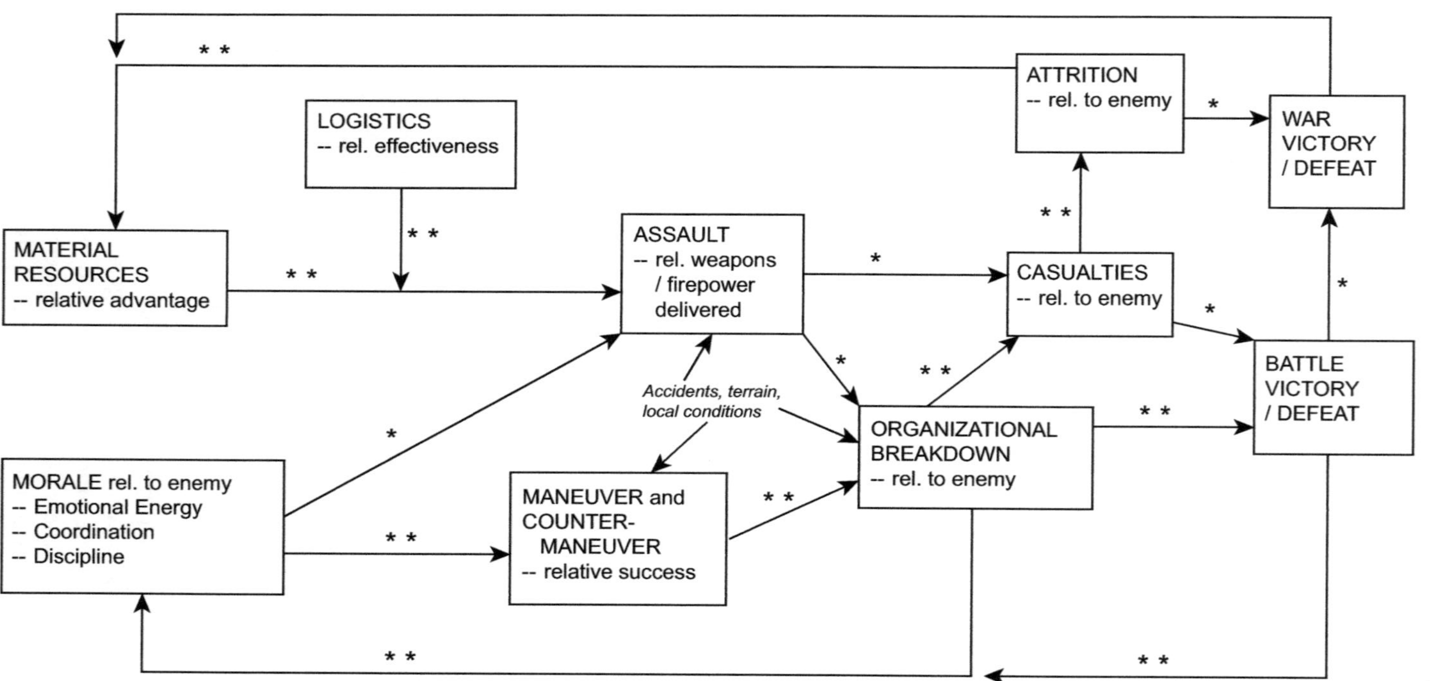

Figure 10.2 Battle victory and defeat: feedbacks

Notes: ** = strong causal path; * = moderate causal path.

proportion of victories, although casualty levels in the Union army were very high (Long 1971). This implies that victory has a stronger effect on raising morale than casualties do in depressing it. Evidence calculated from desertion rates following battle victories or defeats with varying levels of casualties supports the point (Denig 2010; Noe 2010).

There is also a feedback from BATTLE VICTORY/DEFEAT to MORALE; this is in addition to the loop from ORGANIZATIONAL BREAKDOWN, since there is another path leading into BATTLE VICTORY/DEFEAT from the level of CASUALTIES, which also affects the intensity of victory/defeat. The intensity of victory and its effect on morale can be independent of organizational breakdown inflicted. For example, Sherman's march through Georgia in late 1864 involved little fighting. Since the Northern army had an overwhelming force ratio over the enemy, 6 to 1, the enemy did not disintegrate so much as avoid battle, while Sherman's troops engaged in massive destruction of material resources. This victory was largely through the material pathway. But this victory too—widely celebrated when Sherman reached the sea—greatly enhanced Northern morale, and depressed the Southerners, large numbers of whom surrendered soon after (McPherson 2005). Here, the inability of the Southern army to prevent its material resources being destroyed, generated a strong sense of emotional dominance.

Consider now the upper feedback loops in Figure 10.2. ATTRITION leads directly into WAR VICTORY/DEFEAT, independent of the path from BATTLE VICTORY/DEFEAT. (ATTRITION relative to the enemy is read as a positive quantity for the side that has the advantage.) Losing a war is not merely a matter of losing battles; one can also lose because attrition mounts, so that resources are run down and the army is no longer capable of fighting. Lee's army in Virginia continued to win most of its battles, even after the disastrous defeat at Gettysburg in July 1863, but eventually gave up when its material resources became too palpably overmatched. Lee's only major defeats happened when he went on offensive campaigns into the North, at Antietam, Maryland, in 1862, and Gettysburg, Pennsylvania, in 1863. On his home turf, Lee continued to fight a series of defensive battles during 1864, in which he almost always inflicted heavier casualties on the enemy, kept possession of the battlefield, and repelled the enemy. But Grant, pursuing a strategy of attrition, kept bringing increasing numbers of troops and advancing obliquely toward the Confederate capital. Finally, in 1865, Lee's numbers and logistics were reduced so low that a small defeat that blocked him from his remaining supply lines forced him to surrender (McPherson 2005).

And even before a war ends, ATTRITION feeds back into MATERIAL RESOURCES. For an army taking casualties, this is a negative feedback, running down one's resources; but the overall balance between the opponents depends on the level of resources replenished by each side minus the amount of attrition each suffers. Attrition on some occasions can become a positive feedback for the other side, in the case where an army captures supplies or military equipment from the enemy.[4]

Figure 10.2 adds another long-term feedback, from WAR VICTORY/DEFEAT to MATERIAL RESOURCES. Distinct from whatever destruction and capture takes place during the war, the aftermath of victory can involve annexing territory, or stripping conquered territory of its assets. Here we shift to the geopolitical realm of long-term processes, whereby war victors gain cumulative advantage that makes them stronger for the next war, and the defeated lose assets that increases their chances of future defeats.

Sometimes the resources gained or lost are not just equipment and supplies but troops themselves. In ancient wars of the Persians, Macedonians, and Romans, and in ancient and medieval wars in China, Korea, and Mongolia, conquering armies generally absorbed defeated bodies of troops into their own armies. This way of generating a positive feedback loop of forces has largely disappeared since the rise of nationalist ideologies.

The Link between Battle Dynamics and Geopolitics

Battle dynamics determine victory and defeat in the short run, and in the somewhat longer run, war victory and defeat. As noted, winning or losing a war feeds back, positively or negatively, into a society's pool of material resources. Geopolitical theory is even more macro and long-term, explaining the shifting patterns of the territorial power of states (Collins 1978; 1995; Turchin 2003). The model of battle dynamics can be nested inside a larger geopolitical model. A composite model would add links from such macro factors as territorial size and population, natural resources, geographical position and distance from other state regions, flowing into the main variables on the left side of Figure 10.1. Since material resources enter battle dynamics by being transformed into specifically military resources (trained soldiers, weapons, munitions, transport, etc.), a sub-model for the strength of the economy in each state would be needed; this would include not only the extent of market relations, and the level of industrial production, but also financial structures, and the fiscal apparatus of the state.[5] Hobson (1997) shows that during World War I, England had a more effective system of taxation than Germany, which in turn was more effective than Russia; hence their material resources were extracted for military purposes at different rates, affecting overall performance in the war.

A full-scale model linking geopolitics with battle dynamics would be quite complex. As a pragmatic matter of theory building and testing, only segments of this can be managed at any one time.

Reversals and Negative Feedbacks

Modeling battle processes solely in terms of positive feedback loops carries the danger of historically unrealistic runaway processes, in which small initial advantages expand cumulatively without possibility of reversal. Greater realism is introduced in four ways:

1. Conditions of weather, terrain, and other accidents can be modeled as random variations in the strength of the causal pathways. How strong the role of chance is could be tested by fitting models with large or small random components.
2. Exogenous conditions enter into the model (although not explicitly indicated in Figures 10.1–10.3). Most importantly, MATERIAL RESOURCES can be replenished, and one side may have deeper reserves than the other. Thus, in WWII, German resources were eventually used up on the Eastern Front despite initial victories, whereas Soviet resources from deep in its territory were eventually mobilized, turning the tide into a cumulative process in the opposite direction.
3. A negative feedback loop is introduced from BATTLE VICTORY/DEFEAT to LOGISTICS. More specifically, when victory leads to territorial conquest, the advancing army takes on greater logistics costs, whereas the retreating army reduces its logistics costs as it shortens its distance from its resource heartland. This was an important process in the Russian civil war of 1918–1920, where both the White and Red Armies alternated in making long advances into enemy territory, advances which were stopped and reversed by the difficulties of long logistics lines (Klusemann 2010). This feedback loop operates in addition to other pathways in the model; the Red Army eventually won, in this instance, as its level of resources came to outweigh those of the Whites.
4. Territorial conquest produces a negative feedback loop in an additional way: alien troops engaging in resource-stripping, looting, and humiliating the conquered population tend to enrage the losing side. Thus, a more complex version of Figure 10.2 would add a negative path from BATTLE VICTORY/DEFEAT to MORALE. Morale of the defeated army rises following these atrocities, increasing their desire for vengeance. Morale of the victorious army also tends to fall, if it relies heavily on looting, since this reduces army discipline and makes soldiers more concerned with their material fortune (this is described both by Tolstoy for the French army occupying Moscow in 1812, and by Klusemann for the 1917–1920 civil war in Russia between the Red and White Armies). However, this negative feedback loop appears to have a distinct time-pattern; morale swings from response to atrocities operate in the medium run, perhaps up to one year; but if conquered

territory is held for a long period (perhaps 5 years) resignation and loss of morale set in. These time-patterns can be more precisely measured.

The Attrition Sub-Model

Figure 10.3 gives a partial model to make clear the pathways that flow into ATTRITION. Casualties caused by the enemy are generally the strongest but are not the only source of attrition of troops and equipment. An additional, moderate source comes from MANEUVER. Troops became exhausted on rapid marches, drowned, hurt in traffic accidents, get lost or find opportunities to desert the field of battle. Some are shot or imprisoned by their own officers or battle police. In pre-mechanized history, horses died, just as vehicles break down or collide. Most routes of maneuver are strewn with casualties and debris.

ATTRITION is also fed by LOGISTICS. On the whole, logistical transfer of supplies and equipment is like MANEUVER, subject to the same problems although usually with less hurry (suggesting that the rate of attrition during maneuver is higher, per volume moved). Traffic accidents cause a considerable portion of lives and injuries; estimates are on the order of 15–20 percent of all casualties (Keegan 1976; Collins 2008); the era of helicopter transport continues to keep this ratio high, since these are intrinsically dangerous forms of transportation, especially under military conditions, where flight schedules are ad hoc and easily disrupted. Moving munitions is a particularly dangerous source of attrition via logistics; a substantial number of non-combat casualties come from accidents in transporting explosives, or fires or other accidents in storage areas. A major danger of combat is not simply the enemy; the combination of large numbers of heavy equipment and lethal weaponry creates the potential for very destructive accidents. So-called friendly fire, when troops are hit by their own forces, is included in the path from ASSAULT to CASUALTIES. Not all combat casualties are caused by the enemy; the inaccuracy of fire generally causes a modest but relatively constant proportion of losses inflicted by one's own side, whether soldiers are accidentally shot, either by oneself or by fellow troops. These are another result of the high emotional stress of combat, and may be especially high during organizational breakdowns.

Under the heading of logistics we may add another source of attrition that was extremely common until the twentieth century: the hazards of camp life between battles created conditions of poor sanitation, exposure to weather, crowded quarters, and poor supplies of food and water that caused many losses through sickness. Such losses have become uncommon in modern armies with abundant material resources. The underlying issue is to deliver sufficient supplies of life-sustaining necessities to troops in the field. During a defeat, even a modern army may find these conditions unavailable, as in the huge losses that occurred in the Soviet,

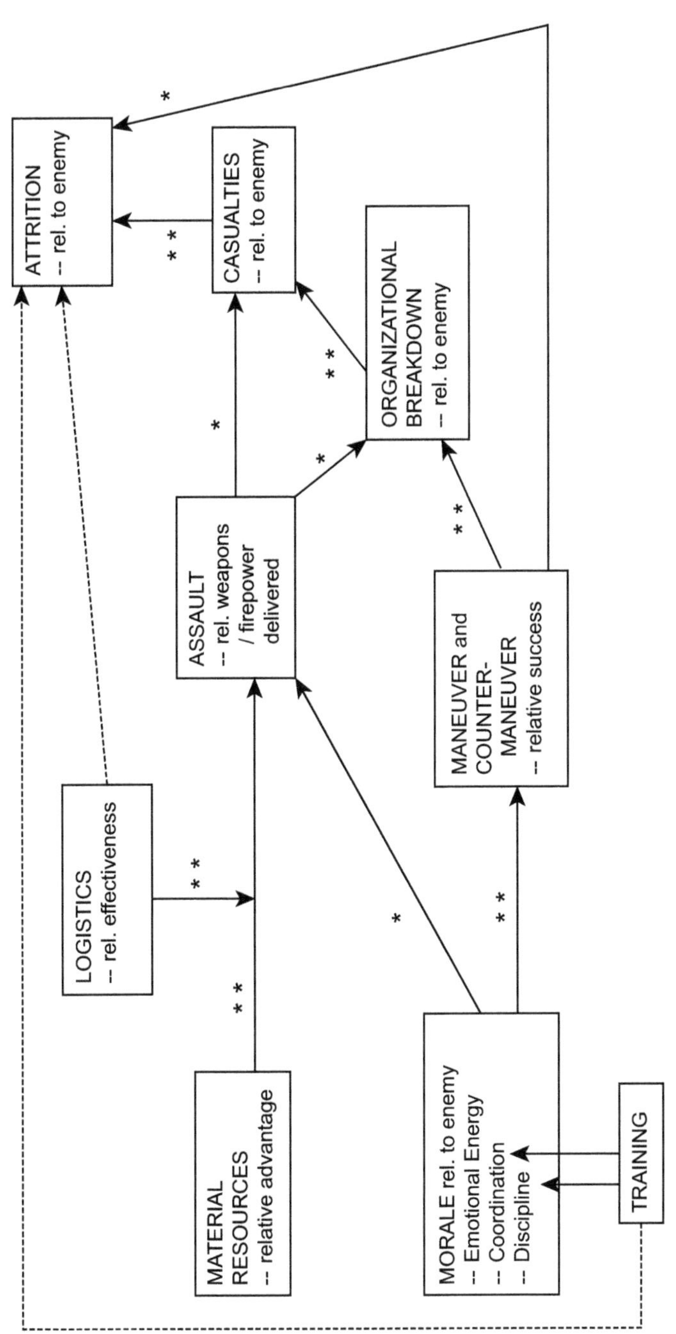

Figure 10.3 Attrition: full model

Notes: ** = strong causal path; * = moderate causal path; --- = weak causal path.

German, and Chinese armies during World War II through logistics shortages (Keegan 1997).[6]

Finally, there is a non-negligible path from TRAINING to ATTRITION. Modern armies place great emphasis on training to produce coordination and discipline; thus casualties here fall under the basic process of building up the MORALE box. A proportion of troops are injured and killed during training, for roughly the same reasons that attrition happens during logistics operations.

Innovations in Military Technology

Figure 10.4 models the portion of the basic processes that are affected by technological innovation. Technology is a long-term factor, not much affected by short-term battlefield feedbacks.

Throughout the twentieth century, and with increasing emphasis from World War II onwards, military and political leaders have stressed the crucial importance of having a technological advantage over the enemy. This was dramatized particularly by German V-1 and V-2 rockets, and by the development of nuclear weapons, leading to the tendency to regard possession of the ultimately powerful weapon as overriding all other conditions of victory and defeat. Superiority of fighter aircraft (easily measured by ratios of air combat victories to losses in numbers of aircraft destroyed) also added to the obsession with technological superiority of weaponry.

By the 1990s, US military doctrine was emphasizing technological innovation transforming all aspects of weaponry as well as coordination,

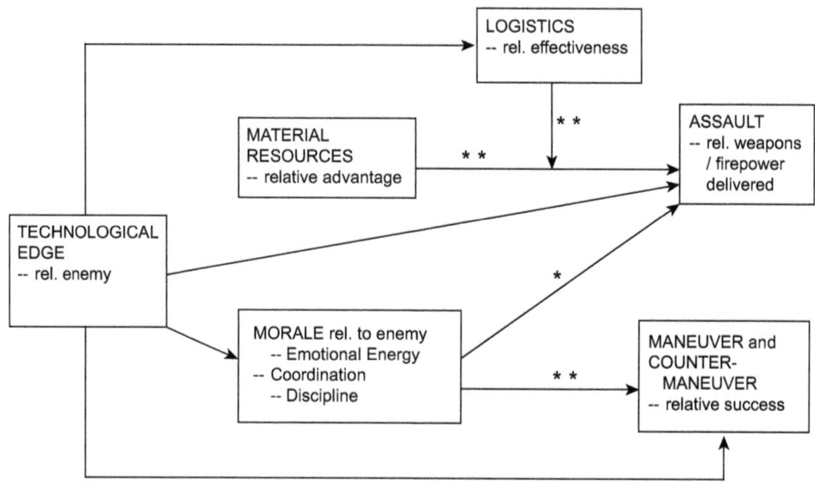

Figure 10.4 Technological innovation

Notes: ** = strong causal path; * = moderate causal path.

command and control: precision-guided munitions; targeting by lasers, infra-red heat signatures, and computer-processed optics; surveillance and precise geographical positioning from satellites and other aerial vehicles; and the use of computers for fire control and organizational processes. It was argued that these technological changes amounted to a "Revolution in Military Affairs" (RMA), so sweeping that the principles of warfare were now changed, outdating all previous military doctrine (McIvor 2005).

Nevertheless, inspection of Figures 10.1–10.3 suggests that technological innovation can be modeled in general terms that do not require changing any of the basic components of the flow-charts. Historically there has always been a technological aspect to warfare. This can be modeled, abstractly, as a single factor, TECHNOLOGICAL EDGE. Like other factors in the battle dynamics model, it is a relative quantity: the relationship between the effectiveness of one side's technology and the enemy's technology.

As we see in Figure 10.4, TECHNOLOGICAL EDGE affects every major component on the left and central parts of Figure 10.1, with one exception: TECHNOLOGICAL EDGE does not affect MATERIAL RESOURCES, since (as defined here) that consists of sheer numbers of troops and numbers of various kinds of equipment. Technological innovation, however, may indirectly affect aggregate levels of material resources. It can reduce material resources, when new weapons become much more expensive, hence relatively few can be produced (e.g. the American B-2 stealth bomber cost over $1 billion each, so that only 20 have been built). Or technological innovation can increase material resources, when effort is put into making them easy to build and they have low maintenance costs, e.g. the Kalashnikov AK-47 automatic weapon, which has spread worldwide. I do not attempt to model these connections in Figure 10.4, since that would involve expanding the model to include economic production processes, financial resources, etc. A more elaborate model could be constructed as desired.

TECHNOLOGICAL EDGE affects material resources as effectively delivered in combat, however, via LOGISTICS. Thus, innovations such as steamboats, railroads, trucks, airplanes, helicopters have made it possible to move troops and equipment faster and longer distances to battlefields. Again, the question of relative effectiveness needs to be examined in detail; high-tech innovations may also produce more logistics burdens, such as fuel for transportation equipment. Thus, with the advance of technology, the size of the actual combat forces compared to the logistical component (the so-called "tooth-to-tail ratio") has grown, from on the order of 1-to-4 in nineteenth-century armies, to 10-to-1 in early twenty-first-century high-tech armies. (In guerrilla armies the ratio is not known precisely, but likely is close to that of traditional armies.) And technological innovation in weaponry (as distinct from innovation in logistics) can also add to the logistics burden. A US army M1A1 tank with virtually indestructible ceramic armor and enormous firepower weighs 60 tons, and thus cannot be transported more than one at a time by the largest cargo plane; hence, during the 2003 Iraq invasion, an armored division had to be slowly transported by ship (Gordon and Trainor 2007). It cannot be taken for granted that technological innovation—giving an edge in defensive and offensive battlefield power—necessarily gives an edge in logistics or other components.

The usual focus on the effectiveness of military technology is to compare weapons in battle. This is the path from TECHNOLOGICAL EDGE to ASSAULT. High precision munitions, with their accompanying sensor and targeting systems, have increased the accuracy of long-distance fire (by aerial bombing, rockets, artillery, armored vehicle fire, etc.) to a level much higher in the 2003 US/Iraq War than in the 1991 Gulf War, and that in turn is much higher than bombing and firing accuracy in WWII (Murray and Scales 2003). Much of the improvement has been in accuracy rather than in destructive power of explosives per se, which was already high at the time of WWII and even WWI (Biddle 2004).

Accuracy of long-distance weapons is one way of remedying the major problem of all infantry in close range combat: the tendency of most soldiers not to use their weapons at all, or to fire wildly (Marshall 1947; Collins 2008). Long-distance weapons such as artillery did not suffer from the emotional effects of confrontational tension/fear; but such weapons were intrinsically rather inaccurate. MORALE was thus traditionally more important for close-range ASSAULT than for long-distance firing. Current weapons technology tries, in effect, to turn all weapons into long-distance weapons, with higher degrees of accuracy.

Nevertheless, as we have seen, the paths from ASSAULT to CASUALTIES, ORGANIZATIONAL BREAKDOWN, and ultimately BATTLE VICTORY/DEFEAT are not the strongest paths to those outcomes. Increasing sheer firepower does not necessarily guarantee battle victory. This set of relationships is obscured by the fact that technological innovation can also affect all the social/emotional/organizational components of an army, hence the empirical effects are hard to disentangle.

To illustrate this from the turn-of-twenty-first-century "Revolution in Military Affairs" (RMA), consider the pathway from TECHNOLOGICAL EDGE to MORALE. Computerization has affected the latter, especially via its subcomponent, coordination. Highly centralized computer controls, connecting every front-line weapons platform (i.e. tank, vehicle, artillery piece, aircraft, etc.) with a command-and-control structure, has been used increasingly. It has been argued that computer links make for better coordination in all phases of a battle, eliminating costly errors that played a major part in Clausewitzian friction. The verdict is still out on the extent to that this has happened (McIvor 2005; Watts 2004).

My conclusion is a wider one: technological innovation can (as in the case of RMA) simultaneously increase ASSAULT firepower, generate LOGISTICS benefits and costs, and change coordination (in the MORALE) box. If battlefield victories or defeats change (e.g. the rapid conquest of Iraq in March 2003; but also the long struggle for pacification in the 16 years—or more—that have followed), we cannot easily attribute this to just one component, such as widely-touted high-precision bombs, or more recently, remote-controlled drones. Every path in the overall model (Figures 10.1–10.4) needs to be investigated empirically, before we can assess their relative contribution to battle outcomes, and long-term war outcomes.

Finally, there is a path from TECHNOLOGICAL EDGE to MANEUVER. Computerization of communications makes it possible for forces to move on the battlefield in complex maneuvers, and a technological edge here makes the difference between a fast-moving force (such as US forces in March 2003), and a slow-moving or stationary opponent (Iraqi forces) (Murray and Scales 2005). Thus TECHNOLOGICAL EDGE does not necessarily shift battles away from classic tactics of maneuver, and onto an exclusive reliance on superior firepower (the crude image of a super-weapon that devastates the enemy). Several conclusions follow:

1. A high-tech army may simultaneously attempt to maximize the advantages of ASSAULT and MANEUVER; this was the strategy of US commanders both in the 1991 Gulf War and in the 2003 Iraq invasion. General Schwarzkopf's "left hook" from Kuwait into Iraq in 1991 was directly modeled on the 1863 battle of Chancellorsville. In general, US military doctrine incorporates all the components of Figure 10.1 (McIvor 2005). Its goal is not only to destroy enemy forces (CASUALTIES) but to bring about "systemic collapse" including the command-and-control systems of the enemy, in effect, to precipitate ORGANIZATIONAL BREAKDOWN.
2. MANEUVER can compensate for shifts in the strength of ASSAULT. Biddle (2004) presents evidence there is no sudden shift in the effectiveness of firepower with the RMA of the 1990s. Artillery and massed infantry fire (machine guns) were already so lethal in World War I that tactics had to be modified. Frontal assault on defensive positions guaranteed heavy casualties to the attacker. By 1918, a solution was found, to break up the massed formations of traditional armies, and to disperse into small independent units that took advantage of local cover and concealment, in order to infiltrate enemy positions (Biddle 2004). In effect, this was a shift to MANEUVER and away from ASSAULT. World War II also placed great emphasis on maneuver, chiefly via mechanized warfare and *Blitzkrieg*. In this progression, the technology of extremely lethal munitions (through precision targeting) since 1990 has produced even more dispersion. An army that is inferior in

ASSAULT—because it lacks the TECHNOLOGICAL EDGE—can compensate by increasing MANEUVER.

As I will discuss in Chapter 12, this is guerrilla war. Guerrilla tactics disperse forces to an extreme degree, infiltrate enemy positions in small numbers, attack isolated targets, and quickly disperse again into positions of hiding. The objects of attack are vulnerable components of the enemy organization, especially in its logistics train—comparable to the goal of classic maneuver to break through the enemy's front into the supply lines. The shift to guerrilla war and so-called terrorism, touted by some as an unprecedented new era in the history of war, is a predictable adjustment to greater lethality of ASSAULT. In the multi-causal model of Figures 10.1–10.4, a weakness in one component can be compensated elsewhere. This is what happens in the shift to guerrilla war in response to very great inferiority in TECHNOLOGICAL EDGE.

This is not the only possible configuration. Two armies may both have a high degree of technological modernity, including precision-guided weapons systems, computer controls, etc. A conceivable example would be a war between the US and China in the middle of the twenty-first century. This would not be an asymmetric war (between high-tech and low-tech forces, and hence between very centralized and very decentralized war styles), but a symmetrical war. A likely scenario is that both sides would use the full array of their firepower (ASSAULT), initially in long-distance precision munitions, resulting in high levels of CASUALTIES on both sides; my conjecture is that victory or defeat would hinge upon the more volatile (and less predictable) tipping-point conditions via the pathway from MANEUVER to ORGANIZATIONAL BREAKDOWN. A parallel here would be the German invasion of France in 1940. Considerable technological modernization had taken place in both armies; both had approximately the same number of tanks and other weapons as well as total forces. German victory resulted from using tanks for rapid maneuver, whereas the French kept their tanks dispersed in infantry formations (Keegan 1997).

In sum: all historical periods of military technology can be encompassed in Figures 10.1–10.4. Technological innovation does not call for a separate model, and does not give grounds for asserting that the basic principles of battle dynamics change with different technological epochs. The characteristics of particular technological regimes, however, can be more clearly specified by showing how they affect the pathways in this composite model.

But What About the Digital Age?

The digital revolution since the turn of the twenty-first century has seemed so overwhelming in all aspects of life that older modes of warfare must surely be on their way out. Chapter 11 examines this question in detail.

Notes

1. Each such variable is determined at a particular moment in time, and changes as quantities are used up or enhanced through feedback and exogenous replenishment.
2. For instance, Robert E. Lee's early battle at Cheat Mountain (western Virginia, September 1861), had an elaborate plan for a five-prong attack, but the movements were poorly timed and the attempt was abandoned (McPherson 2005: 30–31).
3. Peter Turchin (personal communication) suggests an important pathway from long-term morale to the degree of resistance to organizational breakdown. Troops with more cohesion stand up better at the crisis of battle. The pattern was often noted in Caesar's *Gallic Wars*, where Roman troops held their defensive formation, protected by their shields, while larger but more individualistic armies of Gauls displayed berserker-style battle frenzy in front of them. This path can be added in the full model but is omitted from Figure 10.2 for visual simplicity.
4. Demoralized troops can even sell their weapons to the enemy, a notorious pattern in the Vietnam War, where US weapons were passed on by ARVN (South Vietnam) troops through a huge black market and acquired by the Viet Cong (Gibson 1986). Similar arms transfers to the enemy took place in Iraq preceding its sudden collapse to an ISIS (Islamic State) offensive at Mosul in June 2014, where 60,000 Iraqi forces were defeated by 1500 attackers; the former apparently had sold off much of their ammunition and supplies to the latter, before retreating in panic. The process happened again among the fragmented anti-regime forces in Syria, where advanced US weapons supplied to supposedly democratic factions ended up in the hands of Islamic militants. The term "corruption" applied to such sales is better explained through the causes of high or low morale and solidarity. On illegal arms transfers generally, see Naylor (2004).
5. The causal chain would also include the degree of state penetration into society (discussed in Chapter 2), which affects not only extraction of material resources, but national mobilization in the MORALE box. One limitation of Collins' (1978; 1995) earlier geopolitical theorizing is that it is largely confined to inputs into MATERIAL RESOURCES in specific geographical locations, and neglects inputs into the lower half of Figure 10.1 Turchin (2003) remedies this emphasis.
6. Victorious armies were often shocked to find that soldiers held in prisoner-of-war camps were starving when advancing forces liberated them. This was not necessarily a deliberate atrocity. Being defeated breaks down logistics, and large groups of prisoners suffer most dramatically from lack of supplies, since they are lowest priority in the supply chain. The pattern was observed both in WWII and in the American Civil War.

References

Biddle, Stephen. 2004. *Military Power: Explaining Victory and Defeat in Modern Battle.* Princeton, NJ: Princeton University Press.

Collins, Randall. 1978. "Long-term Social Change and the Territorial Power of States." In Louis Kriesberg (Ed.), *Research in Social Movements, Conflicts, and Change.* Vol. 1. Greenwich, CT: JAI Press, pp. 1–34.

Collins, Randall. 1995. "Prediction in Macro-sociology: The Case of the Soviet Collapse." *American Journal of Sociology* 100: 1552–1593.

Collins, Randall. 2008. *Violence: A Micro-Sociological Theory*. Princeton, NJ: Princeton University Press.

Denig, Carl. 2010. "The Sense in the Slaughter: State Solidarity and the Second American Revolution." Unpublished MA thesis, Department of Sociology, University of Pennsylvania.

Gibson, James William. 1986. *The Perfect War: Technowar in Vietnam*. Boston: Atlantic Monthly Press.

Gordon, Michael R., and Bernard E. Trainor. 2007. *Cobra II: The Inside Story of the Invasion and Occupation of Iraq*. New York: Random House.

Griffith, Patrick. 1989. *Battle Tactics of the Civil War*. New Haven, CT: Yale University Press.

Hammes, Thomas W. 2004. *The Sling and the Stone: On War in the 21st Century*. St. Paul, MN: Zenith Books.

Hobson, John M. 1997. *The Wealth of States*. Cambridge: Cambridge University Press.

Keegan, John. 1976. *The Face of Battle*. New York: Random House.

Keegan, John. 1997. *Atlas of the Second World War*. London: HarperCollins.

King, Anthony. 2013. *The Combat Soldier: Infantry Tactics and Cohesion in the Twentieth and Twenty-first Centuries*. Oxford: Oxford University Press.

Klusemann, Stefan. 2010. "After State-Breakdown: Dynamics of Multi-Party Conflict, Violence, and Paramilitary Mobilization in Russia 1904–1920, Germany 1918–1934, and Japan 1853–1877." PhD dissertation, Department of Sociology, University of Pennsylvania.

Long, E. B. 1971. *The Civil War Day by Day: An Almanac 1861–1865*. New York: Doubleday.

Marshall, S. L. A. 1947. *Men Against Fire: The Problem of Battle Command*. Norman, OK: University of Oklahoma Press.

McIvor, Anthony D. (Ed.) 2005. *Rethinking the Principles of War*. Annapolis, MD: Naval Institute Press.

McPherson, James M. 2005. *Atlas of the Civil War*. Philadelphia, PA: Running Press.

Murray, Williamson, and Robert H. Scales. 2003. *The Iraq War: A Military History*. Cambridge, MA: Belknap Press.

Naylor, R.T. 2004. *Wages of Crime: Black Markets, Illegal Finance, and the Underground Economy*. Ithaca, NY: Cornell University Press.

Noe, Kenneth W. 2010. *Reluctant Rebels: Confederates Who Joined the Army after 1861*. Chapel Hill, NC: University of North Carolina Press.

Shils, Edward, and Janowitz, Morris. 1948. "Cohesion and Disintegration in the Wehrmacht in World War II." *Public Opinion Quarterly* 12: 280–315.

Tolstoy, Leo. 1869 [2005]. *War and Peace*. New York: Penguin Group.

Turchin, Peter. 2003. *Historical Dynamics: Why States Rise and Fall*. Princeton, NJ: Princeton University Press.

Van Creveld, Martin. 1977. *Supplying War: Logistics from Wallenstein to Patton*. Cambridge: Cambridge University Press.

Watts, Barry V. 2004. *Clausewitzian Friction and Future War*. Washington, DC: Institute for National Strategic Studies, National Defense University.

Chapter 11

High-Tech War in Theory and Reality

Introduction

Since the 1990s, the US and to a lesser degree other leading militaries have undergone what was initially called RMA—revolution in military affairs; and now is simply called "transformation." Behind the terminological screen is what claims to be the biggest change ever in the history of warfare: the elimination of Clausewitzian friction. If true, the basic principles of how wars are won and lost have changed. These are fundamentally sociological principles: war is a form of organization; winning is an effort by one organization to make the other organization break down. In large part, military high tech transformation means the Information Technology revolution; so military transformation is showing us what happens when organizations are massively computerized.[1]

The chapter is organized as follows. First, we consider Clausewitzian friction and the principles of how battles are won or lost; then a pattern of military change that has already been going on for over a century, increasing lethality of weapons and resulting dispersion of the battlefield (this is Stephen Biddle's (2004) counter-theory to the RMA argument). These are the main problems that computerization attempts to overcome.

Next, how IT has affected all aspects of war: command, communications, targeting, intelligence, logistics, etc. High tech is traditional in at least one aspect: it is expensive. A long-standing principle of geopolitics and war continues to operate: the side with more resources will win, unless its resources get destroyed in the war; or otherwise cannot be mobilized (especially through political difficulties). An expensive high-tech war tends to degrade back into more traditional low-tech war, i.e. friction increases the longer a war goes on.

Computerization connected to an array of high-tech sensors should provide complete information about the battlefield. Does this mean surprise (a main factor in maneuver war) is no longer possible? I suggest conditions under which surprise, or something like it, still operates.

Until war is completely taken over by robots, the human element remains. There are various high-tech efforts to control soldiers more

DOI: 10.4324/9781003245629-15

precisely, including monitoring their bodily signs of emotions. At the same time, recognition of the battle for hearts and minds—enemy and civilian emotions—results in stricter rules of engagement, with unintended consequences of generating new forms of combat stress and human breakdown.

The final step is to eliminate the human element. What would all-robot war look like? The human element would come in at another point, especially the morale of human technicians who service and repair robots. We will also have to look into the political emotions of all those affected, both on and off the battlefield.

Friction, or the Fog of War

In war, General von Clausewitz wrote, everything is simple, but carrying it out is hard. He should know; he was with the Russian army beaten by Napoleon on the way to Moscow in 1812, and he watched Napoleon's army dwindle away on the long cold march back through the Russian winter. This difficulty Clausewitz ([1833] 1976) called friction, the grinding of heavy forces as they move across the surface of the earth, rubbing against each other every step of the way.

In another metaphor, this is the fog of war. Originally it was the smoke of gunfire that covered the battlefield and made it impossible to see where anything was. No general could be sure his orders would be carried out or if the foe would be where he was supposed to be. No soldier could be sure who he was firing at, and a sizable portion of casualties came from accidents and being hit by one's own side. The victories and defeats in the American Civil War of 1861–1865 were fought under a dense fog of war.

Twentieth-century wars had better intelligence and communications, but friction did not disappear. Planes still bombed civilians; unanticipated enemies popped up in sudden maneuvers. Tanks ran out of fuel and rumbled to a halt on the fields of France or the deserts of North Africa. Ammo was exhausted in the midst of battle. Helicopter strikes aborted for lack of repairs or from sand in their engines.

To this physical friction and informational fog must be added a third kind: the emotions of human beings. Soldiers under stress of combat did not always fire and didn't often hit their targets when they did fire. Officers did not always give realistic orders and troops did not always carry them out. Soldiers would forget to bring drinking water with them into combat, and supply officers could fail to provide warm clothes in the winter cold.

The idea gathered momentum that science and technology could do a better job of fighting than human beings. Already in the Vietnam War, Secretary of Defense McNamara used statistical controls to calculate air strikes and enemy body counts (Gibson 1986). By the 1990s, the transformation of the US military was under way. Precision bombs and missiles were guided to their targets by computers in their noses. If humans were fallible, satellites with global positioning system (GPS) coordinates, transmitting intercontinental messages, and hooked to an array of sensors and weapons could hit targets with great accuracy, while their operators sat thousands of miles away, out of the danger and the stress of combat.

The fog of war was disappearing. Though enemies hid and adopted guerrilla tactics of hit-and-run, their cloak of invisibility was being penetrated. Soon the murky battlefield would be fully revealed in the clear electronic light of day.

Effects of Friction on Victory and Defeat

Friction has three forms: physical drag; informational fog; and human emotions. Many aspects of the IT transformation of the military are attempts to overcome these different kinds of friction. Notably there are attempts to overcome informational fog by relying on non-human sensors and computerized communications to evaluation and command centers far from the stress of battle. There are efforts to take most of the targeting and firing decisions out of the hands of humans who are in the weapons platforms (read: tanks, aircraft, etc.) or on the ground.[2]

Human emotions are especially important for the sociology of violence, since I have assembled evidence that violent conflict generates confrontational tension/fear (CT/F), and this causes most of the irrational or horrific features of fighting, including low accuracy, hitting the wrong targets (friendly fire, bystander hits), contagious confusion and panic, as well as massacres of helpless victims (forward panics) (Collins 2008). If informational fog and human emotions are eliminated or at least greatly reduced, what effect does this have on the causes of winning or losing wars?

Friction has been the key to what happens to both sides in combat. Victory occurs when one organization imposes friction on its opponent; more precisely, since both sides are undergoing friction, the winner imposes more friction on their opponent than they suffer themselves. Winning means having a better organization than your opponent. The things that you do—attacking; resupplying; moving around the battlefield—have less friction than the enemy has. Your organization wins, even if it is breaking down, as long as it breaks down more slowly. Virtually all military stories are about how things screw up; but if the enemy is screwing up worse than you are, you win. This is generally not noticed until a tipping-point is passed, when the various kinds of friction—including physical drag and informational fog—generate a surge of the most serious kind of friction: emotional friction, the contagious loss of social cohesion in the enemy organization. It is when one side perceives itself as having become much more disorganized than the enemy that it goes into an organizational breakdown. In extreme cases this takes the form of precipitous retreat: (the disintegration of a materially still very strong French army under the German *Blitzkrieg* breakthrough in 1940); the surrender of massive forces that feel themselves in no position to continue fighting (the Russian Front in 1941); continuous retreats from the inability to form a defensible battle line (British losses to the Japanese advance in Asia in early 1942, when most of South-east Asia was overrun in four months) (Liddell-Hart 1970).

Here the macro scale of war operates by the same principle as the micro-sociology of violence: emotional domination comes first, and most physical casualties and material damage are inflicted on the side that has lost their emotional energy to continue the confrontation. Official US military doctrine (and in other national armed forces as well) recognizes a version of this principle: the aim of an attack is not to kill the enemy or destroy equipment, so much as to destroy their center of command, to disorganize the enemy, so that their troops can then easily be defeated. (This is what happened in the spring 2003 US-led invasion of Iraq; Murray and Scales 2003; Gordon and Trainor 2007). When a military organization is unable to make the enemy disintegrate, the result is protracted war, hinging on total resources, attrition, and political willingness to continue to fight.

There are two main ways battles and wars are won: either by sheer attrition—the side with deeper pockets logistically (more troops and weapons, bigger population and economic base) grinding down the other until they eventually give up; or by maneuver—moving one's forces more rapidly, to hit a weak spot in the enemy organization, disrupting its logistics, and above all causing organizational breakdown. In the American Civil War, the Southern generals were better at maneuver, and defeated the resource-richer Northern forces. Finally, the North went into a relentless attrition strategy under Grant, who kept up pressure even when tactically defeated, until the disparity in resources made it impossible for the Confederates to continue. World War II had a similar pattern; the Germans won many early victories through superior maneuver, but Britain and Russia held out long enough until the superior resources of the Allies were fully mobilized. Thus, attrition war and maneuver war both factor into the overall determinants. These might be described as long-term grinding friction (including the crude friction of being hit by enemy firepower) and short-term dramatic organizational disruption.

Maneuver is a combination of surprise and momentum. Surprise can be disruptive, but in moving very large forces (the 1940 German *Blitzkrieg* again), the surprise is gone after a day or two, and it becomes a matter of one force getting a lead in moving its organization where it wants it, while the other side is always playing catch-up. Maneuver thus has its main effect by disrupting enemy organization, especially its sense of being capable of counter-maneuvering to meet its enemy. Maneuver materially disrupts supplies of fuel and ammunition, but even more disastrously it affects the contagious emotions of the troops and their officers. Maneuver above all imposes emotional friction in the form of loss of solidarity and emotional energy, and thus willingness to fight.

The bottom line: all the main forms of military practice have been built around trying to protect one's own organization from friction, and to impose various forms of friction on the enemy. That is, up until now, historically. What happens when friction is eliminated?

Increasing Lethality and Dispersion of the Battlefield

The problem of friction has gotten worse over the past 150 years because of a trend analyzed by Stephen Biddle (2004), *Military Power: Explaining Victory and Defeat in Modern Battle*. Weapons have become more accurate and more powerful, and therefore more lethal. Before 1870, small arms were rarely accurate beyond 50 meters; artillery in Napoleon's day could reach a mile, but its effect was at best a slow, random attrition of enemy ranks. Both for offense and defense, troops were massed in large compact ranks; this helped solve one of the main organizational problems, cohesion and discipline, as well as making up for poor aim by coordinated volleys of musket or rifle fire. But with the invention of the machine gun and high explosive artillery shells, massed formations became suicidal. The lesson was learned by the last year of World War I; troops had to disperse, taking advantage of small ground contours and cover, to infiltrate enemy positions rather than attack them by frontal assault. One result was that methods of social control of troops had to change; troops needed to be given more initiative, and a variety of morale-boosting efforts were made, including nationalism, ideological indoctrination, and reliance of small group ties (King 2013).

As Biddle points out, the trend to increasing lethality of weapons continued throughout the twentieth century and into the present. Air power initially added another angle of attack with plenty of friction in the form of inaccurate aim, but brought more firepower to the battlefield, along with relatively safe bases from which to deliver it; targeting devices like radar improved; machine guns reached the point where all foot soldiers carried automatic weapons. The result was that armies had to disperse their forces more and more, both on offense and defense. Already by the early twentieth century, battle fronts were shaped in layers of lines backing each other up with a mile or more between; forces could not be risked in one big mass such as characterized the Napoleonic wars, and breakthroughs in one line were to be anticipated and counteracted by deeper lines. This long-standing tendency to disperse became even more extreme by the early twentieth century. One hears of the "non-linear battlefield" where hypothetically any spot can be attacked from any other spot. This is an exaggeration; but the battlefield is essentially a checkerboard, regions of relative concentration, with staging areas and logistics points, surrounded by much empty space. It is easiest to recognize this in a resource-rich military which has an abundance of air bases (including aircraft carriers) at a long distance from the fighting; nearer in, armored helicopters are used to make sudden incursions, but also to resupply outposts.

Dispersion solves some problems but creates others. Dispersion brings its own vulnerabilities, chiefly in logistics and transportation. These become increasingly vulnerable targets for the enemy to hit; and a reason why warfare keeps getting more expensive, even though the size of armies has been decreasing.

Transformation by IT

Information Technology (IT) has affected all aspects of war. Much of what officers previously did in preparing and directing combat is now done by computers. What used to be called C&C (command and control) has been computerized; and the entire package of military administrative functions has been reconfigured as C4ISR (command, control, communications, computers, intelligence, surveillance & reconnaissance—and constantly expanding acronyms).

Military organization has become quite self-consciously a system of inputs and outputs. Both sides of the system, and their interface, have been turned over to hardware as much as possible. What used to be done by human eyes and ears is now being done by electronic and chemical sensors; what was done by human hands wielding, aiming, and firing weapons is done increasingly by the system of wired-together machines integrating inputs with calculations of maximally destructive effects on the enemy.

Although it is easiest to think of this as the computerization of the military, these computers are also linked to new high-tech sensors, transforming not only the organization's brain but its senses. Another buzzword is precision munitions, but more generally it is a connected system of devices for precision targeting. Sensors include:

- *GPS coordinates*: the target is located precisely and the munition is aimed or guided to the exact spot.
- *laser tagging*: the target is located by a team of spotters who mark it with a laser signal guiding the weapon's aim.
- *IR (infra-red heat signature)*: the heat of a body or vehicles is detected and used as targeting information.
- *radar homing*: an enemy device that emits radar signals is detected, and its signals are used to locate precisely where that device is, making it a target for counter-fire.
- *optical images*: what the enemy target looks like is taken in by telescopic photography, and identified by being compared with images in a computer archive; such images come from a version of CCTV

(closed circuit television), which may be in fixed locations on the ground, mounted on vehicles, or flying at various altitudes above.

Strictly speaking, precision targeting is a combination of sensors, computers, and weapons platforms. This sounds jargon-y but it underscores the point that artillery, tanks, helicopters, fixed-wing aircraft flying off of ships or land bases, ground vehicles carrying foot-soldiers, etc. are all components of a weapons system. They don't stand alone, and to an increasing extent they are interchangeable for each other—they are all ways of delivering firepower to enemy targets with maximal precision.

A growing tendency is to add mini-computers on the weapons themselves to the larger electronic network that receives information from the array of sensors. Many of the larger munitions carry onboard computers—the nose of a bomb (dropped from an aircraft) or rocket (fired from a ground launcher, from a fighter/attack aircraft, etc.) may contain a mini-computer that guides it toward its target, using continually updated information about its own position and the position of the target.

All this means that weapons depend on a supporting infrastructure: satellites, aircraft, drones, and/or ground spotter teams. The latter remain one of the few human components in the system, the Special Forces who infiltrate near enough to enemy targets to put laser tags on them, send GPS coordinates, or even eyeball the enemy.

The tendency of the battlefield to spread out, to disperse in response to the lethality of enemy firepower, is thus further increased by the far-flung system of sensors, near-instantaneous communications, sites for integrating information, and electronic orders aiming and guiding weapons to their destinations. The weapons themselves are physically carried for tens, hundreds, or thousands of kilometers to the vicinity of their targets where they are fired or propel themselves to their targets. This dispersion shows up not just in dramatic separations in space like directing the 2003 invasion of Iraq from an air base in Florida, or drones in Afghanistan being directed by pilots in Nevada, but in every aspect of military organization.

To get a more concrete sense of how the system operates, consider what things look like over a modern-day battlefield.

A couple of Boeing 707s, the ordinary vehicle of coast-to-coast airline travel, are droning rather slowly just under 30,000 feet, making a mere 350 miles per hour. A little odd, since airliners generally fly in the mid-30,000s, and their timetables usually keep them over 500 miles per hour, hurrying to an on-time arrival at LAX or JFK. These Boeings are not in a hurry, not going anywhere in particular; if we could hover in the air like angels, we would see they are accompanied by a ring of fighter planes like the palace guard surrounding the queen. These are the aerial centers of the air battle: AWACS, Airborne Warning And Control System.

Each AWACS plane is surmounted by what looks like a giant Frisbee disk elevated on struts a dozen feet above the fuselage—one reason why the plane is relatively slow. It is a rotating radar dome 30 feet in diameter, which can track any plane at any altitude up to 200 miles away. Inside the plane, where normally 200 passengers would sit, a dozen electronic specialists are tending equipment that can sort friendly aircraft from enemy aircraft, sending out information that guides the friendlies on their flight paths—and keeps them from colliding with each other as they zoom through combat—while targeting their weapons on the hostiles. Other equipment brightens the radar signals, straining out ground clutter that would confuse a lesser radar system. Pilots of air-to-air combat fighters, and of the F/A (fighter/attack) ground attack fighters that act as flying rocket launchers, are just along for the ride, since AWACS in effect do all their targeting for them, and can even take over the firing and flying the planes. The pilots, as they say sardonically, ride along as a back-up in case something goes wrong.

Each AWACS usually has its own area of operations, but it also is sending a torrent of information back to computers at battle headquarters, where the data will become mixed and matched in an even larger picture.

Headquarters mega-computers are becoming increasingly like an autonomous brain at the center of all the inputs and outputs. Radar is only one mode of perception, one sense; the evolving headquarters computer has all five senses of a human being, and more. It is not just an eye, but a brain—if a brain is the locus where all the sensory circuits intersect, and connect with the motor circuits that execute action and in turn provide feedback on the updated situation—and so on endlessly in the loop that makes up conscious thinking.[3]

Five senses: classically, sight, sound, smell, taste, and touch. The computerized battle system shows there are many more senses than this. Radar is a kind of sight, but it is something like the sight of a bat—although that is really sonar, sending out sound waves of high pitched squeaks and listening acutely for their echoes, which the bat-brain forms into an image of the world—blind in some dimensions, hyper-acute in another. Radar can see through clouds, fog, storms, day or night, any weather. But it sees in blurry images, and sees best when its target is moving.

Another set of eyes, besides AWACS, are circling the battlefield higher up, above 40,000 feet. These too are Boeing 707s, called JSTARS, but instead of a Frisbee dome towering over its tail, each carries a sleek canoe-shaped cylinder slung under the front of its belly. This looks like a torpedo or a rocket, but it is another kind of radar antenna. Like a bat, it sends out signals and then reads them on the rebound, in this case reading the frequency shift of the returning signal for clues as to what it has encountered. JSTARS means Joint STARS, but it has nothing to do with astronomy. It doesn't look at the stars but tracks vehicles on the ground. It can see them, electronically, out to 150 miles away, preparatory to attacking them: STARS means Surveillance Target Attack Radar System, and it is Joint because it works jointly with other systems to put together a composite picture from many kinds of sensors.

JSTARS can track 600 vehicles simultaneously, if they are the size of a car or bigger. But its vision, too, is rather blurred, and it cannot tell what kind of vehicles they are—only what direction they are moving and how fast—nor what kind of weapons they are carrying, nor even if they are friend or foe. Other information needs to be jointly integrated into the system to sharpen the picture. And JSTARS is usually blind to stationary objects; something like the way a bird, by playing dead, can mystify a cat, which sees rather poorly (among other reasons, being color blind) and which must wait for the prey to move in order to pounce on it.

To improve on the eyes of JSTARS, we turn to another sensor input. One of these is circling the battlefield still higher up, at 65,000 feet, above the level where most planes can fly. This is Global Hawk. It can stay aloft for two days at a time; and it can skim the lower fringe of outer space, because it carries no human crew. It is a UAV, an unmanned aerial vehicle. It is, quite literally, a robot eye in the sky. Its eyes are much better than human eyes, much better than the radar eyes of the human-crewed vehicles circling so much closer to the earth. It takes video images and beams them back to the ground -- electro-optical (EO) images like photographs enhanced to bring out the significant contours of ground objects viewed from 12 miles up. These are daytime photos, dependent on cloud cover and weather conditions. At the height of battle, there is heavy smoke cover, the original fog of war.

Global Hawk has another set of eyes that can see through the smoke: infra-red (IR) sensors that make images out of contrasts in heat. Successful hits on enemy hardware show up as bright conflagrations under the smoke. Unlike in JSTARS radar images, vehicles do not have to be moving for their infra-red signatures to appear, although the hotter they are, the brighter they glow, so vehicles with their engines turned off have a better chance of evading detection. Human bodies, too, give off an infra-red (IR) signature, but too weak to be seen from thousands of feet in the air. But since IR sensors are ubiquitous in all branches of the US military, there are plenty of sensors nearer the action: on tanks moving up, armored personnel carriers full of infantry ready to dismount to clear the battlefield, each man carrying his own night-vision goggles which give IR images, not to mention IR sensors on their automatic rifles. Whatever enemy troops have survived the aerial assault, wherever they are dug in or hiding, will soon become heat images on the screens of numerous weapons, and data integrated into the electronic files of the battle-control computers.

In very recent years there has been a proliferation of smaller, cheaper drones, launched at local command levels, and sending back images to receivers much closer to the combat zone. These come in different sizes, ranging from Predators carrying not only CCTV cameras but missiles, to the size of model airplanes put into the air by an individual foot-soldier, with others projected the size of butterflies. How these affect the organization of combat is not yet well understood; there is a centralization/ decentralization issue here, among other things.[4]

Counter-Measures: The Cat-and-Mouse Game

To the extent that the enemy also has advanced technology (or some segments of it), it can be turned into a vulnerability. For instance: HARMs (a high-speed anti-radiation missile) locks in on a radar signal and takes it out. Thus, any enemy weapons that are guided by radar—like our own radar-guided artillery, tank and APC (anti-personnel-carrier) guns, aircraft-fired rockets, not to mention AWACS and JSTARS themselves—become targets whenever they fire or even search for a target. HARMs are carried by F/A (fighter/attack) aircraft and fly 1600 miles per hour, about Mach 3, and thus are impossible to escape once it fixes onto you.

Nevertheless, there are some limitations, and thus the possibility of a cat-and-mouse game opens up. HARMs weigh 800 pounds, so heavy that a jet fighter cannot carry more than two of them at a time. Thus they may not be available to counter-attack radar-using targets, on sheer logistical grounds. Or the enemy can use counter-counter measures, such as dispersing fake weapons emitting radar signals, to draw fire until HARMs run out; at this point the enemy's real artillery can open up. The greatest value of weapons like HARMs is in set-piece battles, where one side has the advantage of long planning and build-up of forces to attack a known enemy position. In a fluid combat zone, or with sudden, widely dispersed enemy attacks, this unbeatable anti-weapons weapon is often simply not available when it is needed (as interviews with combat veterans of the Afghanistan War have indicated).

A further problem is that HARMs sometimes mix up which radar they're firing at, and may become diverted if they cross another radar source on the way in. This is especially likely when there is so much radar on both sides of the battlefield, operating in a relatively narrow frequency spectrum. This can cause not only the possibility of missing enemy targets, but in a battlefield of dispersed checkerboard pockets, the likelihood of fratricide—firing HARMs on one's own positions. Weapons designers and operators are aware of this, and efforts are made to signal clearly which are one's own forces, but the combination of glitches and enemy counteractions leaves this part of the cat-and-mouse game still ongoing.[5]

Another key anti-weapons system is the Patriot anti-ballistics system (ABS): it shoots down incoming rockets and aircraft, by self-propelled missiles that chase their targets guided by information from sensors both on the ground and in the tip of their own warheads. This is what it looks like:

The missile encampment is a cluster of flat-bed trucks. The missile launcher is elevated toward the sky on its flat-bed truck, resembling nothing so much as a garbage truck in the act of tipping its load to a maximum angle, except that instead of dumping refuse from the bottom there are four white-tipped missile cones sticking out the top end ready to be discharged into the sky. The launch tubes have a strangely civilian look, four long rectangular boxes up on a hydraulic lift, like packing crates being hoisted to the high shelves in a warehouse discount store. The missile canisters still have factory instructions printed on the side, serving as shipping and storage containers until the long slender rockets go whooshing up to destroy any aircraft within 50 miles, no matter how high it flies.

Another flat-bed truck carries what looked like a portable construction office painted in camouflage—the control center where computers link radar input with the missiles and launchers. The electronic control operators work inside an air-conditioned, bio-weapons-sealed box. There are also outside crews of missile reloaders, repairers, and refuelers. Yet another long flat-bed truck carries the phased array radar, a large flat box mounted on hydraulics at a high angle toward the sky. One side of the box is covered with a large circle like a clock without hands or hours. It sends out a narrow beam that scans the sky with great acuity, capable of picking up anything from a big clumsy helicopter to a Mach-3 jet fighter, reading the low electronic profile of a stealth bomber or identifying the tiny visual streak of a ballistics missile incoming from hundreds of miles away.

Anti-ballistics missile firing is the sexy assignment for Patriot missiles, like sending a mosquito to sting a deadly wasp out of the sky at 5 times the speed of sound. Other battle assignments are more mundane—most of what is up there over the battlefield may be aircraft, and Patriots can act like a high-tech version of the ack-ack gunners of World War II. Only now instead of clumsy swarms of bullets that almost always missed, they fire self-propelled missiles that chase their targets, guided by information from sensors both on the ground and in the tip of their own warheads. In WWII, 90 percent of the bombers got through; now most of what was targeted by a Patriot missile would surely die.

But—this leads to enemy counter-measures (ECM), such as radar jamming. And that leads to ECCM: electronic counter-counter-measures. Against radar jamming, we can use radar warning receiver equipment; Patriots fire anti-standoff jammer missiles to seek and destroy ECM emitters. The sequence recapitulates the development of police radar guns to catch speeders, then drivers' radar detectors, then radar detector-detectors.

Similar weapons/anti-weapons/anti-anti-weapons sequences exist for other kinds of battlefield equipment. Modern tanks are virtually invulnerable to direct hits on their heavy ceramic armor; armored attack helicopters (such as the Apache AH-64) carry Hellfire missiles designed as tank killers, to hit them from above on the most vulnerable spot, the engine under the thinner armor of the rear deck. Hellfires are radar-guided, so they are vulnerable to radar jamming, as both sides attempt to jam each other's electronic communications. But a battle helicopter could fly with its radar turned off until enemy targets are in sight. Attack helicopters also take advantage of terrain masking, flying low to use ground contours and trees to hide themselves from infra-red sensors; and laser tags are no good against rapidly shifting targets.

The strongest defensive weapon against helicopter attack are Stinger portable surface-to-air missiles (SAMs). Stingers have a range out to 3 miles and are guided by infra-red sensors that could spot an enemy helicopter by the heat it emitted even through smoke and bad weather. On the battlefield, they would be seen in pits behind sandbag walls. Each two-man team has a metal tube about 6 feet long, like a section of sewer pipe. The operator holds the pipe on his shoulder, most of it sticking out behind him to keep the exhaust away from his body. The forward end has a signal-enhancing scope for his eyes, and a bird-cage-shaped antenna on top. The whole thing weighs about 30 pounds and it takes a muscular man to hold the loaded launcher while his spotter helps with the loading. The missile itself is a long thin tube fitted inside the launcher, with surprisingly small 3-inch fins in a collar steering it from the front. Once the missile is launched to a safe distance from the operator, the bottom stages drop off as it accelerates to Mach 2—twice the speed of sound. Stingers are finicky, fired by inserting a chemical unit into the handguard; the danger being that the unit could lose gas and malfunction from rough handling and poor maintenance. Like so much high tech weaponry, it is awesome when it works, which isn't all the time.

Stinger SAMs are cheap and mobile, soldier-portable, and vehicle-mounted. Since they are infra-red-guided, they cannot be jammed. Thus, another tactic of the armored helicopter is to get into close range through terrain masking, then revert to more traditional weapons, such as 70 mm rockets—since these are unguided, the enemy can't interfere with the guidance system. Just aim and fire. In the electronic cat-and-mouse game, the winning move is to have multiple types of weapons, and to use the lesser electronic signature of some of them at the right time to make up for the vulnerabilities of others.

Limitations of High-Tech Combat: Expense, Logistics, and Attrition Back to Low-Tech

The bottom line: If everything works as it should, the result should be perfectly efficient warfare. The high-tech combat organization spots all of its targets; its aim never misses; it always destroys the enemy. Can anything go wrong? Is there still friction in the military organization? This is not simply a matter of keeping on perfecting the technology, the belief that if we still have glitches, they can be fixed with a future generation of better technology.

We have seen some of the limits already. First, costs: extremely high-tech pieces of equipment are very expensive, and they often require a great deal of maintenance, and are hard to replace when broken. Thus, they are not always available in combat situations when and where they are most needed.[6] That is to say, high-tech does not eliminate problems of logistics; even though computers can aid in planning schedules and deliveries, they still have to be carried out in the real world, where friction can throw calculations off. Local exhaustion of munitions—such as the limits on the numbers of HARMs that strike fighters can carry—have the effect of taking some of the most advanced weapons off the battlefield, sometimes at crucial moments.

It is not just a question of how advanced one's technology is, but how much of it one has, and whether it can be moved to the right place at the right time. At the outset I noted there are three forms of friction: physical drag; informational fog; and human emotions. Most of the high-tech weapons systems I have been discussing are designed to overcome informational fog (and implicitly to overcome the negative effect of human emotions by taking the firing out of human hands). But sensors and electronic guidance systems can be countered by enemy-created informational fog, in the form of electronic counter-measures. Some low-tech solutions are also used, such as helicopters flying low to mask their movements by terrain, or firing unguided rockets that can't be jammed. High-tech weapons also have diminished some kinds of physical friction: especially by using air transport (long-distance bombers or F/A jets so that horses, tanks, or artillery don't have to traverse rivers and mud). Nevertheless, there remains physical friction: the wearing out of parts of helicopter engines and rotors are exactly that. The super-expensive B-2 stealth bomber, covered with alloys and other counter-measures that make it virtually invisible to enemy sensors, nevertheless has to spend a large percentage of its time being maintained, because every time it is flown, its stealth features degrade. And a B-2 is so expensive that it cannot be risked unless conditions are nearly perfect.

To all this must be added the enemy. The advantages of the side with the most advanced high-tech weapons are most apparent when the war is rapidly decided. Thus, the decision to stop the 1991 Gulf War after four days, although much criticized for failure to finish the job, nevertheless had the effect of making the victorious army look invulnerable. But if the war does not end quickly—either because both sides have enough reserves of equipment and economic resources to replace their losses, or because the weaker side has the political will to keep on fighting, as in a guerrilla/terrorist war—then the sources of friction start to accumulate. Over a lengthening period of time, high-tech military systems physically degrade. When this happens, high-tech war turns back into old-fashioned attrition war.

Is Battle Surprise Still Possible?

Let us assume that the high-tech military system is intact and functioning reasonably well as intended. All the remote sensors are operating, giving a clear picture of where enemy forces are, where vehicles are moving and weapons are concentrated. Does this mean that a high-tech military cannot be surprised by enemy attack? This is an important point in military theory, because maneuver is one of the two main ways of winning a battle. This depends on being able to move one's forces faster than the enemy can respond to them, by hitting a weak spot with superior forces, or by disrupting the enemy organization, so that it becomes incapable of acting as a cohesive unit; it is when the organization falls apart that it becomes vulnerable to massive casualties and equipment losses, or to demoralization and surrender. Without maneuver, combat becomes just war of attrition, slugging it out until the side with more resources has whittled the other side down to where it must stop. But without surprise, there is no successful maneuver. Does this mean that high-tech warfare necessarily turns into attrition war?

This might seem to be the case if both sides are high-tech, so that whatever each side does is transparent and no one can achieve surprise (think of a possible US-China war, directly or between proxies). I will argue shortly that this does not necessarily follow. But what if it is asymmetrical war, doesn't this mean that the high-tech side knows where all the enemy assets are, but they can't see ours, so the advantage is totally on our side, and the war is a swift walk-over? This is how both the 1991 Gulf War and the 2003 invasion of Iraq are usually depicted (Biddle 2004; Murray and Scales 2003). But here too, if an asymmetrical war is protracted, the element of surprise is reintroduced, because high-tech sensor systems still have holes in them; the attacking side is successful to just the extent that it can use patches of the fog of war within which to strike the enemy. This may not defeat the high-tech military but it prevents its victory, and makes possible a long indecisive period of attrition, with eventually political consequences through emotional mood-swings. This all hinges on whether a high-tech surveillance of the battlefield can be made complete.

Local battle surprise is still possible, in part, because there are limits on how well high-tech sensors operate. These limitations include weather, especially electric lightning storms; extreme cold and heat; but also in dry environments, sand storms (which also have bad effects on helicopter flights, and on most equipment maintenance). Another kind of limitation comes from fighting in urban environments.

Can a large-scale offensive be mounted against high-tech sensors? Yes; even when all the sensor systems are working, battle surprise is still possible, for the following reasons:

1. *The haystack of normalcy.* When a huge amount of information is coming in, there is an overabundance of banal and contradictory reports. Enemy movements are reported, but most of these turn out to be trivial and abortive (not surprisingly if the enemy has organizational foul-ups—friction—as well). Most reports turn out to be false alarms; and it is hard to tell these from the ones that presage a serious enemy attack. Bridget Nolan (2016), who has studied counter-terrorism organization, characterizes this as looking for a needle in a haystack of needles.
2. *Boredom of operators.* Operators of surveillance equipment, such as persons who monitor CCTV feed, or video coming in from drones overflying enemy territory, most of the time see little but routine. This is true even in battle conditions. With today's dispersion of forces, battlefields are mostly empty. And in conditions of high-tech armies attempting to pacify a disputed territory, most of the time nothing is happening. A survey of the problems of US troops found the highest complaint was boredom (Ender 2009).[7] One of the best first-hand reports by a soldier in the Iraq War calls it "Killing Time in Iraq" (Buzzell 2006). This is the emotional state that puts enemy forces in a position for a sudden attack. Hypothetically, one might turn over the tasks of analyzing information to computers, which cannot be bored because they have no emotions. But the skills at programming computers to do so, without erring on the side of over-zealousness or over-complacency, seem to be the same skills that real-life soldiers also struggle to find.
3. *Struggle over report channels.* When there are a lot of surveillance channels and many operatives, there emerges a next level of struggle over getting one's warnings through to the command center. We have found a needle, but so has someone else too. Bridget Nolan suggests that more time is spent trying to get one's report cleared and noticed at higher levels, than in originally assembling the report on a terrorist threat. The same applies in battlefield situations; higher command has to balance the various reports, some of which are misperceptions and over-reactions. True, once the enemy attack has already hit, it becomes clear where their forces are; but the key moments are in the hours or days before this point, when the most effective counter-actions could be taken.

These are not just technical glitches. They appear to be deep, intrinsic dilemmas of how military action is organized: action in which two organizations are trying to break each other down by disrupting their coordination. They do this not only by taking advantage of the fog of war, but by trying to impose the fog of war on the other side.

Technologically Controlling the Human Element in War

Today's high-tech military are also aware of the human element, and have become increasingly concerned with applying social science to bolster solidarity and coordination in small combat groups. Thus, even the boots-on-the-ground aspect is being brought into the system of high-tech controls.

There is a move now toward monitoring troops' vital signs, by sensors in their helmets or in their battle dress; a commander would be able to read their heartbeat, blood-pressure, and other signs to see when troops are stressed out. In effect, this is an attempt at measuring morale physiologically, in real time and using such information for combat decisions. Another trend is to technologizing small arms with the same high-tech that makes up the rest of the organizational system; automatic weapons are fitted with IR sensors and electronically-enhanced optical scopes; onboard mini-computers are in the offing, so that each infantry soldier becomes in effect a weapons platform connected to remote communications and controls, just like a helicopter or an armored vehicle. Troops have NODs (night-observation devices), eyeglasses that snap down from their helmets, which enable them to see in the dark by enhancing IR and other signals; these goggles are now morphing into even more interactive remote-communications devices, where maps can be called up on mini-screens, and archived images can be compared with what the soldier actually sees. These are attempts to improve their aim (target acquisition, in military terminology), but also to give more centralized organizational control to what troops are doing in the field.

A special concern recently is on monitoring troops' adherence to rules of engagement (ROE). This comes from the increasingly politicized nature of warfare, a battle for hearts and minds, a propaganda campaign to show humane treatment of the enemy, concern for civilians among whom the enemy is hiding, and to avoid propaganda disasters in the form of massacres and other atrocities. The more surveillance devices troops carry with them, and the more directly these are connected to remote communications, the less autonomy they have in the field. Much of this is for the future, but already the presence of battlefield surveillance from drones has had the effect of revealing combat atrocities. For instance, a squad of marines were put on trial for shooting civilians in Haditha, Iraq, in 2005 when searching houses near the site where a remote-controlled improvised explosive device (IED) had gone off, killing members of their unit. The incident was glossed over by the lower-level combat commanders, who no doubt regarded such events as part of the normal stress of combat (what I have analyzed elsewhere as "forward panic," Collins 2008: 83–112). Scrutiny emerged higher up because a drone overhead had recorded the events of the battle, and the details in the field commander's report did not square with what was recorded by the drone. Thus, surveillance devices are used not only against the enemy, but also to discipline one's own troops.

The unintended consequences of these trends are to put contradictory pressures on high-tech troops. On one hand, they are pressured by the enemy who are adopting a clandestine, hit-and-run approach, while otherwise hiding in the civilian population. On the other hand, they are exhorted to adopt a hearts-and-minds approach, to win over the civilian population, to engage in economy-building and community empowerment. It appears that many American troops are sincerely willing to adopt this approach, to play the role of benevolent charity-workers to the civilians who surround them at the front. But also anything they do wrong is increasingly likely to be picked up by their own command hierarchy, and by the news media, and that in turn propagates it to enemy news media and propagandists, making Western troops increasingly the targets for outrage and revenge. The effort to train local troops to take over the fighting in places like Afghanistan makes US soldiers especially vulnerable to sudden attacks from enemy agents or sympathizers, not just in combat situations but in their backstage routine. Thus, it would be surprising if an emotional mood were not building among US troops, of increasing suspicion and resentment of the hidden enemies around them. Incidents where US soldiers have gone on killing sprees in villages around their isolated forward operating base (FOB), or exacted symbolic revenge by acts like pissing on dead enemy soldiers, are not just individual idiosyncrasies, nor are they simply the result of long-standing and unchanging cultural clashes. Particularly in today's high-tech, high-self-selection military, soldiers want to be good guys and heroes. That they sometimes act the opposite is the result of organizational stress-induced human breakdowns.

Eliminating the Human Element

If human soldiers have so much trouble handling today's high-tech, high-politicized warfare, perhaps the solution is to go further in the same direction, and replace all combat soldiers with robots. For several decades, the US military has been at the forefront of the attempt to create humanoid robots. With the news focused on sheer numbers of casualties, the military is under pressure to keep casualties down.[8] And high-tech has made human presence in the front lines increasing unnecessary. Surveillance robots can be sent into a building where the enemy is believed to be hiding; or to investigate a site where hidden IEDs are suspected. What has not been achieved is a robot that looks like a human: a mechanical human that walks on two legs and holds things in its two arms. Perhaps this goal is the result of lack of imagination; at any rate, it turns out that human legs and feet are extremely complex, and to balance a machine on two legs that can move with the agility of a human or an animal is not worth the trouble. Hence the trend is toward robots that are only minimally human-looking; they can be canisters on wheels or treads; vehicles lacking drivers; airplanes or helicopters piloted by remote control. Since the age of AWACS (already available since the 1980s), pilots have largely just been along for emergency back-up; so the shift to robot-like drones is an easy step to make. As military designers get even more emancipated from the idea that weapons occupying the forward edge of the combat zone have to look like humans, a whole array of new military robots is coming into existence, from remote control tanks to miniaturized mechanical insects equipped with sensors as well as offensive weapons.

How far can this go? Leave aside for the moment the element of cost, and the strong likelihood that human soldiers, for many purposes, will be cheaper than their high-tech robotic version. (This may not be true of some kinds of low-level drones.) What happens when we turn the battlefield over to robots?

Here I want to concentrate on the symmetrical version, where both armies are high-tech and both have combat robots. The asymmetrical version, where a high-tech military full of robots fights a low-tech, guerrilla-style army, has not yet quite emerged either, because the hearts-and-minds doctrine is contradicted by robots.

An all-robot war can well afford to slug it out; politically, there is little concern for casualties, and two armies of robot tanks, mobile artillery, armored helicopters, surface-to-air missile batteries, and drones could all shoot at each other for an extended period of time. Note that all the considerations I have gone through above—counter-measures and counter-counter-measures; weak and strong cyber-war; surprise through information-system failures—are still operative even if there are no longer any humans operating the front-line weapons. On the whole, I have argued that unless one side quickly achieves superiority and ends the war, high-tech battles tend to deteriorate back into attrition warfare. This would be true of all-robot war too. So the side with deeper pockets of economic resources could keep on replacing its destroyed robots, and as long as it did this faster or kept at it longer than the enemy, it would win.

But this leaves out a crucial human element. In combat, equipment tends to wear out, both from damage of enemy hits, and from the wear and tear of moving around terrain and grinding its own moving parts.

In short, sheer physical friction. Robot warriors have less logistical needs than humans, in some respects: they don't need to be supplied with food, clothing, shelter from heat and cold, medical supplies and medical evacuation; but they do need to be resupplied with fuel and ammunition; and so there must be logistics vehicles out of the battlefield tending the robots. (Or else flying robots can frequently return to base; if these are forward operating bases, they too need to be supplied.) The logistics vehicles themselves could conceivably be robot-operated; but because humans are on the whole more adaptive and flexible, and generally faster in operating complex equipment, it is likely that humans would drive the logistics vehicles and do the refueling and reloading ammunition. And since many things are breaking down on the battlefield, there is a need for skilled repair technicians. It seems almost certain that in the early generations of robot warriors, at least, the repair techs will be humans rather than robots.

Putting all this together, we get a picture of an all-robot battlefield: it becomes a war of opposing junkyards. Operative and semi-operative robot weapons are out at the front (in the dispersed checkerboard pattern); logistics vehicles and repair personnel are driving around during the lulls, resupplying and repairing. Near the front are the FOBs where damaged robot-vehicles have been dragged or drag themselves, where human technicians are putting things back together, trying to get damaged computer circuits to work, scavenging some robots to repair others, struggling to get spare parts from rear areas. I would hypothesize that the relative efficiency of the human repair technicians determines the outcome of most robot battles. That brings the human element back in: it is a question not just of how skilled the repair techs are (if we can analytically disentangle that element), but of how motivated they are, how high their morale and confidence—how much emotional energy they have. And since emotions are collective products, coming from shared focus and rhythm, and resulting in cohesion and group identification, even an all-robot battle would hinge, in the end, on the familiar human factors that weigh most heavily in victory or defeat.[9]

There is an additional consideration. The shift to high-tech war has resulted in the rise of terrorism as a major form of war; and terrorism is, above all, a war of mass emotions and political will. This is the topic of Chapter 12.

Notes

1. This chapter, and Chapter 12 which follows, are based on presentations and interviews with military personnel at the U.S. Army War College, the U.S. Military Academy; conferences of US and UK officers of all ranks reviewing lessons learned from the wars in Iraq and Afghanistan in the early twenty-first century; and discussions with cyber-security specialists.
2. Watts (2004); McIvor (2005); King (2013; 2019). Apparently physical drag is the hardest form of friction to overcome. As von Clausewitz ([1815] 2007) realized watching

horses, artillery carriages, and human bodies break down trying to move across Russia, merely moving any part of a military organization from one place to another causes losses, and above all losses in efficiency to carry out plans. There is little indication that ultra high-tech military equipment has less tendency to break down, and indeed the costs of repairing and maintaining things like battle helicopters are one of the major problems of contemporary wars (and a significant source of casualties), even where all the high-tech equipment belongs to one side.

3. Anthony King (2019), who spent several years observing military headquarters in Afghanistan, as well as debriefing commanders in the Iraq War, describes how operations are carried out. Headquarters staff program elaborate scenarios about how campaigns are projected to go, especially in regards to logistics—what amounts of fuel and ammo to stockpile where. The program also schedules limited options for commanders at anticipated decision-points, circumscribing the role of the commander who ostensibly makes the decisions.
4. A problem with computer control structures is how they should be organized: in a highly centralized command structure? Or in a lateral network-centered structure which feeds many computer inputs to local commanders? Both structures have vulnerabilities, suggesting another way that Clausewitzian friction returns. This is the old issue in organizational theory, span of control.
5. Patriot batteries are run by central control. All but the most fast-breaking emergencies are relayed to the Regional Air Defense Commander to check if the target being tracked is hostile or one of their own planes. There were a couple of fratricide incidents in the Iraq War, when allied fighters were shot down by Patriot batteries that misidentified them as hostile, and one fighter had knocked out a Patriot radar unit by interpreting it as an Iraqi missile site (Snook 2000).
6. This is true even in long-planned set-piece attacks; for instance, in the major helicopter assault of the March 2003 Iraq invasion, the number of operative helicopters was drastically limited by problems of maintenance as well as availability of fuel at the advanced battle base (Gordon and Trainor 2007; King 2019).
7. The biggest break in US computer security happened as the result of pervasive boredom in combat zones. Pvt. Bradley Manning, who leaked a large number of classified intelligence reports to Wikileaks in 2010, was a computer analyst at an Iraq base. The prevailing atmosphere in the intelligence post was boredom, and the informal work custom allowed soldiers to bring their own music disks into the closed facility, even though security regulations prohibit anyone from bringing in or taking out electronic media. It was on these disks that Manning smuggled out the information. In 2013, Bradley Manning changed sex and became Chelsea Manning.
8. The practice of military public relations, since the end of the Vietnam War and its enemy body counts, has been to report only the number of American casualties, no longer giving the estimates of enemy casualties that used to be announced as an index of battle success. The effect is that news reports publicize only indicators of American losses, never indicators of victories. This further depresses morale within the military.
9. There are always on-going developments in military technology. The weapons, sensors and control systems described in this chapter are still is use, in some version and somewhere in the world. Very recent developments, as of 2020–2021, include increasing use of drones, flying at relatively slow speeds and low altitudes, and thus able to operate silently and to escape detection by defensive radar systems. Armed with rockets, they act like ultra-precise artillery, able to destroy tanks and to kill soldiers who think they are not visible to the enemy. But these weapons are relatively expensive (the most advanced American ones cost about $300 million each), and they need ground control units and human operators. Thus they are subject to the same problems of logistics and attrition as other high-tech weapons. Unanticipated problems emerge precisely from the

improvement in precision. US drone operators in the early 2010s could track human targets (known terrorists and commanders) through video monitors, but images were grainy and blurred. More recently, high-definition video lets the operators see the face of the persons they are trying to kill; and since they may track them for a long period until getting an opportunity to hit them with a rocket while they are away from civilians, operators get to see them in their ordinary family life, such as with their children. The result is that a considerable percentage of drone operators are traumatized by the memory of the people they have killed, which was not the case when blurred images dehumanized their targets (Phelps 2021). In my 2008 book (Collins 2008: 381–387), I noted that one path around confrontational tension/fear is distance weapons, where one cannot see the target as a human like yourself. Improved high-tech now brings back CT/F.

References

Biddle, Stephen. 2004. *Military Power: Explaining Victory and Defeat in Modern Battle.* Princeton, NJ: Princeton University Press.

Buzzell, Colby. 2006. *My War: Killing Time in Iraq.* New York: Berkeley.

Clausewitz, Carl von. [1815] 2007. *The Russian Campaign of 1812.* New Brunswick, NJ: Transaction Books.

Clausewitz, Carl von. [1833] 1976. *On War.* Princeton, NJ: Princeton University Press.

Collins, Randall. 2008. *Violence: A Micro-Sociological Theory.* Princeton, NJ: Princeton University Press.

Ender, Morten. 2009. *American Soldiers in Iraq.* New York: Routledge.

Gibson, James William. 1986. *The Perfect War: Technowar in Vietnam.* New York: Atlantic Monthly Press.

Gordon, Michael R. and Bernard E. Trainor. 2007. *Cobra II: The Inside Story of the Invasion and Occupation of Iraq.* New York: Random House.

King, Anthony. 2013. *The Combat Soldier: Infantry Tactics and Cohesion in the Twentieth and Twenty-first Centuries.* Cambridge: Cambridge University Press.

King, Anthony. 2019. *Command: The Twenty-first Century General.* Cambridge: Cambridge University Press.

Liddell-Hart, B. H. 1970. *History of the Second World War.* New York: Putnam's.

McIvor, Anthony D. (Ed.) 2005. *Rethinking the Principles of War.* Annapolis, MD: Naval Institute Press.

Murray, Williamson, and Robert H. Scales. 2003. *The Iraq War: A Military History.* Cambridge, MA: Belknap Press.

Nolan, Bridget. 2016. "Information Sharing and Collaboration in the United States Intelligence Community: An Ethnography of the National Counterterrorism Center." Unpublished dissertation, Department of Sociology, University of Pennsylvania.

Phelps, Wayne. 2021. *On Killing Remotely: The Psychology of Killing with Drones.* Boston: Little, Brown.

Snook, Scott A. 2000. *Friendly Fire: The Accidental Shootdown of US Blackhawks over Northern Iraq.* Princeton, NJ: Princeton University Press.

Watts, Barry V. 2004. *Clausewitzian Friction and Future War.* Washington, DC: Institute for National Strategic Studies, National Defense University.

Chapter 12

Terrorist Tactics

Symbiosis with High-Tech

Introduction

During the twenty-first-century wars in Iraq, Afghanistan and Syria, insurgents used low-tech weapons against Western forces and their allies. Typical are suicide bombers who carry explosives right up to its target, and improvised explosive devices (IEDs)- hidden in the roadway and set off by a mobile phone when an enemy vehicle passes. But these have acquired a high-tech component. Spotters who see a vehicle approach do not have to communicate directly with a trigger-man who sets off the bomb; both are connected to a coordinator in an Internet café in Brussels. We can trace the link but we can't do anything about it. The arrangement parallels the command structure of US high-tech military, where spotters can be Special Forces putting laser tags on enemy targets, or silent drones flying overhead, or satellites in space, all sending their information to a remote headquarters, like the Air Force base in Florida that controlled the 2003 invasion of Iraq. This seems ironic but in fact the one process is parasitical upon the other.[1]

The Long Trend: High-Tech Disperses the Battlefield

The pattern of military high-tech has been building up since World War I. Weapons have gotten more lethal, and more accurate at increasingly longer distance. Troops and their equipment could no longer be bunched together, since this makes them too vulnerable a target for artillery. Machine guns made old-fashioned marching into battle suicidal. By 1918, soldiers were being trained to split into small groups, taking cover where they could find it on broken ground while infiltrating enemy positions. The trend has continued with every advance in weaponry. In World War II, the front was typically 5 km from one brigade to another; now it is 150 km, forward operating bases (FOBs), supplied by helicopter and communicating electronically, make a checker-board of mostly empty battlespace.

The digital revolution in the last 30 years has vastly increased targeting information, by aerial surveillance and satellites using an array of sensors

DOI: 10.4324/9781003245629-16

that track vehicle movements and even individual humans by infra-red heat signature; radar; and computer-enhanced photographic imagery which can be compared over time to look for tell-tale changes. Enemy headquarters can be located by its buzz of electronic activity. Enemy rockets or artillery that use radar for their own targeting can be tracked by radar-seeking devices that fire back immediately to destroy the enemy weapon. Super-computers assemble the information into a composite picture of the battlefield, and remote computers increasingly control firing on enemy targets, whether from aircraft, ships or ground-based weapons.

So-called asymmetric war (in which a high-tech military fights a more poorly equipped enemy) has taken its pattern from the same shifts that brought about the sprawling battlefields of symmetrical war between major powers with similar levels of equipment. Both high-tech militaries and low-tech insurgents disperse in order to avoid vulnerabilities to increasingly lethal weapons. The poorer just have to disperse more. Either way, the battlefield expands; and it is no longer so sharply marked off from ordinary civilian life.

Guerrillas and Terrorists Disperse Even More

The shift toward guerrilla war is an adaptation to the increasing lethality of modern weapons. Guerrillas avoid matching firepower with firepower in a direct confrontation, since the weaker side cannot win on conventional battlefields. All armies now disperse, hide, or use speed and long-distance movement to protect themselves from the enemy's lethal weapons. Guerrillas just take this to an extreme. The resource-poor side of an asymmetrical war has responded by dispersing its forces even more, and making hit-and-run attacks on isolated enemy bases and the supply lines between them.[2] Most wars involving Western powers since the Vietnam War have been asymmetrical, a high-tech military versus a low-tech insurgency. Such tactics were called guerrilla war, as long as it attacked military targets; it became "terrorism" when it concentrated on civilian targets, since these are softer, less-protected than military targets. Guerrilla war slides over into terrorism, because between attacks guerrillas hide in the civilian population.

Earlier guerrillas hid in favorable terrain such as mountains and caves. Contemporary guerrillas/terrorists hide in populated areas; the civilian population is their cover. Terrorism has grown in symbiosis with high-tech weapons and electronics, as advanced sensors can locate military equipment in the countryside, and command posts stand out when there are few other humans around sending electronic signals. Cities make better cover for military forces than the open fields where early modern wars were generally fought, segregated from the rest of the population. Now, to the contrary, large masses of human population are the best defense for the lightly-armed, and the most cover against high-tech weapons.

Urban buildings clutter sight lines and other direct sensors; it is difficult to distinguish the infra-red (IR) heat-signatures of civilians from combatants; and high-tech surveillance is evaded by hiding in the electronic jumble of ordinary life. A modern city is full of electronic noise, even in poor countries, since cell phones and other consumer electronics are the features of modernity that diffuse the fastest. The result is to deliberately blur the borderline between military and civilians. Terrorists generally are civilians, and they live among other civilians, and attempt to look like them as much as possible—contravening the long-standing military custom of wearing uniforms, which made possible a distinction between combatants and non-combatants. Blurring this distinction has generated the moral conundrums that make it so difficult for modern democracies to fight terrorists.

Terrorism Is War of Competing Media-Publicized Atrocities

The biggest problem in fighting urban guerrillas is political: they use other civilians as shields; and they welcome civilian casualties because these turn the local population against the outside enemy. This leads to the nastiest aspect of contemporary war, intrinsically a type of war with many civilian casualties. This is one reason why wars have become increasingly political struggles for "hearts and minds." High-tech war was designed to eliminate "friction," including human emotions. But urban guerrilla war reintroduces powerful emotions both in the motivation of frontline combatants, and in the political world that backs them up or lets them down.

The more that humanitarian considerations enter the picture, the more advantage to forces that hide in civilian populations. Democratic regimes with open news and unhindered media cannot avoid having their own military atrocities publicized world-wide. It doesn't matter if civilian casualties are accidents, or forward panics by occupying troops embittered by fighting an enemy who hides and disguises themselves as civilians. Western militaries are surrounded by news networks. Troops have access to their own social media that leak private messages about what happens in the battle-zone; and these easily become scandals that go viral on the Internet. The cell phone photos of American soldiers humiliating and torturing prisoners at Abu Ghraib prison in 2004 occurred at the time that these technologies were taking off; perhaps because new users at the time were not yet aware of how limited on-line privacy actually is. Since then, journalists, political activists of various kinds, and social media enthusiasts have made a deliberate technique of seeking out damaging information about persons in the public eye, especially soldiers in controversial wars, paralleling the ferreting out scandals of word or conduct among celebrities and prominent persons in civilian life.

But aren't the atrocities committed by terrorists equally widely publicized? This is especially so when they attack civilians in foreign countries rather than in the war zone, as in New York, Paris, and London. From the point of view of the attackers (whether hijacking airplanes to fly into buildings, driving trucks into crowds of pedestrians, or firing weapons at people in offices or clubs), these are complicitous citizens of the states that have committed atrocities against them. Such targets just happen to be easier to reach, which fits the general pattern that successful violence is mostly attacking the weak. It also illustrates the counter-escalation dynamic of motivating the next atrocity by the other side's previous atrocity. But this is not entirely a symmetrical process.

As a technique for keeping an insurgency going, committing atrocities is more advantageous to low-tech movements than to the high-tech states. This is true both for Western atrocities on Middle Eastern battlefields, and for terrorist atrocities in the war zone and on the enemy's home turf. Atrocities committed by troops of the Western democracies undermine political support for counter-insurgency (COIN) wars, which can lead to troop withdrawals or even abandoning such wars. Tactically, the aftermath of Western investigations of such atrocities leads to stricter rules of engagement for troops, giving terrorists more leeway to act with impunity on the battlefield and making them more secure while hiding in the population. There is no such response when terrorists kill civilians in their own communities, such as by collateral damage in suicide bombings. Loosely organized terrorists have no command structure imposing rules of engagement; nor do they accord much legitimacy to whatever local officials say in condemning their massacres. Unlike well-organized structures of accountability linking Western armies, governments, and courts, terrorists are mostly off the radar as far as their own societies' capacity to hold them responsible.

Atrocities are also the major recruiting tool for militant terrorists, both those who join forces in the battle zone, and media-activated isolates who launch individual attacks in foreign countries. Some atrocities are deliberately orchestrated and produced for the Internet. ISIS has specialized in filming mass beheadings of captured enemy soldiers or unwilling supporters in their own locales. These are regarded as disgusting by most Western viewers; but it is not the majority viewers that count, but the small proportion of sympathizers for the insurgency who can be inspired to join the fight. On the battlefields of the Middle East, the news may be mostly insurgents' defeats. Defiantly publicizing mass beheadings and other acts of successful violence trumpets the news that we too inflict defeats on the enemy; and that *we have not gone away*. In Western eyes, such atrocities are barbaric, but the throw-back to historical times is an explicit appeal to traditionalists attempting to recreate the moral universe of pre-modern societies.[3] The very fact that such things as mass beheading videos are especially shocking guarantees that they receive wide publicity; and this creates a favorable atmosphere for recruiting militants. Terrorists do not aim at wide popularity, but at recruiting a small number of extremists.

In combination, Western atrocities undermine political will and battlefield victory more then terrorist atrocities motivate counter-escalation against themselves; and terrorist atrocities are the main way that they keep up their own morale and recruit enough participants to keep their insurgency going.

Politically, an insurgency does not have to win battles or take territory, but only to resist pacification by an outside enemy. The Islamic State made the mistake in Iraq and Syria of taking territory in 2014 and a few years onwards, setting up a state structure and using more conventional military tactics, which transformed ISIS into the weaker side of a somewhat more symmetrical war. Similarly, the Taliban in Afghanistan became an easy target when they were a government, but hard to eradicate as guerrillas.

Small numbers of insurgents can keep a war going. Their main resource is advertising their presence by spectacular attacks, even if these are bloody atrocities of their own. As long as their actions are well-publicized, they demonstrate a will to continue the fight. Insurgents expect to prevail over time, above all because foreign occupying forces lose the political will to persist.

Terrorist Command-and-Control Is Parasitical on the Global Electronic Web

Terrorism is media-dependent war in two senses. As noted, terrorism relies on global news and social media for the political war of sympathy, recruitment, and discouragement of its enemies' public support. Terrorism has also evolved into a decentralized, acephalous form because it can use global media as a substitute for organizational structure coordinating military operations.

The on-going growth of world-wide high-tech is shifting the crucial balance of military power to communications, above all, because contemporary war is political war. The irony here is that global communications—both for consumers, and as a major component of the post-industrial economy—mean that every innovation by the rich capitalist countries creates a military opportunity for insurgents. It is not so much that they imitate the most advanced weapons (although they can capture or buy them, especially from the West's so-called local allies), but they can share in digital communications because they are marketed worldwide.

Many of the most advanced surveillance systems are umbrellas covering everything within their range, friend and enemy alike. In Iraq, insurgent fires were coordinated via Internet cafés in Belgium, just as US soldiers could link to Internet cafés or any other sites in the world for private communications with family and friends. Cell phones are used to trigger IEDs, but shutting down the local cell phone network was not feasible, since US commanders themselves use them as a more-reliable alternative to centralized military communication channels. GPS coordinates, pin-pointed by a network of satellites around the Earth, are used both by allied targeting and by insurgents targeting us. The terrorist attack on Mumbai luxury hotels in 2008 was coordinated by a mobile phone from across the border with the aid of the ISI (the Pakistani version of the CIA).

Terrorist fighters might be killed in action, but the main principle of modern military doctrine—to decapitate the enemy by knocking out its headquarters command-and-control and thus destroying it as a functioning organization—has become impossible. There is no command post "in theatre," but on ostensibly neutral foreign soil; and there need not be any clandestine network on the spot to uproot (as the French attempted during the Algerian War). Commands and targeting information are sent out by one-way messages, on the open Internet—its source lost in the morass of ordinary communications. In the Russian semi-proxy war in the eastern Ukraine, the Ukrainian military used the same satellites as the Russians (since they were the same country not long ago), so neither side could disrupt the other's targeting without disrupting their own.

Cyberwar has been growing as a cheap resource for insurgents, because they operate inside the same global communications umbrella as their resource-rich enemies. The US does not have an advantage in cyber-space. By concentrating on digital high-tech, the West is playing in an arena where its advantage in other kinds of military resources do not count. Cyberwar can also be practiced by wealthy states, but it is above all a weapon of the weak. Its physical tools are easily available commercially; skill at hacking requires no great organizational coordination, and is easily acquired by alienated youth all over the world. Fighting a cyberwar is exactly the wrong place for the wealthy states to fight.

Cyberwar: Weak, Strong, or Traitorous

Attempts to deceive and mislead the enemy have gone on throughout the history of warfare. The earliest tribal wars were successful (if at all) largely by ambush and sneak attacks; by the time of the early organized states in China and the Mediterranean, we read of ruses to make small numbers of troops look larger while the bulk of forces attacked somewhere else. This is not in principle different from current air fighters ejecting metallic chaff to deflect electronically-guided missiles. What is new in the IT era is that communications systems become hugely more valuable targets when everything a military organization does is coordinated by long-distance computer networks. And since computers and Internet access are widespread even in poor countries, even in asymmetrical wars the weaker side is closest to their high-tech-rich enemy in cyberwar.

The US military formally set up a Cyberwar Command in 2010. Publicly, it emphasizes defending the American economy from cyberattack. Its military defensive and offensive activities are mostly secret, but it is clear that the military has been concerned with communications security of its computer network throughout its development. The SAGE air-defense project turned computers into rapid decision-makers, while the Atlas missile program promoted the military-industrial-academic complex. The Internet itself developed from time-sharing arrangements among computer scientists on expensive university mainframes, and from the DARPANET, set up in the 1980s to link Department of Defense researchers (Hughes 1998: 293–294). The personal computer revolution began with young hobby-hacker type kids borrowing equipment from Hewlett Packard, at that time a major defense contractor (Furnari 2014). The GPS system of satellites tracking the coordinates of everything in airspace and on the ground was initially created for guiding intercontinental ballistic missiles (ICBM). Both these systems of hardware and electronic design eventually were opened to civilian and economic purposes, encouraged by policy decisions made in the Clinton administration. The era of the RMA/military high-tech transformation has also been an era of outsourcing military functions to civilians, a trend propelled (very consciously on both military and civilian aspects) during the G.W. Bush administration (IDA 2003). The global IT economy created the role of the hacker, making civilian mischief-making and military cyberwar all of a piece.

There are weak and strong versions of cyberwar. Weak versions include deceiving the enemy's sensors or decoying them with false targets; jamming communications channels with electronic noise, or bombarding them with Internet communications in a denial-of-service attack. Military computer networks are shielded from much routine hacking, and there are no reports of military operations per se being shut down or strongly compromised by hackers, who only reach the part of the military system expressly designed to interface with the public. But the resources of civilian hackers are limited compared to what an enemy military could generate; in a full-scale war between high-resource states, it is certain that all-out cyberwar would be launched, probably as the first blow. It is not yet known what would happen in battle situations when both sides are vigorously deceiving and jamming each other's computer networks.

The weak versions of cyberwar are aimed at a particular component of the military network: chiefly the sensors, upon which deception is practiced; jamming and overloading are aimed at the communications channels, where information goes in and orders come out. Weak cyberwar attacks on order-giving channels are the equivalent of traditional espionage, or just battlefield intelligence, with the coup being to capture enemy battle plans. Notable instances happened in the US Civil War—the battle of Antietam; and in WWII—the capture of German attack plans in Belgium from a plane flying off course, which ironically had the effect of decoying the French and British into a false sense of where the attack would come, since the Germans changed the plan. Even better, to crack the enemy wireless code, as US intelligence did to Japanese communications (Keegan 2003). These fall into the category of fog of war, to the detriment of one side but the advantage of the other.

A strong version of cyberwar would be to attack a country's economic infrastructure. This has become an increasing vulnerability as advanced economies (above all the US) use computer links for banking, credit cards and credit checks; on-line sales and deliveries; scheduling transport and ticketing such as airlines; coordinating supply chains; electric grids and power plants; as well as record-keeping in medical, educational, and insurance bureaucracies. Tax reporting, government regulations and their compliance all are heavily computerized. All-out economic cyberwar would go beyond the piecemeal occurrences of hacking, identity theft, financial fraud, and ransom attacks that have become a normal part of daily life. Economic cyberwar has the potential to disrupt finances, logistics, transport; to shut down power; and threaten the necessities of life.

Air travel (and increasingly ground travel) are coordinated by digital networks; so are power grids, hospitals, and police forces; so are most financial transactions, from international banking to personal salaries and bill-paying; so are the now-huge businesses of on-line shopping and delivery. One of the most devastating forms of cyberwar now being worried about is a cyber-attack, not from isolated mischief-making hackers or from thieves, but from an enemy government (or an insurgency), aimed at shutting down the economy of one of the rich capitalist nations. Less advanced economies would be safer from such attack, being less reliant on digital coordination. In fact, the more primitive the economy, the less it would suffer from retaliatory economic cyberwar. Thus there is more incentive for insurgent movements, or hostile governments, in economies nearer to subsistence to attack the advanced economies.

But although this is an extremely dangerous prospect, it is not the most dangerous event that could happen. Since an ultra-modern military is so heavily organized around electronic command and control, the worst threat to its existence would be if an enemy could hack into its links to disable its weapons, its mobility and its logistics—in effect, an electronic giant rendered blind, deaf, and paralyzed.[4] There is even one nightmare step beyond this scenario: enemy hackers leave the operational system of our military intact, but take over controls of our weapons so that our rockets and aircraft are turned about to fire on ourselves. There have been some steps in this direction, as Iranians and others have been able to capture some US-made drones by diverting their remote controls.

The strongest and most devastating version of cyberwar is where the enemy's communication channels are not only degraded, but are actually turned against them. Turning the opponent's weapons against itself is the ultimate nightmare of high-tech warfare. In this scenario, the enemy hacks into one's computer channels on the output side, and inserts false orders. Moreover, as the human element in command and execution is reduced by computer-controlled weapons, there is little stop-gap to recognize when our own weapons are being aimed at our own assets. The archetype here is to turn a missile or an F/A aircraft around and have it attack its own base. Of course, friendly fire has existed, apparently as long as distance weapons have been used. Firing on the wrong troops was one of the dangers of the smoke-covered battlefield of Napoleonic times, and this has probably gotten more prevalent with the long-distance artillery of WWI, the close air support of WWII, and the checkerboard battlefield of recent asymmetric wars. But turning a weapons system against itself, as a deliberate tactic, is something new, different from accidental fratricide which benefits the enemy.

To date, and so far as is known through publicly accessible channels, there are no strong instances of turning enemy weapons by cyberwar techniques. In the Russia-Georgia war of 2008, it is believed that the Russians successfully hacked into Georgian military communications and hampered their troop movements (relatively easy to do since Georgian weapons were Russian weapons). During 2012, it is believed that Israeli cyberattacks (possibly with US help) successfully degraded Iranian nuclear weapons-building—although not to a degree to head off prolonged public discussion of direct air attack. During the 2006 Israel-Hezbollah war in Lebanon, Israeli missiles were apparently hacked by Hezbollah, deflecting them from their targets. The nearest to actually turning a computer-controlled weapon was in 2011, when Iranian cyber-warriors captured an American drone. Iranian engineers were able to access the part of the drone's guidance system that controls what happens if the drone loses contact with its operator; the drone is programmed to land at the nearest base, and the Iranian cyber-hackers were able to reprogram it into "thinking" the nearest friendly base was on Iranian territory.

Such partial successes in wresting remote control of weapons from their operators have led to further counter-measures, and these to an escalating sequence of counter-counter-measures. Rather than try to follow these constantly-changing patterns through scattered reports and projections, let us consider schematically what are the possible outcomes of full-scale cyberwar.

Victory and Defeat

One side successfully disables or turns enemy weapons systems and wins the war. This is most likely to victimize the side that relies most heavily on high-tech, computer-linked weapons systems. Alternatively, one side destroys the enemy's economic network, making it impossible for them to continue to fight. This does not necessarily mean that the victor would be able to invade and occupy the economically disrupted territory. Cyberwar is relatively cheap, a weapon of the weak; such states or movements would probably lack the logistics to mount an invasion. As I have argued, terrorism is a tactic for repelling invaders or occupying forces; its strength is in hiding in its civilian population and holding out until the occupiers give up. Terrorism is not an offensive weapon, in the classical sense of conquest; its attacks on foreign targets are sheer destruction (and morale-building for themselves), not a means of taking territory.

There is a second reason why a cyberwar victor would not likely invade the economically devastated territory. If disruption is bad enough, outcomes could be famine and plague, making the territory uninhabitable for a time. Population movements could be reversed, from wealthy states to poorer ones, at least for a period of years.

Stalemate and Mutual Degradation

Both sides attack and disable the other's military organization system to approximately equal degree. This means the war goes on—and, most importantly, by *reverting to lower-tech modes of warfare*. This would also reduce their vulnerability to cyber-attacks. I will consider this possibility further, after discussing a pre-emptive move that is now being discussed in military circles.

Shutting Down the Internet in Time of War

So what can or will be done about the Great Powers' loss of military advantage in a cyber-linked world? Here we come to an unthinkable solution that the military is actually thinking about: shutting down the Internet in time of war. This is a short-hand way of referring to all the communications devices under the modern world-umbrella that are shared with our adversaries: mobile phones, GPS coordinates, networked computers.

But how could these be shut down, without enormous damage to our own economy, and our contemporary way of life?

If the US military's digital control system were seriously threatened by an enemy, the response now being considered is to shut down the entire digital umbrella. There are two ways this could happen: either the enemy shuts down our digital network or attacks it to the extent that it becomes useless; or we shut it down pre-emptively to keep our enemies from using it.

Probably there would be several levels of shut-down: smallest would be to shut down all mobile phone and Internet activity in a given area (e.g. battlegrounds in Iraq or Syria), by shutting down cell phone towers and servers. Or the Internet and/or mobile phones could be put on one-way broadcast mode; messages going out from a central source (as in some emergency warning systems) but otherwise clearing the network of traffic.[5]

Another choice would be to shut down crucial targeting infrastructure, such as GPS; since this is a satellite-based system, it would affect the entire world. Such plans are being seriously contemplated; the Chinese reportedly are building their own GPS system (based on their own satellites) that would be inaccessible to others.

This seems unthinkable, since GPS is included in all sorts of devices, including ordinary smart phones. But GPS was originally created as a secret project by the US military (as a way of preventing aerial collisions and other blue-on-blue attacks); and was opened up to commercial use in the 1990s. There is precedent for returning GPS to government control; and it may become a matter of military necessity—or what is presented to the public as such. We should not expect that history has one continuous trajectory, and that technologies and social customs surrounding them become impervious to removal once they become widespread. The Chinese government's use of super-computers, complete with facial recognition systems for tracking every move of every citizen, shows what kinds of things are technically possible, although they may be politically repugnant in some countries and not in others. Chinese citizens in the future might well benefit from some kind of emergency that caused the shut-down of its central government computers.

Going Back to Non-Digital Back-Up

But how would the military operate under this unthinkable contingency, shutting down the electronic networks that have become the core of its organization? Planning on this point is proceeding. The essential pattern is to build back-up procedures—how to run a war without the Internet, computer links, GPS, or mobile phones. In fact, there is discussion about how over-reliance on digital networks even now is reducing military efficiency; and how weaning ourselves away from it can be done.

We tend to forget that the ultra-computerized military is a relatively recent thing. Big mainframe computers were developed in the military from World War II onwards; it is the dispersed, omnipresent commercial and private networks and its devices that have become widespread so rapidly since the 1990s and early 2000s. Military officers have commented on the huge increase in computerization since the beginning of the Iraq War in 2003. A company (about 200 soldiers) then had five computers, operated by the Executive Officer and First Sergeant. Now all officers have computers, so much so that they spend 75 percent of their time reporting to headquarters. A US general commented: "Network has become more problem than solution." On Navy ships, the traditional system was a single wireless link under the authority of the ship's captain; now with all sailors in possession of personal computers or smart phones, official channels are surrounded by links used for personal reasons. All news gets out, even if confidential. Officers have become risk-averse, since even minor mishaps are scrutinized; junior officers lose initiative and feel they must clear every decision with higher command.

A similar tendency to centralize control upwards comes with the profusion of information from battle sites, gathered by electronic sensors and relayed to all levels of the command network. The term has developed, "Predator pawns"—as if Predator drones are pawns in a chess game. Since high-ranking officers as well as drone operators can watch the video feed from the drone, the result is a strong temptation to micro-manage.

A similar process has led to higher-level intervention by civilian officials worried about possible news scandals. There are many channels for stories to leak out; politicians are under pressure to achieve results, but also highly vulnerable to criticism for mishaps. All this increases the tendency for politicians to intervene, even at the smallest tactical level. A US commander gave the example of how much time he had to spend going back-and-forth with a high official in Washington about whether a load of small arms could be dropped to a local ally in Syria. Multinational forces are considered politically desirable, but US advisors describe the resulting organizational chart as "a wiring diagram"—and US commanders spend much of their time clearing requests for resources with the National Security Council and Iraqi politicians. A sardonic remark by a US general about the tangled authorities of the International Joint Command: "I spent a year in Iraq and all I fought was the IJC."

The core problem is communication overload. The presence of information technology everywhere results in a situation that one general described as "we've gone from network-enabled, to network-enamored, to network-encumbered." Thus, military planners see some advantages in going back to older forms of command and control—cutting off reliance on cyber, going back to local radio links to coordinate troops. Computers, especially when centralized and taking inputs from a vast area, make it hard to quickly change course. Old-fashioned communications allow for more flexibility and more rapid reaction to local emergencies and sudden opportunities. Historians point to flexibility by aggressive front-line officers as the key to the *Blitzkrieg* successes of World War II (King 2019). Whether this still has application in asymmetrical counter-insurgency war remains to be seen.

Preventing and/or Recovering from Economic Cyber-attack

The prevailing approach to economic cyberwar is to continue along the lines of seeking out vulnerabilities and fixing them with superior software. Most cyber-security experts are pessimistic that hacking attacks can be stopped. This is realistic, given there is a vicious cycle of "black hat" and "white hat" hackers; many of them claim to be doing a service by breaking into computer systems everywhere, exposing their vulnerabilities so that they can be remedied. But the same networks of hackers also facilitate and encourage predatory hackers, aiming for gain, revenge, or ideological and personal satisfaction. It is an endlessly escalating cyber-arms race, in which all advances become platforms for further techniques of attack. This pessimistic realization has led some strategists to conclude that the only way to stop a serious, system-wide attack on the US economy is to engage in offensive cyberwar: to prepare to disable the opponent's computers at the slightest indication that an attack has begun. This is a hair-trigger approach to the cyber equivalent of world-wide nuclear war.

A less harrowing alternative is to do what the military is contemplating: take the most crucial economic components off the Internet. This could take two forms. One is to back up existing computer-linked systems with manual controls, such as in electric grids and manufacturing. Information collected and stored on computers (in finance, commerce, health, etc.) should be backed up off-line. This is prudent preparation, not only for cyberwar, but as defense against ransom attacks and other predators.

The second version would be reconstructing the economic network after a cyber-attack. This is not as unthinkable as it seems. It would mean a return to telephones, fax messages, letters, paper files and books, as means of carrying out financial transactions, scheduling transport, managing production and distribution, work, and its payment. In the absence of a crisis, of course, this seems a needless expense, duplicating what digital wiring does faster and cheaper. But when the entire computerized economy is shut down, people are struggling to find food and medicine, lighting and shelter, there would be an immediate scramble to use telephone and written messages to regenerate some semblance of economic coordination.

This way of thinking about fending off or recovering from economic cyberwar is the same as military thinking about shutting down the Internet pre-emptively in the face of devastating attacks on its own weapons controls. It is possible to survive economic cyberwar, by backing up the economic network with non-vulnerable hardware; or after the fact, going back to non-vulnerable modes of communication and coordination. The duplication would be expensive, but recovering from a devastated economy would be even more so.

The Future of Terrorism, Cyberwar, and Others Not Yet Invented

So far I have discussed the ways cyberwar allows terrorists to take advantage of the shared global umbrella of the Internet, both for coordinating their own military assaults, and for disrupting high-tech weapons and even turning them around as captured weapons. A parallel discussion covers economic cyberwar, and the ways that both economic and military operations can be shielded from cyber-attacks. The solution is to back them up with unhackable hardware (not just software), either in advance preparation, pre-emptive moves in open war, or recovery from cyber-destruction.

I have noted that one possible outcome of cyberwar (and of high-tech war in general) is stalemate and mutual degradation, reverting to lower-tech modes of warfare. The fully-linked, highly computerized military system gets degraded by cyber-attacks; and the most immediate way to effectively respond is to keep on fighting by shifting to weapons that are less vulnerable because they are less linked into the system. Weapons platforms go back to being locally autonomous; human decision-making and traditional communications come back to fill the gap.[6]

There is also the back-to-the-drawing-board response, where failures in high-tech security are expected to be remedied by a next generation of high-tech. But the reversion to lower-tech warfare is always the quicker fix. This was the case when the cutting-edge high-tech invasion of Iraq in 2003 was faced by new problems in 2004, giving way to the revival of boots-on-the-ground tactics. None of this is permanent, and the alternation between these two patterns is likely—high-tech advances; then its vulnerabilities; remedied by reverting to lower-tech warfare. Any modern war tends to be a combination of these several tendencies.

Coda: A Thought-Experiment

I have written my own thought-experiment, a novel about a hypothetical civil war, in which the American military divides and fights itself with exactly the same weapons on both sides. (Just as happened in the American Civil War of 1861–1865.) The novel is called *Civil War Two*. The war begins with cyber-attacks attempting to turn bombers against their own bases. The solution to the cyber-hacking is to shut down the computerized system and build another control system. High-tech aircraft have enormous capacities for locating enemy targets and firing back at their electronic location; but since both sides can do this, the result is to destroy a large proportion of the most advanced aircraft on both sides.

Moreover, the most advanced aircraft are the most expensive, and take the longest time to build, as well as requiring assiduous maintenance between missions. Attrition of such weapons would inevitably result in older weapons being pressed into service. Even a battle between robots would be, most likely, not Hollywood's humanoid giants on two legs, but armored tanks containing no humans, like driverless cars firing at each other. The outcome of such a battle would depend, not on the superiority of one side's robots over the other, but on the skill and energy of humans going out onto the battlefield to repair the damaged robots. My chief conclusion is that a war fought between two very advanced militaries would lead over time to mutual degradation, and a return to earlier forms of warfare.

I have already suggested that remote computerized communications and control would be shut down early in such a war. If both sides have drones, armored helicopters, anti-missile missiles, and robot vehicles, their mutual attrition would eventually result in humans making the difference.

High-tech stalemate will drive combat back to the human level. The idea that has prevailed for about a century—that the state would win which created the next super-weapon before the other side did—will probably not hold in the future. That is because the recent wave of digital technologies, whose initial thrust has come heavily from military inventions, has spread into the civilian economy and ordinary life; and warfare centered on the cyber-sphere gives most advantage to the disrupters of the other side's communications. This is true whether it is asymmetrical terrorist attacks against a military and economic behemoth; or symmetrical war between states with equally sophisticated equipment.

What seems unthinkable now—shutting down the Internet and all the other digital media—in one degree or another is likely to happen. Where we come out on the other side of that crisis will probably become normal to people who live in it, just as the digital devices of the last 15 years have become so normal that we can't imagine living without them. But we probably will.

Notes

1. This chapter and Chapter 11 are based on presentations and interviews with military personnel at the U.S. Army War College, the U.S. Military Academy; conferences of US and UK officers of all ranks reviewing lessons learned from the wars in Iraq and Afghanistan in the early twenty-first century; and discussions with cyber-security specialists.
2. More than 50 percent of US casualties in Afghanistan and Iraq between 2001 and 2010 were in supply convoys to FOBs (*The Defense Monitor* 2019: 6).
3. Beheadings were still prominent in British public life through the 1600s. A gradual revulsion against torture and public spectacles of cruelty built up during the following centuries. Public executions and tortures continued in some Islamic regions of the world up through the present. This historically-based cultural divergence in political moral standards makes the "hearts and minds" struggle irresolvable in the short run, although it could change over time. How much time? Decades, centuries? Can our theory of time-dynamics develop far enough to answer this kind of question?
4. This is the scenario envisioned in P. W. Singer's novel, *Ghost Fleet* (Singer and Cole 2016), where Chinese-made components in American electronics are programmed to put the entire US military out of operation during a surprise attack.
5. An illustration of how this might work comes from the shutdown in summer 2019 by the government of India of all communications in and from Kashmir, including the Internet and cell-phone links, to prevent protest mobilization. It is becoming a standard tactic in authoritarian parts of the world.
6. As mentioned earlier, the cyberwar expert P. W. Singer's novel, *Ghost Fleet*, envisions the US being devastated by a Chinese cyber-attack that incapacitates the US military. In

the novel, the US makes a come-back by resuscitating an old moth-balled World War II fleet, unhackable because its controls are pre-digital; plus creating some advanced weapons that can't be diverted from their targets since they carry no on-board mini-computer to be taken over. Singer (2009) discusses the "robotics revolution" in warfare.

References

Collins, Randall. 2018. *Civil War Two: America Elects a President Determined to Restore Religion to Public Life, and the Nation Splits*. San Diego: Maren Ink.

Furnari, Santi. 2014. "Interstitial Spaces: Microinteraction Settings and the Genesis of New Practices Between Institutional Fields." *Academy of Management Review* 39: 439–462.

Hughes, Thomas. 1998. *Rescuing Prometheus: Four Monumental Projects that Changed the Modern World*. New York: Random House.

IDA. 2003. *Transformation and Transition: DARPA's Role in Fostering an Emerging Revolution in Military Affairs*. Alexandria, VA: Institute for Defense Analyses.

Keegan, John. 2003. *Intelligence in War*. New York: Knopf.

King, Anthony. 2019. *Command. The Twenty-first Century General*. Cambridge: Cambridge University Press.

Singer, P. W. 2009. *Wired for War: The Robotics Revolution and Conflict in the 21st Century*. New York: Penguin.

Singer, P. W. and August Cole. 2016. *Ghost Fleet: A Novel of the Next World War*. New York: Mariner Books.

The Defense Monitor 2019. Vol. 48, April–June, p. 6. Washington, DC: Center for Defense Information.

Part IV

Violence in Everyday Life

Chapter 13

Emotional Domination and Resistance to Sexual Aggression

Introduction

Violence is difficult to carry out. This is the main finding of research on what happens when humans find themselves in situations threatening violence. It runs contrary to our cultural beliefs, and the way violence is depicted in the news and entertainment media. But the news reports violence that happens, not fights that abort, angry quarrels that fritter out, or guns that are pointed but not fired, or fired but miss.

Does this pattern fit sexual aggression? We may think sexual aggression is easy and automatic, a product of male hormones or domineering male culture. But our evidence is mostly sampling on the dependent variable, and lumping different kinds of sexual advances together. Attempted rapes often fail, and many kinds of sexual advances do not get very far.

There are micro-interactional conditions by which sexual aggression can be deterred—locally, on the spot, by participants themselves. The question is whether the micro-processes that make physical violence succeed also apply to sexual aggression. This is a genuine question; there is little systematic research on it yet. But sifting through ethnographic evidence plus news reports—which since the last quarter of 2017 have been suddenly full of graphic detail—indicates that the micro-sociology of violence also explains when and how sexual aggression fails. Just asking the question points the way to better research on the turning points of sexual violence.

Part I Micro-Dynamics of Violent Conflict

The triggers—and inhibitors—of violence are in the emotional details of human interaction. We have seen these before, but I summarize here again in order to check their relevance to sexual violence.

Confrontational Tension and Fear (CT/F)

In situations threatening violence, participants may start out with angry bluster, loud voices, and menacing gesture. But when it comes to bodily

DOI: 10.4324/9781003245629-18

attack on their opponent, even the most aggressive show tension and fear on their faces. *This tension makes most violence incompetent.*

Micro-sociology triggers physiology, and bodily reactions get in the way of conscious intentions. Face-to-face confrontations are socially tense, pumping adrenaline, the flight-or-fight hormone, an undifferentiated arousal that can go either way. Many soldiers in combat do not fire their guns. Like cops in shoot-outs, those who do fire often have perceptual distortions, time slowing to dream-like or speeding up to a blur, a sound-proof tunnel where shooters can't hear their own guns. Some freeze; some hit their own side in friendly fire; some go into a frenzy where they can't stop firing in an overkill of bullets until they have emptied their magazine. The same applies to fists, kicks, or knife-stabs. The common denominator is high adrenaline levels, which mobilize the large muscles of the body but desensitize fine motor control of hands and fingers.

What happens in a confrontation depends on the relative levels of adrenaline on both sides. If one side can stay in the zone of medium arousal while the other loses bodily control, the more competent performer at violence will beat the incompetent performer. At the extreme, one side becomes paralyzed at very high adrenaline levels, making an easy target for the opponent still capable of attacking.

To be skilled in violence is to keep your own adrenaline level down to medium levels, while driving up your opponent's to high levels that make them incompetent. If adrenaline levels are equal, neither side performs worse than the other, and the confrontation stalls out, the fight aborting or winding down by losing momentum. We see this also in sexual aggression.

Attacking the Weak

One barrier that aggressors have to overcome if they are to deliver any violence is confrontational tension and fear. There are several ways around this barrier. The most common pattern is attacking a weak victim: someone who is physically much weaker; someone who is unarmed when you are armed; someone who is running away. Outnumbering the opponent is a major confidence-booster. Without this advantage, evenly matched fights usually are stalemates, coming to nothing or quickly aborting. Having even one supporter on the weaker side shifts the emotional balance.

The advantage is not so much physical but *emotional domination.* Robbers with guns are nevertheless wary of hold-ups where one is a lone individual outnumbered by victims and bystanders; most successful robberies consist of two or three robbers against an isolated shop-keeper. Back-up in robberies is confidence-building, and a way to establish emotional dominance over the victim. Successful violence comes from establishing the mood and rhythm from the outset, driving the opponent into passivity.

Audience Support

Onlookers who encourage a fight help overcome CT/F and enable fighters to carry on much longer than they would if there were no one watching. How long and severe the fight is depends on the size and attitude of the audience: most destructive where a large audience is unified in cheering on a fight; shorter and less harmful when the audience is divided or unsure; when bystanders ignore a fight, it soon peters out.

Confrontation-Minimizing Tactics

Another way around the barrier of CT/F is to avoid the main source of tension: threatening the other person face-to-face. Eye contact makes the encounter tense. Robbers and muggers find it easiest to attack from behind, where the two sides cannot see each other's eyes. Wearing masks and hoods emboldens the attacker and disconcerts victims by making the attacker appear un-human. And in the modern high-tech world, cyber attacks are psychologically easy, since they involve no human confrontation at all.

Violence as Fun and Entertainment

Fights are particularly likely on occasions of leisure and fun: parties, drinking places, holidays, crowds at games and concerts. These are carousing zones where normal routines are suspended and special excitement is expected. Violence on these occasions still requires overcoming CT/F, finding emotional domination over weak victims, and/or support of an audience.

Do the Conditions for Successful Violence Apply Also to Sexual Violence?

Sexual Confrontation/Fear

Like all aggression, sexual arousal pumps adrenaline. Sexual advances which are risky and uncertain generate the excitement-equivalent of the flight-or-fight arousal that can go either way. We would expect to find some jittery rapists, and other sexual aggressors who lose their nerve.

We lack systematic evidence on most of these points, so the generalizations here are tentative. But I will cite research where available, and supply illustrations from news accounts and from my own interviews.

> [Interview 1] A young man in his late teens followed an attractive middle-aged woman into her apartment building, by hurrying through the security door behind her. No one else is in the lobby. In the elevator he pulls a knife and threatens to rape her. Although a

small woman (5 foot 2 inches), she is a top executive in a non-profit organization, used to exercising authority. She says disapprovingly, what would your mother think if she knew what you are doing? When the elevator door opened, he runs off.

[Interview 2] A tall (5 foot 9 inches), attractive woman in her mid-twenties is running in an outdoor area, when a man about her age runs up behind her and grabs her. She turns around and swings at him, knocking off his glasses and breaking them.

[RC: What did he look like?]

About six feet tall, long hair and mustache, medium build. He immediately starts apologizing. She steps on his glasses, and glares at him as he retreats.

The tables turned when the rapist fails to establish emotional domination. In the previous case, the attacker has a knife, but as in hold-ups, a weapon is not enough to be successful unless the victim is intimidated.

Short of rape, milder forms of sexual aggression often fail, perhaps most of the time. David Grazian's (2008) research on night clubs found that male patrons often engage in "the girl hunt," seeking pickups. But these young men did more talking among themselves about the women they saw than actually making contact with them. Generally, they lowered their sights to getting phone numbers, not too successfully at that; and groups of young women who went to clubs together often gave them fake numbers. In other words, even in venues explicitly themed for sexual encounters, most of the "girl hunters" stayed on the sidelines, did not approach aggressively, and were rarely successful.

Is this true across the spectrum of sexual aggression? Accounts in the news media focus on aggressions that succeed, but even here we find most aggressors do not get far.

A Distant-to-Close Scale of Sexual Violations

1. *Sex talk*: including talk about sex in general; talking about one's own sexual experiences and thoughts; talking about sex in regard to the listener on the spot.
2. *Sexual exhibition*: from the most distant to the most personal, this would include showing pornography; sending or showing nude photos of oneself; exhibiting oneself in front of someone else; at its most extreme, performing sex acts like masturbation in front of someone else.
3. *Sexual touching*: ranging from any body contact at all; to touching bare skin; touching that approaches genitals and breasts; actual groping. Also along this continuum are various kinds of kissing, from air

kisses to mouth kisses to tongue kissing. Hugging is also a continuum depending on what kind of body contact and how forceful.

4. *Coerced sex acts*: including vaginal, oral, and anal.

Narratives of sexual aggression often claim this set of behaviors is a progression, aggressors trying out (1), (2) and (3) as precursors to (4). An alternative theory, based on the micro-situational theory of violence, is that the more conditions for overcoming CT/F are present, the further along the scale sexual aggressions take place.

Let us see what the evidence is. My generalizations are based on analyzing news and online accounts of 85 victims/accusers of Hollywood producer Harvey Weinstein, and of 76 victims/accusers of entertainment and political celebrities; 8 interviews carried out by myself with women about their experiences of attempted rape; plus existing research.

Attacking the Weak

Sheer size and muscular domination sometimes show up in the accounts of sexual harassment.

A hip-hop record producer (Russell Simmons) offered a young screenwriter a ride home from a restaurant. The car doors were locked and he told the driver to go to his apartment. She testified:

> I desperately wanted to keep the situation from escalating. I wanted you to feel I was not going to be difficult. I wanted to stay as contained as I could . . . he did not punch me, drag me, or verbally threaten me. [But when they got to his building, he] . . . used [his] size to maneuver me quickly into the elevator.

In the apartment, he moved her into a bedroom and did not stop when she said, "Wait." "At that point, I simply did what I was told."

Here physical pressure without actual violence produces emotional domination. But sometimes overt force fails: The leader of a labor coalition (Mickey Kasparian), talking to a county employee in his office, pinned her down on a sofa and lay on top of her. "I felt like I was being raped," she said. But the attempt failed. On another occasion, he asked her to participate in group sex with himself and two other women; she successfully declined, although she did visit his hotel room where he had just finished sex with another woman. Four more advances happened over three or four years, including touching her breasts and genital areas through her clothes in a parked car. She had initially approached him online because she liked his pro-family labor policies and wanted to pursue a career in labor politics; she regarded him as her mentor, and saw him frequently at union-related meetings and social events. This woman eventually sued him. Another woman who worked for him had a long-term sexual relationship with him—although he was married—from the time she was hired in 2001 until she retired in 2016. She eventually joined the round of law suits in 2017.

The chief creative officer of a New York advertising agency was on a business trip to France in the 1990s with a senior art director. He pushed her onto a hotel room bed and tried to kiss her. She pushed him off. Several months later she complained to the agency president. Six months later she was fired, as "not the right fit for the agency."

At the NFL Network, a wardrobe stylist (i.e. she dressed on-screen speakers backstage) charged a former football star with pinning her against a wall, demanding oral sex and pulling his pants down. She accused an executive of sending nude photos of himself, rubbing against her, and trying to coerce her into having sex with him. Two other former football players at the NFL Network sent nude photos or videos of themselves and propositioned her on multiple occasions. All these approaches failed. When the sex scandals broke out in October 2017, she filed suit for wrongful termination.

Another successful rape was again by the hip-hop producer, when he took a 17-year-old model to his hotel room and tried to force her to have intercourse. "I fought wildly," she said later. Eventually he relented, when she agreed to perform oral sex on him. "I guess I just acquiesced." Feeling disgust, she took a shower, when he walked up behind her in the shower and briefly penetrated her. She jerked away, and he left.

Not all violent rapes succeed.

> [Interview 3] A medium size, attractive woman was attacked in her bedroom by a burglar; a trial lawyer, she was able to talk him out of raping her. Thereafter she always slept with a pistol at her bedside.

Differences in Rank

In high-profile sexual harassment cases, strength and weakness are mainly through rank and prestige. Aggressors are film producers and directors, famous actors, successful politicians, orchestra and opera conductors, advertising agency executives, newscasters and TV personalities. Victims/targets are generally their employees, lower staffers, young interns or career-seekers.

> [Interview 4] In the 1970s, a woman holding high rank in a state government heard from her young female interns that when they carried reports to a high-ranking legislator, he would stick his hands up their mini-skirts. Furious at this treatment of her protégés, she barged into the legislator's office—past his protective secretary—and

angrily denounced him: "Next time, pick on someone your own rank!" He was cowed, and desisted—no public charges being thinkable at that time, when women were just entering politics. Like an experiment, the case shows equality of rank makes a difference.

[Interview 5] An attractive woman hospital chain executive, very talkative and friendly, attended a conference of professional peers. After a convivial dinner, she went to her hotel room where she found one of the men from the dinner had gotten inside with a key he picked up from the desk. Although he was large and intoxicated, she locked herself in the bathroom and called security to get him out. [This was her main example when asked if she had ever been sexually harassed.]

But not just rank difference alone is operative; reported incidents show a pattern of times and places that favor the aggressor and weaken the victim.

Backstage Privacy in Work Settings

Rehearsals in professional entertainment are a favorable site for sexual touching by high-status persons. New York Metropolitan Opera director James Levine was accused of several homosexual advances over several decades in such venues. London orchestra conductor Charles Dutoit was accused of groping and kissing singers and musicians. The situation combines the ritual veneration given to musical maestros, with a backstage, out-of-sight atmosphere, and performers who spend most of their time practicing alone, thus are socially weak and isolated targets. And elite musicians are often on the road.

Home Turf Advantage

Sexual aggressions happen especially where an important person works at home, surrounded by female assistants; or where they put in very long hours at the office, into the small hours of the morning when no one else is around.

Independent news interviewer/producer Charlie Rose worked mainly out of his estate 60 miles from New York, with a personal assistant and young interns. A 21-year-old assistant recalled a dozen instances when he emerged from the shower and walked nude in front of her; he also telephoned her repeatedly to describe his fantasies of her swimming nude in the mansion pool. In the most serious charge, a young job applicant was invited to his estate, where he told her he needed to change clothes after getting his pants wet in the pool. He returned in a bathrobe open at the front, and tried to put his hand down her pants. Later she called it "the most humiliating experience of my life." A total of eight women accused him of unwanted advances and trying to kiss them without permission. Other staffers said he was "often flirtatious, but never inappropriate"—possibly those who did not work at his home.

Hollywood producer Brett Ratner had a mansion where he and his friends would invite aspiring models and actresses for screen tests and film viewings. In this backstage atmosphere, the girl would be isolated from companions and locked in a bedroom. One director (James Toback) asked a woman he had approached for a tryout to show him how she masturbated. "I was afraid that if I didn't do what he said, it would get worse," one said later. "I felt frozen." Finally he humped her leg and ejaculated. In another instance, Ratner groped a young actress in the bedroom. "I was saying, 'No, stop, I don't want to.' And he took his pants off and he was trying to grab my hand, and put it on him—'Just touch it, just touch it, come on.'" When she refused, he masturbated and ejaculated. In both instances, the attackers settled for sexual exhibition and masturbation when rape failed.

Federal Court of Appeals Judge Kozinski demanded a strenuous work pace from his young law clerks, often extending past midnight. By December 2017, 15 women accused him of misconduct, mostly making sexual comments, but including four who said he touched or kissed them inappropriately. One woman said that on at least three occasions he called her into his office to show her pornographic pictures on his computer, asking if she thought it was digitally altered and if it aroused her sexually. (Three other clerks told similar stories of being shown pornography in his office.) He also showed her a chart of the number of women he and his college classmates had sex with. Kozinski had been appointed as a very high-ranking judge in 1985 at the age of 33; apparently he regarded himself as continuing the life of a fraternity boy.

As recently as a dinner in 2017, Kozinski sat next to a woman law professor, told her that he had just had sex, pinched her leg above the knee, and tried to feed her with his fork. This was apparently his idea of recreation, a jokey-silly good timer.

As a high-prestige person, he showed off before audiences. Another woman, who clerked for a different judge, described a luncheon break where court staff were discussing workouts; Kozinski suggested she should exercise naked, and when the group tried to change the topic, kept coming back to it: "It wasn't just he was imagining me naked, but trying to invite other professional colleagues to do so as well. That was what was humiliating about it."

Audience Support

The last is an instance where someone uses an audience to support verbal aggression. In these celebrity cases, audience support for violent sexual assault is rare; one reported instance is when hip-hop mogul Simmons attempted to rape a 17-year-old model in his hotel room while his then-young protégé, Ratner, stood by and watched, adding to her feeling of being outnumbered. When relying on sheer rank and prestige, celebrities generally preferred privacy to audience support.

The pattern differs in the case of fraternity party rapes and coerced sex, where audiences are of the essence (Moffatt 1989; Armstrong and Hamilton 2013; Sanday 2007). Anthropologist Peggy Sanday goes so far as to call these homosocial bonding rituals: the frat brothers not only talk at length about who managed to score at a party, but would barge into a room where a bro was having sex, or view through a window. Although fraternities may tout their reputation as places where there is a lot of action, only an elite minority of their members get sex at any given party. Most of the girls who came with companions leave before their number dwindles—i.e. they use their own audience support to protect themselves from going too far even when they are drinking. Conversely, toward the end, the audience becomes overwhelmingly the drunken bros, who may even dance in a circle around the few isolated women who are left. Adding to the pattern, women party-goers are ranked in prestige: high status goes to women who are engaged or girlfriends of fraternity members, and who only have sex privately. Low status are girls from off campus, and from a lower social class; these are the ones who stay until they are the only females left. This is the pattern for fraternity gang rapes, serial sex "trains," and the sex-on-display-for-the-bros scenes described above.

Confrontation-Minimizing Aggression

It might seem sexual assault is not possible without body contact. Stranger rapists, like armed robbers, prefer to attack suddenly and from behind. Back in the era when women wore long skirts, a typical move was to pull her skirt up over her head before raping her (Hemingway reports this for World War I and subsequent civil wars). This eliminated face-to-face contact, creating both greater helplessness on the victim side and greater confidence for the attacker.

The cyber era has made possible new forms of long-distance sexual advances. Letters and phone calls, in the past, also served this purpose, but sending nude photos of oneself makes it more graphic. From the number of scandals of this sort, apparently it is more frequent, although perhaps just easier to document.

At NFL Network, a wardrobe stylist reported at least three former players and executives sent her nude photos of themselves, one of them a video of himself masturbating in a shower. Sending nude selfies was a fad, probably regarded as cool and edgy, in the period when cellphone cameras and email photo attachments were coming in. Rep. Anthony Weiner (married to Hillary Clinton's aide) got into repeated scandals when he sent nude photos of himself to several young women. Rep. Joe Barton got in trouble when nude photos he had exchanged with a woman who approached him on-line were publicized after their affair broke up. This case had no allegation of sexual aggression, but in the atmosphere of spreading scandal in autumn 2017, all sex scandals were lumped together. Women staffers for Rep. Blake Farenthold routinely discussed male lobbyists who sent pictures of their genitals. In this office, men and women chatted about strip clubs and whether newscasters had breast implants. Here nude photos were not regarded as a threat (perhaps because they came from low-ranking persons); also because the office atmosphere included much sexual banter and "off-color jokes." A press secretary said the "workplace culture was more like a frat house than a congressional office."

It appears that sending nude photos of oneself was rarely taken as a serious offense by recipients, unless it went along with in-person physical advances. By itself, nude photos over the Internet were unsuccessful in getting sex.

Sexual Aggression as Fun and Entertainment

It is striking how many scenes of sexual aggression are times of sociability and carousing. This is especially true for lesser aggressions, verbal and touching, rarely forceful rape. Self-regarding cut-ups and party animals (Judge Kozinski, Rep. Farenthold) mostly operate in this zone.

A top executive for Visa credit cards, regarded as a rainmaker and ace negotiator of crucial deals, was reprimanded and then fired in December 2017 for having consensual relationships with mid-level employees. He ran a high-profile division, with a "work hard, play hard atmosphere." "To be in the inner circle, you needed to party with the inner circle, going out for drinks. Most of the women who joined the circle were go-getters. They wanted face time with people who make decisions. To spend time with those men is to be looked upon as a rising star."

Rosabeth Kanter's *Men and Women of the Corporation* (1977) describes the era when women were just becoming accepted into management, mainly by helping their husband's career through sociable contacts, but sometimes by loyalty to a boss who pulled her along with him. Joining the coattails of a 'water-walker' was how men advanced, too, getting highly visible assignments and building their corporate resumé. Zooming back to the present, adding a sexual element, plus a work-hard-play-hard atmosphere, makes a volatile mix.

Jobs that involve a lot of hanging around in bars create opportunities for sexual fun, sometimes leading to serious public trouble.

New York Times reporter Glenn Thrush was accused and fired at the height of the fall 2017 scandals for the following: while in a bar hangout of news employees, putting his hand on a woman's thigh and kissing her; kissing a female colleague on the street after leaving a bar; surprising another colleague with an unexpected kiss.

More serious sexual advances have gone unpunished. A 23-year-old lobbyist in a state capital (in 2005, as she recounted it in 2017), was drinking with an important legislator, then he masturbated in front of her in the bar bathroom. She never revealed his identity, for fear of retaliation; she is still a lobbyist.

Travels Away from Home Base

Trips to exotic places give a sense of freedom from normal constraints. This is a network effect; sexual aggressors are less concerned about their reputation; sexual targets are away from their social support.

The chief creative officer of a major New York advertising agency began advances on a female copy-editor accompanying him on assignment in LA in 2011 to shoot a commercial. She rejected his advances, but days later he invited her to his hotel room to discuss business. After a short conversation, he got naked, got into bed, and said, "You decide what you want to do." She gave in, saying later she felt she had no choice. On a 2012 trip to Cannes, an executive producer at his agency reported, he offered her a key to his hotel room, but she rejected his advances.

NBC host Matt Lauer began an affair with a co-worker covering the 2014 Winter Olympics in Sochi, Russia, continuing after they returned to New York. She made a public complaint in November 2017, leading to other complaints and his rapid dismissal from his high-profile TV show.

Many of the political scandals over sexual harassment take place because elected officials work in a national or state capital, away from their home, and where there is a constant round of quasi-official socializing. Rep. Farenthold drank heavily, and aides accompanying him to Capitol Hill social functions joked about having to keep him from getting in trouble with attractive women. This is the context for news revelations of female Members of Congress and staffers "groped from behind" by Congressmen, who "grinded up against her and stuck his tongue in her ear." Rep. Bob Filner, who was forced out as Mayor of San Diego in 2013 after his staff sued him for aggressive hugging and kissing, was known in Congress as someone female members of Congress would avoid getting into an elevator with.

Special events among politicians are especially likely venues for sexual advances. Long-standing Rep. John Conyers invited the head of his Michigan office (57 years old at the time) to a three-day Congressional Black Caucus event in Washington, DC in 1997. She said she "felt honored to attend." He came to her hotel bedroom, called room service, and ordered sandwiches. I had my nightclothes on. I was scared to death. He sat in the bedroom taking his clothes off. I didn't say anything and he didn't say anything." Nothing happened. "He didn't go naked. He was down to his skivvies. He sat there eating sandwiches and then he stormed out and slammed the door. I was so embarrassed and ashamed of myself for being so stupid. I needed a job. He didn't put his hand on me, but the message was loud and clear." She said incidents of unwanted touching happened the following year, when he was driving a car on a road trip.

Another former aide said Conyers invited her to his Chicago hotel room to discuss business. "He pointed to the . . . genital area of his body and asked me, you know, touch it." Apparently she refused.

The case of Senator Al Franken, one of the sensational news stories of November–December 2017, combines elements of these situations. In 2006, as a famous TV comedian, he was on a USO Christmas tour entertaining troops in Afghanistan. He wrote a skit in which he would kiss a young radio broadcaster (30 years younger than himself). Although she explicitly planned to turn her head and not be kissed on the mouth, during rehearsal, "he mashed his lips against mine and aggressively stuck his tongue in my mouth."

What happened next sounds like escalation against her resistance. On a military plane flying out, Franken had his picture taken with his hands on her breasts—she is asleep, wearing a flak jacket and helmet, safety precautions in the combat zone—while he turns to the camera with a comic leer. After the trip she was given a copy of the photo along with other mementos of the trip, apparently all to be taken in good humor. This good humor broke down 11 years later, in the midst of the spreading scandal about producer Harvey Weinstein's casting couch. It also happened at a time of intense political maneuvering over tax reform, when Republicans held a slim majority in the Senate; and coincided with a scandal about Alabama Republican Senatorial candidate Roy Moore dating and kissing teenage girls 40 years earlier. It was a perfect storm for Senator Franken, deserted and pressured to resign by most of his liberal friends without going through an official hearing. Franken was the poster child of the sex scandals, above all because the embarrassing photo was circulated so widely. It might well be called: "what we did on vacation."

Social Greeting Ritual

Finally, we should add a category that has no counterpart in the sociology of violence, unwanted hugging or touching. Ostentatious full-body greetings that came into style among the fashionable elite from the 1980s onwards, and have become more or less obligatory in such circles, gave opportunity as well as excuse for this kind of sexual touching.

John Lassiter, creative chief at Disney Animation, went on leave at the height of the controversy in November 2017. He was known for prolonged hugging, both in public and privately. Some former employees said "it made people feel awkward or uncomfortable." Because hugging was a central part of his public persona, employees felt "it would be difficult to ask him not to do it." One employee said he would hold her arm in public without asking permission, and hug her for extended periods of time that made her uncomfortable. She also said that several years ago during a meeting, he put his hand on her thigh underneath the table.

A week later, comedian Garrison Keillor was banned by Minnesota Public Radio (MPR), for an incident in which: "I put my hand on a woman's bare back. I meant to pat her back after she told me about her unhappiness. Her shirt was open and my hand went up it about 6 inches. She recoiled. I apologized. I sent her an email of apology and she replied she had forgiven me and not to think about it." Keillor says he is not a person who follows the hugging style. Her accusation came out during the rush of #MeToo charges. MPR subsequently announced that one female colleague had accused him of multiple verbal incidents and touching.

Part 2 Success and Failure Rates of Sexual Aggressions

Taking together all the high-profile cases reported in the news during fall 2017, and listing the types of sexual aggressions charged: a total of 76 specific accusers charged 36 perpetrators with 44 instances of sexual talk; 77 instances of touching, 25 of sexual exhibition, and 12 coerced sex acts or rapes.

The proportion of sexual aggressions that led to coerced sex was 12/76, or 16 percent. If we exclude the 4 homosexual rapes (all by one man), 8/72 sexually harassed women were raped (11 percent).

The surprising result is that only a small proportion of sexual harassments result in rape. If we expand the definition of coerced sex to include being forced to witness or perform masturbation, the figure rises to 18 percent. There is some good news in this figure, however approximate it may be: the large majority of women experiencing sexual harassment have managed to escape.

If the celebrity figures are not representative of the population, in which direction is the statistical bias? Elites in entertainment and politics have usually good opportunities for sexual harassment. The rates of sexual aggression are likely to be lower, perhaps much lower, in other occupations. This is an empirical question; it needs research, asking about specific kinds of aggressions and particular occasions.

The summary just given does not include Harvey Weinstein, the subject of lengthy news reports starting October 5, 2017, which set off the cascade of accusations against others. Is his pattern representative, or an outlier?

A total of 85 women accused Weinstein of sexual aggressions: 56 instances of sex talk, 62 of touching, 31 of sexual exhibition, and 19 coerced sex acts. If Weinstein was looking for sex with each of these beautiful actresses and assistants, his success rate was 21 percent. In detailed scenarios, it appears he settled for making them watch him masturbate when he wasn't successful, as a sort of consolation prize for himself. If we include witnessing masturbation, his success rate rises to 25/85 or 29 percent. Weinstein was the most powerful sexual predator, able to offer elite career opportunities, and supported by his wealth and organization. Even so, most of the time he failed.[1]

Is Weinstein typical of the elite? He made explicit sexual propositions in 52 percent of the cases, as compared to celebrities in 14 percent; he used physical restraint or violence in 32 percent, celebrities in 16 percent; his rape rate was twice as high, 21 percent to 11 percent. Harvey Weinstein is not the tip of the iceberg, but more like an iceberg himself.

Emotional Domination as Turning Point

In sexual aggression, as in other violence, there is usually a micro-turning point: whether emotional domination is established or not.

- Aspiring actress asked by a movie director to show him how she masturbated: "I was afraid that if I didn't do what he said, it would get worse. I felt frozen."
- A job applicant approached by a celebrity TV producer, naked beneath an open robe, who put a hand down her pants: "Why didn't I hit him? Why didn't I run inside? I was completely wracked with guilt and self-hatred." Humiliation at the very moment made her passive. The underlying process is like soldiers who are massacred after they get tangled up trying to find cover on the battlefield; they become paralyzed with fear, which is what happens at very high surges of adrenaline, in a situation where one is unable to decide which way to move (Collins 2008: 102–104).
- A law clerk shown pornography by Federal Judge: "I felt like a prey animal—as if I had to make myself small. If I did, if I never admitted to having any emotion at all, I'd get through it."
- A staffer for a high-ranking member of Congress: "I was scared to death. I didn't say anything and he didn't say anything . . . He didn't go naked . . . He sat there eating sandwiches and then he stormed out and slammed the door." This is similar to how threatened fights peter out: by keeping the action stalled (typically this happens by repeating the same

insults over and over until it winds down from boredom) and slamming the door (Collins 2008: 337–360).

From the Weinstein Files

Successful Rapes Via Emotional Domination

A college student, approached by Weinstein at a New York club and asked to his office for a casting meeting. He both flattered her and recommended she lose weight to be on his reality show (an emotional put-down). "After that is when he assaulted me. He forced me to perform oral sex on him. I said, over and over, 'I don't want to do this, stop, don't.'

"He's a big guy. He overpowered me. I just sort of gave up. That's the most horrible part of it, and that's why he's been able to do this for so long to so many women: people give up, and then they feel it's their fault … The kind of control he exerted, it was very real. Even just his presence was intimidating."

After being cast as lead in a major movie, a 22-year-old was called to his hotel suite, where he placed his hands on her and suggested massages: "I was a kid, I was signed up, I was petrified."—This is probably literally true, paralyzed by fear and the sense of no way out.

A French actress, invited to his Cannes hotel room. He went into bathroom, and she heard the shower being turned on. He came out with an erection and demanded she lie on the bed. "It was like a hunter with a wild animal. The fear turns him on." —Like successful armed robbers and bullies, attacker battening on fear.

Rapes by Sheer Physical Power

Former Miramax employee, raped by Weinstein in the basement of his London office: "He grabbed me and he was so big and powerful. He just ripped my clothes away and pushed me, threw me down."

Italian actress left alone with him in French Riviera hotel room; reluctantly agreed to give him massage, then he raped her. "[He] terrified me, and he was so big. It wouldn't stop. It was a nightmare … If I were a strong woman, I would have kicked him in the balls and run away. But I didn't. And so I felt responsible."

Even so, some were without fear, and overcame physical power with psychological preparedness.

French actress invited to his hotel room for drink: "We were talking on the sofa when he suddenly jumped on me and tried to kiss me. I had to defend myself. He's big and fat, so I had to be forceful to resist him. I left his room, thoroughly disgusted. I wasn't afraid of him, though. Because I knew what kind of man he was all along."

Targets Who Eventually Achieved a Turning Point

Actress/producer, at Sundance Film Festival, invited to his hotel room to review script she had written. Half an hour later, he went to bathroom and emerged wearing only a bathrobe open at front. He insisted on listening to her pitch in his hot tub, then asked her to watch him masturbate. When she said she was leaving, he grabbed her arm, pulled her into the bathroom and told her he could green-light her script—if she watched him. "I was on the verge of tears but I pulled it together and quickly exited."

Swedish actress: "I sat in that chair paralyzed by mounting fear when he suggested we shower together. What could I do? How not to offend this man, this gatekeeper, who could anoint or destroy me?" After realizing there was no way he would settle for anything but "an erotic exchange," she managed to get out of the room. "Later I sat in my hotel room and wept."

Model was brought to his hotel room in the south of France, where he emerged naked and asked for a massage: "I did not want to do that and he asked if he could give me a massage . . . I didn't know what to do and I felt that letting him maybe touch me a little bit might placate him enough to get me out of there somehow." Before long, she bolted into the bathroom. He banged on the door with his fists before eventually retreating, putting on a dressing gown and starting to cry.

In these last two incidents, someone ends up crying uncontrollably. The escaped victim has a belated adrenaline discharge, similar to what happens after one leaves an angry situation where you couldn't express yourself. And the frustrated rapist melts down, too, in frustration, suggesting that, for all the bluster, he was a nervous rapist.

Successful Resistance Throughout the Encounter

TV actress invited to his room to show her a script, told him: "I'm not interested in anything other than work, please don't think I got in here with you for any other reason." He was "furious" and walked her back to the elevator, holding her "tightly" by the arm. The encounter "left her in tears and feeling completely powerless"—again, tears once safety is reached.

British singer and TV-host, propositioned by Weinstein during lunch at Cannes Film Festival, told him "(expletive) off" and left the meeting "disgusted and angry."

Some Blithely Avoided Emotional Dominance and Being Caught

Actress, then 17 and unknown: "I was incredibly naïve and young and it did not cross my mind that this older, unattractive man would expect me to have any sexual interest in him. After declining alcohol and announcing I had school in the morning I left, uneasy but unscathed."

Waitress and aspiring actress, lured to hotel, where he waited in a bathrobe in front of what he said were contracts for his next three films—but only if she would have three-way sex with him. She laughed, assuming he was joking. Weinstein grew angry: "You'll never make it in this business. This is how the business works." She fled.

Temporary front desk assistant at his company, said she had to refuse his advances "at least a dozen times." Nothing happened between her and Weinstein—but only because she "escaped five times." (These numbers are presumably rhetorical.) "All I remember was I ducked, dived and ultimately got out of there without getting slobbered over. Well, just a bit."

Micro-Sociological Research on De-Escalating Threatened Violence

Recent micro-sociological research has uncovered some of the conditions by which participants themselves, on the spot, control whether threatened violence will happen or not. (See "Conclusion: Some Optimistic Findings in the Sociology of Violence.") This implies there is a gender-transcending process of conflictual interaction, and it contains turning points that stymie violence, including sexual violence. Extending the argument, there are micro-turning points that deter rapes, as well as less intense forms of sexual aggression.

As we have seen in this chapter, successful instances of sexual aggression follow the same pathways as successful violence in general. The larger field of research shows that participants in violence do not find it emotionally easy, and when they cannot get around the barrier of confrontational tension, their threatened violence fails. The micro-sociology of preventing violence suggests pathways by which women can deter sexual aggression. The common denominators are, extrapolating from violence generally: keep facing your opponent; looking him in the face, head up, as directly as possible; keep calm and strong-voiced as possible; repeat-repeat-repeat to the point of boredom. Even the arch casting-couch rapist, Weinstein, failed in the majority of his documented attempts; and this is consistent with other evidence.

It is striking that so many of the detailed instances I have assembled show extreme sexual aggression is unsuccessful. News reports and accusations publicize the most atrocious instances, but even here, most of what they report fits the pattern that sexual aggression is not easy and is often deterred.

How Often Do Women Pay the Price for Resisting Sexual Advances?

But if women are often successful in resisting, aren't they trapped by retaliation in the form of losing their job or career opportunities? There are some data on this, in the charges reported by Weinstein's 85 accusers. He was successful in raping 18 women, and forced an additional 7 into witnessing him masturbate. Of this total of 25 victims, 11 had successful careers in the entertainment world. Another 58 women successfully resisted or evaded his aggression. Of these, 34 had successful entertainment careers, including 8 who became big stars.

Surprisingly, women who resisted were more likely to have career success (59 percent) than those who were unable to resist (44 percent). But is this surprising, from a micro-sociological point of view? Success in the world of actors, as in most careers, is strongly influenced by emotional energy—one's confidence and pro-activeness (rather than passivity). High EE helps one avoid being emotionally dominated, the turning point to being raped.

There is not enough data to generalize from with confidence, but it does come from the biggest sexual predator of contemporary times, a man who was famous for threatening his victims' careers. We have seen this pattern before, in the realm of violence, where bluster and bluff are common before a fight but don't carry over into winning the fight, unless the recipient believes the bluster.

Nonetheless, more than a third of the resisters did have mediocre or failed careers. Without in-depth research, it is difficult to judge how many of them were never on a career track or had few prospects, and how many were destroyed by Weinstein's retaliation. In the business world, instances are widely alleged where women who complained lost their jobs. Are there any instances where women who resisted had successful careers? Here again, we need better analysis to see whether micro-turning points exist.

The Larger Picture: Multiple Pathways to Rape

The data I have analyzed are unusual because they deal with sexual aggression very broadly, not just sampling on the dependent variable by looking only at successfully-carried out rapes. But these data from public charges against celebrities and political figures do not cover all types of rape. They fall into the category of *acquaintance rape*, the most frequent type of sexual coercion, which also includes date rape (Laumann et al. 1994: 333–339).

But there are other types of rape, *stranger rape* and its sub-types:

- *Serial rapists* are comparatively rare, but highly publicized when they happen. These have a similar pattern as serial killers, an ostensibly ordinary individual with a clandestine life of carefully selecting victims and planning attacks. Serial killers are often serial rapists (Hickey 2002).
- *Rape in the course of robbery or burglary*, especially when a home intruder finds an easy sexual victim. These rapes are impulsive rather than planned (Katz 1988).

- *Political rape*, including revenge rapes in societies with traditional vendettas; ethnic cleansing rapes during genocides; mass rapes in highly ideological wars and civil wars. These are gang rapes rather than individual (Kaldor 2001; Rafter 2016).
- *Party rape and carousing zone rape*—neighborhoods of bars and nightclubs, geographic hot spots for rape, as well as fraternity and gang parties (Ellis 1989; Moffatt 1989; Sanday 2007; Miller 2008).

This is not just an exercise in categorizing, but distinct causal patterns. Do the situational conditions that increase vulnerability to sexual aggression, and those that favor successful resistance, also hold for the various kinds of stranger rape?

Acquaintance rape attempts, on the whole, do not rely on attackers outnumbering the victim. They play more on the presumptions of easy intimacy among co-workers and friends, and attempt to establish emotional domination that makes vigorous resistance seem out of place.

Stranger rapes are more violent, especially when they are solo. Stranger rapists frequently operate in teams; this is always the case in political rapes, where the teams are very large and often organized as military units or rioters. Serial rapists are usually loners, hence they are generally armed (the Boston Strangler, however, was a large muscular man who approached housewives during the daytime, posing as a repair man). Such rapists develop distinctive techniques for locating and approaching their victims, looking for isolated women (street prostitutes; women who live alone) and relying on dramatic intimidation. Rapes in the course of a robbery or burglary rely on the same situational advantages and vulnerabilities as most robbers and burglars (Wright and Decker 1994; 1997): seeking out targets in neighborhoods close to their own, where they feel comfortable in knowing the turf.

These types of stranger rapists play on the same kinds of situational advantages that facilitates violence in general—attacking the weak, team and audience support, emotional domination—but tending toward the more extreme advantages. Where acquaintance rapes and other sexual aggressions use the cloak of normalcy, stranger rapes are much more explicitly intimidating, with shows of weapons, considerable bodily force, and outnumbering the victim. This suggests that the amount of successful resistance to sexual aggression found in my analysis probably is much greater than in stranger rapes.

The two types—acquaintance and stranger rapes—overlap in party and carousing zone rapes. Victims are usually isolated women, including those whose friends have gone home, leaving them easy targets for groups of enthusiastically intoxicated males. Here again, stranger rapes have more group support, suggesting that emotional domination by attackers is harder to resist.

But some stranger rapes fail (in my small interview sample of middle- and upper-middle-class women, the majority—6 of 8—fended off rape attempts). How often this happens, and via what tactics and situational conditions, is a crucial question still to be answered. Not being emotionally dominated remains central.

Summing Up

The best summary takes the form of the kind of surveys we need, systematically asking questions about the situational conditions of sexual aggression, and its outcomes:

- In your experience, how many instances can you recall where you were subjected to unwanted sexual advances?

For each instance:

- What did the aggressor do? Check all the relevant categories of sexual talk, touching, exhibition, and coerced sex acts.
- Were you successful in resisting these advances? What did you do?

Ask about surrounding circumstances:

- Was the attacker bigger and stronger? Did he have a weapon? Was he of higher rank?
- How many other persons were present: your companions? Attackers and their companions? If an audience was present, what did they do?
- What were your emotions at the time, and those expressed by the attacker and others? Did you have a pounding heart beat, shortness of breath, time distortions? Did you feel paralyzed for a while, and how long?
- What kind of location? Was it at work? Was it an entertainment venue, social event, ceremonial gathering, dinner or party, bar, street? What time of day was it? How long did it go on? Was there a home turf advantage? Was it a location away from your usual home base?
- Above all: who got emotional domination and how did they get it? Were there any turning points and what were the details of how dominance shifted?

Coda: Is Male Violence a Sufficient Explanation?

The topic of this chapter concerns whether sexual aggression is an automatic product of male hormones or macho culture. We may ask the question more broadly for all kinds of violence. Males predominate in every form of violence, from the micro-level up through wars and other macro-violence.

Is it because of a biological universal—the testosterone theory of violence? Or an omnipresent cultural archetype of maleness? Statistics would appear to bear this out.

But frequency statistics by themselves do not answer the question. If violence is male by virtue of being a biological universal, it should have no exceptions. That females are under-represented in committing violence, however, shows that women are capable of it. This suggests an alternative explanation: women have been historically denied opportunities to be violent.

On the anthropological and historical evidence, women have been excluded from military and weapons training and combat sports. When combat was confined to close physical proximity ("man-to-man" or "hand-to-hand"), greater male size and musculature gave men predominance, upon which cultural exclusion was built. This was true too when distance weapons (bows, spears, slings) were muscle-powered. As weapons became mechanized, size and strength made less of a difference. Even among men, the Colt revolver was called "the great equalizer," and Billy the Kid could bring down contemporary Goliaths.

The integration of women into armies and police forces has been a long time coming, but for the past two centuries their exclusion has been largely a matter of cultural tradition and male monopolization. These have been worn down in the modern era of mass democratization and the mobilization of social movements.

The ideology persists (although now argued from a liberal pacificist direction) that women are more peaceful than men. Hence society would become more peaceful at all levels to the extent that women gain political leadership. But this does not appear to be true. Throughout history, when women were rulers, their reigns were as likely to be as warlike as males: the heinous religious persecutions of Protestants under Queen Mary ("Bloody Mary") and of Catholics under Queen Elizabeth I; imperialist wars under Queen Victoria and Catherine the Great (also known for engineering assassinations of rivals at the Russian court); the Red Guards urged on by Jiang Qing (Madame Mao); Eva Perón, the Argentine dictator's wife, who avenged social slights with executions; Margaret Thatcher, who repaired her lagging popularity and won re-election by launching the Falklands/Malvinas War. Violence was always easiest to unleash at the level of high command, but modern emancipated women have also been on the front line of political violence: Vera Zasulich who used a revolver to shoot a Russian Governor, setting off the populist ("terrorist") movement that assassinated Czar Alexander II in 1881; Ulrike Meinhof of the Baader-Meinhof Gang in 1970s Germany; Patty Hearst with the machine-gun-wielding Symbionese Liberation Army; numerous women in the clandestine Red Brigades of 1970s Italy; in the contemporary Middle East, women suicide bombers appear to be a way for women to gain some public status among ultra-male-dominated conservative Moslems. In the assault on the US Capitol in 2021, the only violent death was a woman officer (formerly in the Air Force military police) shot leading the break-in. On the personal level, the proportion of women committing homicides and other violent crimes has been steadily rising, suggesting ongoing integration is moving on all fronts.

Such examples show that generalizations of the "Men are from Mars, women are from Venus" variety are useless as explanations. Women have not had the opportunities, the training, or the cultural encouragement to enter potentially violent situations. When these barriers have been lowered, women act very much as men do. Not to say women are merely assimilating into masculine culture. The revelation of empirically-detailed sociology of violence is to recognize that situational dynamics determine what happens—not the background classification of individuals.

Whether the increasing participation of women as activists in the world of violence is a good thing or not is not a question to be decided by sociology. I would point out, however, that it buttresses the argument of this chapter: the success or failure of violence is above all a matter of emotional domination. Women as well as men are capable of both imposing and resisting emotional domination, including in situations of sexual violence. And that surely is a good thing.

Note

1. Is the sample biased, perhaps because women who gave in to him were ashamed to come forward when others did? To raise his 21 percent success rate to 50 percent, another 50 women would have to come forward with rape charges, and no further women charge anything less than rape. To get his success rate to 80 percent, 250 more raped women would have to make accusations. These numbers are implausible.

References

News sources for celebrity scandals, Oct.–Dec. 2017: *New York Times*; *Wall Street Journal*; *Los Angeles Times*; *Washington Post*; *San Diego Union-Tribune*; *AP news* service.

Sources for Weinstein accusers: *USA Today* Oct. 27, 2017; *Washington Post* Oct. 5, 2017; BBC 20 Dec. 2017; Wikipedia.

Armstrong, Elizabeth A., and Laura Hamilton. 2013. *Paying for the Party*. Cambridge, MA: Harvard University Press.

Collins, Randall. 2008. *Violence: A Micro-Sociological Theory*. Princeton, NJ: Princeton University Press.

Ellis, Lee. 1989. *Theories of Rape*. New York: Taylor & Francis.

Grazian, David. 2008. *On the Make: The Hustle of Urban Nightlife*. Chicago: University of Chicago Press.

Hickey, Eric. 2002. *Serial Murderers and Their Victims*. Belmont, CA: Wadsworth.

Kaldor, Mary. 2001. *New and Old Wars: Organized Violence in a Global Era*. Stanford, CA: Stanford University Press.

Kanter, Rosabeth. 1977. *Men and Women of the Corporation*. New York: Basic Books.

Katz, Jack. 1988. *Seductions of Crime: Moral and Sensual Attractions of Doing Evil*. New York: Basic Books.

Laumann, Edward O., John T. Gagnon, Robert T. Michael, and Stuart Michaels. 1994. "Forced/Coerced Sex in Adulthood." In Edward O. Laumann, John T. Gagnon, Robert T. Michael, and Stuart Michaels (Eds.), *The Social Organization of Sexuality*. Chicago: University of Chicago Press, pp. 333–339.

Miller, Jody. 2008. *Getting Played: African American Girls and Gendered Violence*. Albany, NY: New York University Press.

Moffatt, Michael. 1989. *Coming of Age in New Jersey*. New Brunswick, NJ: Rutgers University Press.

Rafter, Nicole. 2016. *The Crime of All Crimes: Towards a Criminology of Genocide*. Albany. NY: New York University Press.

Sanday, Peggy Reeves. 2007. *Fraternity Gang Rape*. Albany, NY: New York University Press.

Wright, Richard T. and Scott Decker. 1994. *Burglars on the Job*. Boston: Northeastern University Press.

Wright, Richard T. and Scott Decker. 1997. *Armed Robbers in Action*. Boston: Northeastern University Press.

Chapter 14

Clues to Mass Rampage Killers

Introduction

Oh no, not again! we keep saying to ourselves, every time there is another mass killing. Almost everything about it is familiar, including the ensuing debate. For one side, the obvious solution is more stringent gun control; ideally this would turn the US into a low gun-ownership country like others where mass killings are rare. On the other side, the immediate reaction is keep our guns: it's our Second Amendment right; banning guns would criminalize many law-abiding people; and more guns on the ground would be the way to hold off these killers. Do we have to wait until the country breaks through political gridlock to do anything about stopping rampage killings in schools, and increasingly in places of entertainment? Rather than relying entirely on politics, micro-sociology can help.

Looking at the details of mass rampage killings, we find key features that distinguish mass killings from other kinds of violence. One of these clues is that potential killers' pattern of amassing guns is different from ordinary gun-owners, and this difference is important as a clue as to who is dangerous and who is not.

Clues that Don't Predict

Mass shootings are very rare events. There are about 15,000 homicides per year in the US; the great majority are single-victim killings. Less than 1 percent are mass killings (four or more victims in the same incident). Spectacular mass shootings, where many persons are killed or wounded, have been happening at a rate of about one or two per year, in the 40 years since 1980, for the most common type, school shootings; mass shootings in other venues, apparently imitating school shootings, have been on the rise. It is their rarity that attracts so much attention, and their out-of-the-blue, seemingly random relationship between killer and victims, that makes them so dramatically alarming.

This rarity means that very distinctive circumstances are needed to explain mass killings, and that widely available conditions cannot be very

DOI: 10.4324/9781003245629-19

accurate predictors. There are approximately 270 million firearms in the civilian population in America, in a population of about 310 million. The vast majority of these guns are not used to kill people. Even if we focus on the total number of yearly homicides by gun (about 12,000), the percentage of guns that kill someone is about 12,000 / 270,000,000, or 1 in 23,000. Another way to put it: of approximately 44 million gun owners in the US, 99.97 percent of them do not murder anyone. It is not surprising that their owners resist being accused of abetting murder.

My aim here is not to enter the political controversy over banning guns. Many people who own guns are gun-cultists, for whom guns are symbolic objects, connected with their identity and lifestyle (analyzed in Collins, 2004: 99–101). The political argument over banning or retaining guns has strong emotional overtones on both sides. Anti-gun-cultists dislike not only guns but the lifestyle and the values of the people who have them; this is evident in the case of anti-hunting movements, including the recently successful anti-foxhunting movement in England. Both sides blur the gun issue with symbolic politics. What can be said analytically is that banning guns is trying to manipulate a variable that is a very weak predictor of mass homicides. It resembles TSA procedures of searching everyone who enters an airport gate area; airplane terrorists are also extremely rare, and thus the vast majority of the persons who are searched are innocent. More successful ways of heading off terrorists have focused on their organizations and networks (Sageman 2004).

In the case of mass homicides, micro-sociology can help by examining the details that make this kind of murder distinctive.

Mass murders are mostly committed by a solo individual, almost never by more than two. Typically their target is a public gathering of 10 to several hundred persons. Not everyone is killed; usually the number of wounded is larger than the number killed; and many escape injury, since mass murderers resemble other violent persons in this respect: they often miss their targets.

In mass rampage killings, the killers are not aiming at particular individuals at all. The victims are anonymous, representatives of a collective identity that is being attacked. Hence mass attacks generally take place in institutional settings: mainly in schools, or work places, although recently also in exercise gyms and in churches. The Aurora, Colorado, attack in July 2012 was unusual (or the harbinger of new settings), in a movie theater; the Norway shooting attack of July 2011 was on a youth camp of a political party. The number actually killed is misleading; the attack is an effort to destroy an institution through the people who belong to it. In that sense it is a symbolic attack—a deadly symbolic attack. The motivation and tactics of the mass killer are very different from most homicides; here it is not a matter of a personal grudge coming from ongoing conflict with a particular individual, as in the nearly half of all homicides which are among personal acquaintances; nor the targeted killing between gangs; nor the instrumental or accidental killings which take place in the course of another crime, such as a robbery or rape. Most other types of homicides are impulsive or emerge from escalated situations; mass rampage killings are elaborately planned in advance.

Rampage killers tend to attack not only a place but an event. The ritualized gathering has a symbolic meaning—in the Durkheimian sense, it is where the group celebrates itself through communion with its sacred objects. Thus, Holmes, the recently failed graduate student who shot 70 people (12 killed, 58 wounded) at a movie theater in Aurora, chose the night of the premiere of an eagerly awaited Batman movie. From a sociological point of view, being an entertainment fan is an important identity in contemporary youth culture. Holmes, by imitating the costumes of characters in the Batman series, was entering deeply into a popular cult. His apartment was decorated with Batman paraphernalia. Without having the details of Holmes's life experiences and personal thoughts, it can still be said that the killer was simultaneously participating in a ritual of popular youth culture, and attacking the members of that cult. (Of the 12 killed, 10 were in the age range 18–32; 7 of them within 3 years of his own age, 24.) The movie theater mass rampage killing resembles school shootings, where the killer is attacking his own institution and its members—the scenario of the rejected member.

Not very usable clues are the patterns that rampage killers are low status isolates, or recent academic or career failures, or introverts. Like the availability of guns, here again the explanatory variable is too common; there are a tiny number of rampage killers, but incidents of career failures are widespread; the number of introverts in the population is probably around 40 percent; victims of school bullying comprise 5–15 percent of students; since there are about 13 million secondary school students in the US, bully victims would total around 650,000 to 2 million (Collins 2008: 173). About two-thirds of school shooters are bully victims, but there are other ways to be low status in the youth culture, so the number would be higher. The correlation of these predictors with rampage killings must be extremely low.

Better clues come from considering the micro-sociology of this kind of violence. Any kind of violent confrontation is emotionally difficult; the situation of facing another person whom one wants to harm produces confrontational tension/fear (CT/F); and its effect most of the time is to make violence abort, or to become inaccurate and ineffective. But the usual micro-sociological patterns that allow violence to succeed are not present in a rampage killing; group support does not exist, because one or two killers confront a much larger crowd: in contrast, most violence in riots takes place in little clumps where the attackers have an advantage of around 6-to-1.

Another major pathway around CT/F is attacking a weak victim. But in almost all violence, the weakness is emotional rather than physical—even an armed attacker has to establish emotional dominance, before he can carry out effective violence. One might think this is simply a matter of using a gun or displaying a weapon, which automatically puts the armed person in the position of strength, the others in a position of weakness. Nevertheless, detailed analysis of incidents and photos of armed confrontations show that groups without guns can emotionally paralyze an armed opponent, preventing him from using his weapon.

Guns provide emotional dominance when an armed individual threatens a peaceful group and they try to hide or run away. This depends on the style of the victims. When rival street gangs clash, they do not turn their backs; they are used to gesturing, with and without guns, and most such face-to-face confrontations wind down. Running away has the effect of confirming emotional dominance; it is easier to shoot a person in the back than in the front; and turning away or attempting to hide one's face has the effect of removing one's greatest deterrent: eye-contact with the opponent. Thus, the hundreds who piled on the floor in the theater at Aurora, or who ran from the attacker on the Norwegian island, may have saved some percentage of themselves; but they collectively could have saved more than ended up being killed or wounded, if they had used their superior numbers to confront the attacker. I don't mean just the possibility of physically overcoming him, but taking advantage of the fact that groups are always emotionally stronger than individuals, if they can keep themselves together and put up an emotionally united front: they could probably have made him stop shooting.

If this sounds implausible, consider how rampage shootings usually end: in a 1997 school shooting at Paducah, Kentucky, the solo killer, a 14-year-old boy, who opened fire on a prayer group in the school hall, allowed a teacher and the prayer leader to come up to him and take his gun away as soon as he had shot eight girls and boys (who were facing away from him). I will discuss this case in detail below. The Aurora theater killer gave himself up to the police without resistance after he left the theater. Even Breivik, the Norwegian killer, who stated a strong ideological motive for his killings, gave himself up without a fight once armed authorities arrived on the island, although he had plenty of ammunition left. The key point here is not simply that the Norwegian police were armed, and the teenage campers were not, but rather that the police confronted him, while the teens ran away and turned their backs. Rampage killers almost always give themselves up peacefully, or else commit suicide. The Columbine duo, unusually, exchanged fire several times with the police, at long distance and ineffectually, but then killed themselves in a lull in the action. This is another respect in which rampage killers differ from other types of violent persons.

Why Rampage Killers Are Not Suicide Bombers

Rampage killers do not approach their victims in an angry or threatening mode; they give no warning until they start firing. In this respect, their pathway into violence is not at all like disputes that escalate into violence; nor like confrontations among gangs or other ostentatious tough guys, who often do more blustering than actual violence. Rampage shooters are more similar to suicide bombers, whose tactical advantage is pretending that the attacker is just an ordinary, innocuous person until the last moment when the bomb is set off. Political organizations that use suicide bombers do not select belligerent persons, but the most mild-mannered, self-controlled individuals. Rampage killers are even farther at the end of this continuum.

But rampage killers differ from suicide bombers in ways that reveal what is central to their motivation. The suicide bomber kills him/herself at the same moment as the victims; this has the advantage of not seeing the carnage one has caused. Suicide bombers are usually idealistic individuals who believe in a cause, and have never engaged in violence before; so the tactic is ideal for keeping any notion of violence out of their mind—the most successful pathway is to keep one's mind focused on the normal details of routine activity, or on one's ideological message (see Collins, 2008: 409–411, for analysis of the last dialogue of suicide bombers, including a recording in the cockpit of the airline downed on 9/11). But rampage killers are obsessed with their attack; they want to see the token representations of the hated institution die. A minority of rampage killers commit suicide, but only after they have experienced the process of killing that they have fantasized about for so long.

Motives and rituals of confrontation also affect the weapons they use. A remote bombing attack—where the attacker places a bomb at the target and detonates it later from a safe distance—does not fit the psychological scenario the rampage killer seeks. Disgruntled students often fantasize about blowing up the school, and this is perhaps their most common form of rebellious rhetoric, but it is entirely verbal ritualism (and circulation of a cultural cliché), since virtually all mass killings in schools have been carried out by shooting rather than bombs. And this is so even though many of the killers collect an arsenal which includes bombs; for instance, the two killers at Columbine High School in 1999 brought nearly 100 explosive devices, and managed to explode between eight and ten of them, but caused all their casualties by shooting. It appears that bombing is not sufficiently confrontational for the psychological scenario that a mass institutional killer seeks.

Suicide bombers belong to an organized group, a movement with a long-term goal that they hope to advance, beyond the deaths of individual contributors, whereas rampage killers engage in purely personal revenge. Why should this affect the scenarios they choose? Suicide bombers have an abstract agenda; rampage killers are persons who have been personally humiliated. What they want is to reverse the scenario that has dominated their lives—being looked down upon by others in that institution; the habitually dominated seek a moment of dominating others. This fills their horizon; the rampage killer rarely plans what happens next. In all his elaborate planning, he has made no plans for escape. The mass killing is the final, overwhelming symbolic event of his life. Jack Katz (2016) noted that rampage killers want the last scene to be witnessed as they dramatically restore their damaged self.

Insulating Oneself from Face-to-Face Confrontation

Even when an armed individual threatens a large unarmed group, he needs to circumvent CT/F—the debilitating tension that makes violence so hard. He needs a technique for insulating himself from the persons he is going to kill. There are several ways to do this, and recent massacres show some of the techniques.

The Aurora killer wore an elaborate black costume, assembled from military and police supply businesses, including helmet, gas mask, throat guard, assault vest, leggings and gloves. This somewhat resembled Batman—who is also an ordinary person with a secret identity—who goes into violent action transformed into a bulked-up dark costume and head covering. Holmes's costume also let him fit in with the crowd of fantasy fans, as the style of dressing as comic-story characters has become popular at youth-culture gatherings (e.g. Comic-Con in San Diego—his home town—which took place just a week before the Aurora shooting). Before donning his helmet and gas mask, Holmes displayed his flamboyant shock of hair dyed bright red; this attracted attention but eased him into the role, as he told people he was the Joker—thus imitating both the arch-villain and the super-hero. He waited until the action of the film was under way before tossing smoke bombs into the theater and starting to shoot. A witness described the atmosphere: "smoke, explosions—bats flying across the screen because the movie's still playing—it's dark." When the lights came on, Holmes stopped firing and left the theater.

Psychologically, his bulky costume put a layer of insulation between himself and the world, and his bizarre-looking gas mask gave him an artificial face. The normal tendency of a focused interaction between persons is to reflect emotional signals back and forth, so each becomes entrained in the other person's emotions; mutual eye contact and full face-to-face concentration bring a strong sense of the other person's humanity, and make it difficult to carry out violence. The would-be rampage killer needs to *distance his social emotions from his own awareness*; masking or disguising one's own face is one way to do this. In general, masks or hoods either on the faces of the aggressor or the victims increase the amount of violence, by destroying the normal human link in face-to-face eye contact. Later I will describe a case where the killer, just before opening fire in a school, puts on shooting-range earplugs; these have no practical value but insulate him from the sounds and sensations of normal social interaction.

Breivik, the Oslo killer, followed an even more sophisticated pathway. He likewise took on an alien role, wearing a police uniform with a helmet and face shield that obscured his face. In preparation, he practiced meditation techniques, to keep himself detached from the human reactions of the persons he was preparing to shoot. He also extensively practiced violent video games; of course, tens of millions of other youth did too. But Breivik incorporated it as preparation for a real-world attack; unlike the usual frame in which game-players recognize what they are doing as unreal, he consciously connected it with the need to steel himself from any pangs of human sympathy; in effect, he recognized CT/F as an obstacle he would train himself to overcome.

Deep Backstage

Almost everyone has a backstage, a region of privacy (the bathroom, your own bedroom, etc.) where you prepare for and recuperate from the frontstage social interaction that is typically the center of your life. Some individuals—introverts, isolates, the socially excluded—spend much of their time in the backstage. Many persons build elaborate fantasy backstage lives that becomes a substitute for successful interaction rituals on the frontstage, especially in today's world of the Internet and electronic games. This is particularly common among young males, the upper age rising from teens through thirties in recent decades with the postponement of adult careers, inflation of educational requirements, and underemployment relative to aspirations. The demographic is the same as most rampage killers, although only a tiny proportion becomes violent. Information-technology-obsessed "gamers" have become a recognized category among teenagers—a low status at the far end of the spectrum from the extroverts and athletes who dominate school and leisure activities.

Mass rampage killers—and an unknown penumbra of wannabes—go even further. Their obsessive backstages have two distinctive features. First, their private obsessions concentrate on their vision of a personally inimical world: not the standardized war and fighting fantasies of mass-marketed games, but their own real-world hatreds and institutions. They become increasingly drawn into preparing their counter-attack.

A second feature is that a rampage killer makes his backstage into a super-successful ritual, while also keeping it ultra-private.[1] It resembles a personal religious cult, with its own ceremonies, sacred objects, and moral standards. Of course, many innocuous pursuits can also be built up in private into a quasi-religious obsession. The would-be rampager's success, in building an emotionally compelling world that is completely antagonistic to other people's, is so extreme because he has found a unique source of emotional energy: *clandestine excitement*.

Ordinarily, motivations are generated socially, by successful interaction rituals; mutual focus and emotional entrainment with other people build up collective effervescence; an individual's emotional energy (EE) is tied to an arena of successful social membership, and to its collective symbols and moral standards which guide action. Spin-off rituals exist, such as solitary prayer or artistic creation, but such practices are first learned in a group that fills them with sacred significance, so that individuals can take them further in privacy. But clandestine solitary rituals are not like this; they are never shared with a group, and collective ritual can't give them a jump-start. So how can a totally solo ritual generate enough emotional energy to outshine every other motivation?

The answer is clandestine excitement: the energy that comes from successfully keeping other people out of one's backstage. The backstage of the would-be mass killer is illicit; he knows it cannot be revealed to others without provoking severe condemnation. This distinguishes it from other kinds of obsessive backstages; boys caught up in video games and electronic cults do not generally hide what they are interested in, and multi-player games and on-line contacts subject them to a degree of social control, reinforcing a standardized construction of social reality. The would-be rampager is playing a much more exciting game, hiding from others his horrendous plans; and this excitement feeds the emotional input that drives his private ritual. His backstage ritual is in a deepening spiral, a unique source of emotional excitement: as the prospective rampager gets into increasingly serious preparations, the excitement level rises. It is not just the excitement of what he is going to do, in the great showdown event—this may actually be frightening to contemplate. The positive energy comes from the ongoing adventure of doing something illicit, collecting weapons and hiding them, making specific plans—the excitement is that of carrying out a secret mission. From an alienated life, the future rampager now has many moments of excitement, every time he has to fool someone who might notice what he is doing. On the whole, these are easy tasks, risks that he can handle. His daily life of clandestine planning now gives a feeling of confidence, initiative, enthusiasm—the very definition of EE. The preparing rampager gets a buzz from successfully duping persons around him while going through the motions of everyday life. He is playing a higher-order game of social attunement—pretending to be attuned to them so he can control their perceptions of what he is really doing.

The Backstage of a Young Teen Killer

We can follow the construction of a deep backstage in a high school shooting in Paducah, Kentucky, in December 1997 (investigated in detail by

Katherine Newman et al., *Rampage: The Social Roots of School Shootings* (2004); quotes from pp. 25–26). A 14-year-old boy, Michael Carneal, opened fire in the school lobby on a Christian prayer circle just at the beginning of the school day, killing three and wounding five.

The sequence of events begins with struggle over low rank in the social hierarchy of the school. In all known school shootings, the perpetrators were outside the popular group; many of them had been manhandled, punched, trapped in a locker or thrown in a garbage can, taunted and jeered at. For Michael, the worst was when a gossip column in the school paper implied that he was homosexual, precipitating a further barrage of taunts. Like most school shooters, Michael was unathletic, unattractive, and easily dominated: a clear counter-ideal by which the teenage status hierarchy could remind itself of what is and is not, and an easy target for attacking the weak. He did not fight back when attacked.

Rampage shooters are not only humiliated by the school hierarchy, they hide their humiliation. They try to go on faking it on the outside, not admitting that the bullying and put-downs are getting to them. This gives an additional significance to the pattern that they rarely confide in teachers or parents, much less their compatriots, about their feelings of humiliation. This is not just an instrumental issue of failing to get help; being unwilling to confide is in fact a realistic assessment, if the problem is regaining status in the student hierarchy, this is lost by enlisting adults as allies against students. But this cuts off an avenue of expressing shame which could have turned the emotional dynamics away from the cycle of bypassed shame and humiliated rage (emphasized by Scheff and Retzinger 1991).

Bullied rampage shooters are not entirely passive nor entirely isolated; generally they have some friends, rather outside of school than in it. Although they do not fight back against being attacked, or meet taunts with counter-taunts, they may attempt of their own. Michael, who was repeatedly hazed by the school band members—the one organization he did belong to—also carried out pranks to annoy the teachers and other students, episodes of clowning, ostentatious noise-making and mild physical intrusions like slapping other's heads as he walked by their seats. He responds to victimhood by taking on the role of the clown, simultaneously staging the impression that he is not humiliated but takes it all in fun, while also attempting to get the group's attention. This is Goffmanian frontstaging, leaving the humiliation hidden on the backstage. And it is a strategy that fails; higher-status students find it annoying, and retaliate by increasing their harassment. Hence a build-up of taunting, physical attacks, and character assassination, as the dominants defend what they feel is their legitimate status hierarchy.

A deep backstage gets constructed from a spiral of backstage activities. In middle school, Michael was already involved in a number of personal backstages: the fact that he did not fight back against bullying nor express his feelings about it, kept these feelings reserved for a private backstage. He was also adept at presenting himself to adults as normal and well-adjusted, including covering up for his own pranks.

His backstage manipulation of frontstage impressions took a further turn when he moved to high school, and tried to gain admission to an alternative counter-culture group. These were the Goths, ostentatiously dressing in black, displaying pagan religious symbols, and rhetorically challenging the dominant school status hierarchy. Michael as an awkward freshman received little status in the Goth circle either. He tried to bribe his way into the circle, stealing money and a fax machine to give to them. So far he was stepping into the criminal pathway. But, in fact, he did not go far in this direction; his backstaging took another twist when he began to pretend to steal CDs (alternative music being the central interest of the Goth subculture) to give to them, but in fact taking them from his own collection. Michael was now trying to impress the Goths with his criminality, itself a pretense; he was not even a real thief.

Around this time Michael became acutely conscious that other people had hidden backstages. He was impressed with the Goths' charges that the Christian prayer group which met in the school lobby every morning was itself just a show. Behind the façade of pious purity, the Goths said, they were just as sexually dissolute as anyone else. This was just the most obvious form of hypocrisy. The ostensibly altruistic Christians upheld the school status hierarchy of athletes and popular sociables that mercilessly put down nerdy kids like Michael. Around the same time, Michael wrote a short story in which he declared, "there is a secret in my family that my parents and my sister know . . . I am always excluded from things . . . I overheard my parents debating whether they should tell me or not." His perception was not entirely fantasy. The school status hierarchy is omnipotent in its time and place; children who have friends in their neighborhood or through family networks nevertheless may be ignored by the same friends at school because of their different ranks in the school status hierarchy (Milner, 2004). Michael's older sister, who belonged to one of the popular groups, treated him very differently at home and at school.

Michael was becoming obsessed with backstages, recognizing that others had a backstage just as he did. Now he was formulating layers of his own backstages, deep backstages on which he contrived to pretend to belong on more conventionally alienated backstages like the Goths; he was descending into an inner world in which he was suspicious of the layers of staging everywhere.

His final round of backstage activity was to develop a plot around guns. During Thanksgiving holiday, after taking part in the ritual dinner with his family, he visited the home of a neighborhood buddy at a time when he knew the family would be away having dinner with their relatives, using his insider knowledge of their doings to find an opportune time to break in. He must have been secretly observing details of the layout for some time beforehand, since he was able to find the hidden key to the gun case, and take several weapons, which he hid in a duffle bag and carried home on his bike.

> Affecting a nonchalant air when he arrived at home, Michael parked the duffle bag by some pine trees outside his bedroom window, and went in to greet his parents. "I'm fine," he said, when they asked about his day. Once upstairs, he locked his door, climbed out the window, and retrieved the bag, stashing it under his bed. Michael carefully screened the weapons from view by moving Lego boxes in front of the bag. He went downstairs to watch TV for a while but was too excited to sit still for long.

He returned to lie on his bed.

This is a significant detail. In previous months, Michael had developed a phobia about sleeping in his bedroom, believing that a monster was under his bed who would drag him under while he was alone; instead he slept on the living room couch. But he used his bedroom to store his possessions, and now it hid his cache of guns. The monster no longer threatens him; it has merged with himself, or rather with his weapons, which are stored in just the place where he imagined the monster to be.

> Lying awake on his bed later that evening, Michael felt a satisfaction that had eluded him for a long time. "I was feeling proud, strong, good, and more respected. I had accomplished something. I'm not the kind of kid who accomplishes anything. This was the only adventure I've ever had," Michael later told a psychiatrist.

This is an extension of his earlier backstage activity of stealing, or pretending to steal, gifts for the Goths. The plotting, breaking and entering, disguising the guns to transport them on the street, sneaking them into a hiding place in his room, interspersing these moves with normal appearances before his parents to avoid suspicion—all this was an antinomian adventure. He is excited by the backstage action; it is the same kind of appeal that exists whenever someone has a clandestine backstage and a secret hiding place, whether it is drugs, pornography, stolen property, or weapons; Katz (1988) shows that the allure of shop-lifting is chiefly in the staging excitement, not in the intrinsic value of the items stolen. Carrying out backstage activity in front of unsuspecting audiences is itself a thrill. Michael seems to have deliberately repeated the thrill during the weekend, sneaking the guns out of his house again, carrying them hidden in the duffle bag on his bike to another friend's house, where he displayed them, and even took turns shooting in their backyard. On Sunday afternoon of the vacation weekend (the night before school would begin Monday morning), Michael displayed his cool by playing chess with his father; at night he took two more guns from his father's closet and added them to his cache under the bed.

Monday morning, there was more clandestine action:

> Michael came downstairs with the rifles bound together with duct tape, covered by blankets. On top of the blankets he piled the sheets from his bed and, when asked, told his mother that the cat had thrown up on them and that he was taking them to the laundry room. Michael went into the laundry room and deposited the sheets, but then went directly outside and put the bundle of guns in the trunk of (his sister's) car. The pistol and ammunition were stuffed into his backpack. He got into the car with his sister and rode off to Heath High, eager with anticipation.

Michael is full of clandestine excitement. This is no ordinary backstage. He is evading detection while under the gaze of those who might detect him; he is taking advantage of his usual condition of low status and remoteness from the center of attention to build a threat that only he knows about. He is enjoying his backstage, no longer furtively withdrawn into it, but purposively and agentfully. More emotional than the ordinary backstage, we might call it a deep backstage; it is the thrill of carrying off on the backstage what would be a difficult confrontation on the frontstage. Michael's confrontational tension and fear are ordinarily so high that he cannot respond to ordinary bullying and taunting; now he has turned that tension into clandestine energy. His months of activity on various fronts have made him an expert at backstages. In this arena at least, he has some emotional energy: the confidence to carry out his fantasy of overcoming confrontational tension/fear.

Is there a precipitating moment? Michael has planned and fantasized about guns for months. But it is not clear when he is riding in the car to school that he will shoot anybody. Even if he has fantasized about it, there is still the barrier of CT/F to overcome. Many violent confrontations abort at the last minute; it may well happen that he will change his mind.

Michael arrives at the school and carries his bundle of guns into the lobby. To a teacher, he says that it contains his English project. He is not yet ready to confront. He heads for the group of Goths, five or six boys standing in a circle on one side of the lobby. Nearby the Christian prayer group is forming. Michael is between the two groups: both of them ritual groups, indeed performing counter-rituals to each other. After a contingent moment, he will turn from the first to the second and fire at them. He is making a choice between ritual loyalties. As he drops his guns to the floor, making a metallic clank, the Goths pay him scant attention.

The leader of the group says, apparently sardonically, "Sounds like guns to me." Do they actually know Michael has guns? In the past they have engaged in plenty of violent talk, which Michael has attempted, without much success, to join. They are primed to interpret more talk about guns from Michael as a ritual; even bringing guns into the school, in itself a serious violation, an antinomian act of rebellion, is probably perceived by them as an act of bluster, an attempt to raise his status in the counter-culture group. Two sides of the Goths' perceptions converge here: on one side, they might well interpret Michael's presentation as indeed bringing guns into their presence, since they fantasize about it rather openly themselves; on the other, are a series of reasons not to treat him seriously: that he is a young nerd trying once against to raise his status in their group; that their own talk about guns is bluster and no more; that to go any farther with the guns would get themselves in trouble, whereas their bluster is end enough in itself. They turn their backs on Michael and proceed to talk about punk music CDs.

This is the situational turning point. Michael has now been doubly humiliated: by the mainstream status system of the school, epitomized before his eyes by the prayer group a few yards away; by the counter-culture group, who put him at the bottom of their own status hierarchy, reject his best efforts to live up to their antinomian standards, and now literally turn their backs on him at what he had intended as his moment of greatest impressiveness. No one looks at him as he reaches into his backpack and puts on a pair of bright orange earplugs which he has pilfered along with the guns and ammunition. This is the paraphernalia shooters wear on firing ranges to protect their ears from the blast of the shot. No one in either group looks at him as he takes out the pistol, loads a clip, and raises it into firing position, following the posture of the shooting range. Probably all these moments are on the cusp of the turning point, but still no one gives him any attention. He waits until the last words of the prayer are finished, and pulls the trigger, first in a quick burst of three, then deliberately finishing the rest of the clip.

Why does he stop shooting? Students watching the scene describe it as a mixture of shock and unreality as the bodies fall. The pistol in the enclosed space sounds to one of them like little popping noises of firecrackers. This is in keeping with the experience of soldiers and police, for whom the situation of firing, the apex of confrontation, is dissociated from their normal senses; a large majority of these shooters report the sound of their own guns, or of guns fired at them, sound tiny and far away, perhaps not even heard at all (Artwohl and Christensen 1977). The earplugs are not really necessary, since Michael probably would not hear the shots anyway. The chief effect of the earplugs is to heighten the sense of unreality, cutting out normal sounds that make other bodies in the vicinity seem active and real, not just pictures on a screen. He has reached the point of isolation from all social feedback. Of course, he had been heading that way for months, with his succession of backstages; now he has reached the bottom of the tunnel.

As soon as he finishes his clip, he starts to come back into the social world. Although he has plenty of guns and ammunition, he makes no effort to reload. He takes off the earplugs and turns passive as authority figures—the big senior male who leads the prayer group, the school principal—confront him. Now his backstage has turned into frontstage, his emotional energy has disappeared; the confrontational barrier becomes real again, and he freezes, unable to shoot any more.

The Strongest Clue: A Hidden Arsenal

Most of the characteristics of mass killers—low status isolates, bully victims, school failures, gun owners, players of violent games, even persons who talk or write about fantasies of revenge—are far too widespread in the population to accurately predict who will actually perpetrate a massacre. A much stronger clue, I suggest, is amassing an arsenal of weapons, which become the center of an obsessive ritual; the arsenal is not just a practical step toward the massacre, but has a motivating effect that deepens the spiral of clandestine plotting into a private world impervious to normal social restraints and moral feelings.

School shooters and other rampage killers generally amass an arsenal of weapons, bringing far more to the shooting site than they actually use or need. Michael Carneal brought a total of eight guns, wrapped up in a unwieldy bundle as well as in his backpack: a 30–30 rifle, four .22 caliber rifles, two shotguns, and a pistol, and many boxes of ammunition; but he used only the pistol. The pair of 11- and 13-year-old boys who killed 5 and wounded 10 on a school playground in Jonesboro, Arkansas, in 1998 carried 7 pistols, 3 rifles, and a large amount of ammunition, of which they fired 30 shots.

The two shooters at Columbine HS carried a semi-automatic handgun, a carbine, two sawed-off shotguns, and almost 100 home-made bombs; they fired 96 shots from the carbine, 55 from the handgun, and 25 from one of the shotguns; their magazines held 240 rounds, of which they still had about 100 rounds, plus 90 of the bombs, when they committed suicide. In the first 20 minutes of their rampage, they killed 13 students and teachers and wounded 21. Then their emotional energy seemed to run out—they even laughed sardonically that the thrill of killing was gone. They left 34 students unharmed out of 56 who were hiding under desks in the school library, and merely taunted other students while they wandered the halls firing aimless shots, before shooting themselves 25 minutes later, synchronizing their last action with a chant: "One, two, three!"

Holmes, the Aurora killer, carried a shotgun, an automated assault rifle, and two handguns; previously he spent four months amassing equipment in his apartment, including multiple ammunition magazines and 6000 rounds, of which he used only a small part. He also constructed 30 explosives out of aerial fireworks, refilling them with chemicals, a task that must have taken many days.

Breivik had four guns, two of which he took to the island. He spent two years acquiring the weapons, since guns are hard to get in Europe, and Norwegian regulations are strict. Nevertheless he persevered through the official steps for a hunting license and undergoing training at a police-approved shooting club to get a pistol permit. To create a massive car bomb (which he used in the first phase of his attack, at a government building in Oslo), he spent several years acquiring a remote farm as a front for buying fertilizer and chemicals. He was busy in his hidden backstage, video-game training, writing propaganda, and making a fake police uniform and identification. On the island, he used his police persona to assemble the youths, ostensibly to announce precautions, before starting to shoot them at close range. He brought over 400 rounds with him, fired 186, and still had over half remaining after fatally shooting 67 persons and wounding 33. He too seemed to waver toward the end of his 70-minute shooting spree, making several phone calls offering to give himself up (at 40 minutes and 60 minutes), but then resuming shooting until the police finally arrived.

The stockpile of weapons is symbolic overkill. These guns are for showing off—both to intimidate others, but mainly to impress oneself. They are the sacred objects of the private backstage cult that builds up the rampager's obsessive motivation to the massacre. Once at the sticking point their emotional energy never seems to carry them far enough to use all their weapons. Whether they bring all their weapons to the massacre or not, their primary significance has been during the build-up, i.e. the guns they bring are from the focus of their cult activities—they are a kind of security blanket.

The crucial details repeat themselves across cases. I have singled out for detailed analysis the December 2012 Sandy Hook Elementary School shooting in Connecticut; the July 2012 Aurora, Colorado, theater massacre; the July 2011 mass shooting at a Norway youth camp; the 1999 Columbine High School shooting, and at a high school in Paducah, Kentucky, in 1997. A similar example is a student at a community college in Roseburg, Oregon, who kills nine students and teachers, and when the police arrive, kills himself (October 2015). All these cases show the long pattern of obsessive preparation of a clandestine scenario, centered on collecting a weapons arsenal. Like the rest of them, the Roseburg shooter had assembled far more weapons than he actually used. He carried six guns with him to Umpqua Community College, along with five magazines of ammunition and a flak jacket. At home in his mother's apartment, he had seven more guns and large amounts of ammo. It looks like the same symbolic overkill, the same pattern of obsessive clandestine preparation over a period of months.

There are a number of parallels to the Sandy Hook shooter. In both cases, the shooter lived alone with his mother, who was devoted to caring for him. Both shooters had Asperger's syndrome, and both mothers strongly indulged their strange behavior. Both mothers were themselves enthusiastic gun-owners. Both took their sons shooting at gun ranges; the Sandy Hook mother regarded it as one of the successful things they could do together. The Sandy Hook mother bought all five of the guns that her son used (including the gun with which he killed her), as well as his other paraphernalia of weapons, and his massive supply of ammunition. Everything her son did, she interpreted as a manifestation of his illness. The windows in his room taped shut with black plastic were to her just a sign of sensitiveness to light—even though he could go outdoors when he wanted to. The possibility that he was hiding something in the rooms she was forbidden to enter was masked in her own mind by the feeling that she must do everything possible for her son.

At Sandy Hook, we find all the worst ingredients combined. Some of them are already visible in the Roseburg case. The socially isolated son; the single care-giving mother; the diagnosis of mental illness that she is trying so hard to counteract. The young man becoming obsessed with the pattern of previous mass shootings, building up an arsenal, even imitating some previous features such as asking victims if they are Christians.

Could these mass killings have been stopped before they started? Yes, clearly the care-giving mother was in a position to read the warning signs. That they did not is a pointer to the direction we need to go: much greater awareness of warning signs, especially among ordinary gun-owners.

To be clear about the diagnosis: I am not saying that anyone who collects guns is a potential mass killer. The crucial signs are: first, *the guns are kept secret*, part of a deep backstage. In contrast, most gun-owners are quite open about them; they may be involved in a cult of guns but it is a public cult, visible as a political stance, or a well-advertised pastime such as hunting or target shooting (Kohn 2004). It is the hidden arsenal that is dangerous—*psychologically dangerous*. And the rampage killer amasses a large, unrealistic collection of weapons as far as their actual use is concerned. This symbolic aspect also sets them off from other kinds of criminal users of guns.

The symbolic aspects of weapons go beyond their sheer physical availability. Hand-guns are widely available through illegal channels in lower-class urban areas; but they are not used for mass school shootings, but typically in street crime or gang vendettas. Up to 22 percent of inner-city students say they could get their hands on a gun; and between 4 and 12 percent report they have brought them to school; overwhelmingly their stated reason is protection against other students, i.e. in the gang milieu of these communities (Klewin et al. 2003). Many of these claims may be exaggeration and bluster for the sake of the local status system; and some of the gun-carrying students use them not for defense but to intimidate or retaliate against others; but in fact they rarely use them in the school itself, and virtually never in mass institutional shootings but only in targeting specific individuals. (From 1992 through 2000, 234 students were killed at US schools and 24,406 away from school, a ratio of less than 1 percent (DeVoe et al. 2004).) The school is not their turf; their violence has a different symbolic focus and ritual location: their rival streets. In contrast, virtually all the institutional mass murderers have been middle-class whites, and recently, high-achieving Asians.

Guns in the hands of gang members and their youth cohort counterparts are potential murder weapons. But these young men are not potential mass murderers, nor institutional rampage killers. They do not stockpile weapons in hidden caches, secretively protecting them with fake-normal behavior; on the contrary, they show them off to each other at every possible occasion (Wilkinson 2003; Collins 2008: 232; Bourgois et al. 2019). They don't have a clandestine backstage the way a nerdy rampager does. They don't need it, because their emotional attractions to violence, or at least ritualized bluster, are part of their public interaction rituals. By the same token, their interaction rituals push them toward intermittent individually-targeted killings, but not impersonal mass rampages against unarmed members of hated institutions.

Why split hairs? Why not say, all guns are potentially dangerous; the solution is to get rid of all of them? I will not repeat the practical arguments made at the outset; and the Breivik case shows that even very strict regulations can be evaded by a sufficiently obsessed perpetrator. If we are looking for ways to actually prevent violence, in the sequence of events and emotions that make up people's lives, we need to be aware of the pathways leading to particular kinds of violence.

Three Crucial Warning Signs

There is a very strong set of clues that a massacre is being prepared: an isolated individual (or possibly a duo) engaged in an obsessive clandestine ritual around a hidden arsenal of weapons.

A Long Period of Clandestine Preparation

Most other kinds of violence happen rather abruptly. Quarrels which escalate into fights; domestic disputes that boil over into hot rage with whatever weapons are at hand; street-crimes and robberies that hinge on sudden opportunities; rapes at carousing parties: most of these violent events would be unexpected a few hours in advance. Mass killings of the kinds that happen in schools, work-places, and more recently in theaters, gyms and churches, are planned much further back, typically over a period of weeks or months.

This period of clandestine preparation is not just a time of getting the logistics together and working out a rational plan of attack. The mood is much less matter-of-fact than a kind of private ecstasy, a fantasy-land of smothering oneself in the details of revenge for felt social slights. Everything about the imagined revenge scenario is something to brood over and to savor—researching past rampage killings, fixing a target, imagining the scenario, acquiring an arsenal complete with costumes and side-equipment.

An Arsenal of Symbolic Overkill

Mass rampage killers almost always amass far more weapons and ammunition that they need in their attack. They carry more guns, magazines, and bombs than they actually use, and when they are shot, captured, or commit suicide, they still have plenty more they could have used to continue the fight. Another sizeable portion of the arsenal is left behind, at home, or in their car. Clearly they have an obsession with weapons—the more guns the better, a 14-year-old killer said—but most of it is superfluous power in a practical sense; it is part of their psychological preparation. Symbolic overkill is what gives them the emotional strength to carry out this horrific action that cuts them off irreparably from the human community.

Clandestine Excitement

From previous case studies, we have seen that this period of working in one's private underground—either alone or with a small number of conspirators—is the high point of their lives. "It was the only adventure I've ever had," the 14-year-old Paducah, Kentucky, school killer said. Life has been a downer of social isolation or shame; now the tables are turned, and I—the future killer-in-preparation—am doing something far more significant, far more powerful than the people I am going to kill. What needs to be emphasized here is that this high point is in the period of clandestine preparation. What the actual moments of the massacre are like is hard to tell, since few perpetrators survive, but motivation is in the present of on-going time, and it is clear that they are enjoying the build-up to the mass shooting. The very fact that it is hidden away from other people, that there is a danger in being found out, makes it an adventure. This clandestine excitement gives purpose to their lives. And it gives them emotional energy, the forward-moving confidence and momentum that propel them down the emotional slope that leads to mass killing.

Gun-Owning Adults Are Best Placed to Head Off Mass Killings

Ordinary gun-owners are not like this. They don't spend long periods working out a scenario of using their guns. They don't spend months obsessively planning the details of when and where the shooting is going to take place. It is not difficult to distinguish an ordinary gun-owner from someone who is preparing a mass shooting; the pattern of their daily life and state of mind are quite distinct (Kohn 2004).

Ordinary gun-owners are not involved in symbolic overkill. On the whole, they do not amass arsenals so huge that they never could be of any use. True, there is some symbolism in having guns and historic weapons; it says something about one's self-image. But the key difference is that ordinary gun-owners are not so intensely focused on their weapons collection as potential mass-killers are. It is not the center of their self-image, the most important thing in their lives; it is not tied to an obsessive plan for action that is building up in the middle-range future.

Ordinary gun-owners are not full of clandestine excitement. Their guns are clearly on display; or if they are locked away in gun cabinets, their existence is not a secret; there is no excitement about hiding them while looking forward to the day they will be used. The emotional atmosphere is different. Seen up close, there is little danger of mistaking an ordinary gun-owner for a rampage killer.

Once a mass killing has taken place, public scrutiny soon zeroes in on the lead-up to it. Retrospectively we learn about the killer, his (almost always a male) sense of social grievances, his obsessive revenge planning and arsenal-collecting. What we need is for someone to see the warning signs, while it is still in the stage of fantasy killing, before it turns into real killing.

The persons who are in best position to do this are those close to the potential killer, members of his family, neighbors, and acquaintances. This is especially important when the people nearby in his network are gun-owners. For one thing, gun-owners are usually the ones who have introduced the potential killers to guns, have given them knowledge about them; often they have been the source of guns (as in the case of the Sandy Hook mother who bought guns for her son), or because their guns were stolen by the perpetrator.

Gun-owners bear a special responsibility for those in their immediate social network who might get access to guns. And this goes beyond conventional gun-safety training. It is not just a matter of trying to ensure that guns are not fired accidentally or in the wrong direction; it becomes a matter of making sure someone with an alienated world-view doesn't fire guns at all at their chosen target.

Gun-owners need to become alert to the warning signs: social alienation, mental illness, and above all their combination with a young person's clandestine obsession with guns over a long period of time, accumulating symbolic arsenals, and centering one's life around the clandestine excitement of a scenario of violent revenge. Discerning this isn't easy; there are plenty of alienated youths, and today's entertainment culture is full of fantasy violence. It isn't playing the violent video games that is the problem; it is the accumulation of a real arsenal with all the paraphernalia of a mass murder scenario. When this goes on for months, in one's own home, a concerned family member should get a sense of it.[2]

The issue of gun control in the United States has been mainly treated as a matter of government legislation. That pathway has led to political gridlock. That does not mean that we can do nothing about heading off school shootings until guns are banned. Gun-owning parents are closest to where this is most likely to happen. Gun-owning parents need to encourage each other to look for the warning signs, and to take action when they see them.

Appendix: More Guns on Site Mean More Casualties All Around

It is often argued that mass killings can be stopped, with limited damage, if more people are authorized to carry guns in vulnerable sites like schools, shopping malls, and places of entertainment. Instead of the only weapons being in the hands of the killers, citizens can quickly fight back and shoot the invaders. On the balance, lives would be saved. But would they? This kind of argument ignores the basic pattern of violence: people in violent situations are not very accurate. They are full of confrontational tension and fear, pumped up with adrenaline. Like police and soldiers, they are prone to wild firing, over-firing, and perceptual distortions (indeed, probably worse, since some proportion of professionals have learned to be cool-headed under fire). In addition, in the chaos of an attack, it is usually not clear who or where is the perpetrator, and whether he or she is alone or has accomplices; teachers in classrooms may have guns, but they could just as easily shoot students or each other. As noted in Chapter 15, about 10 percent of police casualties in general are from friendly fire; and the more persons with guns present, the greater the chances that someone will be hit. In carefully staged fantasies like cowboy movies, the good guy always hits the right target; but real life is not like that. We lack statistical data comparing attempted mass attacks when the number of guns in civilian hands varies; but what we know so far indicates that more guns on site would produce more casualties.

Notes

1. I use the male pronoun in this analysis as the scenario is overwhelmingly male.
2. Awareness of this sort may be picking up. Florida parents found that their 27-year-old daughter had a large arsenal of bombs and guns in her bedroom, along with many books

and DVDs about previous attacks at Columbine High School and Oklahoma City, and called the police (*New York Times*, October 6, 2019).

References

Sources: news reports; Wikipedia; U.S. Bureau of Justice Statistics; http://sociological-eye.blogspot.com/2013/12/sandy-hook-school-shootings-lessons-for.html.

Artwohl, Alexis, and Loren W. Christensen. 1997. *Deadly Force Encounters*. Boulder, CO: Paladin Press.

Bourgois, Philippe, Laurie Hart, Fernando Montero, and George Karandinos. 2019. "The Political and Emotional Economy of Violence in US Inner-City Narcotics Markets." In Elliot Weinberger, Annette Lareau, and Omar Lizardo (Eds.), *Ritual, Emotion, and Violence*. New York: Routledge.

Collins, Randall. 2004. *Interaction Ritual Chains*. Princeton, NJ: Princeton University Press.

Collins, Randall. 2008. *Violence: A Micro-Sociological Theory*. Princeton, NJ: Princeton University Press.

DeVoe, Jill, et al. 2004. "Indicators of School Crime and Safety." Washington, DC: U.S. Dept. of Education.

Katz, Jack. 1988. *Seductions of Crime: Moral and Sensual Attractions of Doing Evil*. New York: Basic Books.

Katz, Jack. 2016. "A Theory of Intimate Massacres: Steps toward a Causal Explanation." *Theoretical Criminology* 20: 277–296.

Klewin, Gabriele, et al. 2003. "Violence in School." In Wilhelm Heitmeyer and John Hagan (Eds.), *International Handbook of Violence Research*. London: Kluwer.

Kohn, Abigail. 2004. *Shooters: Myths and Realities of America's Gun Cultures*. Oxford: Oxford University Press.

Lankford, Adam. 2015. "Mass Shooters, Firearms, and Social Strains: A Global Analysis of an Exceptionally American Problem." Paper presented at Annual Meeting of American Sociological Association.

Milner, Murray, Jr. 2004. *Freaks, Geeks and Cool Kids: American Teenagers, Schools and the Culture of Consumption*. New York: Routledge.

Newman, Katherine S., Cybelle Fox, David Harding, Jal Mehta, and Wendy Roth. 2004. *Rampage: The Social Roots of School Shootings*. New York: Basic Books.

Sageman, Marc. 2004. *Understanding Terror Networks*. Philadelphia, PA: University of Pennsylvania Press.

Scheff, Thomas J. and Suzanne Retzinger. 1991. *Emotions and Violence: Shame and Rage in Destructive Conflicts*. Lexington, MA: Lexington Books.

Wilkinson, Deanna, 2003. *Guns, Violence, and Identity among African-American and Latino Youth*. New York: LFB Scholarly Publishing.

Chapter 15

Cool-Headed Cops Needed (and Cool Heads on the Street)

Heart Rate Monitors Can Help

Introduction

Virtually all controversial police shootings arise from misperception and over-reaction to the situation. These are results of bodily tension and high adrenaline levels, which in turn cause perceptual distortions and out-of-control shooting. The good news is that adrenaline levels can be recognized and monitored on the spot. And methods now exist for reducing one's adrenaline to a manageable level.

Tension, Adrenaline, and Perceptual Distortion

From studies of violent situations, we have learned the following. Face-to-face conflict raises bodily tension. At high levels, antagonists become clumsy and inaccurate. This happens through a sudden rise in levels of adrenaline and cortisol, the stress hormone. These are triggered by the primitive fight-or-flight center of the lower brain, an undifferentiated arousal for rapid action that can go either way. (I've discussed this point before; but the technical details are crucial, so I'll repeat them here.)

Heart rate is an easily accessible measure of adrenaline arousal. Ordinary resting heart rate is about 60 BPM (beats per minute) in adults, about 100 BPM in moderate exercise. Optimal athletic and physical performance is around 115–145 BPM. As heart rate goes up, the big muscle groups are energized, while fine muscle coordination is progressively lost. You can see this for yourself at the gym on a machine that monitors heart rate: trying writing with a pen when your heart rate is 145 or more. The effect of emotional tension and fear are stronger than vigorous exercise alone.

At levels around 175 BPM, perceptual distortions tend to happen. These experiences are frequently reported by combat troops and police who have been in shoot-outs (Artwohl and Christensen 1997; Grossman 2004; Klinger 2004). Time becomes distorted—both speeded up or seemingly slowed down to dreamlike walking under water. Hearing tends to shut down—a cocoon-like experience in which one can't hear the sounds

DOI: 10.4324/9781003245629-20

of one's own gun, or the voices of people around you. Vision becomes blurred, surroundings are lost, tunnel vision narrows in, making you oblivious to cues other than the most threatening ones.

Infamous cases in the news usually show signs of these perceptual distortions.[1] A 2016 traffic stop in Minnesota when the officer misperceives the driver (Philando Castile) reaching for his wallet as reaching for a weapon. In the Tulsa, Oklahoma, shooting of Terence Crutcher in September 2016, the officer said she temporarily lost her hearing just before she fired—even though there were sounds of sirens and a police helicopter overhead. I am not addressing the point here of whether this makes her legally culpable or not, but noting that it fits the pattern: perceptual distortions are the immediate flashpoint for out-of-control shootings.

Having more police on the scene increases the chances of uncontrolled shooting. Tension is contagious. Cops who are tense tend to make the other officers around them tense.

On New Year's night 2009, in Oakland, California, a white police officer put a gun to the back of the head of a young black man (Oscar Grant), who was lying of the ground being arrested, and killed him with one shot. The incident began with reports that groups of young black men were fighting on the train; at the station, four police began making arrests. There was much loud shouting on both sides, about who was or was not involved in the fighting. The young men argued and struggled with police officers; one of the four cops, not the officer who did the shooting, was particularly aggressive, throwing black youths against the walls, pushing them down, and yelling the word 'nigger' at them. The officer who eventually shot his pistol was relatively restrained, trying to calm both the excited cop and the men being arrested; one photo of him, a moment before the shooting, shows a perplexed expression on his face. The officer said afterwards he thought he was reaching for his Taser but pulled his pistol by mistake. In a state of high adrenaline arousal, this is entirely plausible. If the most out-of-control cop in the group had been calmer, the killing most likely would not have happened.

Some officers get impatient about what they feel as indecisiveness or confusion, and act to resolve the situation by opening fire. This is apparently what happened in the Charlotte, NC, September 2016 shooting of Keith Lamont Scott, a black man who was apparently high on drugs, possibly displaying a gun, and ignoring police orders. The shooting officer had initially been calm, waiting until other police business had been taken care of. Several officers first watched their suspect before finally attempting to get him out of his car. As the situation became more stalemated, it also became louder. More officers arrived, as well as the suspect's wife who kept telling the officers he was harmless and also on medication. One officer (a plain-clothes black cop) who had been there since the outset apparently grew exasperated to the point where he couldn't control himself.

To these kinds of distractions, add the effect of adrenaline arousal on hearing. In the cocoon of high tension, voices disappear. The more people who are present—cops, suspects, friends and family members, vocal bystanders—the more likely sounds blur into a babble of raised voices. Clear communications break down.

With more people on the scene, the higher the tension of the police officers, and the higher the chance that one of them will begin firing. This can set others off as well: the sound of firing may be misperceived as coming from the suspect, or directly by emotional contagion. In the Charlotte incident, the standoff comes to a climax just after another officer (who has arrived to support) tries to break the windshield of the suspect's vehicle with his baton—a loud crashing noise. The officer who has been on the scene the longest now fires a burst from his pistol, even though the suspect has made no sudden move. When heart rate races to 150 beat per minute or more, hearing often goes out so that voices become incomprehensible. It is a situation ripe for miscommunication and misperception.

Such circumstances are also dangerous for the police themselves. When a suspect is surrounded by large numbers of police in different directions, police sometimes shoot each other, especially when they are in plain clothes. About 10 percent of police killed or wounded on duty are victims of friendly fire.

A sign that the shooting is caused by out-of-control adrenaline is overkill: when an officer fires many more shots than necessary to disable the apparently threatening suspect. In New York City, February 1999, four undercover police looking for a rapist saw a man (Amadou Diallo) duck back into a hallway, then reach for what turned out to be his identification. The four cops rushed from the car and fired 41 shots at a range of 3 meters; 19 of those shots missed. Both the poor aim and the overkill are results of adrenaline rush, amplified by contagion among the four officers.

Adrenaline-produced distortions explain why shooting incidents happen where it turns out the suspect did not have a gun, or was reaching for an ID; situations where stops for trivial reasons blow up into killings. Trigger fingers produce wild or uncontrollable firing. Since adrenaline takes time to subside, the cop may empty the magazine of his gun, even after the suspect is motionless on the ground. Catching these details on video certainly looks like an atrocity.

Overkill usually brings public outrage, and usually is interpreted as evidence of police racism and malice. Whatever else it is, overkill is a sign of adrenaline rush. The two explanations are not incompatible. But it is the adrenaline rush that is the immediate cause, and the one we can most easily do something about.

Adrenaline Rush With or Without Racism

Black suspects are shot much more often than whites; blacks are 12 percent of the US population but one-third of victims of police shootings. But counting the percentages of black or white victims can only show one component of an explanation, and is far from explaining when police shootings happen and when they do not. Looking at these same statistics from another angle, given that millions of police stops of minorities occur every year, and granting that racial coding is widespread, it must be the case the racist officers do not shoot black people in the great majority of their encounters.

Framing the issue as racism doesn't solve it. Cops without racist attitudes, under these kinds of tense situations, and with their adrenaline out of control, can trigger off violent atrocities. Black and other minority police officers have been involved in the same kinds of scenarios. The answer isn't in the attitudes; it is in the micro-techniques of how to behave in confrontations.

Individual officers vary widely in their use of force. About 10 percent of police account for the bulk of all force reports; and less than 1 percent fire their guns in multiple incidents (Collins 2008: 371; see also Moskos 2009; Hunt 2010). The polarized viewpoint sees cops in general as being out of control; but the real issue is to make better officers out of the fraction that cannot control their emotions and physiology.

The large majority of the police do not shoot anyone. Among those who do, some are unlucky in being in a bad place at the wrong time; some are the workaholics of the force; some are tough guys looking for action; some have poor control over their tension levels. Many cool-headed cops exist, who have better situational awareness, better control over their tension levels and adrenaline arousal. Our aim should be to increase the proportion of cool-headed cops.

Raising and Lowering the Tension

After every highly publicized incident, whether the casualties are among the people or the police, mainstream figures call for calm and reconciliation. These calls have little effect on de-escalating the overall situation. Most violence and conflict in all forms is carried out by small fractions of the population. There is always an array from the most militant fringe, through the seriously committed partisans, to those who are less involved. Between the two sides of a conflict, those nearer the center are the ones most willing to listen to a message of reconciliation. But it is the extremes who carry on the fight, and drive the level of escalation.

The flashpoint is the police on the streets. Cops are under tension every time they stop a suspect. Tension is higher if conflict has been escalated recently by previous incidents; higher if it is a neighborhood with a high crime rate; higher if there has been a chase, or alarming reports over police radio links.

Tension rises sharply when the citizen isn't cooperative or is defiant. Jonathan Rubinstein (1973), a sociologist who joined the Philadelphia police force, reported that the first thing an officer wants in any encounter are signs that the person will not make trouble. He insists on taking the initiative, and controlling the situation in little details, since these are the warning signs for bigger trouble. Donald Black (1980), who pioneered ride-along observations in patrol cars, calculated that the chances someone would be arrested did not depend on race *per se*, but on whether the person was defiant—and, in the 1960s, black persons were more defiant to the police (not surprisingly, since this was the era of the civil rights movement). Car chases and running away increase officers' tension even more, since these are also acts of defiance, as well as fast-action adrenaline pumping in their own right. Citizens who turn their backs and refuse to stop are acting defiantly, even if the initial order was something trivial like "move to the sidewalk" (the first step in the 2014 Ferguson, Missouri, shooting, which began when a officer encountered Michael Brown, Jr. walking in the street). Adding together any or all of these factors increases tension, and the dangers of out-of-control adrenaline.

The key to preventing such incidents is training cops to keep their bodily tension under control. Sociologists Geoffrey Alpert and Roger Dunham (2004) found that officers who are better at controlling the escalation of force have a more deliberate and refined sense of timing in the moves of both sides. More attention to such micro-details should train more police officers up to a high level of competence.

Practical Steps for More Cool-Headed Cops

1. Recognize the danger of perceptual distortions in high-tension situations. Recognize the danger of getting confusing non-verbal messages and emotional contagion from fellow officers on the scene, and from other people present.
2. Check your adrenaline level and bring it down to the level of effective performance and clear perception.
3. Wear a heart rate monitor. These are easily available on wrist devices used for exercise.
4. Practice observing your own heart rate in various situations. You can train yourself to recognize high adrenaline levels by the feeling in your body—especially the feeling of your heart pounding and the quality of your breathing.

5. Learn the method for reducing heart rate via controlled breathing. (The following is from US Army psychologist Dave Grossman 2004):

    a. Breathe in four counts.
    b. Hold your breath four counts.
    c. Breathe out four counts.
    d. Hold your breath four counts.
    e. Repeat until heart rate comes down.

This does not mean simply "take a deep breath." The key is to repeat the entire sequence until a slower bodily rhythm is established, creating feedback to bring down the adrenaline level. The periods of holding your breath between breathing-in and breathing-out are crucial.

In a tense situation, check your heart rate, and bring it down if necessary.

But what if there is no time for this? What if it is an immediate, kill-or-be-killed situation? In police work, sometimes this may be the case. But such situations do not arise very often. Many instances of police shootings—and especially those which turn out to be based on misperceptions—take time to develop. The Charlotte, NC, confrontation built up over an hour, and could have been resolved peacefully with better management of emotions.

Checking your heart rate and controlling it by a breathing exercise may not be possible in some fast-moving situations. And some victims collude in their own death, in suicide-by-cop, by pretending to aim a weapon at officers in order to be shot. Some such events may be inevitable. But even here, very situationally-aware officers can sort some of them out.

Some officers speed up the situation unnecessarily. In Cleveland, in November 2014, the officer who shot a 12-year-old boy (Tamir Rice) carrying a toy gun on a playground had raced to the scene and fired within 2 seconds after jumping from his car. And the cop who shoots Tamir is still highly alarmed even after the boy falls to the ground, since he rushes to take shelter behind the police car. This indicates that he is still in a condition of high adrenaline surge, and cannot perceive the reality of the situation. From military combat, we know that adrenaline surges can take ten minutes or more to return to normal (Collins 2008: 83–89). Better-trained officers would be aware of their own body signs and the danger zone of perceptual distortion, and would not attempt to fire until they had a clear view of the situation.

Rumors Transmitted by Police Dispatchers and Patrol Cars

The Tamir Rice shooting illustrates another source of high tension and distorted perception of allegedly very dangerous persons: not only in the cops on the scene, but in police communications. The sequence that led to the shooting of Tamir Rice began with a 911 call from an onlooker about a child on the playground with a toy gun. The dispatcher leaves out all other detail (child, toy gun, lack of emotional alarm by the caller), and relays only that there is a gun on the playground and the person is black. She then conveys this truncated account to another dispatcher who sends out a highest-level radio alarm to police cars. When the officers nearest the scene get the call, all realistic information about the context of the situation has been dropped, and the officers are put in a state high of tension and alarm.

The mechanism has been shown in the psychology of rumors (Allport and Postman 1951). In experiments where a message is repeated orally from person to person along a chain, the message gets reduced to its simplest and most familiar form. In the links from one person to the next, detail is progressively eliminated, leaving out any special qualifications and turning nuance into cliché.

A particularly dangerous form of rumor-amplification occurs when eyewitness reports are filtered through police dispatchers and from one police radio to another. Citizen calls to the police may say, someone *might* have a gun; or someone *might* be engaged in a burglary. The dispatcher turns the call into a simpler form, there is a gun or a burglar. The notorious arrest in 2009 of Harvard Professor Henry Louis Gates, in his own home, began with a passer-by calling 911 to report what she said, hesitantly, was probably a minor incident of someone having trouble unlocking their door, but was transformed by the dispatcher into a racially-coded burglary.

When messages are transmitted from one patrol car to another, the process by which rumors are propagated takes over. In the case of police transmissions, the more cars called to a scene, the more likely the message is to turn into an extreme threat. This is another reason why calling more police to the scene usually creates tension and more likelihood of police violence. Weapons are definitely asserted to be present when the original report did not say so. Hostages are mentioned whether they exist or not, and the suspect becomes reported as saying he won't die alone—a cliché that gets into the official rumor chain, producing deadly consequences (Collins 2008: 113).

Reform of police practices should include retraining police dispatchers to become aware of the distortions they introduce into messages. Since dispatchers are usually civilian employees, not sworn officers (with a license to use force in enforcing the law), dispatchers receive little training, even compared to what police receive. There also should be better training of patrol officers to become aware of rumor-like exaggeration in their own chains of messages to each other.

Interactionally-Aware Police Training

Police training should incorporate more explicit awareness of the distortions caused by tense confrontations. Weapons training tends to go in the opposite direction, stressing quick reaction, and training for automatic "muscle memory" in the default scenario that saving lives depends on rapid action. Police are trained for extreme situations rather than clear assessment and self-control. Police training needs to be thoroughly investigated and reformed.

Police shootings of unarmed or unresisting persons have brought huge controversy. Most proposed solutions focus on more body cameras, more release of video data to the public, and more criminal prosecution of officers. These proposals have spiraled into more conflict, in the form of demonstrations, riots, and angry politics on both sides. In the balance of political forces today, none of these has been successful in reducing police shootings.

Another route can be tried. Rather than reacting after police shootings happen, and concentrating on ways to pin the blame in court, we can take steps so that out-of-control behavior in police encounters does not happen in the first place. We do not have to solve huge problems like racism or political gridlock to achieve this.

The answer is not so much after-the-fact criminal charges and court trials—these rarely result in conviction, and focus on punishing individuals rather than on the improvements that can be made in police procedures. Even rare verdicts of police homicide, as in the 2021 trial of Derek Chauvin for killing George Floyd—under tremendous public attention and following months of demonstrations—did not stop police shootings and other violent arrests from happening in the following weeks and months. Since police are acutely aware of such news, there must be an unconscious, difficult-to-control process which triggers off such police violence. Out-of-control adrenaline surges are an obvious mechanism.

Better training can be undertaken at local initiative by police forces willing to do so. Especially important are techniques for becoming aware of one's own adrenaline level and heart rate; and techniques such as breathing exercises for getting adrenaline under control. It is in the interest of all police officers to ensure that their tension-control skills are high. Individual cops do not have to wait until a government agency, or their own police chief, orders them to wear a heart-beat monitor. Everyone can get one easily enough; and do your own training in controlling heart rate and adrenaline level.

And Not Just Cops: Everyone Can Learn to Control Their Adrenaline

What about the other side of the counter-escalation, the anger, hostility, and defiance in the black community? I have focused on what can be done by police to control their use of force, because this is where public policy might be implemented. But escalated conflict is driven by the extremes at both ends of the distribution, and the tough guys of black and Hispanic communities would be harder to reach. Nevertheless, the message is much the same. Be aware of one's own adrenaline, one's rush of emotions, the situational blurring of attention to everything but the impulse to dominate. And be aware of the same processes going on inside the person on the other side—awareness of how to calm police down rather than rile them up. A glimmer of optimism comes from group psychology programs in California prisons, where convicted murderers learn to re-experience the events that led to their imprisonment, and to focus on better control of their emotions. Prisoners who completed the program and were released on parole had a re-arrest rate much lower than usual.[2] It is not impossible that, in the future, self-training in micro-situational awareness could spread even in the most violent part of the population. The more widely knowledge is spread about these micro-techniques—among the police, and on the street—the less damage all of us will cause.

Thinking outside the box is often advocated. But most policy people automatically think in terms of top-down solutions. It is at the bottom level—each moment people encounter each other on the street—that the problem arises. Better emotional awareness can help to head it off, on the spot.

Notes

1. Data on the cases described here are from news reports and on-line accounts referenced by name of victim.
2. Bowen Paulle, personal communication.

References

Allport, Gordon, and Leo Postman. 1951. *Psychology of Rumor*. New York: Russell and Russell.

Alpert, Geoffrey P. and Roger G. Dunham. 2004. *Understanding Police Use of Force*. Cambridge: Cambridge University Press.

Artwohl, Alexis, and Loren W. Christensen. 1997. *Deadly Force Encounters*. Boulder, CO: Paladin.

Black, Donald. 1980. *The Manners and Customs of the Police*. San Diego, CA: Academic Press.

Collins, Randall. 2008. *Violence: A Micro-Sociological Theory*. Princeton, NJ: Princeton University Press.

Grossman, Dave. 2004. *On Combat. The Psychology and Physiology of Deadly Combat in War and Peace*. Belleville, IL: PPTC Research Publications.

Hunt, Jennifer C. 2010. *Seven Shots. An NYPD Raid on a Terrorist Cell and its Aftermath*. Chicago: University of Chicago Press.

Klinger, David. 2004. *Into the Kill Zone: A Cop's Eye View of Deadly Force*. San Francisco, CA: Jossey-Bass.

Moskos, Peter. 2009. *Cop in the Hood*. Princeton, NJ: Princeton University Press.

Rubinstein, Jonathan. 1973. *City Police*. New York: Farrar, Straus, and Giroux.

Conclusion

Optimistic Discoveries in the Sociology of Violence

Introduction

Although sociology mostly delivers bad news, research on the process of violence provides some important exceptions. Good news shows up when we observe the span of time starting from when violence is threatened, to see whether it happens or not. Most times it does not. But our optimistic findings are mainly on the micro-level. Macro-organized violence—in big organizations involving chains of hundreds, thousands, or millions of persons—is more difficult to contain, unlike the action of individuals interacting closely in small-scale situations. Nevertheless, even on the macro level we find practical lessons for how the damage can be limited or headed off.

Face Confrontations Can Be Handled

Jackson-Jacobs (2013) provides an ethnography of a group of several dozen young white males in a Southwest city, who seek out fights in order to escape from their middle-class ethos, seeking underground prestige. Although they often go looking for fights at parties, they seldom get them. When an occasional fight happens, they talk about it excitedly for weeks thereafter—being beaten is OK, as long as they were in the action. One might think that starting fights would be easy, since they don't look for easy victims and relish (or at least brag about) confronting tough guys. But in fact bumping into someone, staring at them—all the usual marks of disrespect—do not get automatic pushback. Jackson-Jacobs details the micro-moves that both sides have to make before they tacitly agree to a state of fighting. Tough-guy "respect" and looking for action are not enough; most of the time the belligerent moves remain abortive.

Levine, Taylor and Best (2011) use CCTV data (now ubiquitous in British pubs) to examine incipient quarrels and fights. Although these are sites of heavy drinking and a macho ethos (usually supposed to be instigating conditions for violence), the great majority of pub fights rarely get beyond the insulting and pushing stage. Third parties frequently intervene, and

DOI: 10.4324/9781003245629-21

are largely successful in breaking up fights. High-density locales and big crowds did not foster fights (hypothetically this would happen via anonymity or crowding); on the contrary, big crowds are segmented into familiar networks that provide the third-party interveners who break up fights their friends were involved in. Liebst, Heinskou and Ejbye-Ernst (2018) using CCTV from another heavy-drinking city, Copenhagen, found that third-party interveners were not only successful but that they rarely got hurt themselves breaking up a fight. These findings indicate that carousing groups tacitly regulate themselves so that fights are mostly harmless; they operate on two levels, a verbal level of belligerent masculinity, and a tacit level of group controls that keep them from going too far. The tacit substrate is ubiquitous CT/F—which is never admitted consciously; but actions speak louder than hostile or bragging words.

Elijah Anderson (1999) presents the "code of the street" as a Goffmanian frontstage performance. Bluster is a ritual that constrains violence, putting on the gestures and bodily postures of being a tough guy, and thereby hoping to head off attacks. This sounds menacing, but when both sides do it in tacit awareness of the ritual, it creates an emotional equilibrium that avoids escalating the situation. Krupnick and Winship (2015) show in detail how this works. Joe Krupnick's participant observation among the fragments of gangs on Chicago streets (after the huge mega-gangs were broken up in the early 2000s), show how gun-carrying gang members manage to pass members of opposing gangs on the streets without starting fights. They follow an etiquette of "fronting": when a potential enemy approaches, avoid eye contact, appear nonchalant and absorbed in something else like beat-boxing to music; keep your hands in plain view, not in your pockets; make brief eye-contact when your enemy passes, give a fist-bump or say something casual; after passing, don't look back—being overtly vigilant is read as looking for a fight, even defensively. Violating these rules is called "slipping" and will get you beaten up, if not shot. The choreographed performance is generally successful in avoiding gun violence; where shootings do happen, it is usually by misunderstandings and accidents. Even in drug disputes or robberies, the cool response when someone catches a "Hustla" unawares is just let the man with the drawn gun get away with it; this is considered appropriate etiquette, doesn't damage your reputation, and even typically winds up with the robber closing the encounter with a ritualistic fist pound or slap on the back. Keeping the common rhythm is keeping the peace, even when it isn't friendly.

Jooyoung Lee (2016) did participant observation as a rapper/street dancer, along with making video recordings of ad hoc gatherings of amateur street rappers. As Anderson has shown about the code of the street, the culture of violence is not so much about real violence but about blustering and dramatizing one's capacity for violence. Playing the part is usually enough to satisfy standards of respect and personal identity. Lee adds two important developments: one is that the rap culture, with its insulting and violence-laden lyrics and its threatening vocal tone, is a form of bluster, developed into explicit entertainment. Outsiders see rap as encouraging violence; in the immediate situation, however, it makes bluster an end in itself, so that violence is unnecessary—indeed, violence would destroy rapping as entertainment, so the performers themselves work to keep rap/ bluster from going over the edge. For them, rapping is a path toward commercial success, and thus a pathway out of the world of gang violence.

Rap performers do get angry at their co-performers and rivals; mock battles can threaten to turn into real violence—not so much because of the insults as because of interruptions of one's rhythm. But there are micro-interactional techniques that they use to signal awareness of danger points, and moves they can make to defuse the danger. This happens less on the explicit verbal level but in tacit communications through shifts in rhythm, touching, eye gaze and emotional expression.

Tyson Smith (2014) makes a similar point about the hyper-macho performance of pro wrestling. That it is staged and rehearsed we have already suspected, but what we did not know is the extraordinary degree of cooperation that goes into it. Front-stage performance in the arena is not just showy violence but joint emotion work, in the over-the-top form Smith calls passion work. Projecting hyper-macho performance requires a backstage of protective cooperation—working together in their rehearsed antagonism so that their apparently hard aggressive bodies are actually soft and yielding, hyper-sensitive as lovers so that they don't cripple each other. It is more akin to ballet than battle, except that all the effort goes into giving the opposite impression. It is, more or less literally, the code of the street on steroids.

The research studies of Krupnick, Lee, and Smith extend Anderson's understanding of violence-threatening bluster as a front-stage performance. When the ritual is successfully performed, it reduces violence in the here-and-now situation. Even if the local culture values violent masculinity, ritual performance is enough to satisfy the cultural gods. The micro-nuances of how to perform and recognize the performances of others is "street smarts" that heads off much (if not all) violence.

Deflecting Sexual Aggression and Failed Robberies

Analyzing a range of sexual aggressions, Chapter 13 showed that the large majority of these incidents did not proceed to rape or forced sex. Even when the sexual threat was explicit, most women successfully resisted it, not so much by fighting back but by refusing to be emotionally dominated. From the point of view of the micro-sociology of violence, this is not surprising, because it is consistent with the pattern in all violent threats: emotional domination is the key, rather than force per se. But these data are chiefly about acquaintance rape, which may not be the pattern in stranger rapes. Yet even then, forceable rape is sometimes successfully deterred. Research is needed on how often this happens in attempted rapes by strangers, and in what interactional circumstances.

We do know that an analogous situation of violent threat, armed robberies, also shows micro-turning points. Analyzing CCTV of store robberies, Nassauer (2018) and Mosselman et al. (2018) found that holding weapons is not a guarantee of compliance, and armed robbers can lose their nerve and retreat. As in getting street respect, flawless bluster is the key to armed robberies. Women are among the clerks who deter robbers by not falling into their rhythm—showing again that women are not intrinsically helpless victims by virtue of their relative size. Resisting emotional domination is a practice available to everyone.

On a macro-level, we know that mass rapes have been common in past wars. In recent decades they are often reported in civil wars, ethnic cleansing, and ideological militias who sustain themselves by kidnapping for ransom and forced recruitment of child warriors. Such rapes are a group activity, where individual women are separated out and gang-raped, or raped under the eyes of a group that greatly outnumbers her. These are the same conditions under which violence of all kinds succeeds: an isolated victim; coordinated group procedures of violence; a supportive audience. Here it is extremely difficult to resist emotional domination. Ordinary confrontational tension, which inhibits violence, and which the targets of attack can sometimes increase by keeping eye-to-eye contact with the attacker, is an escape route that is cut off if the victim has her face covered or head averted—the same principle that makes fraternity party rapes emotionally easy for the attackers when the woman is very drunk or passed out. Hemingway reported that in the civil wars of the 1920s and 1930s, the sexual assault would usually began with the attackers pulling the woman's skirt over her head; just the tactic that eliminates the human link of eye contact and dehumanizes the victim.

Nevertheless, we should not jump to the pessimistic conclusion that mass rapes are never deterred. Omar McDoom reports that in the genocidal massacres in Rwanda during April 1994: "Killers . . . confronted their victims face-to-face and overwhelmingly in groups. Sexual violence against women was commonplace . . ." (2021: 5). But not everyone who was personally threatened was killed,[1] and this was apparently also the pattern of sexual violence. As yet, we have not looked closely at threatened mass rapes, to see what micro-situational features keep rapes from happening. Sampling on the dependent variable guarantees seeing the worst-case scenario. Even here, we can hold out some hope for practical techniques that provide nick-of-time escapes.

Klusemann (2012), analyzing similar data, noted that as we zoom in from regional statistics to detailed descriptions of death-threatening encounters, in many instances threatened killings did not happen. In Rwanda, in communities where the majority were moderates, violent activists from outside were fended off by even a small display of group resistance; here the activists confined themselves to sending threatening messages and clandestine attacks on Tutsi houses and killing their livestock. In areas where the Hutu population became radicalized, a small number of soldiers sent by the national government created an atmosphere of intimidation by noisy gunfire. But few persons were killed by guns. Most were hacked to death with machetes—a particularly gruesome process, making it unsurprising that most audiences shied away from actually joining in.

Klusemann finds similar patterns in Rwanda massacres and those in Bosnia (former Yugoslavia) in 1995. There the killings started after a long military stalemate ended with victory of Serbian militia, when resistance by Bosnian Muslims suddenly collapsed. In the atmosphere of celebration, both captured soldiers and civilian men were taken to forest areas and gunned down, while Serbian civilians from local villages jeered the victims. After this went on for some hours, Muslim women were pulled from the refugee compound and gang-raped. Nevertheless, the majority of women escaped being raped. This does not diminish the horrors of the event, but it does show there are some situational conditions for whether threatened mass rapes succeed or fail. One of these is the time-pattern that, as Klusemann showed for Bosnia, emotional crowds lose their intensity after a number of hours of spectacular destruction. Possibly victims can take advantage of this by prolonging the period of indecision.

"Blaming the Victim"

In recent decades, it has become conventional to label any analysis of women's resistance to coercion as "blaming the victim." This argument was first made about rape trials, where defense lawyers argued that it was the victim's fault for not resisting hard enough or for putting herself in a situation that made her a target. The point I am making is a different one. We can document turning points to successful or failed rapes, clearly enough on the micro-level. The pattern that stands out is that rapes are successfully resisted by disrupting the attacker's rhythm, and by not being emotionally dominated.

Sociologists like myself who make this analysis are not in the business of blaming, but in the business of explaining patterns and turning points. Nor am I in the business of excusing; I don't testify in court trials one way or the other. What we ask as sociological researchers is to analyze the evidence and find the patterns, without being denounced as morally on the wrong side of the fight.

In the controversy over "blaming the victim," the predominant assumption is that the proper way to deal with sexual aggression is by punishment. But as a practical matter, prevention is better than punishment, heading off more damage in both the short and the long run.[2] Durkheim ([1895] 1982: 100) argued that punishment rituals do not so much deter crimes as recreate the conditions for more punishments, in an endless cycle. People are attracted to trials, verdicts, and punishments, not because they actually reduce the incidence of crime, but because these are rituals that focus public attention, and give us a feeling of emotional solidarity and self-righteousness as we collectively condemn deviants. Turning our attention away from the punishment ritual and onto the micro-tactics individuals can use in their own lives seems to many people a moral failing. When almost everyone is caught up in the blame game, the Durkheimian social dynamic demands that everyone join in. Any other stance is regarded as taking the side of the enemy. This is the familiar dynamic of polarization, driving out neutrals and demanding conformity in the most heated judgments.

To blame and punish, or to explain and exculpate, are not the only alternatives. Public morality is not going to collapse if sociologists with a steady eye look closely at the patterns and point out situational dynamics that allow people on the spot to attempt to control their own destiny. The moralizing mode has blinders. Sometimes we have to step outside of it to find more optimistic pathways.

Awareness of the Adrenaline Distortion Zone

As we have seen in Chapter 15, out-of-control violence happens when participants' heart rates accelerate to a high level, driven by an adrenaline surge. At this level, their fine motor control is lost, their perception is distorted by tunnel vision, temporary deafness occurs, and losing track of how much time is elapsing. It is in this adrenaline distortion zone that most atrocities happen—police who shoot the wrong target or empty their guns in overkill; soldiers who commit massacres in combat; and many incidents in riots, domestic violence, and other ferocious attacks. I have suggested that if police wore heart-rate monitors, and trained themselves to bring down their adrenaline before rushing into violent action, many atrocities would be avoided.

The same could apply to the other side. People in street gangs, or in frequent confrontation with people they considering threatening—including the police—can also raise their awareness of the danger of being in an adrenaline distortion zone. To some extent, the street code incorporates awareness of this kind of thing. It could be sharpened by publicly encouraging people in dangerous situations to be aware of their adrenaline by focusing on one's own heart rate, and to lower it by breathing exercises (and possibly other ways still to be discovered).

But what if you are facing someone else who is "in the adrenaline distortion zone"? They are out of control; what can you do about it? We can recognize that persons in the rush of a rampage shooting are probably in the distortion zone (Chapter 14). But not everyone in the target population gets killed; what makes the difference? We know the details of a few cases where potential victims confronted the killer and survived.

In a mass shooting on May 31, 2019, at a Virginia Beach city government building, an employee who had just quit after being told he would be disciplined for getting into altercations and scuffles with other employees, returned in the afternoon and killed 12 people and wounded 4 others, before being killed by police. (In keeping with the general pattern of rampage shooters, he had an arsenal at home of four handguns plus attachments.) Two clerks, casual acquaintances of the shooter, encountered him three different times during the rampage without being targeted. One clerk was calm, thinking it was a drill; while performing his assigned task of monitoring stairwells, he suddenly turned a corner and came face to face with the gunman.

> He had the gun down at his side. He was so close to me, he swung his arm out, he damn near hit me with it. That's how close we were . . . But he never raised the gun at me. He looked up at me briefly . . . By the way he walked past me, he barely gave me a glance, and never broke stride.

In a second encounter five minutes later, another clerk saw the shooter standing in his office with a gun and said,

> "Dwayne, stop!" He turned and looked straight at me, but he didn't see me. He looked straight in my face and he did not see me standing there because he didn't raise the gun. He didn't even make an indication that he saw anyone there.

A third time, both clerks were hiding in a room with an interior window; the shooter looked through the window but passed on (sources: Associated Press, June 3, 2019; *Washington Post*, June 3, 2019; *New York Times*, June 2, 2019).

Apparently, the shooter was in the distortion zone; but his encounters with the two clerks did not raise them to the status of targets. The first clerk did not act as if it were a dangerous confrontation, thinking it was a routine drill and that the shooter was just acting a part; the second clerk did not act frightened (the first clerk was also present), and the shooter showed no sign of paying attention to him even though they locked eyes. This is in keeping with the power of eye contact, in a calm and unthreatening way, to deter attacks.

In another, highly publicized incident in Decatur, Georgia, August 2013, a man broke into an elementary school but was quickly engaged in a shootout with police. He took cover in the office of a school clerk, who was on the phone—hence we know the details of their conversation from the recording,[3] analyzed by Sorge (2016). She was initially terrified, but as they talked, their tone shifted to a "we-together" mode, as she spoke of how they both needed to protect themselves from being shot by the police. Within 24 minutes, he calmed down and peacefully surrendered. The shift from antagonistic confrontation, to shared rhythm and common rapport, constituted a micro-turning point, and apparently brought him down out of the adrenaline danger zone.

Greater awareness of this bodily/emotional danger zone, both on one's own part and in others, promises methods for de-escalating many instances of violence. This would have to be carried out by each person involved—some have saved themselves while others reacted in ways that did not emotionally disarm the attacker.

At Columbine High School in April 1999, the attackers killed 13 and wounded 20 within 16 minutes, but many others they encountered in hallways and classrooms were not shot, even though the killers still had plenty of ammunition when they committed suicide 25 minutes later.[4] By a leap of imagination, put yourself in the shoes of the attacker: you've taken the plunge, you don't expect to get out of this alive; what do you think your heart beat is going to be? How clear is your vision, your hearing, your bodily self-control? The two Columbine killers were recorded as laughing hysterically, a sign of being physiologically and subjectively out of control. Faced with such a person, how would you turn their lack of self-control to your advantage, enabling you to escape?

Awareness of Violent Turning Points in Protest Demonstrations

The same underlying mechanism of adrenaline spikes is at work in larger-scale events, in crowds of hundreds or more where tension builds up and micro-moves trigger violence. Research on when political demonstrations turn violent or stay peaceful, by Anne Nassauer (2019) on protests in the US and Germany, and Isabel Bramsen (2017; 2018) on Arab Spring protests, have zoomed in on turning points. Using videos, police radio traffic, and interviews with protestors and police, Nassauer found that tension can be gauged on both sides by the tense or relaxed body postures and gestures as well as in facial expressions and tones of voice. As we have seen in Chapter 4, rising tension collectively in these groups is the first step toward violence; it is triggered off when one side shows sudden weakness, and the other goes into a forward panic, no longer distinguishing between those who are threatening and those who are not. A practical result of such research is that both crowd control forces and demonstrators could learn to recognize these danger signs. The lesson deserves to be widely publicized.

Nassauer also shows there are micro-techniques, practiced by some participants, that are successful in defusing violence, even if it has already begun. The optimistic news: at such moments of tension, and even when a local cascade of violence is unleashed, participants can cool their opponents down, or at least provide immunity for oneself. Protestors (or cops) can achieve this by directly facing the opponent (not turning one's back, which creates a weak target inviting attack), and calling out in a strong, clear voice, a message such as: "We are peaceful, what about you?" There is a crucial micro-detail here. Screaming the same message hysterically, with an expression of terror or rage, does not deter violence, but just adds to the emotional atmosphere. It has to be done with voice, face, and body postures strong and calm.

But although this may happen in the relatively civil protest traditions and policing tactics of contemporary Western democracies: what about in societies where demonstrators aim for maximal disruption, and regime forces brook no defiance and are authorized to use maximal force? Surprisingly, Bramsen (2017; 2018) shows that even here, local conditions of time and emotional mood determine when and how much violence will occur on either side. Although the spectrum is shifted toward more violence overall, nevertheless there are moments of emotional equilibrium when demonstrators and regime forces let each other go through ritualized displays without using violence; and moments when tension rises uncontrollably into situations of local advantage and hence violence. At times in her Arab Spring cases, protests fall into a dance-like equilibrium, repeating the same circuit around the streets; moments of shouting and even of stone-throwing and tear gas become predictable; the conflict becomes ritualized, expectable, and for the most part, emotionally under control. Many of the demonstrators in Bramsen's analysis were women cloaked in traditional Arab dress, who nevertheless sometimes got into stand-offs with Arab men. Women in German and American protests can confront the police successfully, or give the wrong micro-signals and get beaten up. Even gender stereotypes can give way to situational rhythms.

Limits and Dangers of Prolonged Conflicts

As we have seen in the duration of protests (Chapter 4), over a period of weeks and months the number of participants declines and violence rises. There is a shift from mostly peaceful demonstrators to an increasing preponderance of violent activists, bringing out the counter-escalation pattern of violence from and with the police. This combines with another vicious circle, as violence drives away the non-violent participants, and tactics of disrupting transportation and the local economy turn early protestors into neutrals and neutrals into opponents. Recent peace research has shown that non-violent tactics have a better track record in regime change than violent tactics. But awareness of this by some does not convince militants, as their emotional dynamics become focused on settling accounts with the police—the war of competing atrocities at the core of C-escalation.

Here we seem to encounter a theoretical contradiction. On one hand, mass mobilization and its solidarity-through-conflict follows the 9/11 pattern of rapid ascent, three-month plateau, and three-to-six months decline, i.e. the first months are the high intensity solidarity-and-hysteria zone, and conflict starts exhausting itself after three months. On the other hand, longer protests become more violent and drive the counter-escalation process higher. The optimistic conclusion of the first point contradicts the pessimistic conclusion of the second. The contradiction is resolved if we view both as time-spans: the second is nested in the first. The shift to increasing violence takes place in the middle of the three-month zone; upon reaching the three-six months period where everything is declining, not only non-violent participants but also violent participants and hence total violence drops off too. Beyond that point, a tail of dedicated violent activists may continue, but their model has shifted: no longer mass public demonstrations with their moral claim to *We the People*—to clandestine guerrilla tactics.

Sánchez-Jankowski's (2016) research on conflict between black and Hispanic students in high schools shows a similar pattern: the size and frequency of violent incidents grew during the fall (approximately the first three months), but declined by late spring (the second three months). Over the events of a year, the usually un-mobilized majority of students who are peaceful rather than fighters became collectively organized to show their disapproval of large-scale fights by walking out of the school in what Sánchez-Jankowski calls a "stampede." The power of audiences to control the severity of violence, resulted in a collective tactic that cut off incipient violence and eventually de-escalated it. As I have shown previously, the duration and intensity of small-scale fights are heavily influenced by the attitude of their audience. For larger riots, merely curious on-lookers are taken as tacit support by the violent fraction, but in the goldfish bowl atmosphere of a high school, and with a repetitive pattern of school riots, the let's-get-out-of-here stampede carried an emotional message that eventually demobilized the hot-heads.

But some kinds of conflict go on beyond three-to-six months even though popular enthusiasm declines; the 9/11 pattern of popular support for national symbols was in that time-frame, but the wars in Afghanistan and Iraq that followed lasted for years. This is a shift to greater organization on the macro-level; conflict is taken over by the government and military, coordinating logistics, ramping up troop levels and military hardware. Even setbacks and defeats do not necessarily deter macro-organized conflict; it is organized for the long run, and can regroup and try again. Its efforts do not depend on popular enthusiasm in the way that demonstrations and riots do. In effect, when the militant minority controls the government, even unpopular conflict does not de-escalate.

A crucial turning point in World War I occurred in late 1916, when the Western Front was at a costly stalemate, with huge casualties for French, British, and Germans alike. Early enthusiasts on all sides had expected a brief, decisive war; instead it had become a grinding war of attrition, now 2½ years long. This was apparent to most of these populations and in the armies themselves; politicians on all sides developed peace factions, aiming for a negotiated truce. In November and December, the German Chancellor, the Austrian Emperor, and the British Prime Minister all expressed willingness to negotiate, and US President Wilson offered to mediate (Gilbert 1994: 301–304). But in the ensuing cabinet crisis, Lloyd George—who had been included in the all-party war cabinet even though he was from the left wing of the Liberal party—rallied the others emotionally, took over as PM, and redoubled the war efforts. The French government, which had welcomed the 1914 Balkan crisis as an opportunity for revenging its 1871 defeat by Prussia, put down mutinies in the army and pressed on, whatever the cost. French population loss was so great it took a generation to recover. The refractory period, when it came, lasted a long time; anti-war sentiment in France, England, and the US was so strong into the 1930s that little was done to counter German war preparation to avenge their defeat in 1918. On the emotional level, the mounting number of lives and property destroyed become sunk costs, an argument to continue—even though the rational strategy is to cut further losses as soon as possible.

Time-Forks: Macro-Turning Points to End or Prolong Violence

All this fits the pattern of time-forks: conflicts ranging in scale from protests to revolutions and wars are least destructive if there is a decisive victory or turning point early on. Failing this, conflict becomes lengthy attrition. A decisive turning point requires a central location where all attention is concentrated; when conflict is dispersed in far-flung riots or civil war, it becomes a costly grind, where victory, if any, goes to those with deep resources to commit and persistence to wear down the other side. The most decentralized kind of war is worst in this respect; far-flung battlefields become a war of attacking logistics lines (whether shipping at sea in WWI and WWII, or guerrilla wars attacking transport to isolated Forward Operating Bases in Afghanistan and Iraq). This kind of war on logistics tends to spread the war to more participants, as illustrated by the entry of the US into WWI because of the sinking of a supply ship.

Guerrillas are the counterparts of protest demonstrators who won't give up even if the mainstream movement drops out; a small number can keep the conflict going almost indefinitely by hiding in the civilian population and resorting to terrorist tactics that prolong the emotional war of competing atrocities. In urban demonstrations, the danger is die-hards shifting from fighting the police, to becoming underground cells insulated from public opinion and plotting to keep the revolution going by spectacular acts of violence (Orsini 2011).

All this is pessimistic. Nevertheless, we find some optimism in cases where seemingly endless conflict is brought to an end. The end of the English Revolution (see Chapter 6) shows a repetitive pattern of intermittent coups and battles between mutually distrustful, ever-shifting factions. It is finally brought to an end—after 19 months—in a sudden mood-swing: a temporarily victorious general, instead of seeking his own dominance, enters negotiations to bring back the monarchy as a unifying power standing above politics. In the emotional exhaustion with endless conflict, this proved to be a widely popular move, transcending the ideologies of the conflict. A key to avoiding die-hard resistance was a non-vindictive new regime. Except for a few token executions, the mood of the new monarchy was to forget the past, its atrocities and grudges. As in the Thermidorian Reaction in France following the end of the Reign of Terror, the English Restoration became a period of easy-going hedonism—rebounding from the harsh hatreds and fears of the years of militant strife.

A similar pattern is found in the Red Guards movement in China (1966–1968) and its aftermath (Walder 2009; Yang 2016). Whatever the initial motives were for launching the Red Guards, it became a self-propagating conflict. Different groups of Red Guards soon split and turned their thought-reform tactics on each other; the factions were based not on ideologies but on tactics, accusing each other of too much harshness, or not enough. It was a decentralized organized conflict (even if encouraged from the top of the government), spreading by imitation from one institutional and economic sector to another. It must have become apparent to the student militants that conflict was spreading out of their control, hence their attacks on each other for what they regarded as mistaken tactics. It was, in effect, endless conflict, spreading throughout the country and undermining authority everywhere. After 2½ years of this, Mao stopped the movement by declaring victory and sending the young Red Guards to the countryside; he also shut down their rallying bases, the schools. The result, after seven more years of political struggle among the Communist Party elites, was another Thermidorian Reaction, in which the mood shifted to economic entrepreneurship, hedonism and consumerism—whatever their moral qualities, it was an antidote to self-consuming conflict.

Thus we find yet another time-pattern on a level that involves years and decades: Conflicts which are kept going beyond the usual three-to-six month pattern of popular enthusiasm—because they lose the character of simple two-sided conflicts, spinning out of control by repeated internal splits among mutually mistrustful factions—build up what we might call *mega-exhaustion* with the apparent endlessness of it all. The resulting Thermidorian Reactions are deeply felt and can go on for decades. From the point of view of keeping down violence, this counts as another gleam of optimism—if political actors can learn the lesson.

Cyber Conflict Is the Most Heartless of All

Modern war is turning into cyberwar. On battlefields, long-distance targeting and control of weapons, as well as coordination of logistics and troop movements, have made the high-tech military a huge computerized network. Such a military organization becomes vulnerable to enemy disruption, not so much on the battlefield but from cyberwar from far-flung and inaccessible locations; worse yet, potentially, taking control of opponents' weapons and turning them against themselves. Computerized networks in the civilian economy become another target for devastating economic warfare, including the possibility of creating epidemics and famines.

This is bad news, located at the extreme macro end of the spectrum. It also fits the general principles of violence. At the micro-level of face-to-face conflict, urges to violence come up against confrontational tension/fear. This is the main reason why micro-level conflicts so often get derailed. But one of the pathways around CT/F is to avoid face-to-face conflict, by attacking from a distance. We see this in artillery firing or bombing which never sees its human target: the pilots who dropped atom bombs on Japanese cities spoke of nothing but technical matters; enemy casualties not coming into view at all, absorbed in the polarized stereotypes of the evil enemy.

This is true also of small-scale cyber-conflicts, like on-line bullying, engaging in character assassination even if it drives victims to suicide. It is a perfect medium for avoiding CT/F, which means avoiding human sympathy. It is the same with stealing from individuals and organizations by on-line scams, siphoning off funds, or ransom attacks. These have become the easiest form of conflict, escaping any emotional pangs.

Human morality has its roots in the propensity to fall into rhythm with other persons in face-to-face contact, leading to shared emotions, recognizing the other as a human being. But cyber-conflict, at all levels from on-line bullying to the worst ravages of economic and military cyberwar, is the extreme of insulation from human faces, or even seeing the human bodies afterwards.

This is bad news indeed. Is there any way out?

In war, one pathway out of the extremes of inhumane cyberwar is the tendency for war, if it goes on at length, to fall back from high-tech to earlier methods. As we have seen, high-tech weapons are the most expensive to build and maintain, and thus are most subject to attrition on the battlefield. Mutual cyber-attacks on both sides of a war could degrade each other's capacity, putting us back into relying on older means (just as the German *Blitzkrieg* in Russia in WWII tended over time to fall back on using animals as vehicles and fuel became scarce). Old-fashioned warfare is bad enough, but at least it is a possible escape from the blind omni-destructiveness of cyberwar.

Military officers are now considering the possibility of shutting down the Internet in serious military crises. This would apply as well to domestic networks; the hope is to reduce economic and public health vulnerabilities by backing up coordination with low-tech arrangements, or at least off-line alternatives (which could be a new form of high-tech). Life without the Internet seems unthinkable, but it has become ubiquitous for only about 15 years (since the early 2000s). The vulnerabilities of cyberwar in a totally networked world may well lead to breaking it up. History would once again turn in new directions.

The Bottom Line

On the whole, there are a number of optimistic developments in our analyses of violent conflict. In some areas, optimistic prospects are strong—especially on the micro-level, if new practices for limiting face-to-face violence are adopted. In other areas, mere awareness of favorable and unfavorable time-dynamics will not prevent some of the more destructive forms of conflict, but there are patterns where these conflicts become self-limiting. Even the apocalyptic prospects of all-out cyberwar have potential solutions. We are not used to good news in the study of conflict; but it is here. Realism and pessimism do not have to go together. The sociology of violent conflict is becoming increasingly a field of discovering ways out.

Notes

1. McDoom (2021: 376) concluded that 420,000 Hutus (about one-quarter of the adult male population) participated in killing 500,000 Tutsis (two-thirds of their entire population, men, women, and children). This implies each participant killed, on the average, 1.2 victims. We would not expect killing to be evenly distributed; in violence of all kinds elsewhere, between 2 percent and 10 percent constitute a violent few who do almost all the violence (Collins 2008: 370–380). The rest chiefly provide crowd support and emotional domination. In Rwanda, McDoom's surveys indicated that enthusiasts for killing Tutsi were at maximum 2–4 percent of the community. This is in line with the research of Strauss (2006: 112): attack groups numbered in the hundreds, but 70 percent of participants said they did not personally kill anyone; only 5 percent said they killed more than two people. This matches another estimate that actual killers were 25,000, about 6 percent of the attack crowds. All this is consistent with a pattern in which many individuals escape being killed, even when vastly outnumbered; for instance, when a

crowd contains few violent militants, and the rest confine themselves to threatening and harassing their targets.

2. The same line of argument applies to my suggestions for heading off police violence.
3. *Atlanta Journal-Constitution* (2013). "Antoinette Tuff's 911 call at McNair Discovery Learning Academy in Decatur." YouTube.com, August 21. 2015. (www.youtube.com/watch?v=s6mtcRnUGRg) (accessed August 8, 2015).
4. www.history.com/topics/1990s/columbine-high-school-shooting

References

Anderson, Elijah. 1999. *Code of the Street*. New York: Norton.

Bramsen, Isabel. 2017. "Route Causes of Conflict: Trajectories of Violent and Non-Violent Conflict Intensification." PhD dissertation, University of Copenhagen.

Bramsen, Isabel. 2018. "How Civil Resistance Succeeds (or Not). Micro-Dynamics of Unity, Timing, and Escalatory Action." *Peace and Change* 43: 61–89.

Durkheim, Emile. [1895] 1982. *The Rules of Sociological Method*. New York: Free Press.

Gilbert, Martin. 1994. *The First World War*. London: HarperCollins.

Jackson-Jacobs, Curtis. 2013. "Constructing Physical Fights: An Interactionist Analysis of Violence Among Affluent Suburban Youth." *Qualitative Sociology* 36: 23–52.

Klusemann, Stefan. 2012. "Massacres as Process: A Microsociological Theory of Internal Patterns of Mass Atrocities." *European Journal of Criminology* 9: 468–480.

Krupnick, Joseph, and Christopher Winship. 2015. "Keeping Up the Front: How Black Youth Avoid Street Violence in the Inner City." In Orlando Patterson and Ethan Fosse (Eds.), *The Cultural Matrix: Understanding Black Youth*. Cambridge, MA: Harvard University Press.

Lee, Jooyoung. 2016. *Blowin' Up: Rap Dreams in South Central*. Chicago: University of Chicago Press.

Levine, M., P. Taylor, and R. Best. 2011. "Third Parties, Violence, and Conflict Resolution: The Role of Group Size and Collective Action in the Micro-Regulation of Violence." *Psychological Science* 22: 406–412.

Liebst, L.S., M.B. Heinskou, and P. Ejbye-Ernst. 2018. "On the Actual Risk of Bystander Intervention." *Journal of Research on Crime and Delinquency* 55: 27–50.

McDoom, Omar. 2021. *The Path to Genocide in Rwanda*. Cambridge: Cambridge University Press.

Mosselman, Floris, Don Weenink, and Marie Rosenkrantz Lindegaard. 2018. "Weapons, Body Postures, and the Quest for Dominance in Robberies: A Qualitative Analysis of Video Footage." *Journal of Crime and Delinquency* 55: 3–26.

Nassauer, Anne. 2018. "How Robberies Succeed Or Fail: Analyzing Crime Caught on Camera." *Journal of Crime and Delinquency* 55: 125–154.

Nassauer, Anne. 2019. *Situational Breakdowns: Understanding Protest Violence and Other Surprising Outcomes*. New York: Oxford University Press.

Orsini, Alessandro. 2011. *Anatomy of the Red Brigades*. Ithaca, NY: Cornell University Press.

Sánchez-Jankowski, Martin. 2016. *Burning Dislike: Ethnic Violence in High Schools*. Berkeley, CA: University of California Press.

Smith, R. Tyson. 2014. *Fighting for Recognition: Identity, Masculinity, and the Act of Violence in Professional Wrestling*. Durham, NC: Duke University Press.

Sorge, David. 2016. Unpublished paper, Department of Sociology, University of Pennsylvania.

Strauss, Scott. 2006. *The Order of Genocide: Race, Power and War in Rwanda*. Ithaca, NY: Cornell University Press.

Walder, Andrew. 2009. *Fractured Rebellion: The Beijing Red Guard Movement*. Cambridge, MA: Harvard University Press.

Yang, Guobin. 2016. *The Red Guard Generation and Political Activism in China*. New York: Columbia University Press.

Index

Page numbers in *italics* refer to figures.

For Product Safety Concerns and Information please contact our EU
representative GPSR@taylorandfrancis.com
Taylor & Francis Verlag GmbH, Kaufingerstraße 24, 80331 München, Germany

www.ingramcontent.com/pod-product-compliance
Ingram Content Group UK Ltd.
Pitfield, Milton Keynes, MK11 3LW, UK
UKHW021450080625
459435UK00012B/436

* 9 7 8 1 0 3 2 1 5 7 7 0 2 *